INTERSECTING AESTHETICS

INTERSECTING AESTHETICS

Literary Adaptations and
Cinematic Representations of Blackness

Edited by
Charlene Regester, Cynthia Baron, Ellen C. Scott,
Terri Simone Francis, and Robin G. Vander

UNIVERSITY PRESS OF MISSISSIPPI / JACKSON

The University Press of Mississippi is the scholarly publishing agency of the Mississippi Institutions of Higher Learning: Alcorn State University, Delta State University, Jackson State University, Mississippi State University, Mississippi University for Women, Mississippi Valley State University, University of Mississippi, and University of Southern Mississippi.

www.upress.state.ms.us

The University Press of Mississippi is a member
of the Association of University Presses.

Any discriminatory or derogatory language or hate speech regarding race, ethnicity, religion, sex, gender, class, national origin, age, or disability that has been retained or appears in elided form is in no way an endorsement of the use of such language outside a scholarly context.

Copyright © 2023 by University Press of Mississippi
All rights reserved

∞

A previous version of "Burbanking Bigger and Bette the Bitch: *Native Son* and *In This Our Life* at Warner Bros." by Elizabeth Binggeli was originally published in *African American Review*, Volume 40.3 (Fall 2006).

Library of Congress Cataloging-in-Publication Data

Names: Regester, Charlene B., 1956– editor. | Baron, Cynthia, editor. | Scott, Ellen C., 1978– editor. | Francis, Terri Simone, editor. | Vander, Robin G., editor.
Title: Intersecting aesthetics : literary adaptations and cinematic representations of Blackness / Charlene Regester, Cynthia Baron, Ellen C. Scott, Terri Simone Francis, Robin G. Vander.
Description: Jackson : University Press of Mississippi, 2023. | Includes bibliographical references and index.
Identifiers: LCCN 2023033387 (print) | LCCN 2023033388 (ebook) | ISBN 9781496848840 (hardback) | ISBN 9781496848857 (trade paperback) | ISBN 9781496848864 (epub) | ISBN 9781496848871 (epub) | ISBN 9781496848888 (pdf) | ISBN 9781496848895 (pdf)
Subjects: LCSH: African Americans in motion pictures—History—20th century. | African Americans in the motion picture industry—History—20th century. | African American motion picture producers and directors—History—20th century. | African Americans—Intellectual life—20th century. | Race in motion pictures. | Film adaptations—History and criticism.
Classification: LCC PN1995.9.B585 I58 2023 (print) | LCC PN1995.9.B585 (ebook) | DDC 791.43/652996073—dc23/eng/20230830
LC record available at https://lccn.loc.gov/2023033387
LC ebook record available at https://lccn.loc.gov/2023033388

British Library Cataloging-in-Publication Data available

CONTENTS

Preface. VII
Acknowledgments IX

Part I: Black Literary/Film Adaptations in Scholarly and Historical Contexts

Chapter 1. Introduction:
Cinematic Adaptations Representing Blackness 3
CHARLENE REGESTER AND CYNTHIA BARON

Chapter 2. Glimmers of Hope, Dreams Deferred, and Diminished
Desires: Early African American Literary Figures and the
Cinema Industry 16
CHARLENE REGESTER

Part II: Colonial Anxieties and Reclaimed Identities

Chapter 3. The Devil's Wanga: Representations of Power and
the Erotics of Black Female Planters in *The Love Wanga* (1936)
and *The Devil's Daughter* (1939). 45
TANYA L. SHIELDS

Chapter 4. Filmic Migrations of the Carmen Figure: *Karmen Geï*
and Its Implications for Diasporic Black Female Decolonization. 67
KIMBERLY NICHELE BROWN

Part III: Hollywood's Problematic Reconstructions

Chapter 5. Imagining the Haitian Revolution in *Lydia Bailey*:
Kenneth Roberts's 1947 Novel and Darryl F. Zanuck's 1952 Film 95
JUDITH E. SMITH

Chapter 6. Refusing to Be "Somebody's Damn Maid":
An Examination of Space in Billie Holiday's Autobiography
and Biopic *Lady Sings the Blues* 115
CHARLENE REGESTER

Part IV: Black Literature's Challenge for Screen Adaptations

Chapter 7. Burbanking Bigger and Bette the Bitch:
Native Son and *In This Our Life* at Warner Bros. 145
ELIZABETH BINGGELI

Chapter 8. Frank Yerby and the Art and Discipline of
Racial Sublimation 168
ELLEN C. SCOTT

Part V: Black Auteurs Defying Dominant Norms

Chapter 9. Adapting Black Masculinity in Melvin Van Peebles's
The Story of a Three Day Pass 205
PRISCILLA LAYNE

Chapter 10. Black Autonomy On Screen and Off:
Gordon Parks's *The Learning Tree* (1969) and *Shaft* (1971) 225
CYNTHIA BARON AND ERIC PIERSON

Chapter 11. *Devil in a Blue Dress*: Aesthetic Strategies That
Illuminate "Invisibility" and Continue Black Literary Traditions 247
CYNTHIA BARON

About the Contributors 265
Index 268

PREFACE

The volume has five parts that illustrate distinct themes and considerations. Part I, Black Literary/Film Adaptations in Scholarly and Historical Contexts, provides a context for the anthology's research and a background for evolving Black efforts to penetrate the mainstream film industry. Part II, Colonial Anxieties and Reclaimed Identities, analyzes literature and cinematic adaptations that naturalize white colonial anxieties and, at other times, challenge and dispel the first-world gaze. Part III, Hollywood's Problematic Reconstructions, documents the complications that ensue when Black historical and biographical narratives become the terrain for contests between progressive and conservative white ideological factions in Hollywood. Part IV, Black Literature's Challenge for Screen Adaptations, examines Hollywood's circuitous methods for adapting literary works featuring Black characters whose stories reveal systemic inequities. Part V, Black Auteurs Defying Dominant Norms, presents three case studies that explore the agency and aesthetic choices of Black writers and directors working in disparate production contexts.

ACKNOWLEDGMENTS

This project evolved from the work of several colleagues and scholars who represent a wide range of disciplines from African American film history, cultural history, women's studies, gender studies, popular culture studies, and adaptation studies, who came together to assemble this collection, which we saw as long overdue and as providing valuable insights related to the Black experience as it coincided with film and literature adaptations. Initially, the volume was more narrowly focused on Hollywood productions, but we discovered that it was necessary to include works that reflected colonial perspectives and those of Black American filmmakers who produced works outside the US.

Considering the range of chapters in this volume, we believe it contributes to and invites further historical inquiries into film/literature adaptations that relate to the Black experience both within and outside the US. Moreover, the volume poses questions and raises concerns that invoke discussion and debate surrounding ways that marginalized voices struggle to be heard. When their voices and experiences are reproduced on screen, to what extent are they accurately reproduced? When these narratives are mass-produced for wider consumption, to what extent is their authenticity compromised? Many of the chapters in this collection reflect ongoing research that contributors have launched and continue to pursue as they document the contributions of literary figures, filmmakers, artists, and performers.

The volume could not have been completed without the tenacity of coeditor Cynthia Baron along with the commitment of coeditors Ellen C. Scott, Terri Simone Francis, and Robin G. Vander. Working with such skilled scholars makes the process easier and enhances the strength of the work. Other people involved in reading and editing the material include Emily Baron, who interrupted her schedule to assist. Ellen C. Scott recommended material for the volume. Other contributors and coeditors read chapters to ensure they accomplished what was intended and adequately reflected the author's ideas. Maria DeGuzman and Tanya L. Shields worked on chapters to improve the quality and strength of the work, and to both, I will always be grateful.

Institutional support was provided by the Department of African, African American, and Diaspora Studies at the University of North Carolina at Chapel Hill, with chair and professor Claude Clegg providing funds to subsidize the cost of securing photographs included in the volume. I am grateful to the AAAD Department for a spring 2023 Research and Study Leave, which allowed me to complete the final stages of this project. Others within the department who extended their support in a variety of ways include Lola Tasar and Velvet Catoe. The Institute of Arts and Humanities at UNC–Chapel Hill provided additional grant funding to purchase photos. New York's Photofest was instrumental in allowing us to access photos from their archive, and they made the process simple for acquiring images; we are grateful for their assistance. Eric Browning aided in creating frame captures.

Davis Library, the graduate library at UNC–CH, was instrumental in locating sources that were difficult to access; over the years, its staff members have always extended themselves to retrieve materials through Interlibrary Loan or the Microfilms Division for research purposes. The Robert B. House Undergraduate Library at UNC–CH also provided their services to locate rare materials necessary to complete the project. Within the undergrad library, the Media and Design Center staff, including Fred Metz (head librarian), Katelyn Anders, and Justin Dorazio along with student workers, were incredibly resourceful in locating films and giving me access to the media lab in their facility. Furthermore, I want to thank the African American Institute in the Sonja Haynes Center for Black Culture and Research at UNC–CH, where I served as interim director in spring 2022, for supporting my work on this project.

Finally, I would like to thank the contributors whose commitment and excellent work led to chapters that strengthen the volume's theme and focus; they include Judith E. Smith, Tanya L. Shields, Ellen C. Scott, Eric Pierson, Priscilla Layne, Kimberly Nichele Brown, Elizabeth Binggelli, and Cynthia Baron. On behalf of the coeditors and contributors, I would like to thank Emily Bandy and the production and marketing teams at the University Press of Mississippi for ushering this project through its various phases. We also want to thank the anonymous readers who provided insightful critiques of the book prior to its publication.

CHARLENE REGESTER

Part I

Black Literary/Film Adaptations in Scholarly and Historical Contexts

Chapter 1

INTRODUCTION

Cinematic Adaptations Representing Blackness

CHARLENE REGESTER AND CYNTHIA BARON

Laughing out loud, camouflaging pain, circumventing assaults, internalizing rejection, challenging political affronts, demystifying preconceived notions, and living vicariously through reconstituted identities are among the myriad motivations that propel Black writers to give voice and visibility to Black life. Crafting narratives that distill these lived experiences, Black writers and filmmakers have also fought for Black realities to be visualized on screen. This collection highlights Black artists' groundbreaking efforts and a selection of Black stories adapted to film during the twentieth century. The chapters examine literary explorations of colonial dynamics, cinematic depictions of biographical and historical narratives, adaptations that covertly dramatize Black life, and the work of Black auteurs who retain control over their productions. Reflecting our title, *Intersecting Aesthetics*, the volume's chapters are in conversation with one another as they analyze instances in which literature, cinema, and racial representation intersect.

Taken together, the collection's chapters illuminate cultural and material trends shaping Black film adaptations produced over the course of the twentieth century. Contributors consider how Black literary and filmic texts become sites of negotiation between dominant and resistant perspectives in racialized societies. Case studies disclose the powerful effects that bigotry and patriarchy have on film adaptations. Evidence reveals that race-inflected tropes and cultural norms influence both studio and independent film depictions of colonialism's legacy and gendered complexities. The chapters also illustrate ways in which self-censorship and industry censorship affected Black writing and adaptations of Black stories in mid-twentieth-century America; archival evidence indicates that commercial obstacles led Black writers and white-dominated studios to mask historical and contemporary Black experiences through transposition into costume dramas and white-centered narratives. Other chapters document instances in which Black writers and directors navigate dominant norms and material realities to realize their visions in literary works, independent films, and studio productions. Uncovering patterns in Black literary/film adaptations, the case studies in *Intersecting Aesthetics* illuminate themes, aesthetic strategies, and cultural dynamics that rightfully belong to accounts of film adaptation.

METHODOLOGY OF *INTERSECTING AESTHETICS*

The book's contributions to studies of literary/film adaptations emerge from its central research question: what insights about society, cinema, and literary works become visible when the scholarship concentrates on film adaptations involving Black writers, directors, or stories? The volume's research also rests on the shared methodological perspective that literary sources and film adaptations cannot be analyzed in isolation from cultural-aesthetic realities. For all the contributors, textual, archival, and contextual evidence has clarified that literary and filmic works reflect social and institutional hierarchies and that decisions in the adaptation process become more clear when one examines cultural factors surrounding film and literary works, censorship policies, literary and filmic genre conventions, production conditions, and financial considerations.[1] The chapters in this collection demonstrate that race is an irrefutable factor influencing the creation, distribution, and reception of Black literature and cinematic adaptations depicting blackness. Thus, the chapters frame literary works as existing within specific historical circumstances and identify source material as one of many influences on Black film adaptations. In addition, the volume's contributors deconstruct ideological perspectives in both literary and filmic texts. They present source material as reflecting, negotiating, and challenging a social and material world in which racial hierarchies sustain cultural power structures. Similarly, they discuss film adaptations as documents that shed light on their production, distribution, and reception contexts. *Intersecting Aesthetics* features archive-based analyses that advance scholarship on "how adaptations come to be [and] how the various institutional, commercial and legal frameworks surrounding adaptations influence the number and the character of adaptations in cultural circulation."[2]

The overwhelming evidence that Black literary sources and Black film adaptations exist in cultural and material contexts has also influenced contributors to set aside evaluation and instead analyze intersecting aesthetic choices along with external factors shaping audience responses. Contributors' use of archival records concerning censorship, marketing, and press coverage of Black film adaptations has further encouraged them to approach analysis in nonevaluative terms. The noncanonical source material featured in *Intersecting Aesthetics* has also fostered the contributors' exploratory, rather than evaluative, approach to literary and filmic choices that generate overt meaning *and* allow for interpretations based on against-the-grain readings. The case studies' literary sources include travelogue and autobiography as well as the fiction of Black authors such as early twentieth-century novelist H. G. (Herbert George) de Lisser; mid-twentieth-century writers Richard Wright, Ann Petry, and Frank Yerby; and contemporary author Walter Mosley. Contributors examine independent race films *The Love Wanga* (George Terwilliger, 1936) and *The Devil's Daughter* (Arthur H. Leonard, 1939); Melvin Van Peebles's little-known first feature *The Story of a Three Day Pass* (1967); the Senegalese film *Karmen Geï* (Joseph Gaï Ramaka, 2001); studio-era films *In This Our Life* (John Huston, 1942), *The Foxes of Harrow* (John M. Stahl, 1947), *Lydia Bailey* (Jean Negulesco, 1952), *The Golden Hawk* (Sidney Salkow, 1952), and *The Saracen Blade* (William Castle, 1954); and post-studio-era films *The Learning Tree* (Gordon Parks, 1969), *Shaft* (Gordon Parks, 1971), *Lady Sings the Blues* (Sidney J. Furie, 1972), and *Devil in a Blue Dress* (Carl Franklin, 1995).

SCHOLARSHIP ON BLACK FILM ADAPTATIONS

Despite the extensive scholarship on film adaptation, remarkably few studies examine screen adaptations of Black literature, writings on Black experiences, or works with central Black characters. Documenting that reality, Sara Martín's 1999 survey of work published in *Literature/Film Quarterly* discloses the field's keen interest in "adaptations of Shakespearean plays" and its limited attention to artistic works that explore race or ethnicity.[3] This pattern continues into the twenty-first century. As Deborah Cartmell, Timothy Corrigan, and Imelda Whelehan observe in their 2008 overview of film adaptation scholarship, the "study of literature on screen has largely concentrated on canonical texts," with "Shakespeare on screen and, more recently, Austen on screen [becoming] disciplines in their own right."[4] Writing in 2012, Simone Murray makes a parallel point, suggesting that "adaptation studies has traditionally [focused its] greatest attention on the nineteenth-century and Modernist literary canon."[5] The field's sustained interest in a delimited selection of source materials is visible in contemporary work such as Yvonne Griggs's *The Bloomsbury Introduction to Adaptation Studies: Adapting the Canon in Film, TV, Novels, and Popular Culture* (2016), which examines adaptations of standards like *Jane Eyre* and *The Great Gatsby*. Thomas Leitch's 2017 anthology *The Oxford Handbook of Adaptation Studies* includes new research on Bollywood films, telenovelas, comic books, and videogames but does not bring Black narratives into the volume's project of updating adaptation scholarship. Revealing the field's emphasis on a circumscribed set of literary sources, William H. Mooney's *Adaptation and the New Art Film: Remaking the Classics in the Twilight of Cinema* (2021) examines new dimensions of adapting canonical literature and does not consider the work of Black writers or directors.

The work of Griggs, Leitch, and Mooney follows established patterns in scholarship. Black literary/film adaptations have minimal representation in encyclopedic volumes such as Tom Costello's *International Guide to Literature on Film* (1994), John C. Tibbetts and James M. Welsh's *The Encyclopedia of Novels into Film*, 2nd edition (2005), and Barry Keith Grant's *Books to Film: Cinematic Adaptations of Literary Works: Volume 1* (2018). Anthologies that do not discuss Black film adaptations include Robert Stam and Alessandra Raengo's *A Companion to Literature and Film* (2004), Deborah Cartmell and Imelda Whelehan's *The Cambridge Companion to Literature On Screen* (2007), Colin MacCabe, Kathleen Murray, and Rick Warner's *True to the Spirit: Film Adaptation and the Question of Fidelity* (2011), and Jørgen Bruhn, Anne Gjelsvik, and Eirik Frisvold Hanssen's *Adaptation Studies: New Challenges, New Directions* (2013). James Naremore's *Film Adaptation* (2000) includes a chapter on *How Tasty Was My Little Frenchman* (Nelson Pereira dos Santos, 1971), a film that examines questions of race and colonialism. Deborah Cartmell's *A Companion to Literature, Film, and Adaptation* (2012) includes a chapter on screen adaptations of Shakespeare's *Othello*.

Deborah Cartmell and Imelda Whelehan's anthology *Adaptations: Critical and Primary Sources* (2022) vividly illustrates the white norms in contemporary adaptation studies. Among the eighty chapters in the three-volume set, only one touches on the work of Black writers or filmmakers: the introduction to Robert Stam and Alessandra Raengo's multicultural anthology *Literature and Film: A Guide to Theory and Practice of Film Adaptation* (2005) appears in volume two. Tellingly, the three other chapters that constitute the anthology's consideration of Black stories feature white artists and characters: volume one reprints Harriet Hawkin's 1993 chapter on *Gone with the Wind* (Margaret Mitchell's 1936 book, Victor Fleming's 1939 film); volume two includes the introduction to Thomas Leitch's *Film Adaptation and Its Discontents: From Gone with the Wind to The Passion of the Christ* (2007), which examines the intertextuality of literary sources rather than racial representation in *Gone with the Wind*; volume three reprints Douglas M. Lanier's 2012 chapter on *Othello*.

Contemporary monographs that overlook Black film adaptations include Kamilla Elliott's *Rethinking the Novel/Film Debate* (2003), Linda Costanzo Cahir's *Literature in Film: Theory and Practical Approaches* (2006), Jennifer M. Jeffers's *Britain Colonized: Hollywood's Appropriation of British Literature* (2006), Christine Geraghty's *Now a Major Motion Picture: Film Adaptations of Literature and Drama* (2008), Linda Hutcheon's *A Theory of Adaptation*, 2nd edition (2013), Kamilla Elliott's *Theorizing Adaptation* (2020), and Jae-Seong Lee's *Awakening through Literature and Film* (2021). Robert Stam's *Literature through Film: Realism, Magic, and the Art of Adaptation* (2005) does discuss *Macunaíma* (Mário de Andrade's 1928 novel, Joaquin Pedro de Andrade's 1969 film), based on a parable featuring a Black character. Julie Sanders's *Adaptation and Appropriation*, 2nd edition (2016), considers *Black Orpheus* (Marcel Camus, 1959) and *O* (Tim Blake Nelson, 2001), which have Black characters.

Journals and anthologies have isolated articles on *The Color Purple* (Alice Walker's 1982 novel, Steven Spielberg's 1985 film), *Beloved* (Toni Morrison's 1987 novel, Jonathan Demme's 1998 film), and *If Beale Street Could Talk* (James Baldwin's 1974 novel, Barry Jenkins's 2018 film). Adaptation scholarship of *Intersecting Aesthetics* authors includes Charlene Regester's "African-American Writers and Pre-1950 Cinema" in *Literature/Film Quarterly* (2001); Elizabeth Binggeli's "The Unadapted: Warner Bros. Reads Zora Neale Hurston" in *Cinema Journal* (Spring 2009); Ellen C. Scott's "Blacker than Noir: The Making and Unmaking of Richard Wright's 'Ugly' *Native Son* (1951)" in *Adaptation* (February 2013); and Kimberly Nichele Brown's "Decolonizing Mammy and Other Subversive Acts: Directing as Feminist Praxis in Gina Prince-Bythewood's *The Secret Life of Bees*" in *African American Cinema through Black Lives Consciousness* (2019).

Some anthologies feature research on Black literature and film. Robert Stam and Alessandra Raengo's 2005 anthology *Literature and Film: A Guide to Theory and Practice of Film Adaptation* has three chapters on Black film adaptations: Paula J. Massood's "*Boyz N the Hood* Chronotopes: Spike Lee, Richard Price, and the Changing Authorship of *Clockers*"; Mia Mask's "*Beloved*: The Adaptation of an American Slave Narrative"; and Mbye Cham's "Oral Traditions, Literature, and Cinema in Africa." Mireia Aragay's *Books in Motion: Adaptation, Intertextuality, Authorship* (2005) includes Lindiwe Dovey's chapter on *Fools* (Njabulo S. Ndebele's 1983 novella, Ramadan Suleman's 1997 film). James M. Welsh and Peter Lev's *The Literature/Film Reader: Issues of Adaptation* (2007) includes John C. Tibbetts's "W. C. Handy Goes Uptown: Hollywood Constructs the American Blues Musician." R. Barton Palmer's *Nineteenth-Century American Fiction On Screen* (2007) has a chapter on "Readapting *Uncle Tom's Cabin*." His *Twentieth-Century American Fiction On Screen* (2007) has chapters on the film adaptations of *Beloved* and *The Color Purple* along with two chapters on narratives with Black supporting characters, *The Member of the Wedding* (Carson McCuller's 1946 novel, Fred Zinnemann's 1952 film) and *Intruder in the Dust* (William Faulkner's 1948 novel, Clarence Brown's 1949 film).

Jack Boozer's anthology *Authorship in Film Adaptation* (2008) includes a chapter on *Devil in a Blue Dress* (Walter Mosley's 1990 novel, Carl Franklin's

1995 film), one of the case studies in this volume. Timothy Corrigan's *Film and Literature Reader: An Introduction and Reader*, 2nd edition (2012), has an excerpt from Mark A. Reid's *Redefining Black Film* (1993), which discusses the 1961 adaptation of Lorraine Hansberry's 1959 play *A Raisin in the Sun*. In Linda Cartmell and Imelda Whelehan's *Teaching Adaptations* (2014), contributors Alessandra Raengo, Natalie Hayton, and Rachael Carroll have chapters that examine race and representation. Julie Grossman's *Literature, Film, and Their Hideous Progeny: Adaptation and ElasTEXTity* (2015) has a chapter on *Imitation of Life* (Fannie Hurst's 1933 novel, John M. Stahl's 1934 film, Douglas Sirk's 1959 film).[6] Shelley Cobb's *Adaptation, Authorship, and Contemporary Women Filmmakers* (2015) concludes with a discussion of Prince-Bythewood's film adaptation of *The Secret Life of Bees* (2008). Allen H. Redmon's anthology *Next Generation Adaptation: Spectatorship and Process* (2021) has a chapter that relates Spike Lee's *He Got Game* (1998) to Langston Hughes's poem "I, Too" (1926).

Other scholarship has considered Black film adaptations in various contexts.[7] Emmanuel S. Nelson's *Contemporary African American Novelists: A Biobibliographical Critical Sourcebook* (1999) references Terry McMillan's novel *Waiting to Exhale* (1992) and Forest Whitaker's adaptation (1995), along with her novel *How Stella Got Her Groove Back* (1996) and Kevin Rodney Sullivan's adaptation (1998). Lindiwe Dovey's *African Film and Literature: Adapting Violence to the Screen* (2009) discusses films such as *Cry, the Beloved Country* (Zoltan Korda, 1951, Darrell Roodt, 1995), *La Genèse* (Cheick Oumar Sissoko, 1999), and *Karmen Geï* (Joseph Gaï Ramaka, 2001); *Karmen Geï* is discussed in this volume. Robert E. Terrill's anthology *The Cambridge Companion to Malcolm X* (2010) and Dennis Bingham's *Whose Lives Are They Anyway?: The Biopic as Contemporary Film Genre* (2010) chronicle the fraught process that eventually led *The Autobiography of Malcolm X* (1965) to be translated into *Malcolm X* (Spike Lee, 1992). Barbara Tepa Lupack's *Literary Adaptations in Black Cinema: From Micheaux to Morrison* (2002) surveys American film from the silent era to the present, critiquing mainstream representations and articulating the perspectives of Black authors and filmmakers.

Jonathan Munby's *Under a Bad Sign: Criminal Self-Representation in African American Popular Culture* (2011) analyzes Chester Himes's novels and their Blaxploitation film adaptations. Anne Crémieux, Xavier Lemoine, and Jean-Paul Rocchi's collection *Understanding Blackness through Performance* (2013) includes a discussion of Sapphire's *Push: A Novel* (1996) and Lee Daniels's adaptation *Precious* (2009).[8] James J. Ward and Cynthia J. Miller's anthology *Urban Noir: New York and Los Angeles in Shadow and Light* (2017) features chapters on *Devil in a Blue Dress* and *Cotton Comes to Harlem* (Chester Himes's 1965 novel, Ossie Davis's 1970 film), which are discussed in this volume. Elizabeth Reich's *Militant Visions: Black Soldiers, Internationalism, and the Transformation of American Cinema* (2016) includes a chapter on *The Spook Who Sat by the Door* (Sam Greenlee's 1969 novel, Ivan Dixon's 1973 film). Michael T. Martin, David C. Wall, and Marilyn Yaquinto's *Race and the Revolutionary Impulse in The Spook Who Sat by the Door* (2018) features contributors who offer a comprehensive look at Greenlee's novel and Dixon's film. Taking a different approach, Salvador Jimenez Murguía's *The Encyclopedia of Racism in American Films* (2018) includes brief accounts of Black adaptations in its survey of films that sustain or expose systemic racism in American society.

BLACK TWENTIETH-CENTURY LITERARY/FILM ADAPTATIONS

Intersecting Aesthetics adds to the evolving scholarship on Black film adaptations through a coherent set of case studies grounded in historical, cultural, and material evidence. Consistently placing literary and filmic texts within larger contexts, the research highlights how multiple factors affect production and reception. The approach illuminates patterns in literary, cinematic, and social history. When considered together, the collection's case studies move adaptation scholarship beyond the insights offered in isolated articles and chapters that ostensibly provide diversity in publications that tacitly sustain the link between whiteness and prestige art.

Part I, Black Literary/Film Adaptations in Scholarly and Historical Contexts, includes the chapter you are reading and chapter 2, "Glimmers of Hope, Dreams Deferred, and Diminished Desires: Early African American Literary Figures and the Cinema Industry." In the chapter, Charlene Regester discusses Black writers whose work led to independent film adaptations, garnered transitory interest from Hollywood, or was adapted in compromised ways. Writers whose work attracted independent filmmakers' interest include Paul Laurence Dunbar, Charles Waddell Chesnutt, and Oscar Micheaux. Authors who became screenwriters or whose writings were considered for screen adaptations include Wallace Thurman, Langston Hughes, Zora Neale Hurston, and Ann Petry. Writers who had their literary art compromised when adapted to the screen include Frank Yerby, Willard Motley, and Richard Wright. In both independent and studio settings, the adaptation of these groundbreaking writers' work often involved the fraught cultural and material dynamics examined in subsequent chapters.

Part II, Colonial Anxieties and Reclaimed Identities, features studies of independent film adaptations that complicate colonial perspectives through the depiction of "unruly" Black women who challenge the images of blackness constructed in the literature. Introducing a point that the entire volume makes, the chapters on independent film adaptations from the 1930s and the turn of the twenty-first century suggest that, over time, Black screen adaptations increasingly reflect Black perspectives. In chapter 3, "The Devil's Wanga: Representations of Power and the Erotics of Black Female Planters in *The Love Wanga* (1936) and *The Devil's Daughter* (1939)," Tanya L. Shields analyzes *The White Witch of Rosehall*, the 1929 novel of Jamaican author H. G. de Lisser, and two independent race films, *The Love Wanga* (1936) starring Fredi Washington and *The Devil's Daughter* (1939) starring Nina Mae McKinney. In these texts about female planters, spiritual power is one path women pursue to inhabit the realm of ownership. Yet the ideological terrain of ownership, steeped in imperial notions of masculinity, takes on a ferocious manifestation when connected to women. The films use women to sexualize the Caribbean and convey its instability: as voodoo practitioners, they are tied to the primitive; as landowners, they are an indication of the region's disturbed social hierarchy. De Lisser's novel and the two films highlight fears and desires that dominate the white colonial imaginary and are displaced onto the "throbbing drums" that recall Africa. In the films, Haitian "degeneracy" is mapped onto Caribbean spaces to suggest that they all need the management of white imperial powers.

In chapter 4, "Filmic Migrations of the Carmen Figure: *Karmen Geï* and Its Implications for Diasporic Black Female Sexual Decolonization," Kimberly Nichele Brown reconsiders the story of transgressive female sexuality that *Carmen*, Prosper Mérimée's 1845 novella, made famous. Given the novella's many reinterpretations, Brown sees Carmen as a migratory figure whose mythology traverses cultural and national boundaries, including *Karmen Geï*, the 2001 film by Senegalese director Joseph Gaï Ramaka. While not the only film to feature an all-Black cast or a Black woman as Carmen, *Karmen Geï* offers an especially progressive rendering of Black female erotic agency that challenges the white Western gaze and calls for a reevaluation of critical approaches that position African gender politics as atavistic and stagnant. The film adaptation reshapes a prescriptive morality tale into one that articulates and visualizes sexual decolonization for its Western and Senegalese viewers. In *Karmen Geï*, Ramaka reframes the discourse of love to include self-actualization and civic responsibility, thereby modeling what sexual liberation might look like for its Black female viewers throughout the Diaspora.

Part III, Hollywood's Problematic Reconstructions, has case studies that examine films made after World War II or during the civil rights era, when progressive white producers were motivated to make studio films that celebrated Black resistance and artistry. The chapters document and contextualize complications that arose in the process of adapting Black narratives on screen. The scholarship amplifies the discussions in Part II; one chapter provides additional insights into colonialism's legacy, and both chapters analyze depictions of Black women in white patriarchal cultural and material environments. In chapter 5,

"Imagining the Haitian Revolution in *Lydia Bailey*: Kenneth Roberts's 1947 Novel and Darryl F. Zanuck's 1952 Film," Judith E. Smith documents the development, production, marketing, and reception of *Lydia Bailey*, a Hollywood film that depicts the Haitian Revolution. The chapter draws on private studio memos and public press discussions to analyze debates over racial representation, colonialism, and decolonization in the late 1940s and early 1950s. Smith uses these records to show how white supremacy eventually shaped the film's production and promotion. The chapter draws on archival production files and various trade publications, white mainstream papers, and Black newspapers to document the racial divide shaping the film's production and reception. The *Lydia Bailey* production reveals a moment in which transnational Black history and Black struggle became more public and legible in the wake of World War II antifascism and internationalism, but these concerns faded when white Americans turned their focus to Cold War anticommunism.

In chapter 6, "Refusing to Be 'Somebody's Damn Maid': An Examination of Space in Billie Holiday's Autobiography and Biopic *Lady Sings the Blues*," Charlene Regester sheds light on the almost twenty-year history leading to the screen adaptation of Holiday's 1956 autobiography, *Lady Sings the Blues*, coauthored with William Dufty. The chapter analyzes Sidney J. Furie's 1972 film in relation to both Holiday's longtime interest in shaping accounts of her life and the jazz artist's sometimes marginalized screen depictions, as when she was cast as a maid in the Hollywood film *New Orleans* (Arthur Lubin, 1947). It discusses the complications of female-centered biopics, Holiday's experiences working in films starting in the 1930s, her involvement in plans for adapting her autobiography, and the problematic casting and production decisions eventually made after her 1959 death. The chapter features textual analysis that reveals the intersecting but finally disconnected aesthetic choices that separate Holiday's autobiography and production efforts from the Hollywood film that enhanced Diana Ross's image through embodying Holiday. It shows that, in contrast to the autobiography, certain spaces in the biopic emphasize the restraints imposed on Holiday because of her race and gender.

Part IV, Black Literature's Challenge for Screen Adaptations, clarifies that white studio executives in mid-twentieth-century America showed an interest in working with Black writers but were not prepared to depict fully realized Black characters or narratives that exposed race relations in America. The research shows that this impasse caused adaptation projects to stall in development and led Black writers to create Black narratives that were masked, transposed, and sublimated in ways that suited white Hollywood executives. In chapter 7, "Burbanking Bigger and Bette the Bitch: *Native Son* and *In This Our Life* at Warner Bros.," Elizabeth Binggeli provides an illuminating look into decisions of the Warner Bros. story department concerning Richard Wright's *Native*

Son (1940), Ann Petry's *The Street* (1946), and white author Ellen Glasgow's *In This Our Life* (1941). Shedding light on the process that led Glasgow's novel to be produced while the other literary works were shelved or substantially compromised, the chapter analyzes archival documents that describe the protracted debates about Wright's characterization of his central character, Bigger Thomas, and the risks in adapting his story to make it palatable to white audiences. The archival records reveal that Warner Bros. readers found Petry's central character, Lutie, more appropriate than Bigger for a studio picture but that there were sustained debates about suitable ways to create a commercial film adaptation, including the studio's proposal to have white central characters in films based on Wright's and Petry's stories. Warner Bros. eventually found a way to feature a predatory villain and explore the narrative dynamic of miscegenation in the adaptation of Glasgow's *In This Our Life*.

In chapter 8, "Frank Yerby and the Art and Discipline of Racial Sublimation," Ellen C. Scott analyzes the sublimated racial commentary in *The Foxes of Harrow* (1947), *The Golden Hawk* (1952), and *The Saracen Blade* (1954). Using archival studio resources and Production Code Administration records, the chapter contextualizes the adaptation process, censorship, and reception of these films. Scott frames Yerby as a fascinating conundrum in the midcentury literary scene: the short stories of this Works Progress Administration–trained writer were firmly rooted in the antiracist protest tradition of Richard Wright; yet frustrated with his failure to secure a book contract for his protest fiction, Yerby turned to writing "costume fiction" in which racial problems appeared minor. Yerby became the first Black novelist to write best-selling books, popularizing a mode of indirectly dealing with slavery that contrasted with white-authored plantation melodramas. Like other protest novelists and the pulp fiction writers whose work inspired film noir, Yerby wrote with a deep cynicism about white America, even though his genre work rarely allowed him to depict this sentiment directly. Ultimately, Yerby was an artist whose craft was steeped in the discipline of sublimation and who explored the conditions of Black life through other frames.

Part V, Black Authors Defying Dominant Norms, considers Black writers and directors who overturn white norms in artistic works that reflect Black perspectives. The case studies analyze literary and film narratives that explore Black characters' subjectivity, agency, and experiences with racism. The research confirms that twentieth-century adaptations with a Black perspective existed in both independent and commercial cinema and that Black film adaptations can embody conventions associated with both art cinema and popular genre forms. In chapter 9, "Adapting Black Masculinity in Melvin Van Peebles's *The Story of a Three Day Pass*," Priscilla Layne reveals the opportunities for Black expression when an African American artist creates work outside the United

States. Discussing Van Peebles's early career, the chapter explains that during a long stay in France as one of many Black artists in exile, he applied for filmmaker's rights after establishing himself as a novelist with the publication of *La Permission* (1967), the basis for his first feature, *The Story of a Three Day Pass* (1967). The central character, a soldier stationed in France following World War II, is one of thousands of African American men enjoying a breadth of freedom miles away from racist America. Analyzing the texts' intersecting aesthetics, the chapter reflects on Van Peebles's decision to explore postwar American occupation and a Black male character's state of mind only in the novella. Also considering the adaptation in relation to a subsequent Van Peebles's film, the chapter sees *The Story of a Three Day Pass* as revealing the director's interest in taking a more political and confrontational stance on racial politics, making this film a precursor to his more radical production *Sweet Sweetback's Baadasssss Song* (1971).

In chapter 10, "Black Autonomy On Screen and Off: Gordon Parks's *The Learning Tree* (1969) and *Shaft* (1971)," Cynthia Baron and Eric Pierson analyze Parks's first two Hollywood films in relation to his photography work and the films of other Black artists who participated in the Hollywood Renaissance in the late 1960s and early 1970s. Contextualizing Parks's early feature films reveals Parks's enduring ability to create visual narratives that illuminate and comment on the lives of African Americans. Situating the two films within the social and industrial setting of the late 1960s and early 1970s clarifies how Black creative talent contributed to this celebrated era, which has long been identified almost exclusively with white male auteurs. The chapter shows that the adaptation of *The Learning Tree*, Parks's 1963 autobiographical novel, involved the distillation of the book's themes, events, and characters, whereas in adapting *Shaft*, a white-authored piece of racist and misogynistic pulp fiction, Parks transformed the central character and the narrative's perspective to create John Shaft, for whom private detective work is his creative choice of weapon in a dangerous, bigoted society.

In chapter 11, "*Devil in a Blue Dress*: Aesthetic Strategies That Illuminate 'Invisibility' and Continue Black Literary Traditions," Cynthia Baron creates a context for analyzing Walter Mosley's 1990 detective novel and Carl Franklin's 1995 Black noir film through research that frames both works as iterations of Black literary traditions harkening back to Frederick Douglass and reflecting the contributions of early twentieth-century writers Pauline Hopkins and John Edward Bruce, as well as more contemporary authors such as Ralph Ellison and Chester Himes. The chapter contextualizes the novel and the film adaptation using the insights of legal scholar Michelle Alexander and others who highlight the laws and social conventions integral to the systemic racism "invisible" to white Americans. The chapter sees the novel and the film as the work of Black artists expert in using popular literary and film genre conventions to create social commentaries and illuminate Black subjectivities. It analyzes the intersecting aesthetics in Mosley's novel and Franklin's film to describe how the film's choices in music, performance, and cinematography parallel the novel's narrative strategies that convey the subjectivity of the central character and the elegiac mood that gives his everyday experiences the weight of a historical account.

As the chapter overviews suggest, *Intersecting Aesthetics* mines overlooked evidence, consolidates isolated scholarship, and advances research on screen adaptations that depend on Black creative labor. Offering evidence and analyses that contextualize aesthetic, cultural, and industrial developments, the collection's in-depth research projects highlight patterns in Black artists' interactions with white-dominated culture industries and identify shared traits in their literary and filmic choices that negotiate white mainstream anxieties and values. Coinciding with its range of material, the volume depends on scholars from film and media studies, comparative literature, women and gender studies, American studies, and African American studies. Combining insights drawn from adaptation studies and their respective disciplines, these researchers enhance scholarship on film adaptation, Black artistry, and Black experiences. Their work illustrates the value of analyzing source materials and screen adaptations in multiple contexts and shows how the history of adaptation studies is enriched when research moves beyond canonical texts in which whiteness is the invisible norm.[9]

Notes

1. This orientation reflects the priorities for future research articulated by Deborah Cartmell, Timothy Corrigan, and Imelda Whelehan in their introduction to the first volume of *Adaptation* published in 2008.

2. Simone Murray, *The Adaptation Industry: The Cultural Economy of Contemporary Literary Adaptation* (New York: Routledge, 2012), 4.

3. Sara Martín, "Literature and Film: A Bibliography," *Links and Letters* 6 (1999): 122.

4. Deborah Cartmell, Timothy Corrigan, and Imelda Whelehan, "Introduction to *Adaptation*," *Adaptation* 1, no. 1 (2008): 2, 3.

5. Murray, *Adaptation Industry*, 11.

6. For other publications on *Imitation of Life*, see Lucy Fischer, ed., *Imitation of Life: Douglas Sirk Director* (New Brunswick, NJ: Rutgers University Press, 1991); Daniel Itzkovitz, ed., *Imitation of Life: Fannie Hurst* (Durham, NC: Duke University Press, 2004). Grossman's 2015 book belongs to the Palgrave Studies in the Adaptation and Visual Culture series; in 2021, the series included twenty-one other books, none of which consider film adaptations related to the literature, films, or lives of African, African American, or other African Diaspora people.

7. For scholarship that considers Black literature and film, but not adaptations, see Judylyn S. Ryan, *Spirituality as Ideology in Black Women's Film and Literature* (Charlottesville: University

of Virginia Press, 2005); Peter Caster, *Prisons, Race, and Masculinity in Twentieth-Century U.S. Literature and Film* (Columbus: Ohio State University Press, 2008).

8. The film adaptation *Precious* is also analyzed in several academic journal articles.

9. The case studies analyze a handful of the existing screen adaptations of Black literature. Miniseries based on Black authored books include *Roots: The Saga of an American Family* (ABC, 1977) and *The Underground Railroad* (Amazon, 2021). Two Black literary works have multiple adaptations: *Native Son* (Pierre Chenal, 1951; Jerrold Freedman, 1986; Rashid Johnson, 2019) and *A Raisin in the Sun* (Daniel Petrie, 1961; Bill Duke, 1989; Kenny Leon, 2008). Twentieth-century Black film adaptations not mentioned in this chapter include *The Long Night* (Woodie King Jr., 1976), *I Know Why the Caged Bird Sings* (Fielder Cook, 1979), *Sugar Cane Alley* (Euzhan Palcy, 1983), *Antwone Fisher* (Denzel Washington, 2002), *Crime Partners* (J. Jesses Smith, 2003), *Never Die Alone* (Ernest R. Dickerson, 2004), *Their Eyes Were Watching God* (Darnell Martin, 2005), *The Pursuit of Happyness* (Gabriele Muccino, 2006), *For Colored Girls* (Tyler Perry, 2010), *Think Like a Man* (Tim Story, 2012), *12 Years a Slave* (Steve McQueen, 2013), *Hidden Figures* (Theodore Melfi, 2016), *Moonlight* (Barry Jenkins, 2016), *Fences* (Denzel Washington, 2016), *The Hate U Give* (George Tillman Jr., 2018), *Monster* (Anthony Mandler, 2018), *Ma Rainey's Black Bottom* (George C. Wolfe, 2020), and *Passing* (Rebecca Hall, 2021).

Chapter 2

GLIMMERS OF HOPE, DREAMS DEFERRED, AND DIMINISHED DESIRES

Early African American Literary Figures and the Cinema Industry

CHARLENE REGESTER

Exploiting their lived experiences, borrowing from historical moments, writing themselves into existence, or responding to oppressive forces and practices that limited their freedom, African American writers desired to have their voices heard. Articulating these desires, Black voices emanated from the literary works of early writers Paul Laurence Dunbar, Charles Waddell Chesnutt, Wallace Thurman, Langston Hughes, Zora Neale Hurston, and others, but this is not to exclude white writers who similarly believed it was important to expose the Black experience. For example, whites who reconstructed the Black experience in literature and whose writings were adapted to the screen include William Faulkner, Fannie Hurst, Harper Lee, Margaret Mitchell, and Mark Twain. Furthermore, considering that a significant percentage of African American literature coincided with the infancy of cinema, it is certainly understandable that Black life and writings would, ultimately, be transferred to the screen. One of the earliest examples of a literary work that examines Black life on screen is Harriet Beecher Stowe's 1852 best-selling abolitionist novel *Uncle Tom's Cabin*— a novel that filmmaker Edwin S. Porter first adapted as the similarly titled 1903 film. Viewing one version of *Uncle Tom's Cabin* (remade several times due to its popularity), African American Harlem Renaissance writer Dorothy West (author of *The Living Is Easy*, 1948) shares her memories regarding this historical dramatization—a perspective she unveils in her autobiographical sketch "Remembrance." According to scholar David Seed,

> [West] recalled going to see one of the adaptations of *Uncle Tom's Cabin* when she was a young child. The first thing that struck her was the stark

racial difference between characters: "The white people looked happy and the black people looked sad. The white people looked rich and the black people looked poor." Then, as her mother started crying when she saw Tom being beaten by a white man, the young Dorothy tries to soothe her, saying "Don't cry. It's not real. It's make-believe."[1]

Revealing the impact this early visual representation had on West and her mother and considering the film's introduction of the "Uncle Tom" stereotype that film historian Donald Bogle terms "American movies' first black character,"[2] the novel's depiction of blackness was transferred to the country's early motion pictures. As fabricated on screen, scholar Linda Williams argues, the "Uncle Tom" caricature "embodied all the qualities of servility and self-sacrifice for white masters under slavery that blacks had learned to hate."[3] This observation perhaps explains West's emotional reaction to the gross distortions of blackness and exemplifies why she recoiled at the offensiveness embodied in the image. Although West was repulsed by the abuse the Black male character endured and this abuse garnered her sympathies, she was also potentially sympathetic to Eva, the white disabled child. In this production, white characters were "often placed in close proximity to nonwhite characters [so they would] have narrative opportunities to demonstrate their Eva-like tolerance and sympathy for the downtrodden"[4]—demonstrating how whites garnered sympathy for Black victims at a time it was unpopular to do so. But more importantly, for West, reconciling the stereotype's ill-conceived construction led her to refer to the Black caricature as an artificial depiction and to characterize the stereotype as "fraudulent," to use scholar Lauren Berlant's term.[5]

Regardless of what this iconic stereotype signified, the narrative of Black life shown in *Uncle Tom's Cabin* constitutes one of the earliest examples of Black experiences portrayed in US literature and dramatized on screen. Moreover, Stowe's work and the fact that a white abolitionist writer was among the first to have her writings adapted to the screen demonstrates that audiences were interested in Black experiences. This chapter, then, is a tribute to early Black literary figures whose writings on blackness became viable for cinematic adaptation. Of course, the extensive list of writers who contributed to exposing Black life is far too voluminous to be documented in a single chapter. Thus, this discussion covers the period that began in the Depression era, extends through the emergence of the Harlem Renaissance, and continues through the first half of the twentieth century.

To historicize Black writings produced in the first half of the twentieth century, it is necessary to foreground those literary figures whose works were adapted to the screen, considered for screen production, or attracted the attention of Hollywood as screenwriters. This chapter examines African American writers (1900s through 1950s) in three phases: (1) the first generation of literary figures who had their writings adapted to the screen with independent film-makers; (2) the second generation of literary figures who had close encounters with Hollywood but failed to have their works transformed on screen; and (3) the third generation whose works were produced in Hollywood or other major film enterprises but were significantly compromised in the adaptation process.

GLIMMERS OF HOPE: BLACK LITERARY FIGURES ATTRACTED INDEPENDENT FILMMAKERS

While most African American writers failed to attract the attention of Holly-wood producers, several did garner the attention of independent filmmakers. These early writers include Paul Laurence Dunbar, Charles Waddell Chesnutt, and Oscar Micheaux. They represent some of the first Black writers whose literature garnered the interest of film producers for cinematic adaptation, but these literary figures (including Micheaux, who was also a filmmaker) contributed to independent films produced outside of the mainstream industry.

Paul Laurence Dunbar

Dunbar, according to literary scholars Lillian S. Robinson and Greg Robinson, developed a "reputation [that] shifted between . . . a 'race man' and that of an embarrassment before progressing to that of a forerunner and trickster, who possessed the dual, if contradictory, qualities of transgression and respectabil-ity."[6] Despite the fluctuations in his public profile, Dunbar attracted the attention of Robert Levy, a Jewish filmmaker who managed the Lafayette Players and operated Reol Productions. Levy became interested in Dunbar's novel *The Sport of the Gods* (1902) and adapted this fictionalized work to the screen in 1921.[7] He received some $533 for the rights to this novel, which, scholar Christina Petersen affirms, became the largest sum Dunbar ever received for his writings.[8]

Clarence Muse, Black dramatic actor, newspaper columnist, and one-time filmmaker, wrote the adapted screenplay.[9] Following the film's completion, *The Sport of the Gods* (Henry J. Vernot, 1921) opened in Chicago to rave reviews from the *Chicago Defender* newspaper and earned considerable applause from Chicago's film censor board. The picture's New York exhibition at the Lafayette Theater was also warmly received, and its Los Angeles premiere at the Philhar-monic Auditorium garnered enthusiastic praise.[10]

Apparently due to the film's widespread appeal, some three years later it was exhibited in Baltimore, where the *Baltimore Afro-American* newspaper described *The Sport of the Gods* as "an untimely exciting story, mellowed by love and devoted to a climax, when the husband who had been sent to prison for life, returns to find his wife married to another, his only daughter an actress in a questionable cabaret, and his son a drunken gambler. But the unexpected happened. What is it? See this remarkable picture by Paul Laurence Dunbar."[11] Based on the picture's favorable reception in urban areas, *The Sport of the Gods* demonstrates that Black audiences responded enthusiastically to Black narratives dramatized on screen and developed an appetite for Black-centered films. Revealing how these pictures resonated with Black audiences, Petersen finds that "Levy's choice of the first African American novel 'to describe Black life in the northern ghetto' may have struck a chord with northern Black audiences who knew firsthand the vicissitudes of Black urban life."[12]

Charles Waddell Chesnutt

With the success Dunbar achieved as a writer whose work was transformed on screen, other Black writers such as Chesnutt, who was equally important as a literary figure and whose writings attracted the attention of Black independent filmmaker Oscar Micheaux, followed. Chesnutt's three literary works—*The Conjure Woman* (1899), *The Marrow of Tradition* (1901), and *The House Behind the Cedars* (1900)—captured the attention of Micheaux, one of the twentieth century's most prolific Black filmmakers. While Chesnutt's three film projects may not have all materialized, it is certain that *The House Behind the Cedars* was produced in 1924, even though no surviving print of this film exists. Micheaux remade the film under a different title, *Veiled Aristocrats*, in 1932, which is the only surviving version.[13]

In Chesnutt's novelization of *The House Behind the Cedars* and Micheaux's dramatization of *Veiled Aristocrats*, literary critic Susan Gilman contends, "Both novelist and filmmaker chart the crossing of the classic passing plot of discovery and subsequent acknowledgment or denial of 'black blood,' which shapes . . . [their] narratives of legitimacy—legal, social, and professional."[14] While Gilman acknowledges parallels between the two artistic productions, it is possible that Micheaux primarily capitalized on Chesnutt's literary reputation in making the film adaptation. In fact, film scholar Corey Creekmur argues that Micheaux engaged in a "murky" adaptation process wherein

> The twists and (re)turns evident in simply providing the basic facts linking Chesnutt's novel and Micheaux's two films . . . surely undermine the misleadingly straightforward claim that . . . Micheaux's now "lost" silent film *The House Behind the Cedars* (1924/1925), as well as his rediscovered sound film *Veiled Aristocrats* (1932), are adaptations of Chesnutt's 1900 novel. But the comfortable identification of one text as an "original"

and another, or others, as "derived" adaptations frequently oversimplifies the actual multimedia and multidirectional circulation of texts in a zigzag process that at moments might be better described as translation, allusion, deformation, parody, homage, copyright infringement, [and] "Signifying."[15]

Documenting Micheaux's exploitative strategies, unrestrained borrowing, carelessness, and the excessive license he might have taken with others' works is important, and noting the practices he employed to produce pictures certainly warrants mention. Yet Micheaux also deserves credit for bringing Chesnutt's works to the screen. Although Creekmur seemingly chastises Micheaux for his "freewheeling" practices, he acknowledges Micheaux's humble beginnings, limited resources, and ambition to create profitable productions during an era of racial segregation and alienation. Therefore, for Micheaux to be applauded and condemned simultaneously invokes debates about whether the individual should be held accountable for an unequal and unjust system or whether the system of racial segregation itself should be held responsible. To note these questions is not to defend Micheaux's negligence nor excuse his failings, but to consider the destabilizing environment in which he operated.

Veiled Aristocrats reproduces the problematic themes of racial passing and cross-racial desire that were introduced in Chesnutt's *The House Behind the Cedars*—issues that certainly stood to invite the scrutiny and ire of film censors.[16] For example, Virginia film censors, according to historian Jennifer Fronc, "detected subversive content . . . African Americans successfully passing as white, holding professional jobs, and enjoying privileges usually only available to well-off white families, such as household servants."[17] These censors feared the picture "might inspire African Americans to cross boundaries of race and class."[18] In a similar vein, historian J. Douglass Smith reports, Virginia censors regarded the interracial mixing scenes as dangerous since they "might incite . . . crime."[19]

Veiled Aristocrats, aside from provoking controversy with film censors due to its racially charged themes, was promoted in the *Pittsburgh Courier* newspaper as one of "the finest all-star all-colored talking picture-drama[s] ever produced."[20] Considering Micheaux's adaptation of Chesnutt's *The House Behind the Cedars*, the picture is a testament to Chesnutt's skill and popularity as a literary figure, however fraught the professional relationship between Chesnutt and Micheaux might have been. Chesnutt's authorship, like Dunbar's literary skill, demonstrates that Black literary figures could produce viable screen narratives even if they had to do so with independent filmmakers.

Oscar Micheaux

Less widely known for his literary work and more highly revered for his screen productions, Micheaux, among the more prominent Black filmmakers, published some seven novels over the course of his career and exploited his writings for screen adaptation. Micheaux's first three novels—*The Conquest* (1913), *The Homesteader* (1917), and *The Wind from Nowhere* (1941)—are believed to have been reproduced in his films *The Homesteader* (1919), *The Exile* (1931), *The Betrayal* (1948), and perhaps others. Although these novels may have overlapped in demarcating Micheaux's early years as a Black homesteader in South Dakota, it was *The Homesteader* (1919 film, which no longer survives) that led Micheaux to make a precipitous move; he used this production to launch his filmmaking company. *The Homesteader* became Micheaux's first full-length feature; its story parallels events from his own private life in which he implicates similarly named family members, as when he references his first wife, Orlean McCracken, reproduced on screen as Orlean McCarthy, and dramatizes a dispute involving his father-in-law. Exemplifying Micheaux's audaciousness, his exhibition of *The Homesteader* in Chicago was temporarily halted when film censors became concerned that he overtly referenced a prominent minister of the city—incidentally, his father-in-law.

But more importantly, Micheaux's first feature hints at interracial relationships and racial masquerade—themes that seemed to draw audiences into the movie theater. According to *Half-Century Magazine*, the picture "made quite a hit in Chicago. As a motion picture it ranks very high in race motion picture productions. It has played to packed house[s] throughout the Colored district."[21] Despite the success of *The Homesteader*, a picture partially based on Micheaux's similarly titled novel, it is useful to consider Creekmur's suggestion that Micheaux's films are never adaptations, given the degree to which his films transform written material, even when they draw on his own literary works.[22] Creekmur's assessment encourages us to proceed cautiously in making assumptions about Micheaux's screen adaptation(s).

Whatever questionable strategies Micheaux employed in the adaptation process, his struggle to survive as an African American filmmaker (and self-published writer) led him to join this first group of literary figures whose works were adapted to the screen with independent producers. In this first phase, glimmers of hope emanated from Black authors who believed their writings were worthy of screen adaptation even when produced with independent filmmakers who could not compete with mainstream productions due to limited exposure, minimal exhibition venues, reduced promotional campaigns, meager budgets, or restricted audiences.

DREAMS DEFERRED: BLACK WRITERS CONSIDERED BUT SELDOM SELECTED IN HOLLYWOOD

While the first generation of Black literary figures (Dunbar, Chesnutt, Micheaux, and others) demonstrated that their work could be adapted to the screen, it became clear that these adaptations would only be independent productions. Yet when a second generation of Black writers emerged, they attracted the attention of Hollywood (or other prominent film enterprises). This second generation evolved from the Harlem Renaissance, which produced an avalanche of literary figures and coincided with the heightened popularity of cinematic production. Those who attracted Hollywood's interest included Wallace Thurman, Langston Hughes, Zora Neale Hurston, and Ann Petry. These literary figures had close encounters with the mainstream cinema industry and demonstrated that Hollywood could no longer ignore them, given the recognition they received as celebrated authors. However, most did not have their dreams fulfilled and seldom witnessed their writings transformed into Hollywood adaptations.

Wallace Thurman

Emerging from the Harlem Renaissance, Thurman had his writings reproduced on screen following the recognition he received for his novel *The Blacker the Berry* (1929). It was this novel that escalated him to widespread acclaim as a literary figure and garnered the attention of Hollywood producers. Having established himself as a literary figure of distinction, Thurman worked as a screenwriter for MGM, Pathé, and Fox studios in the late 1920s; his play, *Harlem*, was being considered at Fox for screen adaptation. Unfortunately, interest in the cinematic adaptation of his play quickly dissipated when, according to scholar Phyllis Klotman, he was regarded as "too intellectual."[23] Characterizing industry perceptions, Thurman admits, "They had expected me to be like their Negro actors and were a little surprised at my line of talk."[24] Yet in 1932, Thurman's novel *The Interne*, coauthored with white writer Abraham L. Furman, which focused on a New York City hospital's exploitative reproductive practices, was produced as *Tomorrow's Children* (Crane Wilbur, 1934). Bryan Foy, a white film producer who had led "Warner's 'B' picture unit,"[25] in collaboration with white director Crane Wilbur (who coauthored the script with Thurman), adapted the novel to the screen. While Thurman was listed as screenplay coauthor, he was at least credited as the sole author of the original story.[26]

Elaborating on *Tomorrow's Children*, Klotman remarks, "A film about sterilization in which doctors actually explain the procedure for vasectomy, using the term, and salpingectomy [surgical removal of fallopian tube(s)] or fallectomy,"

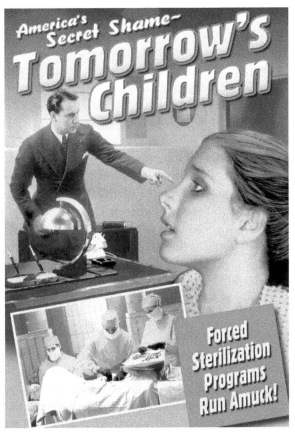

The poster for *Tomorrow's Children* (Crane Wilbur, 1934) utilizes sensational advertising to promote the film based on Wallace Thurman's 1932 novel *The Interne*.

surgical nonremoval of the fallopian tubes, was virtually unheard of in 1934 cinema.[27] That such medical terminology was introduced in a film during this era clearly exemplifies the picture's intrepid proclivity to include medical terms not publicly or widely circulated and hinted at the producers' forthright courage to expose such a procedure to a somewhat "puritanical" society that had judiciously avoided addressing these practices openly. Moreover, the film's release coincided with the popularity of the eugenics movement, which engaged in practices to control marginalized populations deemed "mentally unfit" or "socially undesirable." *Tomorrow's Children* "tells the story of Alice Mason, a young woman whom the US government forcibly sterilizes because she comes from a family with a history of alcoholism, mental illnesses, and physical disabilities, traits that they considered biologically determined and inferior."[28] The film was advertised as "America's Secret Shame" and captioned, "Forced Sterilization Programs Run Amuck."[29]

Apparently, having achieved some degree of success with the picture, Foy Productions again recruited Thurman's talents for a second picture, *High School Girl* (1934/1935). An advertisement for *High School Girl* cautioned, "For Broadminded Adults Only," and the tag line read, "Heedless Youth Speeding through Life with the Throttle Wide Open."[30] Production Code Administration records indicate the film may have been previously titled *Sterilization* or *Lady Beware*, but the picture is described in the following manner:

> The story is an appeal for sex education. It may be classified as definite propaganda.... One of the girls ... is seduced by one of the boys in the school, becomes pregnant and on the advice of a biology teacher, goes with her brother to another city to a hospital to have her child.... The story ends with the boy, who is the father of the child, coming back and making amends by agreeing to marry the girl. Part of the plot revolves around the attempts of the biology professor to discuss sex matters and the "facts of life" [with] his pupils.... The mother ... and her club women friends ... [have] the biology professor discharged from the school.[31]

Although Thurman contributed to both productions, he never saw the fruition of his single-authored work(s) adapted to the screen, due in part to his untimely death in December 1934; he died (at the age of thirty-two) while hospitalized at the New York City hospital on Welfare Island—incidentally, the setting for *The Interne*.[32] Despite Thurman's early death, he became a screenwriter in Hollywood and his contributions were recognized, an achievement that eluded most Black literary figures.

Langston Hughes

While Thurman became a Hollywood screenwriter, Hughes, a more widely known literary figure, had somewhat less success with the cinema industry. A poet, novelist, short-story writer, and newspaper columnist, Hughes garnered literary acclaim for his debut novel, *Not Without Laughter* (1930). In 1932, Hughes, along with twenty-one other African Americans, traveled to Moscow (the capital of the Soviet Union) to work with renowned avant-garde film director Sergei Eisenstein on a proposed film titled *Black and White*. Within two months of the group's arrival, the film project was canceled, a decision some attribute to the American political desire to "compromise ... racial prejudice" for the sake of preserving "American Capitalism and World Imperialism."[33] Hughes concedes the film's cancellation was partially related to the picture's "artistically weak and unsound" script and a "pathetic hodgepodge of good intentions and faulty facts" that a film scenarist created.[34] Whatever factors halted the production, scholar Steven Lee believes Hughes provided a "distorted account of *Black and White* [that] enabled him to turn from radicalism on his own terms, to distance himself from past leftist ties, but in a way that preserved the USSR [Soviet Union] as a beacon of hope."[35] However complicated Hughes's perception, *Black and White* never materialized, and Lee believes Hughes was disappointed with the project's cancellation.

Frustrated about this failed venture, Hughes did not relinquish his desire to work with the US film industry, even though he presumed it was reluctant to adapt the writings of Black authors. In 1934, following the publication of his short story collection *The Ways of White Folks*, Hughes decided to submit his "Rejuvenation to Joy," a burlesque inspired by a famous 1920s Westchester County religious scam, to a Paramount Studios executive. Initially, Hughes was optimistic the work would be adapted to the screen, particularly since white actor Al Jolson (a noted blackface performer) had considered the project and Clarence Muse, an acclaimed Lafayette Players actor, would serve as the film's collaborator. But Hughes's optimism turned to despair when the project was rejected. Hughes's biographer, Arnold Rampersad, reports that Hughes "found the film industry impossible to crack."[36]

Refusing to relinquish his desire for screen adaptation and conceding to the industry's whims, Hughes, along with Muse, cowrote the screenplay for *Way Down South* (Leslie Goodwins and Bernard Vorhaus, 1939); both received credit for developing the original story and screenplay. The project reportedly evolved from Hughes's earlier attempt to rework *St. Louis Woman*, a play that Black writers Arna Bontemps and Countee Cullen conceived for Muse's theatrical group (the Lafayette Players). Unfortunately, even though the project was completed, Hughes was disturbed with the story's stereotypical depiction of southern Blacks. Further complicating *Way Down South*, Hughes was mistreated during the picture's production; after a studio executive refused to join him at a restaurant due to segregated practices, Hughes became disgusted with the industry.[37] Collectively, these events fueled Hughes's animosity toward Hollywood and propelled his belief that while, on the one hand, "Hollywood leaders [were characterized as] ... being anxious not to offend blacks," on the other hand, they were "almost totally ignorant of the offensiveness of most of the movies" they produced.[38]

Regarding *Way Down South*, "The best that probably can be said for the film," according to Klotman, "is that it employed three hundred Black actors and gave Muse an opportunity" to collaborate with white director Bernard Vorhaus.[39] Even though the *New York Amsterdam News* boasted of Hughes's screenwriting efforts,[40] most African Americans were particularly annoyed with the picture's depiction of a kind and benevolent white slave owner's son, who manages to save the plantation from sale but whose benevolence does not compel him to free his slaves. The "stereotypical depiction of a plantation setting," according to scholar Bartholomew Brinkman, "felt to Hughes like a compromise, causing him some degree of embarrassment" even though "the screenplay helped Hughes financially."[41] Confirming Hughes's disappointment, Rampersad insists that he was stung "by the criticism, especially from blacks, and resentful of what he saw as ingratitude and insensitivity after his years of sacrifice for the leftist and the black causes."[42] Hughes's resentment was further amplified when his poem "The Negro Speaks of Rivers" (1921) was considered for screen adaptation but then those plans "never materialized."[43] Conceivably, Hughes consoled himself with the achievement that he had become a Hollywood screenwriter. Although he received other industry writing assignments, in the aftermath of *Way Down South*, he never had any of his original work reproduced on screen.[44]

Responding to the exclusionary practices Hughes experienced in Hollywood as late as the 1960s, he continued to air his grievances with the industry, once adamantly declaring, "When an author of color sells a novel to Hollywood, if ever he does, he is seldom called to California to work on the script. Almost all well-paying jobs in the mass media are still reserved for whites, no matter how celebrated the Negro author may be."[45] Publicly exposing his grievances, however, did not deter his affinity for cinema, because according to Brinkman, Hughes remained preoccupied with the movies, as exemplified in the numerous movie references in his writings.[46] Despite Hughes's challenges in the industry, the award-winning play of Black dramatist Lorraine Hansberry, *A Raisin in the Sun*, with its title from Hughes's poem "A Dream Deferred" (1951), provided the basis for the similarly titled film adaptation (Daniel Petrie, 1961) starring Black actor Sidney Poitier. While Hughes may not have achieved the level of success he desired in Hollywood, he paved the way for others to follow.

Zora Neale Hurston

The career of Black writer Zora Neale Hurston dovetails with the qualified success Thurman and Hughes achieved in the mainstream cinema industry as screenwriters. Hurston is distinguished from these male literary figures in that she was also a filmmaker, although she generally worked outside of the Hollywood industry. However, she parallels Black male literary figures in that she, too, worked as a Hollywood screenwriter and she, too, had her novels considered for screen adaptation, but unlike some of her Black male predecessors, her writings were never adapted to the screen, at least not during her lifetime.

As a folklorist and anthropologist who was driven to produce ethnographic films of Black southern life, Hurston, in this capacity, recorded images of the Black experience. As a filmmaker, scholar Gloria Gibson reports, Hurston "shot ten rolls of motion pictures in the southern United States in 1927–1929 to document logging, children's games and dances, a baptism, a baseball crowd, a barbecue, and Kossula, last of the Takkoi slaves."[47] Analyzing Hurston's ethnographic recordings, scholar Shilyh Warren observes, "In her varied footage, Hurston's position shifts between that of an insider and that of an outsider, illustrating the consistent desire and challenge of generating authentic portraits of Others, even when they are communities to which you sense that you belong."[48] Further interpreting Hurston's ethnographic films, biographer Valerie Boyd reports, "All of the footage—of the black men, women, and children—said as much about Hurston as it did about her subjects: Whoever recorded these images knew black people intimately, the footage insinuated, and loved them intensely."[49]

But not only did Hurston create visual recordings of Black life for ethnographic purposes, her own writings were considered for screen adaptation as early as 1926, when independent filmmaker Micheaux submitted a letter (on company stationery) to the Chicago Motion Picture Censors that listed several "all-star" productions and identified Hurston's *Vanity* as a source that remains unidentified (or does not exist).[50] That Hurston is referenced in this correspondence is significant because it suggests that Micheaux considered her work viable for screen adaptation. Although mentioned, it is unclear or unknown if Hurston ever collaborated with Micheaux on a film project, but certainly Micheaux attempts to embellish his company's profile through linkage to Hurston's literary talent. When Hurston received recognition as a literary scholar "before her time in intellectual circles,"[51] she increasingly became more attractive to the mainstream cinema industry. The literary acclaim Hurston garnered for the folklore published in *Mules and Men* (1935), the Caribbean ethnographic research in *Tell My Horse* (1938),[52] and the publication of three novels—*Jonah's Gourd Vine* (1934), *Their Eyes Were Watching God* (1937), and *Moses, Man of the Mountain* (1939)—captured Hollywood's attention.

Hurston's contact with the mainstream cinema industry may have occurred when she worked as a secretary (and chauffeur) to white award-winning writer Fannie Hurst, who authored *Imitation of Life*—a 1933 novel exploring racial passing that was adapted to the screen in 1934 (John Stahl) and remade on screen in 1959 (Douglas Sirk). The 1934 version of *Imitation of Life* features a white female entrepreneur who achieves wealth and fame through the exploitation of her Black maid's pancake recipe; further complicating the narrative, the maid's daughter decides to pass as white. Considering the racial relationships centered in this production, it is conceivable that Hurston's working relationship with Hurst informed the adaptation, revealed Hurston's literary talents to studio officials, and sparked Hurston's interest in having her own writings adapted. Whatever connection to the film industry Hurston might have had initially, she became directly involved with it when she worked as a Paramount story consultant from October 1941 to January 1942,[53] a position that inspired her desire to have her writings adapted to the screen.[54]

Hurston's employment with the studios was reported in the *Pittsburgh Courier*, but the newspaper misidentified the studio for which she worked. The paper reports, "Although [the] name of the picture on which [she is] working has not been revealed, Zora Neale Hurston, famed novelist is in Hollywood, serving as technical adviser at Warner Bros. Studios."[55] Commenting on her appointment, Hurston unequivocally declares, "This job here at the studio is not the end of things for me. It is a means."[56] Hinting at her studio connections, she allegedly told Carl Van Vechten, prominent Harlem Renaissance writer and photographer, "I have a tiny wedge in Hollywood and I have hopes of breaking that old silly rule about Negroes not writing about white people. In fact, I have a sort of commitment from a producer at RKO that he will help me to do it."[57] Providing evidence of Hurston's association with the studios, scholar Elizabeth Binggeli chronicles Hurston's difficult time in Hollywood.[58] Her novels—*Jonah's Gourd Vine* (1934),[59] *Their Eyes Were Watching God* (1937),[60] *Moses, Man of the Mountain* (1939), *Dust on the Tracks* (1942), and *Seraph on the Suwanee* (1948)—were considered for screen adaptation but never moved into production. "Hurston's desire to see her fiction adapted to film," according to Binggeli, "would continue throughout her life."[61] Her work was finally adapted to the screen well after Hurston's 1960 death and some sixty-eight years after the novel's publication; in 2005, Black female director Darnell Martin made *Their Eyes Were Watching God*.

While there is evidence that Hollywood's racial politics kept Black writers out of the industry, Binggeli believes that "Hollywood did review the majority of works by prominent Black writers of the day, including Arna Bontemps, Jessie Fauset, Chester Himes, Langston Hughes, Claude McKay, Jean Toomer, and Richard Wright."[62] Not defending Hollywood's negligence to capitalize on the writings of these Black literary figures, Binggeli finds that the industry was most preoccupied with the question, "What black stories can we sell?"[63] Hurston represented one of the few Black women to be considered a Hollywood screenwriter, yet she was not the only one; Ann Petry, likewise, had her work considered for screen adaptation.

Ann Petry

Equally prodigious as a writer and similarly attracting studio attention because of her work, Petry wrote her 1946 best-selling novel, *The Street*, which resulted in her being regarded as an "innovator [who managed to break] . . . new ground for the black feminist writers" who followed.[64] Writing for the *People's Voice* (Black politician Adam Clayton Powell Jr.'s paper), the *New York Amsterdam*

News (newspaper), the *Baltimore Afro-American* (newspaper), and *The Crisis Magazine*, Petry's writings drew the attention of Houghton Mifflin publishers, which offered her a literary fellowship to produce *The Street*—her first novel.[65] With the novel's publication, Black historian John Hope Franklin claims, it received "wide circulation and considerable praise."[66] In fact, Petry became the first African American woman to publish a novel that sold over a million copies.[67] The novel was innovative for its resemblance to film noir, according to scholar Paula Rabinowitz, wherein Petry's protagonist, "Lutie Johnson, the maid-turned-nightclub-singer, murders her bandleader when he suggests she sleep with the white racketeer to get money to pay a lawyer to spring her son from reformatory for stealing mail. She flees to Chicago on the train, revisiting the same station where she used to commute to her maid's job in Lyme, Connecticut."[68]

Given the novel's success, Petry attracted Hollywood's attention when African American "Phil Carter, former Metro and Warner Brothers publicist, [took] . . . the option on the [Petry] novel."[69] The *Chicago Defender* reports, "It is Carter's intention to film the book in cooperation with a Hollywood independent producer and release it through a major outlet."[70] In the novel's adaptation process, Binggeli reports that Virginia Volland (a white story analyst for Warner Bros.) claimed Petry's novel "reads with the entertainment value of a whodunit . . . the most satisfactory thing about this author's writing is the feeling of authenticity and life that pervades the pages. This story is real . . . in spite of the fact that it is good entertainment."[71] Furthermore, Volland proposed that the Black "heroine" should be depicted as white (a racial reversal also considered for Richard Wright's *Native Son*) to make the screen adaptation more palatable to white audiences.[72] When Petry's work was recommended to studio superior Tom Chapman (a white story editor), he suggested that Petry was not Black and that she "would have 'possibilities as a writer,'" implying that she could work as a "studio staff writer."[73] Of course, if Petry had become a staff writer, her racial identity would have become known, and this revelation was bound to influence final decisions regarding her work. The fact that Chapman takes the license to appropriate Petry as white reflects, according to Binggeli, that either he was unaware of her racial identity or he attempted to camouflage her identity to have her work seriously considered. Regardless, like many Black literary figures, Petry's novel never materialized on screen.

Remarkably, in 1956, nearly ten years after the novel's publication, the *Pittsburgh Courier* announced *The Street* had been proposed as a film project and a search for Black actresses was under way. The newspaper advertised, "If you're beautiful and blessed with acting ability as well, you stand a good chance of being tapped to play the leading feminine role in Virgo's production of . . . Petry's best-selling novel, *The Street*."[74] This source reported that best-selling white author Harold Robbins, who worked with Universal Pictures from 1940 to 1957, was responsible for the novel's picturization and that producers were in search of an actress who could recreate Lutie Johnson on screen. The film was scheduled to be shot in Harlem, the place where Petry once lived and the inner city she reconstructs in the novel; United Artists was the proposed distributor.[75] Despite these efforts, the film project, like the first proposed version, never developed, but it certainly positioned Petry among the second generation of Black writers (Thurman, Hughes, and Hurston), who became Hollywood screenwriters, worked as filmmakers (Hurston), or had their writings considered for Hollywood screen adaptation.

DIMINISHED DESIRES: BLACK NOVELS ADAPTED TO THE SCREEN BUT SUBSTANTIALLY COMPROMISED

Achieving some degree of success in having their literary works adapted to the screen with Hollywood or other filmmaking enterprises, a third generation of African American writers emerged, and their writings could no longer be dismissed, particularly considering the heightened racial consciousness that erupted during the World War II era.[76] Thus, Black writers Frank Yerby, Willard Motley, Richard Wright, and others had their novels adapted to the screen, but unfortunately, in the adaptation process, their novels were substantially compromised. Certainly, all novels when visualized on screen endure alterations, but the adaptations based on the work of Black writers involved considerable restructuring because the studios changed the narratives to appease white audiences, who they thought were necessary for box-office success.

Frank Yerby

Yerby "was the most successful African American novelist in the . . . [middle of] the twentieth century. . . . He published thirty-three different novels; three were translated to film, one for television; twelve were bestsellers; almost all were selections of the Book of the Month Club."[77] Exploring Yerby's complexity as a literary figure, scholars Bruce A. Glasrud and Laurie Champion explain, the "author of historical romances, known as the 'King of the Costume Novel,' criticized for not exploring race issues, and ignored when he did, Yerby was castigated and condemned by both black and white critics and both affected the directions of his writing."[78] As Ellen C. Scott illustrates in chapter 8, Yerby's first novel, *The Foxes of Harrow* (1946), attracted the cinema industry. With the novel's publication, Twentieth Century-Fox purchased the screen rights for $150,000,[79] and John Stahl served as director. Film producer Darryl F. Zanuck admitted that he bought the story primarily for its "entertainment" value, which a *Baltimore Afro-American* journalist interpreted to mean, "Any elements in the story which did not conform to conventional ideas and myths which America still nourishes about antebellum days had to be either eliminated or glossed over."[80] In the novel's screen translation, its substance, as predicted, was lost or distorted. For example, *Newsweek* magazine characterizes the production as "a rambling story . . . about love, hate, and ambition in nineteenth-century New Orleans. . . . The overall result, however, is a picture which is a little too long and humdrum to have much impact."[81] Further excoriating the film, *Time* magazine reports:

> *The Foxes of Harrow* may easily be confused with the Foxes of Hollywood. . . . All this to-do is expensively and prettily produced as if anyone could possibly care. Probably because the author of the original bestseller, Frank Yerby, is a Negro, the best thing in the picture is a more than ordinary interest in slaves and their lives; but even this feature is drowned in ornateness and theatricality.[82]

New York Times's Bosley Crowther, equally critical, opines:

> We have a strong suspicion that Mr. Yerby spent a lot of time reading *Anthony Adverse*, and, naturally, *Gone with the Wind*. And we also suspect a like attention on the part of Twentieth Century-Fox. . . . But, unfortunately, none of the substance or magnificence of those previous works is to be found in this socially and historically vacuum-packed screen charade. The writing is dull, the dialogue pompous, the settings conspicuously faked and the performances—even those of good actors—are embarrassingly attitudinized.[83]

Black press critics were no more favorable. As *Chicago Defender's* Lillian Scott postulates, the film "will prove a bitter sweet experience to Negroes who see it—sweet in that it is the first Hollywood production of a Negro author's work; bitter in that it is poorly done, and its Negro characters are with minor exceptions the same old 'Southern darkie.'"[84]

Shortly after the film's release, *Crisis Magazine's* Hugh Gloster attributed the film's unfavorable reception to revisions made to the original narrative that resulted in a substantially altered story.[85] Gloster claims, "Writers of the scenario endeavored to please their reactionary audiences by eliminating censor-provoking representations of connubial unfaithfulness and interracial amours."[86] In a similar vein, the *Baltimore Afro-American's* Lois Taylor poignantly insists the novel was grossly distorted: "The prospect of a white wife driven to jealous despair by her husband's honey-colored sweetheart was too much for Hollywood to take . . . and this aspect of Yerby's novel is carefully veiled on the screen."[87] Describing the alterations, Klotman explains:

> The changes from novel to film which do the most violence to the original are (1) the early death of Etienne, thereby assuring that he never has to face the reality of defeat or the loss of power to his former slaves; (2) the aging and whitening of Stephen's quadroon mistress (whom Etienne rapes), who, in the novel, represents the mulatto fixation of the white gentry carried to an art form in New Orleans; and (3) the truncated role of Tante Caleen, whose importance in the novel cannot be overestimated.[88]

Yerby could not stop the substantial alterations made to his work, which scholar Korey Garibaldi attributed to the writer's absence from the adaptation process, since he seemingly "had no role in the [development of the] Hollywood script for *Foxes*."[89] Later, Yerby had two other novels adapted to the screen: *The Golden Hawk*, novelized in 1948 and cinematized in 1952 (Sidney Salkow), and *The Saracen Blade*, novelized in 1952 and cinematized in 1954 (William Castle). Scott's chapter analyzes the complications of these film adaptations. Yerby's inability to exert control over the adaptation process was a fate he shared with fellow Black writers Willard Motley and Richard Wright.

Willard Motley

Enduring a similar experience, Motley's first novel, *Knock on Any Door* (1947), was adapted to the screen, and, like Yerby, his work encountered extensive alterations in the adaptation process. With the novel's publication, Motley garnered considerable acclaim and led scholars such as Robert Bone to characterize his novel as "raceless."[90] Writing a "raceless" novel may have been a strategy Motley deliberately employed to have his work published and to attract the interest of a wider audience; however, in doing so, he produced a novel that seemed completely inconsistent with the predominantly Black Chicago environ from which he emerged.[91] Motley submitted a preliminary version of *Knock on Any Door* (initially titled *Leave without Illusions*)[92] to Harper publishers, which rejected the work, but he received a book contract from Macmillan publishers, which required extensive revisions.

In 1947, when the novel was completed, scholar Alan Wald claims, "The end result was a crime thriller and courtroom drama called *Knock on Any Door*, about Nick Romano, a young, beautiful, and charismatic Italian gangster and ostensibly heterosexual hustler of gay men who provided American culture with the iconic phrase, 'Live fast, die young, and have a good-looking corpse.'"[93] Wald reports that following the novel's publication, Motley attempted to "manipulate his public face. He dramatized his unwillingness to be labeled a 'Negro author' by refusing to have his photograph printed anywhere on his first book."[94] As a testament to the novel's success, former first lady Eleanor Roosevelt applauded the book as "the best-written and most disturbing I have read in a long time."[95] With the novel's widespread acclaim and crossover appeal, the cinema industry, eager to capitalize on its popularity,[96] adapted it to the screen.[97]

Mark Hellinger Productions purchased the screen rights[98] in the fall of 1947, but after Hellinger's unexpected death prior to the year's end,[99] white actor Humphrey Bogart's production company, Santana, produced the picture.[100] (Santana was a subsidiary of Columbia Pictures.) During the adaptation process, the *Chicago Defender* conveyed Motley's reluctance to make major script changes, as he "has never yielded to pleas that the story be altered. It has cost him $250,000, split between two offers to stand by his guns which are still 'smoking.'"[101]

The *Chicago Defender*'s Hilda See believed that many of the adaptation's difficulties were related to the story; she explains, "Certainly [the novel] . . . accuses society of creating the criminals, which is what Hollywood doesn't want"[102] and which may have been in violation of the Hays Code (the Motion Picture Production Code, recognized as the cinema industry's self-censorship system). According to Production Code Administration (PCA) files, Joseph Breen wrote to Walter Wanger at Universal Studios (July 17, 1947) to express his disenchantment with the story. Breen states:

> This story, both in basic theme and in detail, is thoroughly and completely unacceptable under the provisions of the Production Code. . . . It may be argued that the sum total of the story follows the routine thesis that "crime does not pay"—inasmuch as the young criminal dies on the gallows for his crimes. . . . [However,] the story is so filled with unacceptable details as to make it completely unsuited for screen dramatization. . . . We find him, as a young child, blasphemous in speech . . . engaged in criminal activities, illicit sex. . . . The police are shown to be brutal and dishonest.[103]

Of course, many script changes were recommended, leading Breen to correspond with the film's producer Robert Lord in a letter (June 29, 1948) in which Breen advises, "While this basic story may be acceptable under the provisions of the Production Code, there are a number of important details in the first estimating script, which is now under study, which need to be changed, or rewritten, or modified, if the complete picture is to be acceptable."[104]

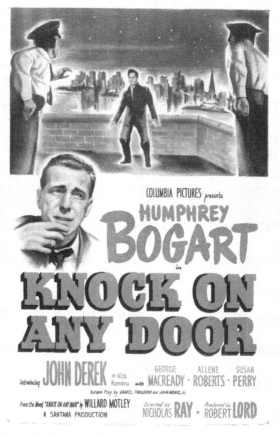

The poster for *Knock on Any Door* (Nicholas Ray, 1949) features star Humphrey Bogart but clearly states that the film is based on Willard Motley's novel *Knock on Any Door*.

Moreover, other problems haunted the picture; as See insightfully reveals, "There are also those who contend that Hollywood's reticence to glorify a Negro as author of a film story is another angle."[105] Implicating Hollywood's racial politics, See nonetheless ends her article somewhat optimistically and insists, "We hope . . . [Motley] isn't denied the quarter million dollars his book merits through Hollywood's outlet."[106] Apparently her comments reference an earlier report that MGM had offered some $125,000 for the adaptation but when the office of Eric Johnston, president of the Motion Picture Association of America, learned of the offer, he banned the film.[107] In the final analysis, Columbia produced the picture at a cost of $1.5 million dollars,[108] and Nicholas Ray became the film's director.[109]

While critics referred to Motley's novel as "raceless," the film was a direct attack on the racial polemics that enveloped Black males in American society.

The characterization of Romano as an Italian criminal is constructed in the guise of an African American who stands in for the disenfranchised Black male in a society that refuses to accommodate him and compels him to lead a life of crime and self-destruction. Therefore, Motley's Italian American Romano becomes the disembodied voice for the Black male who is virtually absent from the film except for a few minor appearances. The film received mixed reviews. *Variety* describes the picture as an "eloquent document on juvenile delinquency; its cause and effect has been fashioned from *Knock on Any Door*."[110] However, the *Chicago Defender*'s Lillian Scott warns, "Those who have read Motley's brilliant, sensitive novel will feel a sense of disappointment, we think. Those who have not, will perhaps, consider *Knock on Any Door* an above average crime film."[111]

Although Motley's novel became a best seller in 1950, having sold some 350,000 copies (selling 47,000 copies in its first three weeks of release), this success was not duplicated in the film's release. Unleashing his displeasure with the adaptation, Motley declared, "It ain't my kid! It's a bastard! . . . People have said they cried when they read the book. I cried when I saw the movie."[112] Expressing his frustration with the mainstream film adaptation, Motley illuminates the dilemma of the Black writer in Hollywood.

Richard Wright

Wright's 1940 novel, *Native Son*, was not adapted until 1951, a delay perhaps related to his efforts to control every aspect of the novel's picturization, having witnessed Yerby's disenchantment and Motley's disappointment with their screen adaptations.[113] Acutely aware of their experiences, Wright assumed a more assertive posture, only to discover that he was no more successful than his predecessors; all had their writings substantially compromised in the adaptation process. Notably, even prior to its publication, *Native Son* was submitted to the studios in 1939 for screen adaptation consideration.[114] The novel was also produced onstage when Wright collaborated with white playwright Paul Green in 1940. Wright accepted Green's involvement, according to historian Kate Dossett, because the way Green handled the Black character in his play *Hymn of the Rising Sun* made Wright believe he could "handle a boy like Bigger," the protagonist in *Native Son*.[115] Despite their best intentions, "the established white playwright and rising Black star came to very different positions on the role of Bigger."[116] Still, the 1941 theatrical production of white director Orson Welles starring Black actor Canada Lee as Bigger Thomas[117] "attracted large Broadway audiences."[118]

Prior to the stage adaptation, Binggeli reports, Wright's literary agent had approached one of the studios[119] for motion picture production, but these early efforts failed to materialize. However, when the novel was transformed onstage, the studios once again became interested: "Wright was approached by the Hollywood producer Harold Hecht who was interested in making a film adaptation, but negotiations fell through when Hecht revealed that he wanted to use an all-white cast!"[120] The *Chicago Defender* affirms that Wright discovered there were some "sticking points" that were nonnegotiable; when he "learned that Hollywood was going to make [the character in] *Native Son* . . . a white person, and change various contents of the book . . . to appease the southern element and other demagogues[,] he quickly refused."[121]

Disappointed with these overtures, Wright relentlessly pursued having his novel dramatized on screen and later met with Pierre Chenal (a French director) and Artillo Mentasti (head of Argentine Sono Films). According to *Ebony* magazine, "Arrangements for *Native Son*'s production was a three-continent deal when consummated. The venture was organized in Paris, contracts signed in New York, exteriors shot in Chicago and filming of the story done in Buenos Aires."[122] In this deal, Wright negotiated retaining the novel's screen rights, controlling the dialogue, serving as collaborator, and playing the film's lead, Bigger Thomas. Attesting to Wright's extensive involvement, Black writer Margaret Walker confirms, "He would write the script, share in financial backing, direct some scenes, and play a major character in the film. He had least to do with the final phase, which he thought was the least effective and successful, but the truth is that all of it was a disaster."[123] In fact, Bogle suggests that Wright's casting as Bigger contributed to the film's failure; Wright was "Too old, too fat, too weary, too middle class and too successful and sophisticated . . . [so he] was thoroughly implausible in the role of a tortured youth."[124] The film received unfavorable reviews. For example, *Newsweek* candidly reports:

> Unfortunately, the net effect of this production (filmed in Buenos Aires and Chicago) is one of disappointment and even embarrassment. As an actor, Wright misses the character that he caught so ably as author-dramatist—that of a man in revolt against the poverty and exploitation that have brutalized him. The embarrassment stems from even more serious ineptitudes: characterizations that have no more reality than stereotypes; acting that is amazingly amateurish; and staging by French director Pierre Chenal that is little better than perfunctory.[125]

Variety castigates the film and proposes, "With a certain modicum of subtlety, the picture seems to have been made with intent to create anti-U.S. feeling. It is rather sad that a number of British and US residents in Argentina (where it was released under the title *Sangre Negra*)[126] should have been enticed into collaborating in this underhand stab at the US."[127]

Richard Wright in the 1951 independent film production of *Native Son*, portraying the alienated young protagonist, Bigger Thomas, who he had created in his landmark 1940 novel.

Considering that Wright was among the most significant voices of the twentieth century and that his acclaimed novel did not succeed as a film, he, Motley, and Yerby demonstrate that Black writers could attract the attention of Hollywood filmmakers, but in doing so, they stood to face substantial alterations to their works. When these writers had their novels adapted to the screen, ultimately their writings were diminished in potency, marginalized in effectuality, stripped of political implication, reduced in artistic expression, and minimized in substance.

Notes

Thanks to University of North Carolina–Chapel Hill librarian Noah Savage, who assisted in navigating online and print sources for this essay.

1. David Seed, *Cinematic Fictions: The Impact of the Cinema on the American Novel up to World War II* (Liverpool: Liverpool University Press, 2009), 7; Dorothy West, *The Richer, The Poorer: Stories, Sketches, and Reminiscences* (New York: Doubleday, 1995), 202–3.

2. Donald Bogle, *Toms, Coons, Mulattoes, Mammies, and Bucks: An Interpretive History of Blacks in American Films*, updated and expanded 5th ed. (New York: Bloomsbury Academic, 2016), 1.

3. Linda Williams, "*The Birth of a Nation*, Melodramas of Black and White, and Early Race Filmmaking," in *Early Race Filmmaking in America*, ed. Barbara Tepa Lupack (New York: Routledge, 2016), 36.

4. Elizabeth Binggeli, "Blood and Sympathy: Race and the Films of Mary Pickford," in *Mary Pickford: Queen of the Movies*, ed. Christel Schmidt (Lexington: University Press of Kentucky, 2012), 201.

5. See Lauren Berlant, *The Female Complaint: The Unfinished Business of Sentimentality in American Culture* (Durham, NC: Duke University Press, 2008), 111.

6. Lillian S. Robinson and Greg Robinson, "Paul Laurence Dunbar: A Credit to is Race?" *African American Review* 41, no. 2 (Summer 2007): 215.

7. Christina Petersen, "The 'Reol' Story: Race Authorship and Consciousness in Robert Levy's Reol Productions, 1921–1926," *Film History* 20, no. 3 (2008): 308–9.

8. Petersen, "'Reol' Story," 309.

9. Petersen, "'Reol' Story," 316; Charlene Regester, "African American Writers and Pre-1950 Cinema," *Literature/Film Quarterly* 29, no. 3 (2001): 212.

10. Regester, "African American Writers and Pre-1950 Cinema," 212.

11. Regester, "African American Writers and Pre-1950 Cinema," 212, 234–35; "*The Sport of The Gods*—Advertisement," *Baltimore Afro-American*, May 2, 1924, 4. *The Sport of the Gods* was also mentioned in *Billboard*, March 19, 1921, 69; *Billboard*, April 16, 1921, 99; *California Eagle*, July 30, 1921, 1; and *New York Age*, May 21, 1921, 6.

12. Petersen, "'Reol' Story," 309–10.

13. Corey K. Creekmur, "Telling White Lies: Oscar Micheaux and Charles W. Chesnutt," in *Oscar Micheaux and His Circle: African American Filmmaking and Race Cinema in the Silent Era*, ed. Pearl Bowser, Jane Gaines, and Charles Musser (Bloomington: Indiana University Press, 2001), 152.

14. Susan Gilman, "Micheaux's Chesnutt," *PMLA* 114 (October 1999): 1080.

15. Creekmur, "Telling White Lies," 148–49.

16. J. Douglas Smith, "Patrolling the Boundaries of Race: Motion Picture Censorship and Jim Crow in Virginia, 1922–1932," *Historical Journal of Film, Radio and Television* 21, no. 3 (2001): 283–85.

17. Jennifer Fronc, "Local Public Opinion: The National Board of Review of Motion Pictures and the Fight against Film Censorship in Virginia, 1916–1922," *Journal of American Studies* 47, no. 3 (August 2013): 740.

18. Fronc, "Local Public Opinion," 741.

19. Smith, "Patrolling the Boundaries of Race," 286.

20. "Screen's Super-Stars in *Veiled Aristocrats* at Roosevelt: Highest-Ranking All-Colored Film Here Next Week," *Pittsburgh Courier*, April 2, 1931, A6.

21. "The Negro on the Stage," *Half-Century Magazine* 4 (April 1919): 9.

22. Creekmur, "Telling White Lies," 150.

23. Phyllis Klotman, "The Black Writer in Hollywood, Circa 1930: The Case of Wallace Thurman," in *Black American Cinema*, ed. Manthia Diawara (New York: Routledge, 1993), 81.

24. Klotman, "Black Writer in Hollywood," 81.

25. Klotman, "Black Writer in Hollywood," 80.

26. Klotman, "Black Writer in Hollywood," 81.

27. Klotman, "Black Writer in Hollywood," 81.

28. Grace Kim, "*Tomorrow's Children* (1934)," Arizona State University Digital History and Philosophy of Science Repository, https://hpsrepository.asu.edu/handle/10776/11531.

29. "*Tomorrow's Children*," Internet Movie Database, https://www.imdb.com/title/tt0220107/?ref_=nv_sr_srsg_0.

30. "*High School Girl*," Internet Movie Database, https://www.imdb.com/title/tt0026470/?ref_=nv_sr_srsg_0.

31. "*High School Girl*, 1935," Memorandum, September 15, 1934, Production Code Administration Records, Margaret Herrick Library, Beverly Hills, CA, https://digitalcollections.oscars.org/digital/collection/p15759coll30/id/5396/rec/134.

32. Klotman, "Black Writer in Hollywood," 90. Thurman was only thirty-two when he died of tuberculosis. See Valerie Boyd, *Wrapped in Rainbows: The Life of Zora Neale Hurston* (New York: Scribner, 2003), 266.

33. Steven S. Lee, "Langston Hughes's 'Moscow Movie': Reclaiming a Lost Minority Avant-Garde," *Comparative Literature* 67, no. 2 (June 2015): 185.

34. Lee, "Langston Hughes's 'Moscow Movie,'" 186.

35. Lee, "Langston Hughes's 'Moscow Movie,'" 187.

36. Arnold Rampersad, *The Life of Langston Hughes: Vol. I 1902–1941* (New York: Oxford University Press, 1986), 309.

37. Rampersad, *Life of Langston Hughes*, 366–68.

38. Rampersad, *Life of Langston Hughes*, 368.

39. Klotman, "Black Writer in Hollywood," 91.

40. "Hughes-Muse Film Okayed: First Feature by Negro Authors Is Given Review," *New York Amsterdam News*, July 29, 1939, 16.

41. Bartholomew Brinkman, "Movies, Modernity, and All That Jazz: Langston Hughes's 'Montage of a Dream Deferred,'" *African American Review* 44, no.1/2 (Spring/Summer 2011): 86.

42. Rampersad, *Life of Langston Hughes*, 371.

43. Faith Berry, *Langston Hughes: Before and Beyond Harlem* (Westport, CT: Lawrence Hill, 1983), 305.

44. Brinkman, "Movies, Modernity, and All That Jazz," 86.

45. Langston Hughes, "Problems of the Negro Writer: The Bread and Butter Side," *Saturday Review* 46, no. 16 (April 20, 1963): 19.

46. Brinkman, "Movies, Modernity, and All that Jazz," 86.

47. Gloria J. Gibson, "Cinematic Foremothers: Zora Neale Hurston and Eloyce King Patrick Gist," in *Oscar Micheaux and His Circle: African American Filmmaking and Race Cinema of the Silent Era*, ed. Pearl Bowser, Jane Gaines, and Charles Musser (Bloomington: Indiana University Press, 2001), 206.

48. Shilyh Warren, *Subject to Reality: Women and Documentary Film* (Urbana: University of Illinois Press, 2019), 45.

49. Boyd, *Wrapped in Rainbows*, 193.

50. Creekmur reports that "no such title now appears among her published novels or short stories." Creekmur, "Telling White Lies," 152.

51. Robert E. Hemenway, *Zora Neale Hurston: A Literary Biography* (Urbana-Chicago: University of Illinois Press, 1977), xv.

52. Warren, *Subject to Reality*, 47.

53. Elizabeth Binggeli, "The Unadapted: Warner Bros. Reads Zora Neale Hurston," *Cinema Journal* 48, no. 3 (Spring 2009): 5. Binggeli reports that Hurston's stint in Hollywood ended in December 1941.

54. Klotman, "Black Writer in Hollywood," 91; Hemenway, *Zora Neale Hurston*, 276.

55. "Zora Hurston Movie Advisor . . . Hollywood," *Pittsburgh Courier*, October 4, 1941, 21.

56. Letter to Edwin Osgood Grover, Paramount Pictures, December 30, 1941, in *Zora Neale Hurston: A Life in Letters*, ed. Carla Kaplan (New York: Doubleday, 2002), 463. Mentioned in Seed, *Cinematic Fictions*, 6.

57. Letter to Carl Van Vechten, November 2, 1942, in *Zora Neale Hurston*, 467.

58. Binggeli, "Unadapted," 4.

59. Boyd, *Wrapped in Rainbows*, 257. Publisher Bertram Lippincott of the J. B. Lippincott Company believed that Hurston's *Jonah's Gourd Vine* would make a good movie.

60. See "*Their Eyes Were Watching God*," Internet Movie Database, https://www.imdb.com/title/tt0406265/?ref_=nv_sr_srsg_0. Oprah Winfrey's Harpo Films produced the 2005 film.

61. Binggeli, "Unadapted," 15.

62. Binggeli, "Unadapted," 3.

63. Binggeli, "Unadapted," 3.

64. Heather Hicks, "'This Strange Communion': Surveillance and Spectatorship in Ann Petry's *The Street*," *African American Review* 37, no. 1 (Spring 2003): 21.

65. Robin Jane Lucy, "'Now Is the Time! Here Is the Place': World War II and the Black Folk in the Writings of Ralph Ellison, Chester Himes, and Ann Petry" (dissertation, McMaster University, 1999), 186–87.

66. Diane Scharfeld Issacs, "Ann Petry's Life and Art: Piercing Stereotypes" (dissertation, Columbia University, 1982), 58. Issacs references John Hope Franklin's *From Slavery to Freedom* (New York: Alfred A. Knopf, 1967), 515.

67. Ann Petry Papers, 1920–2012, New York Public Library Archives & Manuscripts, Archives. nypl/scm/24832.

68. Paula Rabinowitz, "Pulping Ann Petry: The Case of *Country Place*," in *Revising the Blueprint: Ann Petry and the Literary Left*, ed. Alex Lubin (Jackson: University Press of Mississippi, 2007), 55.

69. "Ann Petry's '*The Street*' Optioned for Movie Play," *New York Amsterdam News*, May 31, 1947, 23.

70. "Ann Petry's '*The Street*,'" 23.

71. Elizabeth Binggeli, "Hollywood Dark Matter: Reading Race and Absence in Studio Era Narrative" (dissertation, University of Southern California, 2005), 30; see Binggeli, "Burbanking Bigger and Bette the Bitch: *Native Son* and *In This Our Life* at Warner Brothers," *African American Review* 40, no. 3 (Fall 2006): 475–92; and Binggeli's chapter in this volume.

72. Binggeli, "Hollywood Dark Matter," 31.

73. Binggeli, "Hollywood Dark Matter," 31.

74. "Hunt Beauty for Ann Petry Film: *The Street* to be Filmed Soon," *Pittsburgh Courier*, September 15, 1956, 44.

75. "Hunt Beauty for Ann Petry Film," 44.

76. The NAACP Legal Defense Fund challenged the "separate but equal" policy that began with the 1938 *Gaines v. Canada* case involving Black access to the State University of Missouri's law school.

77. Gene Andrew Jarrett, "'For Endless Generations': Myth, Dynasty, and Frank Yerby's *The Foxes of Harrow*," *The Southern Literary Journal* 39, no. 1 (Fall 2006): 54.

78. Bruce A. Glasrud and Laurie Champion, "'The Fishes and the Poet's Hands': Frank Yerby, a Black Author in White America," *Journal of American and Comparative Cultures* 23, no. 4 (Winter 2000): 1.

79. Lois Taylor, "Movie Version of *Foxes of Harrow*, Omits Many of the Novel's Highlights," *Baltimore Afro-American*, November 15, 1947, M-6. Notably, Ellen C. Scott reports the exact amount remains in dispute.

80. Korey Garibaldi, "*Knock on Any Door*: The Rise and Fall of Integration in American Culture, 1911–1972" (dissertation, University of Chicago, June 2016), 110.

81. "Reviews: The Slow Brown Fox," *Newsweek*, October 6, 1947, 80.

82. "Cinema: The New Pictures-*The Foxes of Harrow*," *Time* 50, no. 15 (October 13, 1947): 105.

83. Bosley Crowther, "The Screen: *Foxes of Harrow*, Fox Film, Starring Rex Harrison and Maureen O'Hara, Bill at Roxy," *New York Times*, September 25, 1947, 35.

84. Lillian Scott, "*Foxes of Harrow* Has Little Appeal as a Movie: Critics Rap 'Uncle Tom' Performances in Mixed Cast Film *Foxes of Harrow*," *Chicago Defender*, October 4, 1947, 17.

85. Hugh M. Gloster, "The Significance of Frank Yerby," *The Crisis*, 55, no. 1 (January 1948): 13.

86. Gloster, "Significance of Frank Yerby," 13.

87. Taylor, "Movie Version of *Foxes of Harrow*," M-6.

88. Klotman, "Harrowing Experience," 220.

89. Garibaldi, "*Knock on Any Door*," 109.

90. Robert Bone, *The Negro Novel in America* (New Haven, CT: Yale University Press, 1965), 178.

91. Wald, "Motley's Men," 47–48.

92. Wald, "Motley's Men," 48.

93. Wald, "Motley's Men," 48.

94. Wald, "Motley's Men," 48.

95. "Film Banned Motley's *Knock on Any Door*," *New Journal and Guide*, August 23, 1947, 18.

96. Anthony Slide, *Lost Gay Novels: A Reference Guide to Fifty Works from the First Half of the Twentieth Century* (New York: Routledge, 2011), 135–36; "Willard Motley," *Encyclopedia of World Biography* Online (Detroit, MI: Gale Publishers, 2021), go-gale-com.libproxy.lib.unc.edu. Motley wrote a sequel in 1958, *Let No Man Write My Epitaph*, which was adapted to the screen in 1960.

97. "*Knock on Any Door* (1949)," *American Film Institute Catalog*, https://catalog.afi.com/Film/25991-KNOCK-ONANYDOOR?sid=1e93fdf4-10F7-4071-a14f-83516011dfe1&sr=15.687 768&cp=1&poso.

98. Garibaldi, "*Knock on Any Door*," 100–1.

99. "*Knock on Any Door*," *American Film Institute Catalog*.

100. "*Knock on Any Door*," *American Film Institute Catalog*; "A Forceful Social Drama," *Orlando Sentinel*, September 16, 1990, 4.

101. Hilda See, "Motley Balks Plan to Rewrite *Knock on Any Door*: Author Demands Script Follow Book to 'Letter,'" *Chicago Defender*, National Edition, March 13, 1948, 8.

102. See "Motley Balks Plan to Rewrite *Knock on Any Door*," 8.

103. Joseph Breen to Walter Wanger (Universal Studios), July 17, 1947, Production Code Administration Records, Margaret Herrick Library, Beverly Hills, CA, digitalcollections.oscars .org/digital/collection/p15759coll30/id/18752.

104. Joseph Breen to Robert Lord (Producer), June 29, 1948, Production Code Administration Records, Margaret Herrick Library, Beverly Hills, CA, digitalcollections.oscars.org/digital/collection/p15759coll30/id/18752.

105. See "Motley Balks Plan to Rewrite *Knock on Any Door*," 8.

106. See "Motley Balks Plan to Rewrite *Knock on Any Door*," 8.

107. "Film Banned Motley's *Knock on Any Door*," 18. Based on an *Ebony* magazine report, Eric Johnston, president of the Motion Picture Association of America, and his office relayed to the studio that the story could possibly be banned as "an attack on society." The film was eventually approved for exhibition.

108. "*Knock on Any Door*: Humphrey Bogart Makes Powder-Puff Film Version of Best Seller," *Ebony* 4, no. 3 (January 1949): 34.

109. "*Knock on Any Door*," Internet Movie Database; "*Knock on Any Door* Cast Has Negro Actor," *New Journal and Guide*, August 21, 1948, 12.

110. "*Knock on Any Door*," *Variety*, February 23, 1949, 10.

111. Lillian Scott, "Motley's *Knock on Any Door* Has Premiere in New York: 'Acting Is Great, Pix Mediocre,'" *Chicago Defender*, National Edition, March 5, 1949, 16.

112. Garibaldi, "*Knock on Any Door*," 125.

113. Bone accuses Motley of plagiarizing Wright's novel with his *Knock on Any Door* and states, "The Truth is that in its main outlines it leans so heavily on *Native Son* as to border on plagiarism." Bone, *Negro Novel in America*, 179.

114. Binggeli, "Burbanking Bigger and Bette the Bitch, 476.

115. Kate Dossett, *Radical Black Theatre in the New Deal* (Chapel Hill: University of North Carolina Press, 2020), 154.

116. Dossett, *Radical Black Theatre in the New Deal*, 155.

117. Dossett, *Radical Black Theatre in the New Deal*, 58.

118. Dossett, *Radical Black Theatre in the New Deal*, 37.

119. Binggeli, "Burbanking Bigger and Bette the Bitch," 476.

120. Mentioned in Seed, *Cinematic Fictions*, 13.

121. Stanley Marshall, "*Native Son* as Film Premieres in Italy: Author in Role of 'Bigger,'" *Chicago Defender*, National Edition, September 2, 1950, 21.

122. "*Native Son* Filmed in Argentina; Screen Version of Best-Selling Novel Is Most Frank Movie Yet Made about U.S. Negro Problem," *Ebony* 6, no. 3 (January 1951): 83. See Ellen C. Scott's article "Blacker Than Noir: The Making and Unmaking of Richard Wright's 'Ugly' *Native Son* (1951)," *Adaptation* 6, no. 1 (February 2013): 93–119.

123. Margaret Walker, *Richard Wright Daemonic Genius: A Portrait of the Man. A Critical Look at His Work* (New York: Warner Books, 1988), 223.

124. Bogle, *Toms, Coons, Mulattoes, Mammies, and Bucks*, 166.

125. "Movies: *Native Son*," *Newsweek* 38, no. 2, July 9, 1951, 94.

126. Seed, *Cinematic Fictions*, 14.

127. "*Native Son*," *Variety*, April 25, 1951, 14.

Part II

Colonial Anxieties and Reclaimed Identities

Chapter 3

THE DEVIL'S WANGA

Representations of Power and the Erotics of Black Female Planters
in *The Love Wanga* (1936) and *The Devil's Daughter* (1939)

TANYA L. SHIELDS

The female planter looms large as both a historical figure and a fictional character, though few discuss her significance in plantation literature. Notwithstand-
ing their minority status, women planters during the antebellum period, most
often widows, existed. And although these women were predominately white,
there were also Black and mixed-race women who owned plantations. This
chapter explores two films from the 1930s that feature Black female Caribbean
plantation owners: *The Love Wanga* (also released as *Ouanga*, George Terwilliger, 1936), starring Fredi Washington, and *The Devil's Daughter* (Arthur H.
Leonard, 1939), casting Nina Mae McKinney and Ida James. That both films are
set *after* the abolition of slavery in the Caribbean is a testament to the enduring significance of the female planter. Indeed, the aesthetic and ideological
order depicted in these films illuminate how Black characters negotiated and
sometimes upended the racialized patriarchal gaze. In examining the films' use
of connotations associated with drumming, local songs, skin color, clothing,
mystical practices, and setting, this chapter shows how *The Love Wanga* and *The
Devil's Daughter* deploy the fraught erotics of plantation narratives exemplified
in the remarkably nuanced examples of Black female authority. The authority
these Black female characters exert is expressed in the ways they wield their
spiritual, sartorial, and sexual power as they navigate the domestic sphere and
move confidently through both their physical and social environs.

THE LOVE WANGA AND THE DEVIL'S DAUGHTER AS LOW-BUDGET PRODUCTIONS

In assuming these liberatory roles as Caribbean plantation owners, Washington and McKinney had previously established themselves as accomplished screen actresses. Washington appeared in *The Emperor Jones* (Dudley Murphy, 1933, with Black actor-activist Paul Robeson) and *Imitation of Life* (John M. Stahl, 1934), while McKinney had been cast in *Hallelujah* (King Vidor, 1929) and *Sanders of the River* (Zoltan Korda, 1935, with Robeson). Yet when Hollywood failed to provide more lucrative roles for these talented performers, Washington and McKinney turned to low-budget independent productions to cultivate their craft and refine their talent as actresses. When these actresses appeared in low-budget productions, it was apparent that such productions were forced to compete with the more polished Hollywood releases, and in order to compensate for their reduction in quality, these independent films provided action, adventure, and "exotic" locations, and they frequently introduced salacious exploitation elements. Indicative of such independent productions, the J. H. Hoffberger Company, which specialized in low-budget genre films, not only distributed *The Love Wanga* but produced other cheaply made productions. For example, this company distributed *White Heat* (Lois Weber, 1934)—a film that explored a white island plantation owner who is involved in an interracial love triangle; *Rangle River* (Clarence R. Badger, 1936)—an adventure story in the "exotic setting" of the Australian outback; and *Shadow of Chinatown* (Robert F. Hill, 1936)—a crime story that occurs in a West Coast Chinatown with a madman (Bela Lugosi) and evil Eurasian dragon lady (Luana Walters). Among other independent distributors, Sack Amusement Enterprises (a company that focused on all-Black cast films), distributed *The Devil's Daughter* (1939), *The Scar of Shame* (Frank Peregini, 1927), *St. Louis Blues* (Dudley Murphy, 1929), *Lying Lips* (Oscar Micheaux, 1939), *The Blood of Jesus* (Spencer Williams, 1941), and others.

To attract audiences to their productions, independent distributors often employed exploitation strategies and implemented publicity campaigns that promised more sensational sex and violence than the films themselves delivered. The distributors for both *The Love Wanga* and *The Devil's Daughter* emphasized the salacious and erotic dimensions of plantation and Caribbean narratives to sell these films. One poster for *The Love Wanga* advertised the film as featuring "the strange loves of queer people." Here, queer is deployed to mean the characters are involved in intimate interracial relationships; it also invokes the dominant culture's assumptions about primitivism in the Caribbean and frames the agency, desire, and culture of Clelie Gordon (Washington) as strange and abhorrent. Posters for *The Devil's Daughter* are equally sensational. One declares, "Magic! . . . Black Magic!! Mystery! . . . Dark Mystery!! Sister Against Sister! In a Burning Drama of Tropical Love and Hate!" It also promotes the film's "Sensational Blood Dance." Another poster for *The Devil's Daughter* promises audiences that the film featured outlawed erotic material and announces, "Forbidden By Law For Years But *Now* You Can See It!! The Blood Dance. Sex-ational Dance of the Damned! For Adult Eyes Only!"[1] In other words, the promotional materials for *The Love Wanga* and *The Devil's Daughter* invoke the racialized erotic connotations of the Caribbean and, especially, Caribbean women. As this chapter will show, meanings generated in narrative design, mise-en-scène, performances, and sound-image relations both support and complicate the stereotypical messages the films' publicity appropriates.

As low-budget independent films, *The Love Wanga* and *The Devil's Daughter* are not licensed adaptations of specific literary works. Instead, the screenplays for both films build on surrounding cultural tropes and borrow liberally from existing works of music, theater, and literature. In fact, George Terwilliger, a white writer-director whose career began in the early silent cinema era, not only authored both screenplays but also used *The Love Wanga* as the basis for the latter screen adaptation of *The Devil's Daughter*. Both films include love triangles involving Caribbean plantation owners, yet in *The Love Wanga*, Washington (Clelie) portrays a jilted mistress who is punished for her attempt to cross the color line, whereas in *The Devil's Daughter*, which features an all-Black cast, the conflicts between the half-sisters McKinney (Isabelle) and James (Sylvia) over land and their shared love interest are resolved, with Isabelle still stigmatized for her "primitive" Haitian lineage, while Sylvia's African American experiences align her with a demure, civilized femininity.

ARTISTIC WORKS INFLUENCE THESE SCREEN ADAPTATIONS

Terwilliger's screen adaptations, however, were influenced by a wide range of artistic works that include an opera, a play, and literary works. For example, the opera *Ouanga!* (1932), which African Americans Clarence Cameron White and John Frederick Matheus composed and wrote, as well as the play, *Pocomania* (1938), which Jamaican author and activist Una Marson created, inform these filmic representations and provide a context for understanding these productions. The opera is the tragic tale of Dessalines (emperor of Haiti), Défilée (Dessalines's lover), and the tensions between modernity and primitivism unfolding through the question of national religion and whether the nation should be Catholic or vodouist. Ouanga, the voodoo[2] charm, is invoked throughout the opera mainly as a warning to Dessalines to refrain from betraying his people by banning vodou. *Ouanga!* is intriguing in that, though it deploys the well-trod tropes of Haiti, it was penned by African Americans who sought inspiration from the first Black republic. Scholar of the opera Michael Largey notes that there is friction between the creators' (White and Matheus) desire to rehabilitate Haiti in the US imagination and their own status as "middle-class African-American intelligentsia."[3] In other words, their political and social agenda sometimes clashed with their prejudices, born of class and nationality, particularly regarding the primitive. Nonetheless, *Ouanga!* was performed in concert in 1932; though not fully staged until 1945,[4] it was in limited circulation in the early 1930s.

Meanwhile, Marson's play *Pocomania* explores an Afro-Jamaican spiritual practice more accurately known as Pukkumina or Kumina, which originates from Central Africa's Kongo region and which was brought to Jamaica by indentured laborers who came after emancipation.[5] Kumina emphasizes the "continuity between 'visible and invisible domains of the human and ancestral world.'"[6] Invested in medicinal healing, Kumina adherents "share a deep African identity consciousness based on a constant awareness of a legacy of African persecution and suffering."[7] The play's protagonist, Stella, is torn between Anglican-sanctioned customs and African-derived traditions. Stella's conflict is reminiscent of those explored in *Ouanga!* Like the opera, Marson's play probes these themes along class lines. The friction between the poor and the powerful manifests in the idea of pocomania, "a little madness" likened to sexual pleasure; the play's ideas on sex, civilization, race, and class are intertwined and expressed through the vehicle of African spirituality. As David, a doctor who loves Stella, opines, "There is too much that is base and erotic [in *Pocomania*]."[8] The play premiered in Jamaica in 1938, a year before filming began on *The Devil's Daughter*. *Pocomania* and *Ouanga!*, which African-descended people wrote, provide somewhat complicated representations of Haiti and African Caribbean spiritual practice. These representations of Creole religion signify the ways in which healing practices like Kumina and other African retentions have been vilified in colonial contexts. *The Love Wanga* and *The Devil's Daughter* continue to deploy disparaging depictions of Haiti, the Caribbean, and African spiritual practices. However, given the commanding screen presences of Washington and McKinney, the films also illustrate their characters' undeniable complexity.

Further informing these cinematic productions, the most visible influences on Terwilliger's screenplays are the popular and widely circulated literary works *The White Witch of Rose Hall* (1929), written by Herbert G. de Lisser, Afro-Jewish editor of *The Gleaner* newspaper, and *The Magic Island* (1929), by William Buehler Seabrook, a well-known white travel writer. Both works are relevant to understanding the aesthetic and ideological choices shaping these films. *The White Witch of Rose Hall* is a novel that fixates on transgressive female power and the dark arts of Obeah.[9] In de Lisser's text, Annie Palmer is a white widow deeply involved in an outlawed African Caribbean spiritual practice, Obeah. An Irish woman raised in Haiti, Annie understands drumming and the "occult possibilities" of voodoo.[10] In Haiti, she learned the force of "the eerie sound of the voodoo drum [that] could be heard stabbing through the silence and the darkness."[11] The drums cloak the night, and everything associated with it, in fear. The drums are a mark of Africanness, danger, transgressiveness, and the occult.

In comparison, Seabrook's travelogue *The Magic Island* reiterates similar menaces. Credited with popularizing the zombie figure in the United States, the book traffics heavily in Haiti as an occult place steeped in superstition and unreason. Seabrook's work, divided into four sections, devotes its first two sections, "The Voodoo Rites" and "Black Sorcery," to his salacious experiences of "voodoo" in the Haitian hills, while his zombie chapter, ". . . Dead Men Working in the Cane Fields," is based on hearsay. Nonetheless, his work was incredibly influential, and phrases taken directly from his travelogue appear in *The Love Wanga*, *The Devil's Daughter*, and even the Hollywood-produced *White Zombie* (Victor Halperin, 1932)—one of the first motion pictures to feature the zombie character. When not sharing his voodoo experiences in the travelogue, Seabrook's commentary is infused with class and color descriptions steeped in and informed by the US racial binary. Seabrook's status as a white US citizen emerges when he discusses the valuable attributes of the US occupation of Haiti. From his vantage point, the United States, despite its own inconsistencies, is the orchestrator of order, peace, and enlightenment. In other words, American troops are conveyers of civilization, building roads and providing stability to a region they have invaded. Seabrook takes pains to mention that some among Haiti's peasantry appreciate US intervention, while many Haitian elites resent such imposition. His articulation of class antagonisms, along with his dogmatic nationalism, feed on each other to represent Haiti as regressive. Therefore, undeniably, the opera, play, and literary works especially strongly influence the narratives of both *The Love Wanga* and *The Devil's Daughter*. The nuanced depictions of the Black female plantation owners that emerge primarily from Washington's and McKinney's engaging screen presences and well-crafted performances, in conjunction with the films' respective depictions of their characters in relation to the stories' physical and cultural settings, result in producing convincing productions.

THE POWER OF DRUMS

When these films were produced, they borrowed from the novel and travelogue in that drums are introduced to symbolize the decadence and primitivism associated with Haiti. In these earlier literary works, during the ritual, the throbbing drums become sensual and excessive and hypnotic to the women who hear them. The women who compel drummers to beat the goatskin become as menacing as the instrument itself. Dramatizing this spiritual power on screen, even if it is a pretense, the drums as an extension of the women's power become a mechanism that allows them to inhabit the realm of influence and all its ecstasies. In *The Love Wanga*, Clelie/Washington, a white-looking Black plantation owner, feels entitled to Adam Maynard (Philip Brandon), a nearby white plantation owner, in part because of her white skin. Despite their prior two-year affair, Adam rejects Clelie and plans to marry his fiancée, Eve Langley (Marie Paxton), whom he brings from New York to his Haitian plantation, which borders Clelie's estate. His plans mean nothing to Clelie, who is determined to have him. Meanwhile, Adam's mixed-race overseer, LeStrange (Sheldon Leonard), is as obsessed with Clelie as she is with Adam and declares that if he cannot have her, no one will because he "will kill [her] first."[12] Fueled by revenge, Clelie plots to kill Eve using voodoo charms, dolls, and eventually zombies. The film begins with a written prelude scrolling across the screen before dissolving into a picturesque backdrop of mountains, marketplaces, and the sea. The intertitle warns that despite the proliferation of science and the scientific method, African Caribbean primitivism, and the belief in bocors, or witch doctors, prevails. A narrator slowly and menacingly intones that when night falls, the people on this island leave their "colorful and primitive occupations" for the "voodoo drums, drums, drums." Thus, the strange love of these queer people is exacerbated by the depiction of the drum as a mesmerizing instrument of excess.

Similarly, drums are impugned at the beginning of the all-Black-cast film *The Devil's Daughter* (originally "Daughters of Jamaica"), when Sylvia Walton (James) cries, "The drums . . . night and day . . . sound different. I know it is only dance music in the hills, but they don't sound friendly anymore. . . . They sound menacing." A newly returned plantation owner, Sylvia is disturbed by the ceaseless pounding near her Jamaican plantation.[13] Meanwhile, the story also follows her recently disinherited half-sister, Isabelle (McKinney), who had been running the plantation while Sylvia and their father lived in Harlem; when Sylvia returns after their father's death, Isabelle goes into hiding as she plots to reclaim her place as owner. The film's central theme is one of sisters clashing over plantation ownership: unbeknownst to Isabelle, Sylvia wants to share proprietorship, while for Isabelle the plantation is her raison d'être. The half-sisters are also caught in a love triangle. Isabelle has been secretly in love with John Lowden (Emmett Wallace), owner of the adjoining estate, but soon after Sylvia arrives from Harlem, John tells Isabelle about his love for Sylvia. Losing her plantation and potential lover prompt Isabelle's sensational efforts to drive the soft-spoken Sylvia from the island. As in *The Love Wanga*, the throbbing,

Marketing emphasized the film's stereotypical messages about the Caribbean and Black female sexuality rather than its exploration of Clelie's power as a plantation owner.

menacing, ubiquitous drums are threats to the civilized woman's sanity and the colonial social order. They are sonic usurpations of a Black presence that is more in touch with Africa than with Europe. For the "refined," the drums fascinate and frighten, but for spiritual practitioners, these barrels are a way of communing with forces beyond this world. The drums bring sacred and sexual bliss and illustrate plantation pressures regarding race, class, and sexuality. As racially coded instruments belonging to the Black and, often, uneducated masses, drums are linked to irrationality. Since these masses are also poor, the drums are identified with class and their percussive pulsations associated with orgasm. Given all these associations, for white, near-white, or genteel women to enjoy (or align themselves with) the barrels, represents their opposition to colonial control. Therefore, banning drums in the colonized Caribbean was about maintaining colonial order; yet as the film suggests, drumming or succumbing to drums, especially those that Caribbean women deployed, reflects a social order in which local women have ideological, political, spiritual, and economic power.

Collectively, de Lisser's novel, Seabrook's travelogue, Marson's play, and White and Matheus's opera, along with the films, *The Devil's Daughter* and *The Love Wanga*, underscore the fears as well as the desires that dominated the white colonial and Black elite imaginary, which were then projected onto the depictions of the throbbing drums that recall Africa. In fact, drums and horns that produced similar percussive sounds were outlawed throughout the Americas during the colonial period.[14] Ordinance after ordinance declared that drums were uncivilized, frenzied, infectious, contagious, and, by implication, carnal. The criminalization of drums was closely tied to outlawing Afro-Caribbean cultural practices. An obsession with drums, Obeah, and voodoo dominated European fears (and those of the colonial elites) of an African unknown. Identifying the Caribbean as indistinguishable from other "primitive" places was linked directly to US aggressions in the region. As Caribbean literary scholar J. Michael Dash argues, the vilification of the drums and negative images of Haiti "justified" US occupation and invasion (1915–1934), creating a political, cultural, and economic rationale for marking the region as regressive. While this was the mainstream view of Haiti, Black intellectuals produced more complicated readings of the territory, even though these complex versions do not inform the conventional narratives in *The Love Wanga* and *The Devil's Daughter*.

FOLKSONGS AND PIGMENTOCRACY IN THESE FILMIC REPRESENTATIONS

In the two films, Black female characters who possess color and class privilege, most especially Sylvia in *The Devil's Daughter*, offer a subtle rationale for (white) empire and the "colored" middle class that would inherit power with independence, since both films deploy Caribbean folk music to signify a "happy darkie" space. As for *The Love Wanga* and *The Devil's Daughter*, the crowd scenes are populated with singing, dancing, and drumming natives. The opening of *The Devil's Daughter* features a short skit of native performers singing two Jamaican folksongs, "Linstead Market" and "Sweetie Charlie." The first song is about a mother who goes to market, cannot sell her ackee, and laments that her children will go hungry. "Linstead Market" merges into the more risqué "Sweetie Charlie," and the dance changes to reflect the sexually suggestive nature of the second song. "Linstead Market" and "Sweetie Charlie" form the movie's soundtrack. The sound of drumming precedes the film's first credits; this is quickly followed by performances (songs and skit) and instrumental snippets that play throughout the action. Like the drums, which establish the menace of the region, the folksongs highlight the picturesque, but the content of the songs, for those who know them, mitigate that simple reading. These moments throw into stark relief the tensions between class, color, and citizenship.[15]

Similarly, pigmentocracy, or color hierarchy, shapes characters' access to legal and social power.[16] Color is one of the collateral (and silent) advantages of ownership and one of the ways in which the racial and socioeconomic politics of the Caribbean and the United States become incidental in these plots. Casting choices and the lyrics featured in the musical numbers indicate the competing gazes and internalized contradictions in the worlds recreated on screen and for spectators. The erotics associated with the "happy dark primitive" contrasts with light-complexioned characters and reinforces notions of beauty, judgment, and reason while at the same time reflecting the ever-present tensions between the primitive and the civilized in the Caribbean and the United States. Thus, the singing native functions as a subtle justification for the earlier enslavement as well as a marketing device to entice the tourist's gaze. In *The Love Wanga* especially, the light-skinned Black female plantation owner (Clelie) is caught between two worlds.

MAPPING COLONIAL TROPES ONTO BLACK BODIES THROUGH CLOTHING: *THE LOVE WANGA*

Coinciding with the end of US occupation in Haiti, the films' racial discourses are vectors for an aggressive imperial agenda that characterized the region as Uncle Sam's backyard; even today, the idea of the merged concept, Haiti-Caribbean, as a place unable to govern itself continues to have influence in the popular imagination of the dominant culture. The formulaic narratives in *The Love Wanga* (as well as *The Devil's Daughter*) suggest that the native voodoo horror can only be contained by white reason and governability steeped in hierarchal logics. These films map colonial rationalizing tropes of empire, ownership, and control onto Black women's bodies. For example, in *The Love Wanga*, after Clelie, the white-looking Black plantation owner, rejects LeStrange, the mixed-raced overseer, he plots to tame (and destroy) her by taking her garments and clothing the corpse of a female field hand. To clarify the implication of his actions, the theft of Clelie's attire is juxtaposed with a party guest explaining to Adam's fiancée, Eve, that this "sounds like the worst sort of voodoo." The guest elaborates: "When the Blacks plan a special revenge," they look for a corpse and "dress the body in some borrowed article of clothing belonging to the person" they wish to curse. "Then, the body dressed in these borrowed clothes is concealed somewhere in the jungle [and] unless the person marked for death can find the body and get their clothes back, it's just too bad. People have become raving maniacs trying to recover their clothes."[17] Travelogue writer Seabrook chronicles various types of ouanga, including this curse, which is in the film almost verbatim.[18] Voodoo, a manifestation of these irrational curses, and "magic" assert Black superstition and degeneracy, which indicates an incapacity and inability to reason, govern, and prosper. Additionally, women who can enchant reaffirm foundational colonial pathologies about white women who lose their minds to Caribbean excess and Creole women's ability to beguile.[19] By using this curse, LeStrange schemes to control Clelie even if it means her death. In this way, LeStrange mitigates some of the power associated with Clelie's stylish costuming and her capacity to claim space and people as a plantation owner. Notably, in *The Love Wanga*, Clelie's defiance of gender and racial codes, as well as her ability to have autonomy over her own body and supremacy over others, indicates the ways in which she, as a Black woman, violates imperial norms.

The characterization of Clelie shows the influence of de Lisser's novel *The White Witch of Rose Hall* since in the novel, the white widow Annie's dressing choices defy gender norms. At night, she wears men's clothes—specifically, "a black suit which had evidently been made for her [because] she was in the habit of riding about the estates at night, habited like a man"; in these scenes, she is described as "a slight figure clothed all in black and like a man."[20] In counterpoint, several times Annie is "clothed daintily in white,"[21] displaying her desirability and fragility in direct contrast to her "evil deeds."[22] Annie's clothing thus evinces male and female associations. She rides about the estate in darkness, dressed in black, like a man. By day, she is fragile and dainty in attire, despite flouting norms of femininity at night. In sum, Annie, as a conundrum and usurper of imperial practices is made most visible via her wardrobe. The novel anticipates representations in *The Love Wanga*, since once again clothing and desirability are both linked to the female plantation owner's corruption and her complex connection to ideals of womanhood. Annie and later Clelie both embody ideal womanhood through their attractive figures and superior tailoring, but at the same time, their exercise of power—spiritual, erotic, and otherwise—make them unacceptable vessels of planter power and (white) womanhood.

In *The Love Wanga*, LeStrange uses Clelie's clothing to conjure the power of the death ouanga, but this challenge takes place only after Clelie has used sartorial control to express her power. As Ellen Scott writes, throughout the film, "dress becomes a means for passing" for Clelie, and "just as [she] has crossed the color line through dissemblance of dress, the film enacts Clelie's punishment through a kind of hanging in effigy whose power is based on costume."[23] Clelie's lynching via the cadaver encased in her dress would have been a familiar sign of control to 1930s audiences about the ways to tame transgressive Black bodies. This extrajudicial mechanism was a means of terrorizing African Diaspora communities, especially in the United States; miscegenation, though a mainstay in all slave societies, became corrupted into the myth of the Black male rapist and used as an excuse to lynch Black men who were perceived as partners or violators of white women. In the film, the dead body in Clelie's clothes is hung because she rejected LeStrange and did not remain among her kind, a constant refrain in the text.

LeStrange attacks Clelie via her clothing because, as Scott contends, she has used fashion to "straddle the line between modernity and primitivism . . . and in the process defying the power of their binary opposition."[24] Thus, beyond the visual trace of US racial politics in the hanging cadaver, Clelie seeks to disrupt multiple binaries. Her costuming asserts the power of her class. As a plantation owner, Clelie strides with confidence in all her outfits, whether it is the sequined two-piece she wears to voodoo rituals or the dresses and suits she wears traversing her lands.[25] As a landowner, not only can Clelie afford to wear the best, but her garments, as Scott explains, illustrate her ability to be on par with the white characters and identify with the power they wield. Clelie's power is Black, white, and mixed. She marshals the mastery of the drums, the wealth generated by her plantation, and the sensual and erotic vigor associated with her near-white blackness.

MIXING HUMANITY, PIGMENTOCRACY, AND ATTIRE TO ASSERT VALUE IN *THE LOVE WANGA* AND *THE DEVIL'S DAUGHTER*

Clelie's color is also a visible form of capital,[26] something Seabrook notes in his writings related to light-complected people of African ancestry. In the travelogue chapter titled "A Nymph in Bronze," he discusses the racial mixtures at play in Haiti's pigmentocracy. He introduces the Baussans, who are part of "the native aristocracy of Haiti, its brains, wealth, and beauty."[27] Writing about Thérèse, one of the Baussans's daughters, Seabrook describes her in minute detail as "a tall, pale-brown-skinned lithe creature . . . slightly darker than mulatto [who] was like a pale bronze nymph come to life."[28] Further, he raves about Thérèse's beauty, her unprocessed hair, and her swaying body, in which "there lurked potentialities neither banal nor restrained."[29] For Seabrook, Thérèse gowned in "'Paris sophistication' was full of the facile small talk [in French, but], some-thing was asleep, yet not asleep, like a caged panther dreaming."[30] Thérèse and the Baussans lead Seabrook to reflect "on the strange biological-hereditary processes that had culminated" in her[31] and the history of miscegenation that though "deplorable morally . . . was biologically sound."[32] To Seabrook, Thérèse is the manifestation of "a fusing of the highest selective elements in both the white and negro races."[33] Seabrook wonders if Thérèse represents some future and superior expression of race mixing (reminiscent of the racial democracy touted in Brazil at the time).[34] With flourish, he concludes that she is "the ultimate product of [ancestral] fusing, this rather gorgeous, poised, modern creature with her crinkly hair, Egyptian-bobbed, and high heeled gold slippers, dancing with the tall blond" Swede.[35] Seabrook's meditation on Thérèse's body as neither "banal nor restrained" and as a caged animalistic panther ready to pounce speaks to the (white) fixation on Black women's sexuality. In other words, Thérèse is an exemplar of the admixture of her class but also erotic and exotic enough to ensnare Seabrook's attention. As evidence of race mixing, Thérèse is not reviled for being racially impure; instead, she becomes the object of lust.

Like Thérèse, Clelie's attributes in *The Love Wanga* find expression in the actress's (Washington's) physical appearance. The actress's ability to visually transgress and engage in racial cross-dressing allows both the character and the actress to disrupt norms and expectations encoded in Black bodies. As Gina Ulysse contends when discussing Jamaica, light-skinned Black female bodies are a form of capital that plays a crucial role in whether the bodies are read as women or as ladies who possess the "degree of humanity" attributed to them.[36] In the color hierarchies that predominate in the Caribbean, whiteness and near-whiteness are highly valued commodities that secure economic, political, and social access and legitimacy. Black women near the top of this hierarchy find affirmation of their personhood. Thus, humanity, pigmentocracy, and expensive attire are intermingled because bodies that are esteemed and well dressed have access to materials that enable them to present as valued persons and all that such a designation entails. The formulaic, sensationalized narrative in *The Love Wanga* sustains the dominant culture's racialized hierarchies at the same time that images of the immaculately dressed Clelie/Washington, who strides confidently across the screen, offers a refreshing alternative to demeaning mainstream representations of Black women.

Similarly, costuming in *The Devil's Daughter* marks Harlem-raised Sylvia (James) as not only human but also refined and delicate. In the actress's (James's) portrayal, Sylvia's clothes are fitted, belted, and stylish with coordinating accessories. Sylvia's exposure to life off the island is made visible through her fashionable wardrobe. On the other hand, Isabelle's (McKinney's) frocks are hewn from patterned fabrics in matronly cuts. There appears to be little tailoring in her pleated skirts, which are closer to housecoats than high-fashion clothing. Yet Isabelle's white peep-toe heels, her most fashionable accessory, necessitate assistance from Philip, the plantation overseer, when she ascends a

Highlighting exotic adventure, the marketing obscured the personhood of both Haitian-born Isabelle (Nina Mae McKinney) and Harlem-raised Sylvia (Ida James).

woodland staircase. Thus, in contrast to Sylvia's fashionable garments, Isabelle's clothes mark her as in between the lower-class Black islanders and the elite class of Black plantation owners disconnected from Haitian-Caribbean traditions.

Regarding the attire of the local people in this film, they are garbed in well-worn textiles. For example, Elvira (Willa Mae Lang), the servant who wants Isabelle to run the plantation and aids Isabelle in her plot against the Americanized Sylvia, wears a madras-like dress and headscarf associated with a "traditional" Caribbean cultural uniform. Because of the unvarying and homogeneous nature of uniforms, they confirm low social status; students, soldiers, and underlings wear uniforms, but someone with mastery over all they survey does not. Enslaved people were clothed in homespun calicos or osnaburg fabric made from hemp; even when they wore cotton, it was an inferior quality because the period's "sumptuary laws prohibited people from dressing in ways that were perceived to be above their station."[37] Using dress, these laws and customs marked which bodies were precious, important, beautiful, and desirable. Generally reflecting the sumptuary laws of earlier eras, clothing choices in *The Devil's Daughter* reveal if or how a character might transgress their position. Isabelle's plaids and stripes signify that she represents a bridge between the plantocracy and the people. Her attire visually connects her to the local community and mark her as the more legitimate heir to the plantation.

Scott shows that, in *The Love Wanga*, fashion allows light-skinned plantation owner Clelie to disrupt and transgress racial and sexual codes. Yet the distinctive features of characters' clothing in *The Devil's Daughter* are not related to transgressing race but instead are codes for identifying characters' degree of alignment with ideal notions of femininity and the colored elites' power; notably, the codes reflect those of former colonial overlords. The tailored ensembles of the Harlem-raised Sylvia reify her as a delicate lady, while the serviceable clothing of Isabelle (born of a Haitian mother) present her as a no-nonsense workhorse rather than glamorous figure. Depicting Sylvia, James's portrayal as a character with a melodic voice and fashionable attire telegraph the character's ideal femininity; she even recounts that their father took her (not Isabelle) to New York for refinement. Meanwhile, depicting Isabelle, McKinney's rough and to-the-point language link her to the unrefined jungle terrain in which she is most often pictured. Once again, sartorial differentiation is a way for a low-budget independent film to signal status, power, and personhood. However, despite the distinctions between Sylvia and Isabelle, the images of a dignified James and a powerful McKinney convey their suitability to portray Black female plantation owners.

ILL-FATED LOVE TRIANGLES AS REFLECTIONS OF COLONIAL POWER

While clothing conveys the characters' race, gender, and station, these films further use conventional narrative tropes to explore carnal relations. Historically, such liaisons, particularly marriages, have been vehicles of patriarchal control, yet in both *The Love Wanga* and *The Devil's Daughter*, race, gender, and sexual desire are used to challenge the lingering effects of colonial power dynamics. Both films revolve around ill-fated love triangles. In *The Love Wanga*, Clelie wants Adam, a nearby white plantation owner for whom she was a companion for two years, while Adam wants Eve (his New York fiancée), and LeStrange (a mixed-race plantation overseer) desires Clelie. As for *The Devil's Daughter*, the romantic triangle involves Sylvia, Isabelle, and John, who owns the adjoining plantation. The friction between the half-sisters continues as Isabelle, capitalizing on Sylvia's fear of the drums, drugs her sister and, while at a fake Obeah (here a stand-in for voodoo) ceremony, orders Sylvia to leave John and the plantation. As in the novel *The White Witch of Rose Hall* and the play *Pocomania*, the relationships chronicled in these two films offer both conventional and unconventional displays of sexual autonomy. For example, as Alison Donnell writes of Marson's play, "the dramatic investment in a woman who wishes to assert her desires and entitlements remains vital [despite an ending that seems] conventional."[38] In both films, conventional and unorthodox sexual spectacles unfold as the characters seek to form heterosexual unions that solidify their plantation ownership. *The Devil's Daughter* concludes with an easy resolution when Philip, the overseer, is revealed to be the villain, while Sylvia and Isabelle, both women of the brown-skin elite, seek to form the national family that will build great wealth and great ladies.

In *The Love Wanga*, Clelie seeks power through union with Adam, who is white. Pursuing him, Clelie insists that he needs a woman of passion and fire and not his pallid fiancée Eve, thus playing on the erotic and exotic rhetoric tied to Black women and light-skinned women especially. However, Adam's "stick with your own kind" discourse and practice reveals that in his (white) view, while Clelie was appropriate as a lover—he even remarks that she is attractive with commendable qualities—it is her "bad" Black blood that makes her an inappropriate wife. Clelie is desirable as a mistress but not as a life companion and potential mother. Her blackness, though phenotypically invisible, is still "inside," as LeStrange says. Clelie's racial taint is a bridge too far and cannot match Eve's racial innocence. Clelie contaminates the marriage and plantation space with her "polluted blood," while ideologically, Adam and Eve are meant to be together. Adam disavows Clelie because her "polluted" Black blood reaffirms his allegiance to whiteness. Yet Clelie is also unable to overcome the idea of white purity linked to ladies. Her emphatic statement "I'm as white as [Eve] is" illustrates that she is willing to disavow her own blackness.

Fueled by the interracial love triangle, *The Love Wanga* dwells on issues of color and race. Despite her racial and economic power, Clelie is frustrated that she is not white. Washington, who famously played the tragic mulatto Peola in *Imitation of Life*, here again portrays a woman with power whose tragic flaw is her "Black blood."[39] Like Peola, who cries, "I want to be white, like I look. Look at me. Am I not white? Isn't that a white girl?" Clelie, frustrated, utters similar lines about her complexion, seemingly oblivious to the power her color and wealth afford her in 1930s Jamaica and Haiti. Speaking to LeStrange, she says, "There is a barrier of blood that separates us." Aligning herself with Eve, she tells LeStrange, "I am white too, as white as she is." Clelie's obsession with Adam centers on his whiteness and perhaps his ownership of the neighboring plantation. In her view, her qualification for his love is her white skin, not her personality, her sexuality, or even her property. She insists that her white skin makes her good enough for Adam and trumps her "Black blood"; at one point she even places her arm next to Eve's to illustrate that there are no visible distinguishing racial markers between the two. Thus, the formulaic narrative in *The Love Wanga* illustrates the complicated social status of a Black female plantation owner who belongs to the Black elite but remains separate from whites.

ZOMBIES AND SUPERSTITIONS AS EXTENSIONS OF (COLONIAL) POWER

In *The Love Wanga*, when Clelie's plan to use a voodoo doll to kill Eve fails and Adam again rejects her, Clelie kneels before him and pleads, "Don't draw away from me as if I were a Black wench in your fields." Yet LeStrange reminds her, "Your white skin doesn't change what's inside you. You are Black, and you belong to me." Clelie responds, "Black, am I? I'll show [Adam] what a Black girl can do!" Throwing down the Black girl gauntlet, Clelie summons two Black shirtless male zombies from the dead. She orders them to kidnap Eve, who she plans to sacrifice at a voodoo ceremony. The zombies' dark skin and clothing that consists of only belted pants conveys their powerlessness. Their unquestioned deference and seminakedness cement their status as being at the very bottom of the racial hierarchy and as men no longer worthy of minimal patriarchal privilege.

The zombies enact the capture and symbolic defilement of the white woman (Eve) that are at the heart of imperial fears concerning white women's sexuality. Scholar Emiel Martens notes that despite being animated by Clelie, the zombies are, to use film historian Donald Bogle's language, "black brutes, inhuman and feral."[40] Like "other black West Indian bodies [they are] also subjected to the objectifying colonial gaze of fear and desire."[41] The Black female plantation owner's near-white body juxtaposed to the dark-skinned Black male zombies illustrates that Clelie is not afraid of the zombies but instead has power over them, and she has the power to control their labor.[42] Significantly, like white planters, Clelie exploits the Black body as laborer. Though she accesses power through voodoo, her desire for white racial power involves a willingness to exploit Black bodies as white planters have. There is no empathy or affinity between the zombies and Clelie: it is all about exerting control.

In both films, the Black female plantation owner primarily demonstrates her authority through her role as (faux) priestess, with Clelie and Isabelle exercising their power through Afro-Caribbean spiritual practices or spiritual trickery. Yet Clelie, Isabelle, and even Sylvia exercise the power they have as economically independent landowners. For example, in *The Devil's Daughter*, Isabelle plots to drive her sister Sylvia mad, and she makes it clear to her coconspirator, Philip, that she is "running the show." When she elaborates on her plans, she tells him what to do and reminds him that she is "on to him." Taking a different but equally entitled approach, Sylvia shows her interest in running the plantation through visiting the docks to witness the loading of bananas[43] and using dulcet tones to tell servants to "do as you are told." However, Isabelle prevails because she garners workers' loyalty through protecting and working closely with them. By way of illustration, Isabelle responds quickly when the overseer Philip calls

The Love Wanga (1936) and The Devil's Daughter (1939)   61

the police to report illegal Obeah activity because her first concern is for her workers ("my people," she calls them). Knowing they would be in trouble if the police found them, Isabelle disperses the crowd and reminds them that if questioned by the authorities, they were "only having a little pocomania," which was perceived as less sinister than Obeah.

As with all plantation texts, loyalty in *The Devil's Daughter* is a complicated notion. Are the servants loyal because Isabelle is a known quantity or a kind mistress? The kindness of mistresses has been debunked by volumes of archival research that indicate that whether Black, white, or mixed race, plantation owners exercised power to ensure that their enterprises were profitable.[44] The myth of the kind mistress and the "happy darkie" are complementary notions that reflect plantation power dynamics and convey the ideology that enslavement was good for Black people. Plantation ownership was "a key signifier of free[dom] and elite status."[45] Whether held in Black bodies or white, plantation ownership allowed women to navigate economic, social, and sometimes political territory. Ownership gave women the type of economic independence that allowed them to be "eccentric." In *The White Witch of Rose Hall*, Annie's overseer, Ashman, tells her, "You are the owner and can do what you like,"[46] which echoes her oft-repeated claim, "This is my property and I am mistress here."[47]

Therefore, in both *The Love Wanga* and *The Devil's Daughter*, Clelie and Isabelle use sorcery to buttress their power as plantation owners; without the "threat" of magic, their elite status can be more readily undermined. However, Clelie's actions differ from Isabelle's because voodoo is not a pretense for her. She uses her power as a voodoo priestess to repeatedly achieve her goals, first hypnotizing Eve's maid, Susie (Babe Joyce), to allow her to torment Eve. Second, she orders her father in the faith, a great bocor himself, to make her an ouanga charm and work as an overseer to the zombie laborers. Clelie tells the papaloi that he must help her raise the dead despite his aversion to her command. She admonishes him "not to fail her" when she sends him and the zombies to kidnap Eve.[48]

Clelie's power is intertwined with her identity as a voodoo practitioner, and while *The Love Wanga* does not deal explicitly with Clelie's economic power, it, too, is an overt presence that reveals the covert ways in which plantation power operates because the property provides Clelie with resources to follow Adam to New York and back. Clelie's elite status as a white-skinned Black plantation owner also gives her power. For example, on the voyage from New York to Haiti, presumably to Port-au-Prince, she passes for white, and Eve's maid defers to Clelie as if she were a white woman when Clelie requests her help prior to bewitching Eve. Moreover, Clelie's "foreignness" also likely allows her to travel even without having to pass as white. While traveling, foreignness and plantocracy align her with wealth and beauty, but once back on the island, Clelie's looks and voodoo associations mark her as degenerate.

Even so, Clelie is not afraid to claim her power. When Adam confronts her in the act of trying to kill Eve through the process of wrapping threads (representing life) around a voodoo doll, she does not recoil in horror. Instead, when Adam threatens to report her to the police, she retorts with a toss of her head, "Why don't you? Now you see my power." Adam takes the doll and burns it but, recognizing Clelie's power, does not report her to the authorities. In de Lisser's novel, Annie also embraces the power of whiteness and voodoo as she confronts the sentiment that "Obeah, even if it is practiced by a white woman is against the law."[49] Annie's disregard for law and custom reveal her debasement. Anticipating the characterization of Clelie, Annie is marked by both her whiteness and foreignness. As scholar Leah Reade Rosenberg argues, Annie's foreignness reflects an emerging Jamaican nationalism based on rationalizing local elite gender, political, and economic norms.[50] Annie's Haitian upbringing and her Irish mother make her a purveyor of the "racialized respectable womanhood,"[51] which de Lisser supports. At the same time, she represents those elements that displace "the plantocracy's brutality during slavery [onto Annie's body, leaving] the plantocracy of [the]1920s innocent of past labor abuses."[52] Nonetheless, Annie uses her voodoo prowess, taught to her by a baroness in King Christophe's court,[53] to her advantage though it may socially undermine her whiteness: "while a white woman might be suspected of murder, no jury would readily believe that she practiced obeah."[54] The idea that murder but not Obeah is within the realm of possibility for white women makes clear that Annie is a debased character. While Obeah may be too foreign for white women, Annie's ability to use it compounds how transgressive she is and simultaneously solidifies her as an agent not confined to social, religious, or gender expectations. At the same time, while Obeah and voodoo extend the powers of plantation owners like Annie, Clelie, and Isabelle, the formulaic nature of low-budget film narratives and their literary influences allow the real social implications of plantocracy to go unexamined.

CONCLUSION

Reflecting their conventionality, *The Love Wanga* and *The Devil's Daughter* pursue the erotics of domestic relations through spatial discourses that repeat the influence of the pigmentocracy and the divisions embedded in the imperial project. The plantation space, one of order, is racialized and sexualized by their female Black owners, whose plantations resemble the well-ordered white world. In *The Love Wanga*, while Clelie is mainly seen on the veranda of her

Big House, she resides in a well-maintained home with her altar, or *houmfort*, in a thatched roof building, separate from the Big House. The film's spatial distinctions continue

> through familiar binary oppositions. Black savagery is . . . the mountain jungle [while] Adam's plantation, beautiful and peaceful, represents modern-industrial, white civilization [and these juxtapositions replicate] the imperial tropes of cultivation and primitivism. [*The Love Wanga* portrays] the plantation as a civilized world of order and refinement—that is, hierarchically segregated—along racial lines, though at all times threatened by black degeneracy, produced by miscegenation and voodoo.[55]

The main house in *The Devil's Daughter* is similarly well ordered; however, neither Sylvia nor Isabelle is seen inside the house, whereas the duplicitous overseer, Philip, has lunch in the house and tries to rob the safe supposedly protected inside the house. The characters' contrasting relationship to the ostensibly civilized space points to ways that both films complicate the simple bifurcation between cultivated and uncultivated land. The Black female characters who own the plantations traverse the jungle/habitation binary; doing so is part of their transgressive authority. In a complicated twist, Clelie, Isabelle, and Sylvia maintain the savagery/civilization binary through their proprietorship but also trouble it via their gender and race.

In *The Love Wanga* and *The Devil's Daughter*, these three female characters are never seen in the Great House because, like the word "plantation," Big/Great House comes with its own associations of power, privilege, and privacy. It is thus not necessary to see the women in the house to understand what Big House evokes. Equally important, to place these Black women in the interior is to domesticate them, and for the African American actresses who often only had roles as domestics, being shown outside the house is a welcome stretch. Moreover, the exterior grounds of the plantation represent expansive power and wealth. Therefore, seeing the women walk the grounds affirms that they have power over all they survey.

The films' depiction of Black female plantation owners emphasizes the ways in which sartorial expression, spatial mobility, and other signs of female authority rupture mainstream depictions of Black female bodies in Caribbean locales. Historically, these bodies have been devalued and exploited, so to see them navigate terrain as landowners, with bodily autonomy and their own agendas, disrupts the white supremacist male gaze found in Hollywood representations. Though this gaze still manifests in depictions of natives as exotic and erotic, there is a pleasure in looking at these plantation owners for Black women audience members. Still, *The Love Wanga* and *The Devil's Daughter* reiterate ideological and aesthetic norms even as they rupture them.

Both films suggest a way of reading the Caribbean through dominant associations with Haiti. Specifically, Haitian degeneracy is mapped onto Caribbean spaces in general and Jamaica in particular to reiterate narratives of horror and dependency as well as the notion that the Caribbean is perpetually in need of external management. The Black female plantation owners, especially the ones who rely on magic, are used to sexualize the region and reinforce its instability. Black women are tied to the primitive, *and* they are plantation owners; both factors suggest that Caribbean societies are pathological. The characters' expression of legal dominion rests on dark and primitive dealings associated with African-based spirituality; the persistence of "this Caribbean"—isles of enchantment with beguiling "devil's daughters"—tacitly justifies imperialistic political, economic, and humanitarian intervention. Yet the films' explorations of color intersecting with class and gender illuminate layers of history, power, and privilege built on distinctions between light- and dark-skinned members of colonial societies. Further, as actresses Washington and McKinney portray powerful Black female plantation owners in *The Love Wanga* and *The Devil's Daughter*, they serve to both dismantle and trouble the racialized imperial gaze of the characters within the film as well as spectators outside of the films.

Notes

1. See Emiel Martens, "Welcome to Paradise Island: The Rise of Jamaica's Cine-Tourist Image, 1891–1951" (dissertation, University of Amsterdam, 2013), 195, 244, 254–55. Martens briefly discusses promotional material in his dissertation, particularly the "erotic and exotic" nature of representations of these characters.

2. I distinguish between the use of black magic or voodoo and the religious practice, vodou, through spelling.

3. Michael Largey, "*Ouanga!*: An African-American Opera about Haiti," *Lenox Avenue: A Journal of Interarts Inquiry* 2 (1996): 35–54, 52.

4. Largey, "*Ouanga!*," 35.

5. Margarite Fernández Olmos and Lizabeth Paravisini-Gebert, *Creole Religions of the Caribbean* (New York: New York University Press, 2003), 148.

6. Olmos and Paravisini-Gebert, *Creole Religions*, 149.

7. Olmos and Paravisini-Gebert, *Creole Religions*, 149.

8. Una Marson, *Pocomania and London Calling* (Kingston, Jamaica: Bouse & Skirt Books, 2016), 44.

9. Obeah and voodoo are interchangeable in many of the texts and are used to signify black magic.

10. Herbert G. De Lisser, *The White Witch of Rose Hall* (Kingston, Jamaica: Macmillan Caribbean, 1929), 127–29.

11. De Lisser, *White Witch*, 136.

The Love Wanga (1936) and The Devil's Daughter (1939)   65

12. George Terwilliger, director, *Love Wanga* (George Terwilliger/Ouanga Productions, 1935), 20:20.

13. Arthur Leonard, director, *The Devil's Daughter* (Lenwal Productions, 1939), 19:19.

14. See Robert Worthington Smith, "The Legal Status of Jamaican Slaves before the Anti-Slavery Movement," *The Journal of Negro History* 30, no. 3 (July 1945): 295; the 1717 act, which prohibited the use of drums and curtailed the ability to assemble, is "An Act for the more effectual punishment of Crimes Committed by Slaves" that forbade Negroes from assembling and from "beat[ing] drums or blow[ing] horns, thus after the manner of their native land transmitting signals 'of their evil and wicked intentions' to confederates upon distant plantations." See also the Negro Act of 1740 in South Carolina, which banned drums and horns and criminalized teaching slaves to read.

15. Curdella Forbes, *From Nation to Diaspora: Samuel Selvon, George Lamming and the Cultural Performance of Gender* (Kingston, Jamaica: University of the West Indies Press, 2005), 6–7.

16. Gina A. Ulysse, *Downtown Ladies: Informal Commercial Importers, a Haitian Anthropologist, and Self-Making in Jamaica* (Chicago: University of Chicago Press, 2007), 28.

17. Terwilliger, *Love Wanga*, 24:08–24:44.

18. William Seabrook, *The Magic Island* (New York: Harcourt, Brace, 1929). Seabrook writes, "One of the most dreaded forms of Haitian-African magic includes the dressing of a corpse in a garment of the person marked for vengeance and then exposing it to rot away in some secret place in the jungle. Men have gone stark mad seeking that jungle-hidden horror, and others have died hopelessly, searching" (51).

19. Leah Reade Rosenberg, "Creolizing Womanhood: Gender and Domesticity in Early Anglophone Caribbean National Literatures" (dissertation, Cornell University, 2000), 134–36.

20. De Lisser, *White Witch*, 104, 206.

21. De Lisser, *White Witch*, 210.

22. De Lisser, *White Witch*, 50.

23. Ellen C. Scott, "More than a 'Passing' Sophistication: Dress, Film Regulation, and the Color Line in 1930s American Films," *Women's Studies Quarterly* 44, nos. 1&2 (Spring/Summer 2013): 77; see 60–86.

24. Scott, "More than a 'Passing' Sophistication," 76.

25. Scott, "More than a 'Passing' Sophistication," 76–77.

26. Ulysse, *Downtown Ladies*, 25.

27. Seabrook, *Magic Island*, 138.

28. Seabrook, *Magic Island*, 139.

29. Seabrook, *Magic Island*, 140.

30. Seabrook, *Magic Island*, 139.

31. Seabrook, *Magic Island*, 140.

32. Seabrook, *Magic Island*, 141.

33. Seabrook, *Magic Island*, 140.

34. Seabrook, *Magic Island*, 140–41.

35. Seabrook, *Magic Island*, 141.

36. Ulysse, *Downtown Ladies*, 25.

37. Karen Lyons, "Rise and Fall of Sumptuary Laws: Rules for Dressing in Shakespeare's England," *Shakespeare & Beyond* (Folger Shakespeare Library), September 8, 2017, https://

shakespeareandbeyond.folger.edu/2017/09/08/sumptuary-laws-rules-dressing-shake speare-england.

38. Alison Donnell, "Introduction," in *Pocomania and London Calling*, by Una Marson (Kingston, Jamaica: Blouse and Skirt Books, 2016), xx.

39. See Scott, "More Than a 'Passing' Sophistication," 74. *Love Wanga* was filmed in 1933 but not released until 1935 in Britain; it had a very limited release in the United States in 1942.

40. Bogle, quoted in Martens, "Welcome to Paradise Island," 247.

41. Martens, "Welcome to Paradise Island," 247.

42. Martens, "Welcome to Paradise Island," 234.

43. Leonard, *Devil's Daughter*, 11:46.

44. See Thavolia Glymph, *Out of the House of Bondage: The Transformation of the Plantation Household* (New York: Cambridge University Press, 2008), 63–96; Stephanie E. Jones-Rogers, *They Were Her Property: White Women as Slave Owners in the American South* (New Haven, CT: Yale University Press, 2019), 1–24. See also Larry Koger, *Black Slaveowners: Free Black Slave Masters in South Carolina, 1790–1860* (Jefferson, NC: McFarland, 1985); Christine Walker, *Jamaica Ladies: Female Slaveholders and the Creation of Britain's Atlantic Empire* (Chapel Hill: University of North Carolina Press, 2020).

45. Walker, *Jamaica Ladies*, loc 6411.

46. De Lisser, *White Witch*, 62.

47. De Lisser, *White Witch*, 52–53.

48. Terwilliger, *Love Wanga*, 37:15.

49. De Lisser, *White Witch*, 212.

50. Rosenberg, "Creolizing Womanhood," 147–57.

51. Rosenberg, "Creolizing Womanhood," 135.

52. Rosenberg, "Creolizing Womanhood," 149.

53. De Lisser, *White Witch*, 136–37.

54. De Lisser, *White Witch*, 160.

55. Martens, "Welcome to Paradise Island," 247.

Chapter 4

FILMIC MIGRATIONS OF THE CARMEN FIGURE

Karmen Geï and Its Implications for Diasporic Black Female Sexual Decolonization

KIMBERLY NICHELE BROWN

Describing the longevity of Georges Bizet's 1875 operatic rendition of Prosper Mérimée's novella *Carmen* (1845), Erich Leinsdorf writes, "No other opera has been rearranged and revised more, which may be taken as further proof of its indestructibility. Not many other operas belong to this exclusive club. They have found favor on every continent, in every city where opera is part of public entertainment."[1] From her inception, both figuratively and literally, the Carmen figure has been a consummate border crosser—she has migrated across continents not only in operatic form, as Leinsdorf states, but also through the mediums of literature and film. Given Carmen's initial migratory status as a Gypsy[2] interloper who upsets Spain's status quo and given how her story has traveled through time and throughout cultures, I read Carmen as a *migratory figure* who, for nearly two centuries, has served as the embodiment of aberrant and transgressive female sexuality.

CARMEN'S HISTORICAL ORIGIN AND BLACK ITERATIONS OF THE CARMEN FIGURE

Originally set in Andalusia, Spain, and written in response to anxieties concerning Romani migration, Prosper Mérimée's novella begins with a damning epigraph from the fourth-century Greek poet Palladas that translates to, "Every woman is as bitter as gall. But she has two good moments: one in bed, the other in death."[3] While on the surface Mérimée seems to castigate all women for having a "dark" nature, a salient feature of the Carmen myth is that her licentiousness is credited to her ethnicity and class status. When the novella's French narrator, a traveler who has recently arrived in Spain, first encounters Carmen, he is unable to tell if she is Andalusian, Jewish, or Moorish. In both Mérimée's novella and Bizet's operatic rendition, as a Gypsy woman, Carmen is both constructed and constricted by the genteel dictates of nineteenth-century Spanish society as she seduces, then discards, Don José, a man from a higher social stratum who enjoys, for all intents and purposes, what contemporary race scholars would consider "white privilege." Following Carmen's rejection, Don José murders her in retaliation, an act that is essentially sanctioned within the opera.

In what José F. Colmeiro would call a "traveling myth," the indestructibility of the Carmen story, in conjunction with her repeated death and resurrection, can be attributed to a basic universal fear of female border crossers, women who eschew or trouble "territorial demarcations imposed by cultural and political norms."[4] Colmeiro identifies two competing tendencies in contemporary cultural studies that reveal the ambiguity of Carmen's mythology. As he explains, "Those informed by feminist theory see her as an affirmation of free will, independence, and liberation; those informed by postcolonial theory seek to unmask the misogynist and racist undertones toward the other, which ultimately neutralize those emancipatory impulses."[4] Not only does Carmen's story lend itself to both readings, but "its fundamental ambivalence about issues crucial in the construction of our modern consciousness, an ambivalence which reveals cultural anxieties about gender, race, class, nation, language, and sexuality" is the "key to its continual renewal and adaptability."[5] However, the diverging tendencies that reflect feminist and postcolonial theory, respectively, converge when adaptations shift from using the Black woman as mimesis to literal representations of Carmen as a Black woman.

It was a Black woman that served as my induction into the Carmen mythos when, as a teenager, I watched Dorothy Dandridge play the title character in Otto Preminger's *Carmen Jones* (1954). And yet, shifting through the annuals of my parents' record collection, I might have caught glimpses of her in Aretha Franklin's version of "Spanish Harlem" and when the Black rhythm-and-blues group the Impressions sang, "I hate to see the lady go / Knowing she'll never know / That I love her, I love her / She was a Gypsy woman."[6] Thinking back to Dandridge and these sixties crooners, I always had my suspicions: was she a *Gypsy* woman? Scholars such as Robert L. A. Clark, Susan McClary, and Phil Powrie have argued convincingly that the dark Gypsy featured in Mérimée's and Bizet's texts is linked intricately to the African Other.[7] In light of Sarah Baartman and the nineteenth-century European fascination with her genitals, documented by scholars such as Yvette Abrahams, Sander Gilman, and

Christina Sharpe,[8] not to mention the subsequent historical vilification of Black women throughout the Diaspora as "Jezebels," it seems inevitable that the defamed Black female body would merge with this fictional embodiment of deviant female sexuality. And yet, despite the insinuated connection one can easily make between the dark Gypsy and the African Other, it is not until *Carmen Jones* that the allusion to Black female sexuality is made overt. Starring Dandridge and Harry Belafonte, *Carmen Jones* distinguishes itself from other operatic and filmic renditions due to Preminger's decision to interpret the story through an all-Black cast. Preminger relocates the well-worn tale of a dark seductress who causes the downfall of an upstanding military man to a US Air Force base that uses civilian workers to make parachutes for the World War II effort.

Since the release of *Carmen Jones*, there have been three additional major adaptations featuring a Black woman as the lead character: Joseph Gaï Ramaka's Senegalese musical adaptation *Karmen Geï* (2001); the MTV-produced *Carmen: A Hip Hopera* (directed by Robert Townsend in 2001); and *UCarmen eKhayelitsha* from South Africa (directed by British dramatist-turned-filmmaker Mark Dornford-May in 2005). Taken together, these millennial adaptations offer a unique insight into how filmmakers have used the Carmen mythos to examine the barriers, parameters, and proscriptions societies place on Black women's attempts to acquire love and freedom. While all the millennial adaptations follow Preminger's lead by having all-Black casts, in this paper I have chosen *Karmen Geï* as my focal text because it offers a more nuanced depiction of global Black female sexual decolonization.

KARMEN GEÏ, TRANSNATIONAL FILMMAKING, AND MIGRATORY STORIES

It is crucial to my analysis of *Karmen Geï* as a model of sexual decolonization for Black women in Africa and its Diaspora to situate Joseph Gaï Ramaka as a transnational filmmaker. Ramaka, born in St. Louis, Senegal, in 1952, would later study visual anthropology at the École des hautes études en sciences sociales and train in cinema at the Institut des hautes études cinématographiques in Paris. Between 1985 and 1989, Ramaka established himself as a filmmaker with the release of three anthropological documentaries on the "rites and cults of Senegalese ethnic groups."[9] Although he currently resides in New Orleans, Louisiana, Ramaka spent over twenty years dividing his time between Senegal and France. Mari Maasilta labels him an "African transnational diasporic filmmaker"; as such, and in light of *Karmen Geï*'s interstitial production history, Maasilta argues that Ramaka caters to national (i.e., Senegalese) and Western audiences. In her article "The 'Monumental' Heroine: Female Agency in Joseph Gaï Ramaka's *Karmen Geï*," Anjali Prabhu contends, "African cinema thus reclaims an African audience, which in turn retains its right to the global as much as it does to the local."[10] Therefore, "in conceiving the globalized context of filmmaking and, particularly, of reception," Prabhu argues that Ramaka "implicate(s) the 'globalized' spectator from home or abroad intellectually," while the film simultaneously "Africanizes a global audience" by resisting an "easy correspondence with African reality even in its most recognizably African aspects."[11] It is because of Ramaka's transnational directorial credentials, the film's production history, and his filmic gestures toward what Prabhu would consider a "universal" blackness that I am emboldened to revisit *Karmen Geï* as a model of Black female sexual decolonization applicable not just to African women but to Black women of the Diaspora as well.

Although Prabhu disavows the political valence of *Karmen Geï* throughout her article, she concedes that in "perhaps enabling the space of the (globalized and thus inclusive of an African) spectator . . . one might potentially locate the politics critics have touted for this film."[12] But even then she cautions that because "the politics of the film are strongly anchored in a mise-en-scène . . . feminism or Afrocentrism or third worldism or postcolonialism can function as little more than points of entry into the film."[13] However, at the risk of using a cliché, *representation matters*, the symbolic matters. As a Black feminist from the United States, I am interested in representations of how Black women throughout Africa and its Diaspora navigate sexual desires through the muck and mire of societal expectations and the historical and global racist maligning of Black women as always already aberrant, excessive, and queer.

When *Karmen Geï* was first distributed, Ramaka mused, "Carmen is a myth but what does Carmen represent today? Where do Carmen's love and freedom stand at the onset of the 21st Century?"[14] In a separate interview, Pauline Malefane (the lead in *UCarmen eKhayelitsha*) alludes to the universal quality of Carmen's story, saying, "It could be anywhere, anytime or anyone. In the 1800s, it still made sense to people living then, and now in the 21st Century, it's still relevant."[15] So here we are, a little over twenty years since *Karmen Geï*'s initial release, and the new millennium is not so new anymore, and yet Ramaka's question still remains valid as Carmen's story continues to circulate. The permanence of migratory stories like Carmen, then, can often be attributed to the need to reinterpret or recreate a universal morality tale or truth that, to be properly ingested by a contemporary audience, must be updated with each adaptation.

When speaking specifically about the effect that actual migration has on societies, Paul White explains, "Migration . . . changes people and mentalities. New experiences result from the coming together of multiple influences and peoples, and these new experiences lead to altered or evolving representations of experience and self-identity."[16] I use the phrase "migratory figure" as antithetical to "migratory subjectivities," Carole Boyce Davies's phrase to define the cross-cultural writings of Black women who must actively renegotiate their identities as they move from place to place.[17] While Boyce Davies's term connotes a certain amount of agency on the part of Black women, Carmen (even when she migrates) neither writes nor narrates her own story and is therefore often acted upon; her sexual agency is thwarted. Although I am tempted to rely on the easy conflation of "migration" and "adaptation," I am struck by the contradiction between the transformative power that real-life migrations enact on societies and the stagnant quality of the Carmen myth that insists generally, in deference to narrative fidelity, on Carmen's death. To what extent, then, is it possible to create a decolonized model of female sexual agency by salvaging a story *that was never meant to set Carmen free?*

RAMAKA'S DECOLONIZATION OF THE CARMEN MYTH

Therefore, I am interested in how Ramaka rehashes the Carmen myth to offer a version of Black female sexual decolonization that exists outside of the parameters of patriarchy and heteronormativity. To this aim, I posit that Ramaka, as a Black male feminist following in the footsteps of Ousmane Sembene, recreates C/Karmen as a Black nationalist feminist. Ramaka relinquishes his desire to be, as Michael Awkward coins it, "ideologically male," which entails giving up "traditional patriarchal desires for control and erasure of the 'female'" and offering instead "sophisticated, informed, and contentious critiques of phallocentric practices . . . in an effort to redefine our notions of Black male (and female) textuality and subjectivity."[18] Ramaka presents an example of Black female sexual agency that defies Eurocentric, patriarchal, and heterosexist privilege; therefore, *Karmen Geï* rejects the phallocentricism associated with the traditional Carmen myth, opera, and Hollywood cinema. Ramaka attempts to redeem Black female sexuality from its maligned history by manipulating plot elements that were originally designed to castigate Carmen as the exotic Other: he dispenses with the use of a frame narrator; he usurps the heterosexual love triangle that has been so germane to the Carmen myth; and he revises Hollywood definitions of the femme fatale.

In Mérimée's novella, Carmen and Don José's story is narrated almost as a travelogue from the vantage point of a French archaeologist who had nearly succumbed to Carmen's charms himself. The archaeologist acts as a framing narrator; he sets up the story and forms his own conclusions about Carmen at the end.[19] Susan McClary explains, "These overemphatic framing devices [such as the use of the French narrator] leave little doubt that this narrative

In Joseph Gaï Ramaka's film, cinematic and narrative choices make Karmen (Djeïnaba Diop Gaï) the central character *and* someone committed to those around her.

concerns threatening encounters with the other: the other primarily understood as woman and gypsy."[20] McClary further argues that when Bizet translated Mérimée's novella into an opera and decided to dispense with the original framing device, he risked unveiling a subversive subtext of Carmen's real erotic power, because the opera simply traces "the humiliation and degradation of a male, white authority at the hands of a woman of color."[21] Therefore, in operatic renditions that forgo such framing devices, Carmen appears free to speak for herself, thus giving the audience the impression that Carmen is indeed acting on her own accord in all instances. However, McClary explains that Bizet made sure to minimize the potentially liberating aspects of Carmen's seduction by employing various techniques to ensure the containment of Carmen's sexual liberation.[22]

In contrast, *Karmen Geï* opens with the camera trained on Karmen (Djeïnaba Diop Gaï), who sits spread eagled and smiling surrounded by a group of incarcerated Black women who have gathered in the prison yard to witness a seduction. Using Karmen as essentially *the* establishing shot, Ramaka dispenses with the male frame and narrator found in Mérimée's novella, thereby forcing the audience to deal with Karmen on her own terms, so that her story is not mediated through a male figure. Wearing a black boubou with high slits that showcase fiery red undergarments, Karmen performs the Wolof *sabar* dance. She enacts a frenzied performance punctuated by pelvic thrusts and a lap dance that culminates in a sensual dance duet between Karmen and Angélique (Canadian singer-actress Stephanie Biddle), the female prison warden she is seducing. Ayo A. Coly explains, "As performed by Senegalese women, the dance is the ultimate expression and homosexual theatricality of erotic autonomy . . . because in the space of the *sabar* an endless unscripting of sexualities occur, erotic allegiances are constantly influx, and it is not unusual that the audience find themselves hailed into and rescripted by the performance."[23] For example, according to Coly, under Karmen's gyrations, "the authoritative representative of the postcolonial commandment moves from stiff spectator and overseer of the dance to a signifying loosened up dancing body as she is hailed into the dancing circle and joined by all the female inmates."[24] The audience quickly learns that the dance is a ruse; shortly after this public spectacle, Angélique summons Karmen to her quarters, where they make love, and then Karmen escapes while Angélique sleeps.

Cheered on by the other female inmates and aided in escaping by a female prison guard, these opening sequences situate Karmen as a model of transgressive Black female sexuality as well as a Black nationalist feminist.[25] The astute viewer understands Karmen's illegal machinations (both the charge of smuggling and the seduction) as subversive tactics enacted to undermine a corrupt government that exploits its impoverished citizens. Additionally, it is important to highlight that the opening scene is shot in a women's prison located on Gorée Island, a former Senegalese slave port that was purported to be the largest on the African coast from the fifteenth to the nineteenth century. Because Gorée Island acts as a geographic metaphor for displacement in terms of the African Diaspora, I would argue that Karmen's actions have wider implications that extend beyond Ramaka's indictment of Senegal's elite; her incarceration can also be linked to the ways in which Black women worldwide have been imprisoned by stereotypes associated with promiscuous and aberrant sexuality. Conversely, Karmen's decision to enact a dance of seduction in public, at a site of contemporary and historical captivity, evokes and troubles multiple looking relationships—the panopticon, the scopophilia, and the colonial gaze—thereby signaling Ramaka's desire to liberate Black women from misogynist and racist schemata that continue to plague us.

Additionally, opera and film can function as markers of "high art" that have historically disseminated problematic renditions of the Black body, as well as genres that have used the colonial gaze to reproduce hegemonic representations that curtail a Black agentic presence. John Rieder explains, the colonial gaze "distributes knowledge and power to the subject who looks, while denying power for its object, the one looked at. This structure [is] a cognitive disposition that both rests upon and helps to maintain and reproduce the political and economic arrangements that establish the subjects' respective positions."[26] Directors like Ramaka, then, are forced to negotiate and dismantle these hegemonic representations in order to render Black characters as agentic subjects rather than as objectified figures. Ramaka seeks to empower Karmen's gaze and to offer alternative looking relationships that do not cast Blacks as consummate victims of the colonial gaze or women as forever prey to the male gaze. He achieves this goal by breaking from the operatic tradition as the method through which to convey Karmen's story.

In *Opera, or the Undoing of Women*, Catherine Clément writes of the infeasibility of merging feminism or Black agency with the goals of traditional opera. Speaking against feminist readings of operas, Clément states:

> Opera concerns women. No, there is no feminist version; no, there is no liberation. Quite the contrary: they suffer, they cry, they die. Singing and wasting your breath can be the same thing. Glowing with tears, their decolletés cut to the heart, they expose themselves to the gaze of those who come to take pleasure in their pretend agonies. Not one of them escapes with her life, or very few of them do.[27]

Many define *Karmen Geï* as an African musical because of Ramaka's decision to fuse African American jazz with Senegalese music, replete with Wolof lyrics. In addition to breaking from the traditional method of telling Carmen's story, his musical decision underscores his position as a transnational filmmaker committed to appealing to a global Black audience. But more importantly, Ramaka's choice essentially decenters opera from its position as high art.

Powrie argues that Ramaka's choice to make *Karmen Geï* into a musical, possibly Africa's first, is his attempt at realism, since the music flows logically from the scene itself rather than the forced way in which music is used in an opera. I would further argue that a direct correlation can be made between Preminger's reliance on and Ramaka's disposal of operatic traditions with the former's tendency to romanticize US working-class Blacks and the latter's desire to present an authentic representation of blackness, or at least one not filtered through white Western traditions. In his article "Black Faces, White Voices: The Politics of Dubbing in *Carmen Jones*," Jeff Smith explains that while Belafonte and Dandridge were both good singers, their voices were dubbed by opera-trained whites who affected a Negro accent—which implies to Smith that Belafonte and Dandridge might have been considered "'too black' to sing opera."[28] In many ways, *Carmen Jones* functions as an elaborate masquerade or parody of blackness that, underneath the surface, reveals racist tendencies that equate Black bodies with base and primitive sexual desire and, by extension, Black voices with low art.[29]

RAMAKA RESISTS COLONIALIST, MASCULINIST, AND NATIONALIST INSCRIPTIONS

While a credible case can be made that Ramaka resists the colonial gaze by switching genres, Saya Woolfalk challenges affirmations that Ramaka succeeds in disassociating himself from scopophilia. She insists that Karmen "never frees herself from the male gaze of the camera."[30] In contrast, Prabhu argues that Ramaka avoids "the classic voyeuristic camera whereby the woman's agency is thwarted by objectification . . . both diegetically and cinematographically" by his reliance on what she terms "the monumental mode of representation."[31] Here Prabhu is not denying that the camera is trained on Karmen or that it isn't privileging male viewership. However, she suggests that the male gaze in this sense should not be thought of as *voyeuristic*. Rather than this male gaze prioritizing the sexual desire of male viewers, this gaze objectifies Karmen by making her a more manageable feminine revolutionary ideal. Instead, according to Prabhu, this aesthetic "'monumentalizes' the heroine by making of her a magnificent, impenetrable entity which . . . simultaneously resists . . . discourses given coherence by feminist criticism, political engagement, or other such particular forms of rationality."[32] In other words, Prabhu seems to find fault with Karmen's portrayal *not* on the grounds of the traditional male gaze but by arguing that the character of Karmen never rises above the level of the "phenomenological" moment depicted in the film, thereby constricting "her cinematic possibility" to "embody or present allegorically, the African woman, let alone anything beyond, even in utopian form."[33] Instead, Karmen is on some levels rendered androgynous; she embodies "the idea of a masculinized collectivity of 'the people' against 'the system,'" while representing "no ultimate triumph for either."[34] So, while Ramaka does not participate in the traditional male scopophilia associated with Hollywood cinema, there is "no demasculinizing of the interpretive position."[35]

What Prabhu identifies as a "masculinized collectivity of 'the people' against 'the system'" might more accurately be interpreted through the framework of Black nationalist feminist ideologies like Alice Walker's "womanism" and Clenora Hudson-Weems's "Africana Womanism" in the United States and Chikwenye Ogunyemi's "African Womanism" for Black women on the continent. These ideologies share an inability to resonate with white Western feminism "because it concentrates solely on the question of gender, while they view gender relationships always in the context of other political, economic, cultural, and social forms and mechanisms of oppression such as racism, neocolonialism, (cultural) imperialism, capitalism, religious fundamentalism, and dictatorial and corrupt systems."[36] Ogunyemi holds space for a gender-free Pan-Africanism, which would differ drastically from the "the separatist, idyllic existence away from the hullabaloo of the men's world."[37] Ogunyemi writes that this Pan-African version of feminism would entail "the unity of Blacks everywhere under the enlightened control of men and women."[38] And while Ramaka's Black nationalist feminism also does not foreground gender separatism, it does privilege Black female sexual desire over nationalist tendencies to render the Black female body in service to the state. Therefore, Ramaka pushes back on what Coly calls the "cautious engagements of African feminists with the sexual female body."[39] Coly states that this repression of the sexual female body "walks a thin line with the gender and sexual politics of . . . nationalism, namely the nationalist conscription of the female body to signify the cultural values of the nation and the nationalist privileging of desexualized motherhood as both virtuous womanhood and proper female citizenship."[40]

For Prabhu, Ramaka does not offer any credible instances of "female sociability," a "possibility of an imagined social fabric in which differently positioned women might be connected," or an "extended female community whose support Karmen draws on."[41] For contrast, she turns to Dornford-May's *UCarmen eKhayelitsha*, in which "Carmen is always in the company of her little entourage, and the strong bonds among its members allow for the mourning of Carmen first by the women and then by the men of the outlaw-gang who join them in horror."[42] However, in addition to arguably privileging feminist ideologies that maintain gender separatism, Prabhu fails to consider how the lionizing of heroic Black female historical figures runs rampant both on the continent and throughout the Diaspora. In her article "She Who Creates Havoc Is Here," Cheryl Stobie specifically mentions Ndèye Guèye, Kumba Kastel (Mami Wata spirit), and Aline Sitoe Diatta as inspirations for Karmen's character. She explains, "All of these African and Senegalese historical and mythic resonances endow Karmen with a host of associations with specifically female physical, emotional, and spiritual strength and power, broadening the character beyond the limits of her predecessor, Carmen."[43]

Additionally, Tuzyline Jita Allan explains, "Walker intends the major themes of womanist epistemology—audacity, woman-centeredness, and whole(some)ness of vision—to be understood as critical imperatives in the effort to fashion a framework of feminist resistance to patriarchy."[44] Womanist ideologies highlight willful behavior as indicative of Black female culture; therefore, many Black women have been socialized to see Black womanhood in monumental terms irrespective of whether an individual chooses to embrace a feminist ideology or not.

In service to her reading of Karmen as monumental, Prabhu discredits and downplays the film's feminist gestures at almost every turn.[45] I argue, however, that Ramaka prefigures Karmen as a Black nationalist feminist, and, as such, her love cannot be understood in individualistic or gender separatist terms.

Instead, Ramaka links her quest for love to her love of "the people." Rather than paint Karmen as monumental, he uses her to challenge compulsory hetero-normativity by redefining our traditional understanding of the femme fatale, by usurping the heterosexual love triangle prevalent in the Carmen mythos, and, finally, by adhering to the affective needs of Black women throughout the Diaspora regarding *misogynoir* and the politics of representation, female solidarity, and beauty hierarchies.

WESTERN INDIVIDUALISM JUXTAPOSED WITH BLACK NATIONALISM

Placing *Karmen Geï* into an intertexual dialogue with *Carmen Jones* in terms of how the director interprets the famous refrain from Bizet's opera, "Love is like a bird which cannot be tamed. If you cage it, it will fly away," reveals a contrast between Western individualism and Black nationalism that also character-izes the distinction between bourgeoise feminism (in the pejorative sense) and Black feminisms in general. Offering two vastly different models of Black female sexual agency, Preminger defines love in individualistic terms, while Ramaka defines it in terms of communal or revolutionary love.

In Preminger's film, parachute maker Carmen (Dandridge) is confronted in the cafeteria by a jealous woman, Cindy Lou (Olga James), who accuses Carmen of stealing her man, Joe (Belafonte), the Don José character. As both a retort and an explanation of her own sexual nature, Carmen sings, "Love is a baby that grows up wild and he don't do what you want him to. Love ain't nobody's angel child and he won't pay no mind to you. One man gives me a diamond stud and I won't give him a cigarette. One man treats me like I was mud, and all I got that man can get. You go for me and I'm taboo, but if you're hard to get I go for you. And if I do, den your through. Boy, my baby, that's the end of you." Carmen, then, inadvertently minimizes her own sexual agency, prefer-ring instead to envision herself as a victim of love's caprice. Later in the same song, Carmen compares love to a bird that cannot be contained. Both images demonstrate the fickle nature of love and, by extension, Carmen. However, despite Carmen's insistence, the audience is not persuaded to blame "love" for Joe's demise; Carmen is seen as complicit in her own murder because her desire has been characterized as self-serving and parasitic.

In contrast, Karmen's ambitions coincide with that of the underprivileged in her community. Throughout *Karmen Geï*, Ramaka recycles the symbol of the child and the bird mentioned in Carmen Jones's signature song. In one scene Karmen intones, "Love is a vagabond child. A child who knows no law. If you don't love me, I love you anyway. And if I love you, be on your guard."

Much like her predecessor, Karmen's version of love is also not predicated on reciprocity; however, Ramaka truncates the original lyrics of "Dat's Love," removing words that equate Karmen's love with a fatalistic predilection for abusive and nonresponsive men. Additionally, Ramaka's switch from Carmen's "wild child" to Karmen's "vagabond child" connects Karmen's discourse of love to the economic plight of contemporary Dakar's poor and disenfranchised in a way that *Carmen Jones* does not.[46]

Ramaka's redefinition of love as communal is most prevalent in the opening scenes where Karmen enjoys female camaraderie with the other inmates with whom she's incarcerated. In an attempt to discredit Lindiwe Dovey's reading of the film as a "feminist argument," given Ramaka's "'nationalization' of the women's bodies through *sabar* dance," Prabhu argues, "The idea of an actual female society beyond the enclosed and forced contiguity of women's bodies within the prison is not raised in this film. There is no gesture to indicate any meaningful female society in terms of reality or myth. Karmen leaves the prison and does not organize her sisters, whom she stirred up through dance—nor does her energy carry the collectivity to action."[47] While the film does not pay homage to any of the feminist organizations prevalent in Senegal, Stobie argues that Ramaka "illustrates the connections between women in the prison as well as their sexual agency, both of which act as alternatives and implicit challenges to heterosexuality, patriarchy, and feminine gender roles of marriage, motherhood, and sexual submission."[48] Ramaka intends for Karmen's sexual freedom to be as much of an aspirant goal for Black female viewers as she is for the female inmates.

It is important, then, that Karmen's seduction of Angélique is carried out in public, that the other women are in on the subterfuge, and that they join in to dance alongside Karmen and Angélique. After her seduction of Angélique succeeds, back in the confines of a shared cell, Karmen celebrates with her sister inmates who sing her praises: "Karmen, there's no one like you. You attract men and make women undo their robes. I like you, you like me. It's all about feeling good. Be careful! Hide your women, hide your men. Karmen has come! She who creates havoc is here." Karmen's queerness is heralded as a marker of true sexual freedom. Their enthusiastic acceptance replaces the antagonism that Carmen Jones encounters from her female coworkers at the parachute factory in Preminger's version.

Stobie notes, "Karmen's difference from others is more a question of degree and heroic charisma than of exceptional behavior, as in addition to Angélique's response to Karmen, the other prisoners graphically and humorously simulate same-sex intimate acts."[49] To label her charismatic rather than "monumental," as Prabhu does, widens the possibility that others can emulate Karmen's subversive actions. For example, Coly evokes Achille Mbembe's *On the Postcolony*

(2001) in order to explain how this opening scene demonstrates "carnivalesque practices of space."[50] According to Coly, "Mbembe describes the postcolony as a theatrical metaparody where all disciplinary norms and signifying practices are eventually fair game for poaching, including relations of power."[51] Later, another prisoner emulates Karmen's actions by also attempting to seduce Angélique; in their estimation, "one slit is as good as another." And while they do not succeed, it is clear that Angélique has lost all credibility as the prison warden, which we can surmise contributes to her eventual suicide.[52]

RAMAKA'S ALTERNATIVE TO THE WESTERN FEMME FATALE

As Angélique's example demonstrates, Karmen does indeed "create havoc," but she does not revel in it. Throughout the film, she exhibits a Black feminist "ethic of care" as further proof of her communal love.[53] Her consideration of how her actions impact others demonstrates Ramaka's shift away from conventional portrayals of Carmen as a femme fatale. Slavoj Žižek argues, "What is menacing about the *femme fatale* is not that she is fatal for *men* but that she presents a case of a 'pure,' non-pathological subject fully assuming *her* own fate."[54] Additionally, Julie Grossman contends that the main appeal of femmes fatales is their "commitment to fulfilling her own desires, whatever they may be (sexual, capitalistic, material), at any cost."[55] However, Saya Woolfalk argues against this labeling for Karmen and opts instead to call her a "political sex icon," explaining that while the Hollywood prototype's sexual liberation is portrayed in individualistic terms, "Karmen, the protagonist of the film, uses her sexual power to obtain not only personal pleasure, but to stimulate cultural subversion and incite political dissent."[56]

Therefore, like Audre Lorde's articulation of "erotic power," Karmen's sexual agency is formed outside of the parameters of Western pornographic ideas about sexuality.[57] Her agency is also not predicated on compulsory heterosexuality that castigates and constricts female sexual desire and fosters competition among women for male attention. To that aim, Ramaka disassociates his alleged femme fatale from labels such as "whore," "gold digger," "man stealer," and so on. For example, Tahar Chériaa argues that in Egyptian melodramas, "The only person who shows her body is the belly dancer; she is always the femme fatale who tries to lead a son from a good family astray; it ends with the son escaping her clutches."[58] Chériaa explains that since the body is "always associated with people's moral turpitude . . . if you want to devalue someone, you denude him, you show his body."[59] If the femme fatale is denuded either literally or by suggestion (I am thinking of the fact that audiences get to see Dandridge in her underwear in *Carmen Jones*), as a way of defaming her character, Ramaka

In *Karmen Geï*, the 2001 Senegalese musical adaptation, Karmen is not a Westernized femme fatale but instead an agent for diasporic Black female sexual decolonization.

must combat the negative connotations of female nudity with "whoredom." When Karmen's juggling of men's hearts, particularly Lamine Diop's (Magaye Niang), is criticized and gossiped about among the smugglers in her ring, that conversation is quickly squelched by Samba (Thierno Ndiaye Doss)—who is the oldest male member of the group. Additionally, in one scene, Karmen discusses the details of a smuggling operation with her male cohorts while taking a bubble bath in plain view of the men. Not only do none of the men seem aroused by her nudity, hidden beneath the bubbles such as it is, when she stands to get out of the tub, the men turn away or avert their eyes while she wraps herself in a towel. This act of deference highlights Ramaka's decision to reject the primacy of the male gaze.

GOOD GIRL VERSUS BAD GIRL

One further example of Karmen's conscientious female allegiance in contrast to the conventional femme fatale, and in reference to Prabhu's objection to the lack of feminist or female solidarity, is found in the dynamic between Karmen and Majiguene (the Micaëla/Cindy Lou figure, played by Aïssatou Diop). McClary explains that Bizet made sure to minimize the potentially liberating aspects of Carmen's seduction by employing various techniques to ensure the containment of Carmen's sexual liberation. An example of such a technique is the creation of the character of Micaëla to act as a good-girl foil to Carmen's bad-girl persona. The casting of the good-girl antithesis can also be found in *Carmen Jones* in which Cindy Lou acts as Carmen's foil. While Cindy Lou is pretty enough, her sexuality is subdued by her plain attire. Her character is a reflection of the anxieties typically associated with Black female sexuality in the United States; she offers the audience a model of respectable, bourgeois Black femininity.

Although equal in beauty to Karmen, Majiguene is deemed more respectable based on her class status; not only does she come from a wealthy family, she is also the superintendent's daughter. Karmen intrudes upon Lamine's wedding ceremony to Majiguene. Using dance as her method of seduction, Karmen wins Lamine's heart by besting Majiguene in a frenzied dance-off. Coly describes this confrontation as follows: "The bride is thrust out of the phallic economy of the postcolony when she joins Karmen on the dance floor and the two female bodies come together in a homoerotic saber dance-off that undercuts the heterosexual wedding. Thrusting her loins forward, Karmen symbolically penetrates the young bride before the husband gets to consummate the wedding."[60] However, I would argue that this dance is very much still a part of the phallic economy. Rather than undercut the "heterosexual wedding," it furthers an understanding of both the marriage and groom as penultimate prizes for women. As the term "dance-off" connotes, they are in competition for Lamine's heart; the best dancer wins. Coly's idea that Karmen "penetrates" Majiguene symbolically only works if Karmen is in competition with Lamine rather than the two women competing against each other.

In attendance at the wedding are also several high-ranking government officials at whom Karmen launches her condemnation: "Let Kumba Kastel's spirit appear. Your rifles cannot bring me down. The eagle soars through the sky. Ramatou, the little bird flies under his wing. You are all evil. . . . You've swallowed up the country. We'll eat your guts." After her victorious dance performance, Lamine is ordered to escort Karmen to jail for her insubordination. However, because of her successful performance, Lamine ultimately sets her free; the scene ends with his incarceration; he has fallen hopelessly in love with her.

The competitive aspects of two women fighting for a man are curtailed, or rather Karmen decides to rectify her previous actions by reconciling with Majiguene; her cooperative spirit also hinders the potential mislabeling of her character as a "man stealer" or "gold digger." Majiguene meets with Karmen to plead that she leave Lamine alone. Not only is their conversation amicable, Karmen gently instructs Majiguene that she cannot force Lamine to love her. When we next see Lamine and Karmen together, she terminates their relationship, in part out of respect for Majiguene. What's more, when Ramaka departs from Preminger's version by having Karmen free Lamine from jail (after she has gotten him into trouble) and then later splitting the proceeds from the smuggling ring with him, Ramaka demonstrates Karmen's selflessness.[61]

Throughout her travels, Carmen has vacillated between her imprisonment in a misogynistic myth in which her sexual agency is chastened and sympathetic renditions that position her as a woman who follows the mandates of her heart and libido despite repressive societal expectations, although she inevitably falls victim to these expectations. In relation to *Karmen Geï*, Amy Harlib argues that the film has an "insufficient development of the implications of what a truly free, independent woman would mean in the story's West African environs."[62] In many ways, then, Ramaka's model of sexual decolonization remains aspirational. Given the social stigma attached to the trope of the sexually liberated woman and the correlation made between Black women and the Jezebel stereotype, Djeïnaba Diop Gaï found it difficult to fully embrace the character. In one interview, she makes sure to distance herself from the role of Karmen, stating,

> I was a very good girl growing up. I loved my father, who was the ultimate authority in our home, and I obeyed him. I am certainly no *femme fatale*. I never even think about my appearance. Karmen is very sure of her sexual appeal. When she enters the circle to dance, she knows she's the best. Me? I never go into the circle. . . . At a nightclub, I just dance for myself, not to attract attention.[63]

Gaï clings to the patriarchal perceptions of what it means to be a "good girl": humility and obedience. Her words demonstrate her fear of being associated with negative interpretations of the role she plays.

It has proven difficult for Black actresses who play C/Karmen to fully embrace the consequences of Karmen's free love.[64] Black actresses must negotiate the impulse toward modeling healthy Black female sexuality with the real-life consequences they might face when they decide to take on such roles. For example, the stereotypes that dogged Gaï also plagued Dandridge. For Dandridge to secure the part of Carmen, not only did she have to train herself to speak in a forced "Black," "southern" "dialect," but she also had to play on Preminger's preconceived notions of what a "Black whore" looked like. Donald Bogle explains that Dandridge became imprisoned in this type of role for the rest of her career.[65] Therefore, despite Ramaka's intentions, Gaï's need to disassociate herself from the sexually liberated model that her character represents challenges the extent to which Black female sexual agency is possible outside of the filmic imagination.

RESEXUALIZING THE PROTAGONIST

The most significant way Ramaka challenges traditional portrayals of the femme fatale, however, is by making Karmen bisexual. Ramaka underscores the primacy of Karmen's desire and story by reformulating C/Karmen as queer, thereby challenging what Cheryl Clarke calls "compulsory heterosexuality."[66] Seduction is a salient feature of the Carmen myth, but *Karmen Geï* disrupts the usual heterosexual love triangle by making Karmen's preferred love interest a woman. In fact, in addition to Angélique, the film supplies three potential suitors vying for Karmen's affection: Lamine (the Don José figure), Massigi (a popular male musician played by El Hadg Ndiaye), and the elderly Samba. Ramaka toys with the assumption that Karmen's true love is a man, as in previous renditions. The tension of the movie revolves around Karmen's choice, as opposed to Lamine's desire. The audience becomes preoccupied with speculating on who it is that Karmen truly loves, so, in reality, Lamine is an incidental character.

Scholars like Prabhu and Alexie Tcheuyap dismiss Karmen's queerness as "directed to a specific diegetic end"—namely, facilitating her escape from prison.[67] And while their relationship began in an opportunistic manner, Ramaka makes it clear from Karmen's discussion with her mother that she has actually fallen in love with Angélique. Prabhu finds Karmen's queerness inconsequential, since it is "so fleeting and underdeveloped."[68] Yet Ramaka's decision to offer some sort of semblance to the Mérimée/Bizet plot results in minimal character development—all of Karmen's relationships are underdeveloped. I am more persuaded by arguments that interrogate why queering C/Karmen is important not just for the story's mythos but in terms of African cinema. For example, Powrie explains how the film destabilizes the heteronormativity of the Carmen mythos that reinforces Carmen as a dangerous femme fatale who usurps patriarchy and thereby also disrupts spectatorial expectations of a faithful rendition of Mérimée and Bizet's narrative.[69] Similarly, Stobie reads Karmen as bisexual in order to underscore "bisexuality as a complex, queer site that destabilizes stereotyped gender role, patriarchy, monosexuality [and] heteronormativity."[70]

Stobie's interpretation is brilliant and compelling, and even as I read Karmen as a queer bisexual, I highlight the ways Ramaka decenters heterosexuality and normalizes lesbian desire specifically, because it is particularly her desire for women that makes her the ultimate outlaw, given the prevalence of African countries that criminalize same-sex relationships. Just as Karmen is not shamed for sleeping with multiple partners, throughout the film, no one frames lesbianism as immoral. Rather than being castigated by her community, Karmen is celebrated and loved. Additionally, both Angélique and Karmen discuss their relationship with Karmen's mother, Ma Penda (Dieynaba Niang). Although Ma Penda warns Karmen that she is "too free," this warning is meant to ensure that Karmen protects her heart in all her romantic encounters rather than serve as a judgment on Karmen's sexuality. These discussions, and the fact that neither Samba nor Ma Penda shun Karmen, upsets the usual characterization of African elders as representations of traditional values that exclude homosexual desire.

CHALLENGING WESTERN BEAUTY STANDARDS

Ultimately, not only does Ramaka decenter the femme fatale, he challenges the Western beauty hierarchy that privileges lighter skin complexions as an affective nod toward a global Black female audience.[71] Prabhu argues that in *Karmen Geï*, "blackness is natural and universal"; she therefore disregards scholars who find the casting of the lighter-complexioned Canadian actress Stephanie Biddle as Angélique significant beyond an "extradiegetic level."[72] Instead, Prabhu reads her inclusion as further proof of Ramaka's "globalized context of filmmaking and . . . reception."[73] While I agree that Ramaka's intended audience is a global one, Angélique is the only woman in the entire film of a lighter complexion; the majority of the women, by comparison, are dark and remarkably fit. She is not lauded for her lighter complexion and instead is Karmen's pursuer. Ramaka is clearly inverting global beauty hierarchies. Rather than laud Angélique as the epitome of feminine beauty, Ramaka privileges darker-complexioned women, showcasing them throughout.

Tcheuyap equates class status with light-skin privilege and argues that lesbianism is employed as a theme representing the clash between traditional African values and that of the bourgeoisie. He states, "The lesbian who has sex with Karmen is mulatto and a senior prison warden, that is, a person of a visibly higher social class."[74] Powrie explains that the reversal of the beauty hierarchy is evident in the power dynamics existing between Karmen and Angélique:

> [Angélique] is played by a Canadian actress . . . who is lighter-skinned than Djeïnaba Diop Gaï. Her name, "the angelic" [is symbolic]; she [not Micaëla] is the "angel" to Karmen's "devil." But her lighter skin also underscores the film's postcolonial perspective: the whiter woman is also, as the name suggests, Christian rather than Muslim . . . and thereby associated with the ex-colonial power; as Warden she holds the power to imprison as well as free Karmen.[75]

Ultimately, it is Karmen who exudes erotic power over Angélique, rather than the reverse. Therefore, I would further argue that not only is the postcolonial perspective challenged, but the entire Western beauty hierarchy is called into question.

As a male director, Ramaka runs the risk of replicating what Laura Mulvey characterizes as voyeuristic tendencies implicit in the male gaze. In "Eroticism and Sub-Saharan African Films," Françoise Pfaff states:

> Since most sub-Saharan African directors are men, frequently the naked female body is the primary object of desire offered to viewers. . . . Naked

female bodies have also been used by these filmmakers in a static fashion, thus heightening their symbolic presence.... Since most West African filmmakers have lived and/or studied in Europe like their western counterparts, and in spite of cultural differences, African cinéastes are very aware of the fact that a prolonged shot of a naked body in motion has highly erotic connotations.[76]

Additionally, prior to filming, Ramaka announced, "I will show many bodies, naked bodies, dancing bodies, young bodies, old bodies, but the camera will seize in them the desire which they inspire rather than the libido they might unleash."[77] Ramaka, then, strategically employs scopophilia to challenge the traditional male gaze. According to Stobie, "Karmen is accorded with the power to destabilize masculine preeminence through her corporeal performativity," and, therefore, "the hegemonic heterosexual male gaze is rendered partial and unsatisfactory, as its instances of privilege are revealed, while modes of engagement offering imaginative entry into alterity from social norms are validated."[78]

Ramaka also makes strategic use of scopophilia to challenge prevailing global beauty hierarchies that privilege white and light skin. It is important, then, that Karmen is cast as a dark-complexioned woman. Since part of Ramaka's mission is to celebrate African beauty aesthetics and the Black female body—a body that has historically been vilified as the "ugly" antithesis to that of white women—the gaze of his camera *does*, in fact, linger over Karmen's body. For example, in the love scene between Karmen and Angélique, rather than make the lesbian sexual intercourse the spectacle, Ramaka's camera remains trained on the buttocks and back of Karmen for a time, thus emphasizing the beauty and darkness of her skin and full buttocks. Given the emphasis on the buttocks as a symbol of Black beauty and erotic pleasure in Black cultures throughout Africa and the Diaspora, this shot valorizes Afrocentric beauty aesthetics rather than Eurocentric ones.[79]

THE IMPLICATION OF KARMEN'S ENDING

McClary offers a challenge to those who would make future adaptations of *Carmen*. She argues that the endless retelling of Carmen's tragic end is pointless unless we "begin taking apart the very structures of identity and difference that permit such pieces to make sense to us as they drive toward their awful conclusions."[80] Arguably, Ramaka's adherence to the death impulse implicit in Carmen's mythology can be interpreted as the foreclosure of the possibility of sexual liberation for Black women as well as the continued hope for a decolonized future. For example, Saya Woolfalk expresses disappointment at the film's ending. She argues that *Karmen Geï* "ends with Karmen crippled and destroyed by the power that made her thrive. At the end of the story, all of the symbols of her sexual authority lose their potency."[81] Prabhu further contends:

> One is tempted to ask whether some of the risqué aspects of representing Karmen on the screen depend precisely on the safety net of her imminent and predetermined death—the lesbianism of Karmen in her relationship with Angélique, Karmen's illegal activities, or even her spiritual and sexual abandon before her lovers—is then reined back quite simply into the realm of plaisir (that which grants euphoria but is linked to a comfortable practice of reading) by the knowledge that these transgressions are expected to be cut short by her imminent death.[82]

Prabhu and Woolfalk make compelling points; if her punishment for defying patriarchy is the same as her predecessors, can C/Karmen ever be truly sexually liberated? To provide some semblance of an answer, I want to offer an alternative reading of the climactic scene.

In *Karmen Geï*, Lamine is depicted more accurately than any of his predecessors—he is coded as pathological because he cannot accept Karmen's right to her own body and stalks her to assuage his humiliation. Costumed in a fiery red evening gown, both a nod to Mérimée's original text and used to underscore her passion for life, Karmen runs from Lamine backstage during a concert featuring Yandé Codou Sène.[83] In a shot from behind what seem to be prison bars, the camera shows Karmen ducking from Lamine; thus, the movie ends as it begins, reminding the audience that Karmen's freedom is once again at stake. Done with running, Karmen confronts Lamine as he brandishes a knife. However, rather than being "crippled and destroyed," as Woolfalk describes, Karmen is defiant to the end. With her hands on her hips in exasperation, Karmen sings, "Love is a rebellious bird, and no one can tame it. If it doesn't feel right to him, it's really no use to call him. There's no use trying. You can't buy it. Love isn't a business deal. If you want to kill me, do it quickly and do it well. Tomorrow's another day." Although she cannot control whether she lives or dies, Karmen does have control over how she faces death. By proclaiming, "Tomorrow's another day," she prophesizes the continued defiance of patriarchal power by sexually liberated women like herself. As the granddaughter of Kumba Kastle, goddess of the sea, perhaps Karmen's spirit will avenge her death or perhaps it will live on in other women who dare to love freely and on their own terms. As Lamine stabs her in the stomach, she looks him straight in the eye. Karmen reserves her final gaze, however, for her audience. When she falls, Karmen is looking directly into the camera; her eyes appear to be fixed on the audience. Will we simply bear witness or rise to the challenge of her death stare? This, however, is not the last scene of the movie. The movie fades to Samba transporting her body to a Muslim burial site. While Prabhu bemoans the absence of Karmen's mother and the rest of the community as a final way to discredit Ramaka's feminist politics, I submit that in having Samba burying a queer woman in a Muslim cemetery, he is marking Karmen not only as a member of that sect but as someone beloved in the eyes of Allah—and therein lies the ultimate subversion.

Notes

1. Erich Leinsdorf, "Opera: What Constitutes Longevity?" *Daedalus* 115, no. 4 (Fall 1986): 95.

2. "Gypsy " is widely recognized as a racial slur against the Romani people. This chapter uses the term in the context of character descriptions within the source material.

3. Justin Hayford, "Giving Misogyny a Bad Name," *Chicago Reader*, January 23, 1997, https://chicagoreader.com/arts-culture/giving-misogyny-a-bad-name/.

4. José F. Colmeiro, "Exorcising Exoticism: Carmen and the Construction of Oriental Spain," *Comparative Literature* 54, no. 2 (2002): 140. Colmeiro argues that Carmen's initial story usurps the following categories: "Gender (she resists male domination); sexuality (her desires are free and uninhibited, and create fears of emasculation); race (as a Gypsy, she elicits fears of miscegenation); religion (she practices occult magic and is repeatedly seen as a devil and a threat to Christian faith); and politics (Carmen not only continually resists both civil and military authority; she also obliterates geo-political borders, defying territorial borders and mocking both Spanish and British law in the process as she takes advantage of the status of Gibraltar as a British colony on peninsular soil). Ultimately, Carmen's smuggling is also an economic threat that subverts governmental regulations and the monopoly of the oligarchy (a threat already suggested by the commotion she causes in the state-run cigarette factory)" (140).

5. Colmeiro, "Exorcising Exoticism," 128.

6. Written by Jerry Leiber and Phil Spector and produced by Jerry Leiber and Mike Stoller, Aretha Franklin released the most famous cover of the song in 1971. "Gypsy Woman" was written by Curtis Mayfield and released and recorded by his group, The Impressions, in 1961.

7. See Robert L. A. Clark, *Local Color: The Representation of Race in Carmen and Carmen Jones* (New York: Routledge, 2006); Susan McClary, "Structures of Identity and Difference in Bizet's *Carmen*," in *The Work of Opera: Genre, Nationhood, and Sexual Difference*, ed. Richard Dellamora and Daniel Fischlin (New York: Columbia University Press, 1997), 115–29; Phil Powrie, "Politics and Embodiment in *Karmen Geï*," *Quarterly Review of Film and Video* 21 (2004): 283–91; Powrie contends that the Carmen story has its roots in Africa; he bases his assertion on the fact that the word "gypsy" is a shortened form of "Egypt" and on a quotation in which Nietzsche concludes that Bizet's opera has an African sensibility; McClary also explains that Bizet's incorporation of an "African-Cuban popular song that became the 'Habañera' worked so well because it was an amalgamation of societal impressions of what an exotic Other 'should sound like,' hip" (120).

8. See Yvette Abrahams, "Images of Sara Bartman: Sexuality, Race, and Gender in Early-Nineteenth-Century Britain," in *Nation Empire, Colony: Historicising Gender and Race*, ed. Ruth R. Pierson and Nupur Chaudhuri (Bloomington: Indiana University Press, 1998); Sander Gilman, "The Hottentot and the Prostitute: Toward an Iconography of Female Sexuality," in *"Race," Writing*

and Difference, ed. Henry Louis Gates Jr. and Kwame Anthony Appiah (Chicago: University of Chicago Press, 1985); Christina Sharpe, *Monstrous Intimacies: Making Post Slavery Subjects* (Durham, NC: Duke University Press, 2010). Note that Abrahams uses one of several spellings for a Khoikhoi woman who was exhibited as a freak-show attraction and called Hottentot Venus.

9. Mari Maasilta, "African Carmen: Transnational Cinema as an Arena for Cultural Contradictions" (dissertation, University of Tampere, 2007), 156. Ramaka's documentary film, *So Be It* (*Ainsi soit-it*) was awarded the Lion d'Argent at the 54th Mostra Internationale d'Art, Cinematographic of Venice in 1997. *And What if Latif Was Right?* (*Et si Latif avait raison?*) was awarded Best Documentary Film at the Festival Vues D'Afriques in Montreal in 2006.

10. Anjali Prabhu, "The 'Monumental' Heroine: Female Agency in Joseph Gaï Ramaka's *Karmen Geï*," *Cinema Journal* 51, no. 4 (Summer, 2012): 84.

11. Prabhu, "'Monumental' Heroine," 82, 84.

12. Prabhu, "'Monumental' Heroine," 84.

13. Prabhu, "'Monumental' Heroine," 84.

14. "About the Film: *Karmen Geï*," *California Newsreel* (no date), https://newsreel.org/video/KARMEN-GEI.

15. Pauline Malefane, "U-Carmen e-Khayelitsha: Mark Dornford-May & Pauline Malefane Q and A," Cinema.com (no date), https://www.cinema.com/articles/4018/u-carmen-e-khayelitsha-mark-dornford-may--pauline-malefane-q-and.phtml.

16. Paul White, "Geography, Literature, and Migration," in *Writing across Worlds: Literature and Migration*, ed. John Connell, Russell King, and Paul White (New York: Routledge, 1995), 1.

17. Carole Boyce Davies, *Black Women, Writing and Identity: Migrations of the Subject* (New York: Routledge, 1994).

18. Michael Awkward, "A Black Man's Place(s) in Black Feminist Criticism," in *Representing Black Men*, ed. Marcellus Blount and George P. Cunningham (New York: Routledge, 1996), 21.

19. McClary reminds her readers that Mérimée ends his text with a "pseudoscientific ethnography" on Gypsies, which is an attempt by the French narrator to culturally distance himself from Carmen and the tragic plot that eventually leads to her murder by Don José.

20. McClary, "Structures of Identity and Difference," 116.

21. McClary, "Structures of Identity and Difference," 118.

22. An example of such a technique is the creation of the character of Micaëla to act as a good girl foil to Carmen's bad girl persona, which I explore in greater detail later. Additionally, nineteenth-century audiences would have castigated Carmen as a whore anyway for her willingness to engage in sexual intercourse outside the confines of matrimony, thereby weakening the potential for any discussion of female sexual agency.

23. Ayo A. Coly, *Postcolonial Hauntologies: African Women's Discourses of the Female Body* (Lincoln: University of Nebraska Press, 2019), 71.

24. Coly, *Postcolonial Hauntologies*, 71.

25. I use "Black nationalist feminism" as an umbrella term, in this instance, which encapsulates Black women-centered ideologies from the United States—such as womanism (Walker) and Africana womanism (Hudson-Weems), as well as Ogunyemi's coinage of "African womanism"—that are committed to separatism. These ideologies also include space for uplifting Black men by offering analytics that explore how both Black women and Black men face oppression under white patriarchal power.

26. John Rieder, *Colonialism and the Emergence of Science Fiction* (Middletown, CT: Wesleyan University Press, 2008), 7.

27. Catherine Clément, *Opera, or the Undoing of Women*, trans. Betsy Wing (Minneapolis: University of Minnesota Press, 1988), 11.

28. Jeff Smith, "Black Faces, White Voices: The Politics of Dubbing in Carmen Jones," *Velvet Light Trap* 51 (Spring 2003): 31.

29. Here it is worth noting that *UCarmen eKhayelitsha* is an opera. The film is spoken and sung in Xhosa. Additionally, many of the film's lead characters are members of Dimpho Di Kopane (formally, the South African Academy of Performing Arts) and thus operatically trained. In some respects, then, Dornford-May corrects the presumptive mistake of Preminger's use of dubbing in *Carmen Jones*.

30. Saya Woolfalk, "*Karmen Geï*: Political Sex Icon," *African Film Festival, New York*, September 25, 2001, https://africanfilmny.org/articles/karmen-gei-political-sex-icon-2/.

31. Prabhu, "'Monumental' Heroine," 67.

32. Prabhu, "'Monumental' Heroine," 67.

33. Prabhu, "'Monumental' Heroine," 74.

34. Prabhu, "'Monumental' Heroine," 74.

35. Prabhu, "'Monumental' Heroine," 82.

36. Susan Arndt, "African Gender Trouble and African Womanism: An Interview with Chikwenye Ogunyemi and Wanjira Muthoni," *Signs* 25, no. 3 (Spring 2000): 710–11. Ogunyemi indicates that some of the points of demarcation between US Black feminisms and African womanism include this attention to religious fundamentalism, dictatorships, and corruption.

37. Chikwenye Okonjo Ogunyemi, "Womanism: The Dynamics of the Contemporary Black Female Novel in English," *Signs* 11, no. 1 (Autumn 1985): 71.

38. Ogunyemi, "Womanism," 71.

39. Coly, *Postcolonial Hauntologies*, 63.

40. Coly, *Postcolonial Hauntologies*, 63.

41. Prabhu, "'Monumental' Heroine," 83, 84.

42. Prabhu, "'Monumental' Heroine," 83.

43. Cheryl Stobie, "'She Who Creates Havoc Is Here': A Queer Bisexual Reading of Sexuality, Dance, and Social Critique in *Karmen Geï*," *Research in African literatures* 47, no. 2 (2016): 95.

44. Tuzyline Jita Allan, *Womanist and Feminist Aesthetic: A Comparative Review* (Athens: Ohio University Press, 1995), 6.

45. I call these instances "gestures" because rather than portray instances of feminist activism or organizing, Ramaka is more subtle; feminist elements are more prevalent in mise-en-scène.

46. Preminger's adaptation underscores the theme of unrequited love and the violent and possibly vulgar romanticism that he would have associated with both the Blues tradition and the Black working class of the 1950s. For responses to Preminger's film, see Smith, "Black Faces, White Voices," 89; Smith notes that after the opera's debut, James Baldwin argued that Preminger romanticized poverty rather than deal with the real violence of the "Negro ghetto." Other critics have argued that Preminger's choice to use an all-Black cast in *Carmen Jones* diffused the ways in which racist oppression hinders Black economic advancement. It is quite possible that, subconsciously, Preminger wanted his white audience to vicariously experience the pleasures of blackness (i.e., wanton sexual abandon) without having to deal with the inequality that Blacks experience regarding economic disparities and racial oppression.

47. Prabhu, "'Monumental' Heroine," 72.

48. Stobie, "She Who Creates Havoc Is Here," 93.

49. Stobie, "She Who Creates Havoc Is Here," 92.

50. Coly, *Postcolonial Hauntologies*, 67.

51. Coly, *Postcolonial Hauntologies*, 67.

52. Perhaps out of a combination of heartbreak and humiliation, Angélique dies by suicide by walking into the sea.

53. See Patricia Hill Collins, "The Social Construction of Black Feminist Thought," *Signs* 14, no. 4 (Summer 1989): 745–73.

54. Slavoj Žižek, *Looking Awry: An Introduction to Jacques Lacan through Popular Culture* (Cambridge, MA: MIT Press, 1992), 66.

55. Julie Grossman, *Rethinking the Femme Fatale in Film Noir: Ready for Her Close-Up* (New York: Palgrave Macmillan, 2009), 3.

56. Woolfalk, "*Karmen Geï*: Political Sex Icon."

57. Audre Lorde, *Uses of the Erotic: The Erotic as Power* (Brooklyn, NY: Out & Out Books, 1978).

58. Tahar Chériaa, "African Cinema and the Headshrinkers: Looking Back at a Strategy for Liberation," in *African Experiences of Cinema*, ed. Ishaq Imruh Bakari and Mbye Cham (London: British Film Institute, 1996), 43.

59. Chériaa, "African Cinema and the Headshrinkers," 43.

60. Coly, *Postcolonial Hauntologies*, 74.

61. Even in Robert Townsend's *Carmen: A Hip Hopera*, Carmen is no longer portrayed as a gold digger or a whore; in fact, she is depicted as an average girl, with above-average looks, who is merely seeking to better herself—as the bookcases cluttered with self-help books in her apartment emphasize. Given that Carmen in this instance is played by Beyoncé Knowles, MTV's fan base would recognize the verisimilitude and interpret the repositioning of Carmen's motives as the desire to be self-actualized because of Knowles's discography, which includes the "Survivor" anthem and "Independent Woman" from the *Charlie's Angels* soundtrack.

62. Amy Harlib, "The Free-Spirited *Karmen Geï*," *Inception Magazine*, http://www.inception -magazine.com/fall06/review_karmen_gei.htm (note: the *Inception Magazine* website is no longer active). Here Harlib might be referring to nearly everyone's easy acceptance of Karmen's bisexuality, particularly in light of the fact that homosexuality is illegal in several African countries—most notably, Botswana, Ghana, Senegal, Uganda, South Africa, and Zimbabwe.

63. Adrienne E. Gusoff, "*Karmen Geï*," *Global Rhythm* (no date), http://www.globalrhythm .net/FILM/KarmenGei.cfm (note: *Global Rhythm* was active 1992–2008; the website is no longer available).

64. See Douglas Century, "NOTICED; Seen the Opera? Experience the Hip-Hop," *New York Times*, May 6, 2001, https://www.nytimes.com/2001/05/06/style/noticed-seen-the-opera -experience-the-hip-hop.html. Beyoncé Knowles also sought to distance herself somewhat from Carmen's rampant sexuality. While she has since gone on to costume herself in much more alluring and scanty attire, at the release of *Carmen: A Hip Hopera*, she explained, "Carmen is not so different from Beyoncé in Destiny's Child as far as her image, but I wouldn't have worn a dress so low or a slit so high."

65. See Donald Bogle, *Toms, Coons, Mulattoes, Mammies, and Bucks: An Interpretive History of Blacks in American Films* (New York: Viking Press, 1973), 168–69. Bogle explains, "Initially, Preminger had thought [Dandridge] too sleek and sophisticated for the role of a whore. But he underestimated the talent and determination of the actress. When it appeared as if she had lost the role altogether, Dorothy Dandridge completely redid her appearance and style. . . . She mastered wildly uninhibited body movements. . . . With her new image perfected, she tossed her hair about her head, made up her eyes darkly, dressed herself in a sheer low-cut blouse and

a long, tight skirt, and then audaciously strutted into Preminger's office. Vivacious, sportive, alluring yet somehow haunted and vulnerable, Dorothy Dandridge was the living embodiment of the director's Carmen."

66. See Cheryl Clarke, "Lesbianism: An Act of Resistance," in *This Bridge Called My Back: Writings by Radical Women of Color*, ed. Cherríe Moraga and Gloria Anzaldúa (Watertown, MA: Persephone Press, 1983), 128–37.

67. Prabhu, "'Monumental' Heroine," 82.

68. Prabhu, "'Monumental' Heroine," 82.

69. Powrie, "Politics and Embodiment in *Karmen Geï*," 287.

70. Stobie, "She Who Creates Havoc Is Here," 86.

71. The other adaptations that feature a Black Carmen, *Carmen Jones* (1954) and *Carmen: A Hip Hopera* (2001), capitulate to beauty standards, which stipulate that lighter skin and thin physiques are preferred by casting actresses Dorothy Dandridge and Beyoncé Knowles, respectively, in the lead roles. For a view on the casting in *Carmen Jones*, see James Baldwin, "*Carmen Jones*: The Dark Is Light Enough," in *Black Films and Film-Makers: A Comprehensive Anthology from Stereotype to Superhero*, ed. Lindsay Patterson (New York: Dodd, Mead, 1975), 88–94; Baldwin was less impressed than general reviewers were with Dandridge's performance of what he saw as "manufactured sexiness." He argued that the casting of Dandridge and Belafonte, two light-complexioned actors, as romantic leads in *Carmen Jones*, and the framing of darker characters like Frankie (Pearl Bailey) and the sergeant (Brock Peters) as comic relief and evil villain, respectively, reinforced a beauty hierarchy that positioned "white" as "desirable" and "good," while "black" was read as "ugly" and "bad."

72. Prabhu, "'Monumental' Heroine," 82.

73. Prabhu, "'Monumental' Heroine," 82.

74. Alexie Tcheuyap, "African Cinema and Representations of (Homo)Sexuality," *Matatu* 29–30 (2005): 152.

75. Powrie, "Politics and Embodiment in *Karmen Geï*," 287.

76. Françoise Pfaff, "Eroticism and Sub-Saharan African films," *Zeitschrift für Afrikastudien* 9–10 (1991): 6.

77. Quoted in Powrie, "Politics and Embodiment in *Karmen Geï*," 285.

78. Stobie, "She Who Creates Havoc Is Here," 94.

79. It is important to note that while Ramaka defies beauty standards in relation to colorism, he still upholds beauty standards in relation to weight. In contrast, *UCarmen eKhayelitsha* is the only adaptation that thwarts Western beauty standards by casting a full-figured actress (Pauline Malefane) as the *femme fatale*.

80. McClary, "Structures of Identity," 128.

81. Woolfalk, "*Karmen Geï*: Political Sex Icon."

82. Prabhu, "'Monumental' Heroine," 82.

83. Yandé Codou Sène (1932–2010) was a Serer griot. She was "the most famous practitioner" who sang in the Serer tradition, and she made an enormous impact on Senegambian music. See Sean Connolly, *Senegal: The Bradt Travel Guide*, 2nd ed. (Guilford, CT: Globe Pequot Press, 2019), 28; Connolly explains that Sène was "once the official state griotte [*sic*] to president Léopold Sédar Senghor and went on to record with Youssou N'Dour in the mid 1990s."

Part III

Hollywood's Problematic Reconstructions

Chapter 5

IMAGINING THE HAITIAN REVOLUTION IN *LYDIA BAILEY*

Kenneth Roberts's 1947 Novel and Darryl F. Zanuck's 1952 Film

JUDITH E. SMITH

In the United States, Haiti's successful revolution (1791–1804) has largely been consigned to historical silence, even as abundant popular literary and filmic representations of Haiti have circulated demeaning, exoticized, and sexualized versions of the Black Republic. The Haitian battle for freedom was central to Kenneth Roberts's best-selling 1947 novel *Lydia Bailey* and provided the setting for director Jean Negulesco's 1952 film adaptation; both novel and film reproduce *and* depart from conventional depictions. This chapter argues that the film adaptation, the first and only twentieth-century Hollywood attempt to represent Haiti's revolutionary period, warrants further examination.[1] In the immediate aftermath of World War II, the period in which the novel was released and its film adaptation proceeded, fierce political debates about democracy, decolonization, segregation, and racial equality were part of public discourse. Archival evidence from the process of adapting, scripting, and filming *Lydia Bailey* documents the ways in which contested political positions on these issues of the director, producers, and screenwriters shaped the resulting contradictory film. Studio publicists also influenced the circulation and reception of the film, promoting it via conventional racist tropes associated with blackness and Haiti, thus overshadowing the film's depiction of Black liberation.

KENNETH ROBERTS AND THE NOVEL *LYDIA BAILEY*

Roberts, a white journalist, turned from magazine writing to historical fiction in the late 1920s. Between 1929 and 1940, he produced six New England historical novels, populated with many characters based on his Maine ancestors and often sympathetic to the British in early US history. His fifth novel, *Northwest Passage*, first serialized in the *Saturday Evening Post*, became the second-highest-selling novel in 1937 and was adapted to the screen in 1940 as an MGM Technicolor film. Widely celebrated for his historical research, Roberts appeared on the November 25, 1940, cover of *Time* magazine.[2] Even before *Lydia Bailey*'s 1947 publication, its selection for a popular subscription book club guaranteed its commercial success. In September 1946, Hollywood studio Twentieth Century-Fox acquired the film rights. Always on the lookout for "presold properties" that would draw moviegoers into theaters, studio personnel saw Roberts's novel as a sure bet, especially since six of Fox's top ten moneymaking films in 1946 were based on popular novels.[3]

As an advocate of white (what he would have called "Nordic") supremacy whose popular writing helped influence the passage of the racialized and exclusionary 1924 Immigration Act, Roberts was an unlikely chronicler of Black struggle.[4] For the novel *Lydia Bailey*, Roberts wanted to follow the historical path of US military and political decisions unfolding in Haiti during the island's victorious revolution for self-rule. Haiti's historical setting required him to describe former slaves successfully resisting Napoleon's attempt to retake the crown jewel of the French colonial empire.

Roberts's Haiti chapters, detailing the adventures of the dashing New England–born hero Albion Hamlin and the title character, a beautiful white expatriate woman Hamlin seeks and courts, reproduce many of the previously established white literary representations of Haiti. These had pictured the world's first independent Black republic variously "as a slave rebellion, an anticolonial war, and an atrocity."[5] Narratives about Haiti "held up the country as the highest model of heroism and race pride or used it as the lowest model of debased primitive beliefs, crushing poverty, and political instability," with many white writers attempting to "prove" that Black self-rule was a failure.[6] During the US military occupation of Haiti (1915–1934), military memoirs, sensational and sexualized travel narratives, and theatrical renderings, which were both supportive and critical of the occupation, popularized Haiti as "exotic." In the 1930s, left-wing African American writers and artists such as Langston Hughes, Arna Bontemps, Jacob Lawrence, and Katherine Dunham challenged the prevailing popular imagery. Their alternative accounts represented Haitians as Black citizens of the world and the Haitian Revolution as part of a Black radical tradition.[7]

Roberts's historical research drew on conflicting accounts. He read and underlined passages in two demeaning nineteenth-century interpretations of Haiti's history. The 1853 British abolitionist John Relly Beard's account of (François-Dominique) Toussaint Louverture depicted Louverture as an exceptional savior of an inferior people. The 1889 memoir of Sir Spencer St. John, *Hayti; or the Black Republic*, was an infamously white supremacist screed making the case for Haiti's history as proof of Black inferiority and barbarity.[8] However, Roberts also read and annotated newer revisionist studies. He consulted anthropologist Melville J. Herskovits's nonexoticized *Life in a Haitian Valley* (1937), which emphasized African and European influences in Haitian culture and offered a nonsensationalist account of Haitian vodou religious practices. In addition, Roberts read and marked passages in Trinidadian historian C. L. R. James's *The Black Jacobins* (1938), which highlighted the developing consciousness of political universalism and anticolonialism, focusing on Black agency in the revolutionary period.[9] Roberts's handwritten comment inside the front cover of *The Black Jacobins*, which refers to James as a "Negro and Marxist," reveals his skepticism about James's personal and political authority.[10]

Lydia Bailey's Haitian chapters borrowed promiscuously from these conflicting sources. The novel provides sensationalized accounts of Blacks engaged in looting, killing white French male colonists, and raping white French female colonists. It also includes descriptions of admirably planned and executed Black military strategies that triumph over contemptuous white French landowners and outmaneuver the overconfident French military forces attempting to retake the island. White newspaper reviewers were particularly impressed with Roberts's vivid descriptions of the chaos exemplified in the "huge and violent scenes crowded with the ferocity and cruelty of a numerous community caught in . . . desperation."[11] Some critics mentioned that the novel had cinematic potential.[12]

The distance between Roberts's fiction and Black accounts that highlight revolutionary Haiti's significance in Black radical traditions is exemplified in the novel's characterization of King Dick, an intriguing and charismatic Black character whose name invokes white mythology about Black men. This character has a central role in the story because he is critical to the successful quest of white adventurer Albion Hamlin. An earlier King Dick character loosely based on a free Black man, Richard Cephas, played a role in Roberts's 1931 historical fiction *Lively Lady*. This character spoke in minstrel dialect and appeared at key moments to enable the New England hero's daring escape from Britain's infamous Dartmoor prison. In *Lydia Baily*, King Dick again assumes the faithful native guide-servant helpmate who assists a wandering white traveler. Following folktale and literary conventions, he appears "as suddenly and as magically as though he'd popped from the ground like the Slave of the Lamp."[13] Recreating this character for *Lydia Bailey*, Roberts felt it necessary to revise "King Dick's manner of speech, which is too n----rish."[14] Reimagined now as a Sudanese king's son, *Lydia Bailey*'s King Dick had traveled to Spain, Surinam, and New Orleans before jumping ship in Cap-Français (later Cap-Haïtien in

Haiti) and becoming a trusted general in Louverture's army. However, Roberts's "Nordic supremacist" views shaped his racialized delineation of King Dick as someone who "preferred white Englishmen and white Americans to people of his own color."[15] Several white press reviewers found the literate, courageous King Dick to be the novel's most compelling character and were startled to find passages advocating racial equality, unexpected in a Roberts novel.[16] In contrast, Black press reviewers used Roberts's novel as an opportunity to emphasize the historical significance of Louverture and the Haitian Revolution.[17]

LYDIA BAILEY AT TWENTIETH CENTURY-FOX

Producer Darryl F. Zanuck, the powerful, hands-on Fox production chief, involved himself directly in the making of the film *Lydia Bailey*. Zanuck was known for commercially successful entertainment: musicals, star vehicles, gangster films, and stories "ripped from the headlines." Prior to the production of *Lydia Bailey*, he made popular adaptations of best-selling social problem novels, including the stories of migrant laborers in *The Grapes of Wrath* (John Ford, 1940) and Welsh coal miners in *How Green Was My Valley* (John Ford, 1941). The rise of fascism in Europe and Zanuck's close friendship with Wendell Willkie, the dark-horse Republican presidential candidate who Democrat Franklin Roosevelt defeated in 1940, influenced his thinking about politics and the films he produced. Zanuck actively supported and greatly admired Willkie, an outspoken internationalist who challenged the fascist aggression that pervaded Europe and who vigorously criticized the racist Jim Crow practices instituted in the United States. After the Japanese attack on Pearl Harbor in 1941 and the US official entry into World War II (1941–1945), Zanuck fast-tracked production of films supporting the Allies. Similarly, Willkie used his new influence in Hollywood to arrange meetings between Zanuck and his personal friend Walter White, chief executive of the NAACP, to lobby for improved African American filmic representations as "part of taking the offensive against the Axis."[18] Pushed by the pressure civil rights organizations applied, wartime discussions of antifascism began to challenge accepted norms of white supremacy, and some Zanuck films began to screen new imagery.[19]

Zanuck returned from his wartime military filmmaking stint committed to making more progressive films, which he envisioned as "vital, thinking men's blockbusters. Big theme films."[20] Addressing the 1943 Writers' Congress, cosponsored by UCLA and the left-wing Hollywood Writers Mobilization (established following the attack on Pearl Harbor in 1941), Zanuck encouraged writers to be part of solving the world's problems. Zanuck was confident that he knew how to use "showmanship" and "entertainment" to make "serious worthwhile pictures palatable to mass movie audiences."[21] He relished the strategic maneuvering required to get controversial material past the censors and adroitly maintained control over storytelling through hands-on involvement with producers, writers, and editors throughout the filmmaking process. His personal productions addressed the social challenges of the postwar world, focusing on the costs of isolationism in *Wilson* (Henry King, 1944), "polite" anti-Semitism in *Gentleman's Agreement* (Elia Kazan, 1947), and racial discrimination in *Pinky* (Elia Kazan, 1949).[22] Zanuck's considerable involvement in *Lydia Bailey* grew out of these experiences.

SCRIPTING *LYDIA BAILEY*, 1947–1952

Immediately, tensions erupted in the adaptation process about how to handle conflicting narrative directions—dramatizing the white adventure/romance, exploiting a crowd-pleasing Caribbean setting, representing the cause of the Black Haitian Revolution, and constructing a plausible anticolonialist stance for the American hero. White screenwriter Milton Krims's initial treatment and script imagined Haiti as a "simmering volcano" and the revolution as a race war.[23] Fox producer Sol Siegel identified "the all important problem"—how to create "a story in which the white people were the principal characters" without sacrificing "the color and history of Haiti."[24]

Filming "blood, thunder, and revolution" with the "Technicolor of dashing action" celebrated by book reviewers promised to be prohibitively expensive at a time when the Hollywood trade papers warned of box-office declines and downtown theater closings. Fox had already set tough budget ceilings on high-end features and encouraged location shooting to limit union labor costs.[25] In addition, a filmic retelling of Haiti's revolutionary history might attract unwanted political attention. Preproduction for *Lydia Bailey* was unfolding just as the House Committee on Un-American Activities (HUAC) began to investigate the film industry, interviewing cooperative Hollywood figures in Los Angeles in May 1947 and holding well-publicized formal hearings to "clean house" and expose "Communist Infiltration" in Washington, DC, in October 1947.[26] After ten "unfriendly" screenwriters and directors challenged HUAC's authority to question their political affiliations, Congress voted to hold the ten screenwriters and directors in contempt. In November 1947, the Motion Picture Association of America (MPAA) issued an official statement declaring that the studios would not employ known communists. At this point, anticommunism became a standard part of film industry policy; those identified as suspected communists or communist sympathizers were targeted as threats to Hollywood and were "blacklisted."[27]

In 1947 and 1948, economic rather than political pressures stalled production of *Lydia Bailey*.[28] In the late 1940s and early 1950s, Zanuck was a reluctant enforcer of the Hollywood blacklist, acting to protect some Fox employees.[29] When the adaptation finally moved forward in the spring of 1948, contentious issues surrounding racial representation continued to dominate planning. Left-leaning screenwriter Philip Dunne, a Screen Writers Guild activist and cofounder of the Committee for the First Amendment, now worked on the screenplay.[30] Dunne, like Zanuck, was interested in producing films that might deepen postwar democracy, dramatizing interracial interactions as a means of promoting supposedly color-blind universality while also attracting Black as well as white ticket buyers across the country.[31]

The multiple drafts of Dunne's *Lydia Bailey* scripts proposed this kind of 1940s race liberalism as an alternative to Krims's depiction of the Haitian Revolution as a "race war." Dunne contrasted what he saw as Haitian leader Louverture's universalism with the racialist views of his successor, the military leader Jean-Jacques Dessaline. In Dunne's first script, Dessaline "hates all whites," while in a later revision, it is Mirabeau, a fictional maroon marauder, who is marked by "race prejudice"; Dunne notes, "If there's anything Mirabeau hates more than a white man, it is a black man who deals tolerantly with whites."[32] Dunne's scripts described Louverture's trusted generals as an interracial group, including Blacks, whites, and mulattoes, as well as a white French general who said that for Louverture, "race melts under his hands."[33]

Dunne's scripts decisively took the side of the Haitian revolutionaries, characterizing the French colonials as driven by racial contempt. The central French plantation owner, D'Autremont, refers to the Haitian military forces in a derogatory manner as "monkeys in uniform" and denigrates them by suggesting they could be bribed "with money, titles, flattery, [and] hatred" to fight on the French side. D'Autremont voices racist platitudes: "There is no logic in blacks. They reason like animals. And need to be treated the same way."[34] Dunne researched Haitian sources to write a detailed vodou ceremony to function as a backdrop for D'Autremont's elderly mother's sympathetic memory of an earlier victorious slave rebellion.[35]

Zanuck continued to monitor the representation of the Black Republic in *Lydia Bailey*, which was referred to as his "personal production."[36] In conferences, Zanuck warned against replicating Hollywood stereotypes. He explained, "We should not show Negro soldiers wearing elaborate uniforms. If we do, they are liable to look like a musical comedy army. . . . The cutting of the bridge [for an escape from the French forces] may become too Tarzan-like."[37] At the same time, Zanuck carefully emphasized Haitian "exoticism" to create distance between Haiti's revolutionary politics and current Jim Crow racial policies in the United States. He proposed, "If we stick to the voodoo thing and show other Haitian customs, our [Haitian] Negroes will look more like natives, and less like Pullman-porters on parade."[38]

At the same time, perhaps influenced by Willkie's American-centered internationalism, Zanuck pushed for the film to fall firmly on the side of Haitian independence over French imperial claims. Zanuck argued, "We should feel that it is a pretty solid government or we won't pull for them when the French try to take them over. We want to believe that they are substantial people who will govern well if left alone." Zanuck criticized scenes that showed "Negro traitors . . . working with Napoleon's people" and asked for cuts related to "talk about Negroes double crossing their own people." He wanted the film to persuade audiences to "believe that the Haitian government is a good government. . . . It is young, and it is growing."[39]

SCRIPT REVISIONS WITH A NEW PRODUCER, SCREENWRITER, AND DIRECTOR

In December 1948, *Lydia Bailey* was on the studio's list of "blockbusters," signaling a high-cost production with commercial potential; the announced budget was $3 million, but preproduction again stalled.[40] When active script work on *Lydia Bailey* resumed in 1950–1951, arguments intensified over how to balance the white adventure/romance story with the Haitian Revolution. A new producer, Jules Schermer; left-wing screenwriter Michael Blankfort; and director Jean Negulesco (Zanuck's personal friend) now worked on the script. Blankfort had come to Fox in the summer of 1949 as the screenwriter of record for the pro-Indian Western *Broken Arrow* (Delmer Daves, 1950), which won the Screen Writers Guild Award for Best Written American Western and was nominated for a Best Writing Academy Award.[41]

Director Negulesco immediately challenged Blankfort's focus on Haiti in a memo to producer Jules Schermer. He asked, "About whom are we telling this story? The Negroes or [the characters] Albion Hamlin-Lydia Bailey and D'Autremont? All of a sudden the background and local atmosphere are predominating. . . . We want to get into Albion's story . . . not making King Dick and his confederates the central story point. . . . I am more interested in an adventure love story told against this Haitian background. . . . I understand why you [Schermer] and Blankfort have done what you have done. You want to show the Negro situation—the Negro attitude."[42]

Screenwriter Blankfort *was* committed to conveying "the Negro situation—the Negro attitude" differently than prior representations on Hollywood screens. Coming of age in the 1930s, Blankfort had immersed himself in the literary and theatrical left. A cofounder of the Theatre Union, he directed the company's electrifying 1934 *Stevedore*, a groundbreaking play about Black and white New Orleans dockworkers, described as showing, "It is *possible* for black and white workers to stand together."[43] Promoting the production in the *Daily Worker*, Blankfort contrasted *Stevedore*'s powerful Black leading roles with the antiquated Black characters on Broadway, which in his estimation included "stock Mammies or night club jazz babies or comic butlers, or any other of the false characters which colored actors or actresses are called on to play in the bourgeois theater."[44] Blankfort had participated in the American Writers Congress (AWC) in 1935, identified as the setting for the first serious Black literary critique within Communist Party circles, and he was a member of the left-wing League of American Writers.[45] After Blankfort moved to Los Angeles in 1937 to work in Hollywood, he continued to associate himself with left-wing organizations that opposed Jim Crow policies, supported labor organizing, and, after 1945, questioned the emerging Cold War. The screenwriter's associations were public knowledge when Blankfort worked at Fox on *Lydia Bailey*.[46]

Negulesco and Blankfort continued to spar over the screenplay's race-conscious characterizations. Negulesco pushed for deepening the white characters Albion Hamlin, Lydia Bailey, and French planter/fiancé D'Autremont. He argued, "Our basic story, if we are going to seek the most box office appeal here, is <u>love</u> and <u>adventure</u>."[47] His goal was to "tell a [silent screen star] Douglas Fairbanks story of adventure and excitement" against what he termed a "bizarre" background.[48] Negulesco preferred a King Dick character who displays "easy going genial charm" to a more powerful and self-determined character.[49] He wanted the white character Hamlin to upstage the Black characters Louverture and King Dick to emphasize the New Englander's courage "as an active participant in the [Haitian] conflict."[50]

In detailed comments on Blankfort's scripts sent to Blankfort and producer Schermer, Negulesco was on guard for anything that seemed "too pointed in political view" or that directly challenged conventions of white supremacy, what he labeled "sudden preaching and in terms of a Negro."[51] He believed that he recognized language that "would offend every Negro in the country"; for the scene after Hamlin has traveled through rough countryside stained with black dye, Negulesco proposed cutting Lydia's command to Hamlin that he go wash because he "smells terrible."[52] But Negulesco's own comments about the characters reveal him to be oblivious to his own segregationist assumptions and racial paternalism. He praises Lydia's concern for her maid as "showing her inner sentiment, how she really cares for the blacks."[53] But he argued that when Lydia finds herself amid refugees fleeing the fighting, "instead of blaming the French for the hatred she sees around her, her first and most natural inclination would be to blame the blacks . . . responsible for the terror and disorder on the island." He insisted that it would take time before Lydia could "bring herself to [view] a black as a human being capable of feelings and the rights which she enjoys." At another point, he argued, "This is asking a lot of her, fraternizing with blacks."[54]

Blankfort forcefully resisted Negulesco's suggestions. His scripts used plot points and dialogue Dunne provided, and he further sharpened the characterizations of King Dick and Louverture. Lydia's sympathy for the refugees remained in the script, alongside Hamlin's newfound identification with Haitians and the Haitian cause: "If I were a native today whose liberty was threatened by Napoleon's cut-throats, I'd kill any white man I could lay hands on."[55] In a memo to Schermer, Zanuck wrote that he was pleased with Blankfort's final script, despite its tendency to emphasize "the political significance of freedom, revolt, liberty, etc." Zanuck urged Blankfort to make Hamlin less "self-righteous," asking "why is he always shouting against slavery: we had slavery in the United States at the same time." Still, these notes signaled hopefulness about the film's potential appeal as

> something more than box office. It is an interesting story and way off the beaten track, and it will have a certain real significance if we do not constantly pound in the significance. After all, this is a romantic adventure story told in terms of excitement and a certain amount of sex.... If we handle them effectively this will be a picture we can all be proud of.[56]

Zanuck and his trusted colleagues continued to revise the final script, explicitly framing the goals of the Haitian Revolution in an American idiom, with Louverture equated with the first American president: "the George Washington of Haiti."[57]

FILMING *LYDIA BAILEY*

Lydia Bailey's sensationalist sequences featured daring escapes through forbidding jungles and across roaring rivers to evade snarling dogs, renegade maroons, and Napoleon's French allies. References to the racial/sexual spoils of empire and the presumed dangers for white people, especially women, on a majority-Black island became explicit. Dialogue emphasized the salacious application of black dye "all over" the white bodies of Hamlin (Fox contract player Dale Robertson) and Lydia (Fox contract player Anne Francis) to enable their travel through the countryside. In the film, transgressing sexualized racial boundaries became possible because of this improbable "blackface" artifice. Camera angles repeatedly spotlighted sexual display in the scenes when King Dick (African American actor-singer William Marshall) introduces his eight

Recognizing the heroism of the Black Haitian revolutionaries, Zanuck sought to depict the stature and agency of fictional character King Dick (William Marshall) in *Lydia Bailey*.

wives, when Lydia appears in costumes designed to feature her breasts and legs, and in the lavish decadence of royal French festivities. The mysterious "voodoo" ceremony popularly associated with Haiti is a spectacular modernist musical dance sequence. Its passions license Hamlin and Lydia's attraction to each other while also enabling revolutionary communication; the vodou priest signals to King Dick when to kill a collaborationist Black general who had been paid off by French colonialist D'Autremont to betray Louverture. Scenes of marauding maroon outlaws torching D'Autremont's plantation are "answered" with the burning of the capital ordered by Louverture, marking the collapse of colonial authority.

After postproduction screenings, Zanuck demanded additional filming. These costly reshoots required the presence of principals and extras and delayed the film's release. Despite Zanuck's supposed prioritization of "the intimate personal story," most of the new scenes for the film's opening and closing showcased Haitian resistance.[58] A new opening introduced powerful close-ups of three different Black drummers, listening for and then passing along information indecipherable by white colonials. Scenes with Louverture and his trusted generals were reshot to "film him interestingly" as he and his comrades, including Hamlin, seriously debate military-political strategy. These scenes feature an explanation of Louverture's military strategy to defeat the French and destroy colonial wealth by burning down the island's French-dominated towns. Hamlin proclaims his support for the Haitian cause: "I know what it is you are fighting for, no different than what men in my country fought for." In the end, Louverture responds to French treachery with the order to burn the capital. The film's reshot finale features the towering figure of a defiant King Dick in front of the city in flames. The script reads, "Camera holds on King Dick, who raises his club and brandishes it. On his heroic figure we fade out."[59] These new scenes shift dramatic momentum toward Black agency and the Haitian Revolution, away from improbable American characters, romance, and sensationalized Caribbean exoticism.

THE STUDIO'S PROMOTIONAL STRATEGY

With the film's completion, responsibility for promoting *Lydia Bailey* fell to Fox's New York publicists. The financial stakes were high; filming extensive spectacle was expensive, and *Lydia Bailey* was the studio's first film to be distributed after enforcement of the antitrust "divorce" of production from exhibition increased competition.[60] In 1950, Fox promotional materials announcing the film had promoted *Lydia Bailey* as a special Technicolor production with "universal appeal," describing the story as "the liberation of Haiti during the Napoleonic era."[61] By 1952, the language of "liberation" disappeared, and was replaced with more sensational and conventionally racialized terms. Publicity repeatedly referred to Haiti's Black Republic as the mysterious dark place of "lush voodoo jungles," utilizing widely circulated words and images carrying the imprint of deeply rooted assumptions of white supremacy.[62] These promotional materials would shape expectations of film reviewers and audiences.

The graphic materials in the "Exhibitor's Campaign book," which presumably white publicists addressed to white exhibitors aiming to attract white audiences, associated the Black Republic with sexuality and violence. Promotional materials identified "the primitive jungle of nineteenth century Haiti" as a space where white characters confronted "intrigue," "insurrection," and "savage rebellion," and where white women were forbidden and prized objects of desire.[63] The visuals and written text in the *Lydia Bailey* pressbook associated Haiti with "vivid passion," "the wild beat of a thousand voodoo drums," "savage ambush," and "magic and terror."[64] Brief mention of "Toussaint" and "Napoleon" represents the only nod to the film's depiction of the "ragged armies" who halted the French invaders.[65]

Because the studio intended (and needed) to bring Black ticket buyers to the theater, they developed Black publicity materials. In an early effort to promote *Lydia Bailey*, the studio previewed the film for *Ebony* magazine, which it recognized as a primary pathway to Black moviegoers. *Ebony*'s extensive preview

Marketing materials for *Lydia Bailey* blithely mobilized entrenched racist tropes and downplayed the reality that Toussaint Louverture led a successful war of independence in Haiti.

of the film, published in January 1952, included five pages of production stills and text emphasizing the historical significance of Haiti's successful rebellion, insisting that the "Character of King Dick Overshadows Movie's [White] Lead."[66] Another Black press writer critiqued the continued dominance of "pale [white] movie stars" in studio films and explicitly praised *Lydia Bailey*'s "minimum [number] of white actors."[67] *Variety* called attention to *Ebony*'s coverage, observing, "Negro pub kudos 20th Century Fox for its production of *Lydia Bailey*[, which] glorifies Negro history for the first time in a Hollywood film."[68] The *Lydia* Bailey pressbook recommended "*Ebony*'s spread" and "lavish coverage" for marketing to Black communities.[69]

SCREENING THE FILM IN 1952

Lydia Bailey's first public screening was its unprecedented world premiere in Port-Au-Prince, Haiti, attended by dignitaries, stars, and US journalists. The event was hosted by Fox and the Haitian government. Most white press covered this event as a junket to an "exotic" tourist destination.[70] In contrast, Black press coverage emphasized the event's political and racial significance, particularly visible in the Black Republic. Black journalist James Hicks's reporting for the *Baltimore Afro-American*, reprinted in other Black newspapers, burned with fighting words challenging US norms of white supremacy. Hicks pointed out how the screening in Haiti itself "made history . . . throughout the four days of the premiere festivities, [because] white people took a back seat to colored people in a manner which has probably never occurred before in the Western hemisphere and which may not occur again for a long time." He suggested that event dynamics might have helped white journalists and other white premiere attendees notice that, in Haiti, "it was more important to be black than white." He emphasized how premiere festivities transgressed segregation's supposedly rigid boundaries, observing that in Haiti, the premiere's Hollywood stars, "tall handsome" African American William Marshall and "beautiful" white Anne Francis, were "inseparable companions, accorded the full privileges and rights of stars such as never could be accorded in America."[71]

In the United States, white newspaper reviews covering *Lydia Bailey*'s opening in first-run theaters described its action-adventure-romance as a racialized exoticized spectacle, although also some called attention to the heroism of its Black characters fighting for the Black Republic.[72] In the words of one southern white reviewer, "Full advantage has been taken of the exotic background, including the blood-maddened voodoo dance for war, to make *Lydia Bailey* the sort of swashbuckling colorful adventure-romance that is hard to resist."[73] Most Black newspaper coverage emphasized the film's monumental representational breakthroughs, their articles illustrated with movie stills showing King Dick planning military strategy with Louverture. While some Black reviewers were critical of the film's divergence from the historical record, others were laudatory, borrowing *Ebony*'s formulation: "For the first time, a motion picture has been built around a black country with giant leaders who had the courage to fight for freedom and independence, to successfully repulse the superior forces of the great Napoleon."[74] One Black reviewer described the film as "the story of the slave revolt against Napoleon and the French and the making of the Haitian republic."[75] Another argued that "not once does the action lose sight of the fact that Haiti is at war with the French and that an attack by Napoleon's General Philippe Leclerc is bitterly contested by the Haitians."[76]

CONCLUSION

In the end, *Lydia Bailey*'s contradictory storytelling could not deliver a commercial success. The film, accompanied by a stage show, had a strong New York opening at the Roxy Theatre; it was also "holding steadily at fair" in London.[77] *Variety* box-office reports for *Lydia Bailey*, such as "Passable" in Chicago, "Mild" in Providence, and "Dull at the Buffalo," told a different story.[78] Exhibitors' reports were unenthusiastic, routinely describing audience interest as average.[79] Although the film ranked in the middle of "Top Grossers of 1952," ticket sales did not cover the film's production costs.[80] Most Black viewers had to wait weeks or even months for the film to open in their neighborhood theaters due to segregated practices that kept them out of the first-run theaters. When Black audiences did see the film, many lauded the picture, voting it third place in the *Pittsburgh Courier*'s film poll.[81] International ticket sales were more robust, perhaps because international distributors could rename the film to attract audiences, emphasizing either Haiti's struggle or the film's exoticism.[82] According to publicity posters, the film was released as *Insurgents' Haiti* in the Netherlands and as *The Revolt of Haiti* in Italy and Spain. The film was called *Black Drums* in Germany and *The Sorcerer of Haiti* in Argentina.

Anticommunist surveillance and the blacklist continued to exert intense pressure on the film industry, and these factors affected individuals involved with *Lydia Bailey*. Charles Korvin, the actor who portrayed the French planter, did not face widely publicized allegations, but because he refused to name names during the Red Scare, *Lydia Bailey* was his last Hollywood film. By 1953, William Marshall's left-wing Black arts activism alongside political activist Paul Robeson made him the target of aggressive anticommunist blacklisting. Even Darryl Zanuck, lifelong Republican, found himself under attack; a substantial article in the conservative *Chicago Tribune* appeared in July 1952 describing Zanuck as "long friendly to internationalist and leftist causes" and accusing him of supporting "the Communist Party line" due to his appearance at the 1943 Writers' Congress and his production of "controversial" films.[83]

So, *Lydia Bailey* and its glimpse of the Black Republic's defeat of French invaders quietly disappeared from Hollywood history. Black artists, however, held on to the goal of dramatizing Haitian revolutionary history on screen. In 1957, at the height of Black actor Harry Belafonte's music and film stardom and shortly after he organized his own independent production company, Belafonte and Black novelist John Oliver Killens pitched a film revolving around the exploits of Haitian Revolution leader Henri Christophe to studio executives. In 1968, William Marshall developed a film script about Christophe, collaborating with Black actor-writer-activist Julian Mayfield.[84] Marshall's subsequent 1972 announcement of his plans explicitly rebuked *Lydia Bailey*. He explained, "The successful revolt of the African people in Haiti, unique in history, was used in *Lydia Bailey* as a backdrop for the love story of two white Americans, and my objective is to bring the backdrop to the forefront."[85] In the 1990s, Black actor Danny Glover began making plans for filming this history, as did Black

Caribbean filmmaker Euzhan Palcy.[86] Yet to date, *Lydia Bailey*'s conflicted film account remains Hollywood's only feature-length narrative depicting the Haitian Revolution. The film stands as a celluloid artifact from those postwar years when anticolonialism's challenge to white supremacy seemed to create the possibility to imagine, even briefly, American heroism emerging in support of the collective Black struggle.

Notes

1. This chapter draws on some material in Judith E. Smith, "Hollywood Imagines Revolutionary Haiti: The Forgotten Film *Lydia Bailey* (1952)," *Historical Journal of Film, Radio and Television* 41, no. 4 (2021): 759–87. On its release, Black publications applauded the film; the tabloid *Jet* described it as "the first picture to depict truly the bravery of Negroes whose love of freedom did not melt in the face of guns, fire, and death." "Lydia Bailey," *Jet*, June 12, 1952, 65.

2. See "Angry Man's Romance," *Time*, November 25, 1940, 93.

3. See "Of Local Origin," *New York Times*, September 25, 1946, 48. *Northwest Passage* (King Vidor, 1940) heroized the American defeat of the Abenaki during the French and Indian War (1754–1763).

4. See Nell Painter, *The History of White People* (New York: Norton, 2010), 302–5, 322–23; Kenneth Roberts's popular journalism aggressively promoted hierarchical racial categories.

5. Philip Kaisary, *The Haitian Revolution in the Literary Imagination: Radical Horizons, Conservative Constraints* (Charlottesville: University of Virginia Press, 2014), 1.

6. Lindsey J. Twa, *Visualizing Haiti in U.S. Culture, 1910-1950* (Burlington, VT: Ashgate, 2014), xviii, xxi.

7. See Mary Renda, *Taking Haiti: Military Occupation and the Culture of U.S. Imperialism, 1915-1940* (Chapel Hill: University of North Carolina Press, 2001), 17–20, 277–85; see Twa, *Visualizing Haiti*, 125–27, 136–38, 171–73, 176–94.

8. The author was a British diplomat. Some sources list his name as Sir Spenser St. John. The first edition of the book appeared in 1884; sources differ on the punctuation in the book's title.

9. Kaisary, *Haitian Revolution*, 5, 21–23, 30–36.

10. Roberts's notation in *The Black Jacobins* on his copy is in the Kenneth Roberts Library book collection, Rauner Special Collections Library, Dartmouth College, Hanover, NH. Dartmouth undergraduate researcher Daniel Fishbein copied Roberts's marginal notes and marked passages in these four sources.

11. Robert Van Gelder, "When the Republic Was Young," *New York Times Book Review*, January 5, 1947, 25.

12. Van Gelder, "When the Republic Was Young," 1; Sterling North, "Ken Roberts' Research, from the Hub to Haiti, Hallmarks Best Seller," *Washington Post*, January 5, 1947, S8.

13. Kenneth Roberts, *Lydia Bailey* (Garden City: Doubleday, 1947), 80.

14. Alan Thomas Lipke, "The Strange Life and Stranger Afterlife of King Dick Including His Adventures in Haiti and Hollywood with Observations on the Construction of Race, Class, Nationality, Gender, Slang Etymology and Religion" (master's thesis, University of South Florida, 2013), http://scholarcommons.usf.edu/etd/4530/68.

15. Roberts, *Lydia Bailey*, 90, 103, 214–15.

16. Edward Laycock, "Roberts Is Back," *Boston Globe*, January 2, 1947, 11; Charles Poore, "Books of the Times," *New York Times*, January 2, 1947, 25; W. R. R., "Kenneth Roberts on the Federal Era," *Christian Science Monitor*, January 2, 1947, 24; "Building a Best Seller on a Basis of History," *Globe and Mail* (Toronto, Canada), January 4, 1947, 8; Walter Havighurst, "Lydia Bailey," *Chicago Daily Tribune*, January 5, 1947, G3; Lewis Gannett, "Books and Things," *New York Herald Tribune*, January 2, 1947, 17A. Statements on racial equality appear in the book's foreword and on 276–79.

17. See Gertrude Martin, "Bookshelf," *Chicago Defender* (national), January 25, 1947, 15; John Jasper, "America Owes Freedom to 50,000 Haitians," *Baltimore Afro-American*, May 3, 1947, M8.

18. See George F. Custen, *Twentieth Century's Fox: Darryl F. Zanuck and the Culture of Hollywood* (New York: Basic Books, 1997). On Willkie's politics and public antifascism, see David Levering Lewis, *The Improbable Wendell Willkie: The Businessman Who Saved the Republican Party and His Country and Conceived a New World Order* (New York: Liveright, 2018); Samuel Zipp, *The Idealist: Wendell Willkie's Wartime Quest to Build One World* (Cambridge, MA: Harvard University Press, 2020). Willkie is quoted in "Willkie Praises Industry at Fete," *The Exhibitor*, March 4, 1942, 11b.

19. On Willkie and White's Hollywood campaign, and Zanuck's films, see Walter White, *A Man Called White: The Autobiography of Walter White* (New York: Viking Press, 1948), 198–203; Thomas Cripps, *Making Movies Black: The Hollywood Message Movie from WWII to the Civil Rights Era* (New York: Oxford University Press, 1993), 35–63; Ellen C. Scott, *Cinema Civil Rights: Regulation, Repression, and Race in the Classical Hollywood Era* (New Brunswick, NJ: Rutgers University Press, 2015), 108–19, 160–69.

20. Leonard Mosley, *Zanuck: The Rise and Fall of Hollywood's Last Tycoon* (New York: McGraw Hill, 1985), 199–209, 210–11.

21. Colonel Darryl Zanuck, "Do Writers Know Hollywood? The Message Cannot Overwhelm the Technique," *Saturday Review of Literature*, October 30, 1943, 12–13.

22. On these films, see Thomas Knock, "History with Lightning: The Forgotten Film *Wilson*," *American Quarterly* 28, no. 5 (Winter, 1976): 534, 538–40; Judith E. Smith, *Visions of Belonging: Family Stories, Popular Culture, and Postwar Democracy, 1940–1960* (New York: Columbia University Press, 2004), 156–65, 117–23, 166–70, 184–98; Scott, *Cinema Civil Rights*, 119–33.

23. Treatment by Milton Krims, April 9, 1947, in Fox Lydia Bailey Collection, Cinema Television Library, University of Southern California [Fox-LB, CTL-USC].

24. Sol Siegel to Darryl F. Zanuck [DFZ], April 9, 1947; "Conference with Mr. Zanuck on April 9, 1947 treatment on April 17, 1947" [Fox-LB, CTL-USC].

25. Thomas Schatz, *Boom and Bust: American Cinema in the 1940s* (Berkeley: University of California Press, 1999), 290, 293, 307–13, 332, 334.

26. Thomas Doherty, *Show Trial: Hollywood, HUAC, and the Birth of the Blacklist* (New York: Columbia University Press, 2018), 62–72.

27. Schatz, *Boom or Bust*, 307–13; Doherty, *Show Trial*, 299–311.

28. "'Lydia Bailey' Back on Sked with Cost Cut," *Variety* (daily), January 23, 1948, 10; Krims to Sol Siegel, January 5, 1948, in Milton Krims Collection, file 32, Special Collections, Margaret Herrick Library, Academy of Motion Picture Arts and Sciences [MH-AMPAS].

29. Larry Ceplair and Steven Englund, *The Inquisition in Hollywood: Politics in the Film Community, 1930–1960* (Urbana: University of Illinois Press, 2003), 326–33; Peter Lev, *Twentieth Century Fox* (Austin: University of Texas Press, 2013), 110.

30. In 1954, members of the Screen Writers Guild, established in 1933, voted to expand membership to include film, television, and radio writers and become a national union divided into geographical regions: Writers Guild of America, West and Writers Guild of America, East.

31. Ceplair and Englund, *Inquisition in Hollywood*, 326–33; Dunne to DFZ, April 19, 1948, in Philip Dunne Collection [PDC], Box 4, Folder 1, CTL-USC; Dunne worked on *Lydia Bailey* scripts from March to November 1948, then worked on *Pinky* scripts November 1948 to May 1949. See Smith, *Visions of Belonging*, 117–23, 184–98; Scott, *Cinema Civil Rights*, 119–26, 177–79.

32. Dunne, LB first draft, May 18, 1948; Dunne, LB draft August 19, 1948; both in Fox-LB, CTL-USC. Dunne produced six *Lydia Bailey* scripts between March and November 1948.

33. Dunne, LB first draft, May 18, 1948, Fox-LB, CTL-USC.

34. Dunne, LB draft, August 19, 1948, Fox-LB, CTL-USC.

35. Dunne wrote, "In these sequences we should follow a voudun [*sic*] ceremony as closely as possible. . . . It would probably be wiser to omit the sacrifice of chickens and goats. . . . It is a scene indescribably primitive and yet with a wild beauty." In LB first draft May 18, 1948, Fox-LB, CTL-USC.

36. "20th's Policy on B's Is Subject to Individual Deals," *Variety* (weekly), September 22, 1948, 16.

37. Conference on First Draft Continuity (October 14, 1948) with Zanuck, Siegel, and Dunne, from Molly Mandeville, October 21, 1948, Fox-LB, CTL-USC.

38. Conference on First Draft Continuity, October 21, 1948, Fox-LB, CTL-USC.

39. Zanuck's statements in Conference on First Draft Continuity, October 21, 1948; Conference on Revised first draft continuity (November 4, 1948), with Zanuck, Siegel, and Dunne, November 10, 1948, Fox-LB, CTL-USC. Zanuck carefully substituted "native" for "Negro" in suggested dialogue.

40. "119 Million in 65 Pix Due to Hit Screen Next Yr.," *Variety* (daily), December 2, 1948, 14.

41. "'Lydia Bailey' Again Revived Project," *Los Angeles Times*, November 19, 1950. See Michelangelo Capua, *Jean Negulesco: The Life and Films* (Jefferson, NC: McFarland, 2017), 7, 69; Negulesco, an artist born in Romania, came to Hollywood via New York in 1934, directing for Paramount, Universal, and Warner Bros. before moving to Fox in 1948. He avoided political activism. See Larry Ceplair, "Who Wrote What? A Tale of a Blacklisted Screenwriter and His Front," *Cineaste* 18, no. 2 (1991): 18–21; the original script for *Broken Arrow* was written by blacklisted screenwriter Albert Maltz, a close friend of Blankfort's since the 1930s. Blankfort accepted the considerable risk involved in serving as Maltz's "front."

42. Negulesco to Schermer, January 11, 1951, in Michael Blankfort Papers [MBP], Box 88, Folder 1, Howard Gottlieb Archival Research Center, Boston University [HGARC-BU].

43. George Streator, "'A Nigger Did It'; About a Play Called *Stevedore*," *The Crisis*, July 1934, 216–17.

44. US House, Committee on Un-American Activities, *Communist Infiltration of Hollywood Motion-Picture Industry, Part 7*, HRG-1952–UAH-002, January 24, 28, February 5, March 20, April 10, 20, 1952, 2338–40, ProQuest *Congressional Hearings Digital Collection*; this excerpt, from Blankfort's article in *The Daily Worker*, April 27, 1934, was read at his public appearance before HUAC, January 28, 1952.

45. Blankfort's contributions to the AWC in 1935 are listed in Henry Hart, ed., *American Writers Congress 1935* (New York: International Publishers, 1935), 26, 188; for the significance the AWC had for Black literary critique, see Robin D. G. Kelley, *Race Rebels: Culture, Politics, and the Black Working-Class* (New York: Free Press, 1996), 271, n. 34.

46. See Blankfort letter to Malin, October 10, 1950, in MBP, Folder 86, MH-AMPAS. In 1950, Blankfort listed his political associations after 1942 as the American Veterans Committee, the ACLU, the American Jewish Congress, the Writer's Guild, and the League of American Writers. He noted that he signed the amicus brief for the Hollywood Ten and every petition to abolish HUAC. Blankfort's affiliations were listed in California's yearly HUAC-like Tenney Commission reports from 1945 to 1949, the 1949 report of the anticommunist watchdog *Counterattack*, and the 1950 report in *Red Channels*.

47. Jean Negulesco to Jules Schermer, January 11, 1951, MBP, Box 88, Folder 1, HGARC-BU.

48. Negulesco to Michael Blankfort, March 3, 1951, MBP, Box 88, Folder 1, HGARC-BU.

49. Negulesco to Schermer, January 11, 1951, MBP, Box 88, Folder 1, HGARC-BU.

50. Negulesco to Schermer, January 11, 1951; Negulesco to Blankfort, January 28, 1951, MBP, Box 88, Folder 1, HGARC-BU.

51. Negulesco to Blankfort, "Attached Commentary on the Script," March 6, 1951, Comments on scene 39, MBP, Box 88, Folder 1, HGARC-BU.

52. Negulesco to Schermer, February 8, 1951, MBP, Box 88, Folder 1, HGARC-BU.

53. Negulesco to Schermer, February 8, 1951, 4.

54. Negulesco to Blankfort, "Attached Commentary on the Script," March 6, 1951, Comments on Scene 174, 201, MBP, Box 88, Folder 1, HGARC-BU.

55. See Blankfort's scripts for *Lydia Bailey* in MBP, Box 35, Folders 5–8, HGARC-BU. Blankfort annotated Negulesco's March 6 "Attached Commentary on the Script" with marginal comments such as "Shit! Over my dead body" and "vomitous." See also Blankfort to Zanuck, March 12, 1951, MBP, Box 88, Folder 1. This dialogue appears in what is probably Blankfort's first script, no date, Box 35, Folder 5, and is spoken by Hamlin in the film. Dunne and Blankfort shared writing credit on the screenplay.

56. Zanuck to Schermer, copy to Blankfort, March 19, 1951, MBP, Box 88, Folder 1, HGARC-BU.

57. Blankfort Revised Final Script (with inserted pages from May 12, June 7, July 17), March 10, 1951, Revised Final April 13, 1951, Shooting Final April 18, 1951, Revised Shooting Final, May 12, 1951 in MBP, Folder 14, MH-AMPAS. By March, Blankfort was no longer employed at Fox. For Production Code Administration objections to Dunne's script and approval of Blankfort's final script, see letters in PCA *Lydia Bailey* file, October 14, 1948 to April 27, 1951; additional letters April 11, 1951 through October 1, 1951; Special Collections, MH-AMPAS.

58. DFZ to Sol Siegel, April 14, 1947, Fox-LB, CTL-USC; "Hollywood Inside," *Variety* (daily), October 4, 1951, 4; see also "Twentieth Revamps 4 Pix," *Variety* (daily), October 10, 1951, 4; "Chatter," *Variety* (daily), October 12, 1951, 12.

59. For descriptions of these new scenes in conference to discuss new scenes and retakes, see screenings, September 7, 11, 1951; combined notes of screenings September 7, 11, 20, 1951; New Ending and Added Scene, September 29, 1951, in Fox-LB, CTL-US.

60. "'Lydia' Starts Coast Scramble for 20th Pix," *Variety* (weekly), June 11, 1952, 5; see also "'Bailey' First 20th Film to Be Put Up for Bidding Here," *Variety* (daily), May 21, 1952, 6.

61. "A Studio Pledge," "Call It Treason," "1950–51 Feature Output Proof 'Movies Are Better Than Ever,'" "Lydia Bailey," "Production Periscope" in *Twentieth Century Fox Dynamo*, April 1950.

62. Twentieth Century Fox advertisement, *Motion Picture Herald* 187, no. 8, May 24, 1952; Twentieth Century Fox "Exhibitor's Campaign Book," cover page, publicity, and artwork, 3, 4, 5, 9; MH-AMPAS.

63. "Exhibitor's Campaign Book," cover page, 3, 4.

64. *Lydia Bailey* pressbook, 2, 12, MH-AMPAS.

Imagining the Haitian Revolution in *Lydia Bailey*   113

65. Twentieth Century Fox, "Exhibitor's Campaign Book," 7, 11, 13; *Lydia Bailey* pressbook, especially Mat 401, 12, MH-AMPAS was reproduced widely in newspaper advertising for the film.

66. "Lydia Bailey," *Ebony* 7, no. 2, January 1952, 39ff; quote on 40.

67. "The Revolt against Pale Stars," *Pittsburgh Courier*, April 19, 1952, 8.

68. "Inside Stuff-Pictures," *Variety* (weekly), December 19, 1951, 14.

69. *Lydia Bailey* pressbook, 10.

70. For example, Charles S. Aaronson, "Haiti Spreads Hospitable Arms to 'Lydia Bailey,'" *Motion Picture Herald*, May 10, 1952, 35.

71. James Hicks, "'Lydia Bailey' Holds Gala World Premiere in Haiti," *Baltimore Afro-American*, May 17, 1952, 7; reprinted as "Negro Actors Steal Film Premiere," *Cleveland Call and Post*, May 24, 1952, 1B, 3B; see also "William Marshall, Other 'Lydia Bailey' Stars Frolic in Haiti," *Plain Dealer* (Kansas City, KS), June 13, 1952, 6; this article features nine ANP wire service photographs of the premiere.

72. For example, Kay Proctor, "'Lydia Bailey' at Two Theaters," *Los Angeles Examiner*, June 28, 1952; Donald Kirkley, "When Haiti Warred with Napoleon," *Baltimore Sun*, June 21, 1952, 8; Marjory Adams, "'Lydia Bailey' in Color," *Boston Globe*, June 19, 1952, 26.

73. Ben S. Parker, "More Problems for Napoleon in Haiti Rebellion—at Malco," *Commercial Appeal* (Memphis, TN), July 23, 1952.

74. For the praise in *Ebony*, see January 1952, 44; this sentiment was repeated in the *California Eagle*, June 19, 1952 and reprinted in the *Los Angeles Sentinel*, June 19, 1952, A9. Black reviewers challenging historical accuracy included Hicks, "'Lydia Bailey' Holds Gala premiere in Haiti," 7; Al Monroe, "Lydia Bailey Is a Good War Film of Early Haiti," *Chicago Defender*, May 17, 1952, 23; Walter White, "'Lydia Bailey' Hailed as Stirring Picturization of Negro on Film," *Chicago Defender* (national), June 21, 1952, 11.

75. "William Marshall Stars: 'Lydia Bailey' All Set for U.S. Bow at Roxy," *Pittsburgh Courier*, May 31, 1952, 23.

76. Monroe, "'Lydia Bailey' is a Good War Film," 23.

77. "Weather Boosts London Film Biz," *Variety* (weekly), June 11, 1952, 11. For New York box office, see "B'Way Soars; Johnnie Ray Tilts 'Heart' to Huge $142,000, 'Lovely' Sock 145G, 'Bailey'-Vaude 78G, 'Beacon' Big 29G," *Variety* (weekly), June 4, 1952, 9; see also "Johnny Ray Keeps 'Wild Heart' Throbbing in 2nd B-Way Week," *Variety* (daily), June 6, 1952, 3; "Heat, New Pix Dearth Slough B'Way, 'Young Man' Slow 7G, 'Cal Conquest' Plus Vaude 13G, 'Lovely' Fine 2d," *Variety* (weekly), June 11, 1952, 9.

78. "Chicago Biz Murky . . . 'Bailey' Moderate 16G," *Variety* (weekly), June 18, 1952, 9; "'Carbine' Fair $12,000 in Prov., 'Baily' Mild 71/2G, 'Shark' Slight 6G," *Variety* (weekly), June 18, 1952, 8; "Buff Hits Skids," *Variety* (weekly), June 25, 1952, 22.

79. "Independent Film Buyers Report on Performances," *Motion Picture Herald*, October 11, October 25, November 1, 8, 15, 29, December 8, 20, 27, 1952.

80. "Top Grossers of 1952," *Variety* (weekly), January 7, 1953, 61. Production costs and rental fees in Aubrey Solomon, *Twentieth Century Fox: A Corporate and Financial History* (Metuchen, NJ: Scarecrow Press, 1988), 246, 224.

81. "Final Tabulation of *Courier* Theatrical Poll," *Pittsburgh Courier*, April 25, 1953, 22. Reader "votes went to *Sudden Fear* (1100) *High Noon* (580), *Lydia Bailey* (570)."

82. Zanuck's assessment: "'Lydia Bailey' (ordinary in the domestic market but will do more than $1,000,000 in the foreign market)," in DFZ to Philip Dunne, "Strictly Confidential," August 1, 1953, in PDC, Box 8, Folder 16, CTL-USC.

83. Charles Korvin, "Letters to the editor: Actors Suffered, Too," *New York Times*, May 4, 1997, H11; "Charles Korvin, 90, Film Actor Who Played Cads," *New York Times*, June 27, 1998, B8. Korvin worked with Herbert Klein and the Film and Photo League on the 1937 Spanish Civil War documentary *Heart of Spain*. Marshall was part of Paul Robeson's circle of left-wing Black arts activists in the early 1950s, appearing with him at the National Negro Labor Council in 1951. *Counterattack*'s publication of his left activism (December 25, 1952) halted his film and television career until the late 1960s. For the attack on Zanuck, see "International Film Set Beats Drums for Ike: Zanuck Profits from Sales Abroad," *Chicago Tribune*, July 3, 1952, 5. For Zanuck's defense, see memo to W. D. Maxwell, July 9, 1952 in Rudy Behlmer, *Memo from Darryl F. Zanuck* (New York: Grove Press, 1993), 209–13.

84. Keith Gilyard, *John Oliver Killens: A Life of Black Literary Activism* (Athens, GA: University of Georgia Press, 2010), 129; for correspondence and scripts for this project, see the Mayfield Papers, Box 4, Folder 8; Box 18, Folders 8 and 9; Schomburg Center for Research in Black Culture, New York Public Library.

85. "Star William Marshall Talks about 'Blacula,'" *Box Office*, August 7, 1972.

86. "Danny Glover Says Producers Told Him His Haiti Film Lacked White Heroes," *Miami Herald*, July 28, 2008; Stuart Jeffries, "Interview: Danny Glover: The Good Cop," *The Guardian*, May 18, 2012; "Danny Glover's Toussaint L'Ouverture Film That Never Was, but Still Could Be, and Other Films on the Haitian Revolutionary," *Shadow and Act*, July 31, 2015, https://shadowandact.com/danny-glovers-toussaint-louverture-film-that-never-was-but-could-still-be-other-films-on-the-haitian-revolutionary.

Chapter 6

REFUSING TO BE "SOMEBODY'S DAMN MAID"

An Examination of Space in Billie Holiday's Autobiography and Biopic *Lady Sings the Blues*

CHARLENE REGESTER

The cinematic representation of African American jazz artist Billie Holiday (Eleanora Fagan) reconstructed in *Lady Sings the Blues* (Sidney J. Furie, 1972) was an ambitious project but one that could not escape its own complications. Moreover, as a biopic, the film's premise was based on Holiday's similarly titled 1956 autobiography, which she wrote with *New York Post* writer William Dufty,[1] wherein Holiday engaged in mythologizing her own image. Affirming that Holiday fictionalized her autobiography, musicologist George Lewis claims, she "never intended this book to be an accurate reflection of her life."[2] In Lewis's estimation, "she was adept at putting on many faces—continually reinventing herself in ways that might aid her musical career, might impress or distress people, or [might have created an image] . . . just for the plain hell-raising fun of it. She was a woman of contradictions."[3] Supporting the assertion that Holiday deliberately contrived inaccuracies in her autobiography, biographer Robert O'Meally suggests, "Surely Billie Holiday's was an invented life, pieced together from myths and dreams/wishes as well as memories. And yet surely, too, she was willing to trade her life story, again and again for cash on the spot."[4]

In its 1956 review of Holiday's autobiography, *Phylon*'s Miles Jefferson wrote:

Billie's personality is not what you would call warm, nor is her choice of words censored. There are many three-lettered and four-lettered words in her book which may restrict circulation. She is vindictive of people she does not like, but reasonably faithful toward those few friends she cherishes. Under that hostile exterior there is an occasional sentimental heartbeat. Toughness covers some tenderness. Her story always rings true, and if it is unpleasant, its honesty insists that you stick with it. The book is not literature; it is a slice of raw life that compels attention.[5]

Vera D. Hunton, *Journal of Negro Education* reviewer, reported:

Although allowing for any weaknesses inherent in the bastardy of a ghosted autobiography, one still misses in the person [that] the book portrays much of the exciting warmth, the stirring earthiness, and the moving melancholia of even Billie Holiday's stage personality. One is left wondering what the "real" Billie is like. Billie is liberal with a steely kind of realistic philosophizing, yet she seems to have remained the romantic idealist who forever refuses to become disillusioned. She sums up with a wistful bit of moralizing on an optimistic note. For one who has endured personal anguish such as she describes, this is indeed remarkable.[6]

New York Times's Gilbert Millstein related:

And, however true are a great many things that Miss Holiday has experienced, it must be remembered that a great many of them were self-inflicted; that she has suffered the psychic wounds and cultivated the attitudes of the deep neurotic. She has few reticences and many biases and there isn't much point in trying to break down the percentages of societal and individual responsibility.[7]

Regardless of the autobiography's misrepresentations, omissions, or flaws and given the complications associated with adapting this literary work to the screen, the film remains significant to Black cinema history. It emerged during the Hollywood Renaissance—an era that occurred in the late 1960s and early 1970s when Hollywood exhibited a level of freedom rarely observed in the industry, resulting in a dramatic transformation of cinematic standards.[8] Therefore, to understand the biopic's historical significance and the connections between Holiday's autobiography and the filmic representation of her life, the current chapter examines the following: *Lady Sings the Blues*, a film that both conforms to and deviates from traditional biopics; Holiday's troubled relationship with the cinema industry; Holiday's imprint or influence on her biopic (even though the film was produced some thirteen years after her death); and the ways Holiday's autobiography exemplifies the liberated spaces she created for herself that are in direct contrast to the restrictive spaces created for her on screen. The chapter's comparative analysis of Holiday's autobiography and biopic reveals that the liberating spaces Holiday depicts in her autobiography convey her adamant resistance to the dominant white patriarchy and its efforts

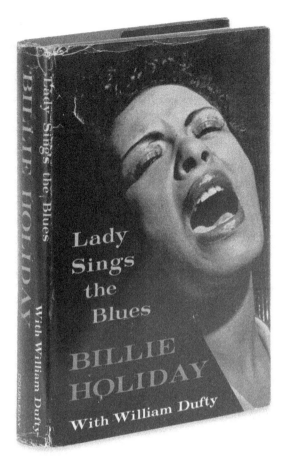

Billie Holiday's compelling and confounding 1956 autobiography, *Lady Sings the Blues*, provided a basis for the similarly titled 1972 film.

to restrain her, whereas the Hollywood biopic sustains those efforts through its emphasis on the restrictive spaces in which Holiday finds herself.

This critique will utilize a variation of Foucault's term "heterotopic spaces" to mean places of difference, where difference refers to physical spaces that are disturbing, incompatible, contradictory, and sometimes restrictive. Most importantly, they are transformative and transgressive spaces that "contain worlds within worlds which scramble the order of dominant society."[9] In her autobiography, Holiday presents heterotopic (contradictory) spaces in narrating events of her complex life, whereas the film often depicts spaces that are simply restrictive. Foucault contends, "In general, the heterotopic site is not freely accessible like a public space. Either the entry is compulsory, as in the case of entering a barracks or a prison, or else the individual has to submit to rites and purifications."[10] Holiday transcends such institutional spaces in her autobiography, while her screen character is not allowed such transcendence. Attempting the daunting task of deconstructing Holiday's complexity as it relates to the physical and sometimes psychological spaces that the autobiography and film protagonist occupies is not to further mythologize the artist but instead is designed to expand the evolving literature on the filmic adaptation of this autobiographical work.

Furthermore, this chapter is not another attempt to ferret fact from fiction in view of the numerous and varying accounts of Holiday's life. It is not an attempt to mark her as a victim, sensationalize her complicated life, or reduce Holiday to her sexuality and/or narcotic addiction. Instead, this chapter employs a different approach to interpreting the biopic and autobiography of a brilliant female jazz artist who left an indelible impression on the male-dominated jazz world despite her failings, the racial politics that prevailed, and her commodification as an artist. To provide a context for analyzing *Lady Sings the Blues* (film), it is necessary to consider how the film relates to her autobiography since film/literature adaptations frequently adhere to cinematic formulations and genre conventions that are not relevant to the source material.

LADY SINGS THE BLUES AS A BIOPIC

Biopics are generally constructed differently when they are centered on women rather than men. Women in biopics "cannot be consistently posed as the objects of male looks and language and also be the subjects of their own stories," according to scholar Dennis Bingham.[11] Instead, female-centered biopics "highlight the contradictions between the public positions—positive and negative—women have achieved and the 'unladylike' activities that have landed them there."[12] When one considers that female-centered biopics reveal how male directors/producers exploit female artists and attempt to control their image and narrative, it is possible to see that male-dominated perspectives impact how representations are constructed on screen. Considering that most of the biographies written on Holiday have been penned by men and that the people who produced, directed, and made decisions about *Lady Sings the Blues* (film) were men—particularly men who controlled her voice and narrative—the male-dominated influence exerted over Holiday's public image cannot be ignored when analyzing this woman-centered film. In a story about a woman who challenges dominant patriarchal norms and in which men control the narrative, the production will highlight the consequences and punishments a nonconformist woman is likely to face for her oppositional voice, views, and behavior.

Supporting this position, scholar Gary Storhoff claims, "Society . . . punishes [Holiday in *Lady Sings the Blues*] for daring to transgress its most covert laws and moral structures concerning women, especially Black women. She refuses her gendered place in society as an obedient daughter who should choose above all else the sanctity of home, husband, and family."[13] That Holiday engaged in nonconformist behavior and defied these expectations is evident when O'Meally observes that she "was decidedly not a member of the Cult of True Womanhood—that nineteenth-century mythic construct that posited the cardinal virtues for the 'true woman' as 'piety, purity, submissiveness, and domesticity'... [even though she] did feel pressured to conform to 'true woman' rules."[14] Constructing Holiday as oppositional when compared to "traditional" women is characteristic of female-centered biopics in which the self-interest of a dominant patriarchy seeks to restrain (and contain) women for the purpose of capitalizing on the exposure and notoriety to be gained from presenting women in this manner.[15]

While *Lady Sings the Blues* (film) certainly demonstrates how patriarchal forces attempt to control the woman in this female-centered biopic, the picture also presents Holiday as a victim—another biopic characteristic. Depicting her as a victim, according to scholar Farah Jasmine Griffin, is a strategy deliberately designed to restrict "and control black women who are multidimensional, talented and ambitious."[16] Not only is Holiday presented as a sympathetic victim, but the film circulates the sentiment that if only she had not become a drug addict or encountered troubles with the law, she would have been hailed as the ultimate untainted star. Relegating Holiday to the margins of society due to her drug addiction (presenting her as someone to be disparaged, rather than recognized for her illness) marks her as immoral or illegal—a bifurcated perspective that leads spectators to participate in blaming the victim or desiring to save her from herself. "If we think of Holiday as a woman who was victimized instead of as a woman who was a perpetual victim," Griffin believes, "our perspectives of her, her achievement, and ultimately of our own possibility, change profoundly."[17] Similarly, biographer John Szwed insists, "Hers was not a victim's story."[18] But Holiday's depiction as victim conforms to female biopics, since these pictures find "conflict and tragedy in a woman's success. A victim, whatever her profession, made a better subject than a survivor with a durable career and nontraumatic personal life."[19] Additionally, biopics examine artists who die early, marking these artists as "preferable to [those with] long lives."[20] Holiday became suitable for a biopic because she met her death in 1959, when she was only forty-four. Without question, Holiday's life conforms to certain conventions associated with biopics, and her story was appropriate for screen adaptation, but to understand this picture's historical significance and how the film intersects with her autobiography, it is necessary to explore Holiday's ill-fated relationship with the cinema industry and unveil her skepticism regarding the industry's ability to adequately reconstruct her life on screen.

HOLIDAY'S TENUOUS RELATIONSHIP WITH
THE CINEMA INDUSTRY

With the publication of Holiday's autobiography, it was well understood that she was interested in having her story transformed on screen, since she "saw the book as an opportunity to make a quick buck."[21] Many assumed that if the book was profitable, then a screen adaptation would be equally successful. The autobiography did achieve some degree of success, but when Holiday named fellow celebrities and artists with whom she had performed, the public attention aroused concerns that their reputations could be tarnished. Fearing that their careers would be jeopardized, some fellow artists alienated and abandoned Holiday.[22] Regardless of those who feared public scrutiny, Holiday was determined to have her story filmed, particularly since she and Dufty owned the film rights, even though many assumed the publisher, Doubleday, controlled the rights.[23] Holiday's enthusiasm for a screen adaptation evolved from her fascination with cinema, made apparent when she admitted, "I don't think I missed a single picture [white actress] Billie Dove ever made. I was crazy for her. I tried to do my hair like her and eventually I borrowed her name."[24] This fascination with Dove encouraged Holiday to pursue the screen and reportedly led her to appear in "mob scenes in a picture with Paul Robeson"[25]—a film that may have been *Emperor Jones* (Dudley Murphy, 1933).[26] According to Holiday, two years later she was recruited for a "real part" in Duke Ellington's movie short *Symphony in Black: A Rhapsody of Negro Life* (Fred Waller, 1935)[27]—a film she describes as "a musical, with a little story to it [that] . . . gave me a chance to sing a song—a real weird and pretty blues number."[28] According to scholar Susan Delson, "Waller's ease with cinematic effects is evident in the cross-fades and other optical treatments used throughout that film."[29] Regarding Holiday's portrayal, O'Meally reports that in one scene she is "pushed to the ground by her two-timing lover," who is played by African American dancer Earl "Snakehips" Tucker, and in another scene, she "sings the 'Big City Blues (The Saddest Tale),'" emulating Bessie Smith's singing style.[30] O'Meally writes, "The elegance of Ellington's arrangement provides just the right showcase for Holiday's delicate but nonetheless powerful contralto. And it is wonderful to see young Holiday in action. Playing the part of an unglamorous street woman done wrong, she is not dressed or made up to flatter her looks. But the diamond-in-the-rough beauty, of both her voice and her body, is deep and irresistible."[31] As for Ellington's orchestra, scholar Arthur Knight notes, the picture provides a "nine-minute 'symphony,' . . . intercut with expressionist images, for a white, concert-hall audience."[32]

In Holiday's early screen appearances, she was conceivably enthusiastic about her representations, but it is also possible that she was concerned about

Holiday's Autobiography and Biopic *Lady Sings the Blues*

being misrepresented, as was certainly the case with *New Orleans* (Arthur Lubin, 1947)—a picture that cast her as a maid. *New Orleans* was reportedly the outgrowth of an earlier production filmmaker Orson Welles developed called *The Story of Jazz*. The project was part of a jazz anthology that never materialized but instead became the nucleus for *New Orleans*.[33] Ultimately, when *New Orleans* was completed, it focused on a white opera singer (Miralee Smith/Dorothy Patrick) who travels to New Orleans with her mother (Mrs. Rutledge Smith/Irene Rich) to cultivate her singing career, and in doing so, the young opera singer develops an attraction to a gambler (Nick Duquesne/Arturo de Cordova). In the film, although Miralee is trained in opera, she gravitates to jazz and ragtime music after her maid (Endie/Holiday) encourages her to explore the music of New Orleans. It is in Storyville's jazz district that Miralee becomes mesmerized with the music emanating from the dives where Louis "Satchmo" Armstrong (as himself) and his band perform.

When Miralee and her mother arrive in New Orleans, they stay at an opulent residence and are greeted by none other than Endie, a Black maid who wears a uniform with a white ruffled headpiece to mark her subservience. The black uniform is accentuated with a white apron, white collar, and white sleeve cuffs. Although Endie assumes the maid role, she immediately redefines or remakes herself as a performer when she plays the piano and sings "Do You Know What It Means to Miss New Orleans?" To further subvert her domesticity, Endie reveals to Miralee that not only is she attracted to blues and jazz music, but she has also developed an affection for the jazz musician Satchmo, who becomes her romantic idol.

Exemplary of how Endie reverses her subservient status and reinvents herself, in the film she discards her maid's uniform and appears in a black dress, wears pearls around her neck, and displays flowers in her hair. She then enters Miralee's room to bring her tea; she picks up Miralee's clothes in a final act of serving as her maid and announces her intent to leave work early so that she can go to Storyville, a place where jazz music dominates. Endie is so captivating that Miralee, who is equally fascinated with the music permeating New Orleans streets, joins Endie in traveling to Storyville. The two, white employer and Black maid, virtually dismantle their racial and class differences when they travel together in secrecy to avoid Jim Crow laws and escape the control of Miralee's mother. Upon their arrival in Storyville, Satchmo greets them, plays his horn/trumpet, and invites Endie, no longer a maid but a performer, to sing her signature song ("Do You Know What It Means to Miss New Orleans?").

In a subsequent appearance, Holiday performs at the Storyville nightclub, and after the city threatens to close this Black cultural space, she sings "Farewell to Storyville," while those in the background sing the refrain. Having abandoned her maid's uniform, which restricted her identity, Holiday is unquestionably transformed into an entertainer; she wears a light-colored suit, black blouse, necklace, and hat. Her presence represents one of her last performances in Storyville, as many of those who frequented this entertainment district are forced to leave the city. Nick (Miralee's love interest) departs New Orleans when a young woman who is infatuated with him becomes involved in a car accident and the city decides to close the Storyville area. Mrs. Smith (Miralee's mother) ensures Nick's departure, coercing him with money to leave the area to thwart her daughter's attraction to the young bachelor. Satchmo is forced to leave the district once the entertainment venues close, and with his departure, Endie feels compelled to leave. At the closing of Storyville's entertainment district, Satchmo and Endie lead the marching crowds of those who must abandon the city.

Storyville, referred to as the "red-light district" in 1917 New Orleans, represented the birth of jazz.[34] Scholar Bruce Boyd Raeburn affirms that Armstrong was appropriately placed in Storyville's history; while the film suggests that he departs the district at its closing, he actually left a few years later.[35] In the film, when Storyville is closed, Satchmo takes his band on tour, while Nick attempts to reinvent himself in Chicago. The three (Nick, Satchmo, and Endie) return to Chicago, where they are reunited, and Nick opens a nightclub that features Satchmo and Endie performing. Endie, unsurprisingly, sings "The Blues Are Brewin," which marks her final appearance in the film. At Endie's finale, it is apparent that she has abandoned the maid's uniform that earlier marked her identity and rightfully claims her role as a renowned artist, who suitably wears a long, jeweled dress, flaunts a diamond necklace, and displays gardenias (Holiday's signature flower) in her hair.[36] The subservient role Holiday initially assumes in *New Orleans* is one that she resisted throughout her career.

Holiday was offended with not only her casting in *New Orleans* but also her recruitment, treatment, and diminishment, which she believed was as an assault on her personhood, considering that she was a wealthy entertainer. Holiday recalls:

> I was working in a Hollywood club when Joe Glaser [talent manager] made the deal. It was an independent picture, produced by Jules Levey, called *New Orleans*. . . . I thought I was going to play myself in it. I thought it was going to be Billie Holiday doing a couple of songs in a nightclub setting and that would be that. I should have known better. When I saw the script. . . . You just tell me one Negro girl who's made movies who didn't play a maid or a whore. I don't know any. I found out I was going to do a little singing, but I was still playing the part of a maid. I was sore at . . . Glaser for signing me for the part. I'd fought my whole life to keep from being somebody's damn maid. And after making more than a million bucks and establishing myself as a singer who had

some taste and self-respect, it was a real drag to go to Hollywood and end up as a make-believe maid. . . . I don't think I am the type for maid parts; I don't feel it. I didn't feel this damn part. How could I, after going through hell to keep from being one when I was twelve?[37]

While Holiday had only a few speaking lines in the picture, she "failed" to convey the maid's lowly status even after working with a dramatic coach. She explains, "About the only lines I had, called for me to say, 'Yez, Miss Marylee [Miralee]. No, Miss Marylee [Miralee],' in twenty-three different . . . ways. So, this coach was trying to brief me on how to get the right kind of [Uncle] Tom feeling into this thing."[38] Exhausted from repeating these lines to comply with the director's expectations, Holiday asked, "Who the hell is this Miss Marylee [Miralee]?"[39] Further illustrating Holiday's disparagement, Dorothy Patrick, the white actress playing Miralee, charged that Holiday stole scenes, but in Holiday's view, "This was a laugh. I was no actress, never had been one, never pretended to be one."[40] At the film's completion, Holiday claims, while "they had taken miles of footage of music and scenes in New Orleans . . . none of it was left in the picture. And very damn little of me. I know I wore a white dress for a number I did in the picture. And all that was cut out of the picture. I never made another movie."[41] To affirm Holiday's assessment, biographer Stuart Nicholson reports, producer Jules Levey and scriptwriter Herbert Biberman were instructed to minimize Holiday's and Armstrong's roles to avoid giving the impression that Blacks created jazz—a deliberate attempt to "whitewash" history. According to Nicholson, Levey and Biberman were forced to succumb to the pressures of the blacklist era (when those in the entertainment industry were targeted as being un-American or communist sympathizers) and placate the prevailing racism that compelled artists to adopt the political agenda of those in power, which ultimately limited their ability to give Holiday and Armstrong better roles.[42] Given her experience with *New Orleans*, Holiday was frustrated with casting that she deemed insidious and that she adamantly refused (according to her autobiography) off screen. Considering the political climate, Holiday's fear of being misrepresented in a biopic becomes understandable.

Redirecting attention to Holiday's filmic contributions, scholar Donald Bogle notes, "Holiday has so much more grace, poise, and style than the white woman for whom she works in [*New Orleans*] that she lays to waste the movie's fundamental tastelessness. . . . Holiday provides us with a rare opportunity to see her at her radiant, vibrant, creative best."[43] Offering an alternative perspective, Black jazz singer Carmen McRae acknowledges, Holiday "wasn't that great [being cast as a maid]. . . . Not that she had any good lines to say. She was *Lady*! The most unlikeliest person to be a maid to anybody."[44] Other criticisms leveled against *New Orleans* suggest, "Instead of the film doing justice to an array of musicians, the emphasis throughout was on whether or not the young white opera singer . . . would give up her career to run off with the gambler and restauranteur."[45] As for Holiday's performance, O'Meally insists, "Holiday, with her slyly subversive eyes, takes over the movie when at last it gives the audience a chance to see her (with . . . Armstrong) in song, telling her story. Her versions of 'The Blues Are Brewin' and 'New Orleans' will last when the rest of the movie is justly forgotten."[46] Yet there were times in the picture when Holiday was erased; Szwed reveals that Black singer Ethel Waters's voice was dubbed for one of Holiday's songs and on another occasion, white protagonist Miralee/Patrick sang another Holiday song. This erasure leads Szwed to conclude, "Jazz had somehow become a lady, and a white one at that."[47] Expounding on these views, scholar Sherrie Tucker contends:

> These performances of bland white characters gaping at creative black musicking are enactments of power; acts facilitated in large part through a particular construction of white womanhood as unaware, or "innocent," of her social power. To [watch] the entire film, rather than just the musical sequences starring the black jazz musicians, compels us to consider the curious efficacy of the "white lady" in that very enactment of jazz appropriation analyzed in jazz studies as a white masculinist routine.[48]

Tucker continues, jazz scholar "Ingrid Monson cautions that the historical problem with 'white hipness' is its tendency to project white desires for affect, authenticity, sexuality, onto black bodies and black music—so that when the 'hipster' is sincere in loving jazz, he or she may be reproducing elements of the very aspects of dominant constructions of race that buoy white supremacist ideology."[49] Excoriating Marilee's characterization, Tucker sees Miralee as an embodiment of what she terms the "Jazz Virgin . . . who is stirred by what she hears in black music—which in this film is construed as sexuality, authenticity, emotion, newness, modernity—while *other characters* serve as her anxious protectors."[50] The troubling merging of the white Miralee character with the Black Endie character becomes especially evident when Satchmo sings "Endie" and the camera incidentally cuts to Miralee as though the white opera singer has supplanted the Black blues singer (Endie) as the object of desire. More than this, Miralee's affinity for jazz culminates at the film's end, when "Miralee woos an all-white concert-going audience" with "Do You Know What It Means to Miss New Orleans?" backgrounded with an all-white symphony orchestra and all-white jazz orchestra "to share her epiphany that this music belongs to them [whites]."[51] Concerning this performance, Tucker concludes that "a white woman presents a nostalgic song about a happy south stolen from her black maid, thus transforming jazz into respectable American culture, and the film swells to its musical big finish without apology."[52] Still, Holiday's *New Orleans* role led to her casting in the movie shorts *Frankie "Sugar Chile" Robinson, Billie Holiday, Count Basie and His Sextet* (Will Cowan, 1950) and *The Sound of Jazz* (Jack Smight, 1957),[53] productions in which she plays herself (a performer) and is not required to act (particularly in a subservient capacity).

HOLIDAY'S IMPRINT ON HER BIOPIC

Considering Holiday's demeaning casting as a maid in *New Orleans* (but redeeming representation as a singer) and fearing that Hollywood would grossly distort her life on screen, Holiday expressed reservations regarding early versions of a screen adaptation of her autobiography. In discussions that occurred in the mid-1950s surrounding a film adaptation, Holiday recognized that she was conceivably "too old," according to industry standards, to play herself, and she recognized the picturization would be left in the hands of others. Acknowledging her inability to depict herself, Holiday still wanted to produce the film's soundtrack. Plans were proposed to record songs for the biopic's soundtrack in France, "but it all fell through when the Algerian crisis forced the French government to close all the concert halls."[54] Although the soundtrack was not produced, several actresses were considered for this coveted role, including African American actress Dorothy Dandridge, the first Black performer to receive a Best Actress Oscar nomination for her role in *Carmen Jones* (Otto Preminger, 1954) and someone who received Holiday's tacit approval.[55] However, Holiday did not support casting white actress Ava Gardner—who played the mulatto character in *Show Boat* (George Sidney, 1951), a part that had been denied to Black actress Lena Horne, Holiday's confidante. In *Show Boat*, white singer Eileen Wilson dubbed Gardner's voice even though Gardner preferred Holiday to sing her songs; Holiday had resisted dubbing Gardner's voice, explaining, "If you want the song sung, get me; why this? . . . I'll be standing in the shadows and there's Ava Gardner out front using my voice—why?"[56] Holiday further stated, "Even if they get a white actress, the character she plays will still be coloured. If they change that, there's no story."[57] Given Gardner's casting in *Show Boat* as a mulatto character and her affection for Holiday, Gardner apparently believed that she (a white actress) could depict Holiday (a Black singer) in Holiday's biopic. Weighing in on these casting considerations, writer James Baldwin affirms that when Gardner asked him if he thought she could play Holiday in a biopic, he responded:

I had to tell [Gardner] that, though she was certainly "down" enough for it—courageous and honest and beautiful enough for it—she would almost certainly not be allowed to get away with it, since [Billie] Holiday had been widely rumored to be black, and she, Ava Gardner, was widely rumored to be white. I was not really making a joke, or, if I was, the joke was bitter: for I certainly know some black girls who are much, much whiter than Ava. Nor do I blame the black girls for this, for this utterly inevitable species of schizophrenia is but one of the many manifestations of the spiritual and historical trap, called racial, in which all Americans find themselves and against which some of us, some of the time, manage to arrive at a viable and honorable identity. I was really thinking of black actors and actresses, who would have been embittered if the role of Billie Holiday had been played by a white girl.[58]

Gardner was not the only white actress who may have considered reenacting Holiday on screen; Lana Turner, an avid Holiday fan[59] and, incidentally, cast as the white mother in *Imitation of Life* (Douglas Sirk, 1959), was also considered for the biopic. Apparently, Holiday was fond of Turner and appreciated her support, as when she acknowledged, "Turner used to come in every Tuesday and Thursday [when Holiday performed at Billy Berg's nightclub on the West Coast]. That girl can really dance, and she did at *Billy's*. She always asked me [to sing] 'Strange Fruit' and 'Gloomy Sunday.'"[60] Although Holiday viewed Turner with some degree of affection, this did not mean that she endorsed Turner to portray her. While these early casting considerations were followed by Holiday's early death, it became clear that a biopic would not materialize quickly. The project did not gain momentum until the 1960s, and this era of heightened Black consciousness made it unthinkable to consider a white actress for this important Black role.

With renewed interest in a Holiday biopic, Black actresses Diahann Carroll and Diana Sands were proposed for a project that garnered Black actor/author Ossie Davis's attention, yet this project failed to develop. But when white film producer Lester Cowan, white Canadian director Sidney Furie, and African American Berry Gordy Jr. (music producer and founder of recording company Motown Records) collaborated, the three ultimately produced the Holiday biopic, which was Motown's first picture. *Ebony* magazine reported that white producer Jay Weston, "who owned the rights to the Holiday biography," was among those involved in this venture.[61] Although Paramount served as the film's financial collaborator, Gordy's company decided to undertake the film's financing and expanded its budget from the initial $2 million offered to some $3.3 million.[62] During preproduction, Gordy was initially reluctant to accept Furie's proposal to cast Diana Ross, the lead singer for the Supremes, as the film's protagonist. However, when Gordy learned that Ross could be nominated for an Academy Award and catapulted from pop singer to international star, Gordy agreed to the casting decision.[63]

The July 1971 announcement that Ross would portray the film's protagonist prompted considerable opposition, particularly from those who remembered Holiday or who were so enamored with Holiday that they believed no one could reproduce her music style.[64] Furie's biographer, Daniel Kremer, recalls, "Most everyone's initial reaction to the announcement was one of doubt, if not pure trepidation."[65] Many were concerned that the Motown-produced Paramount Pictures film would fail to accurately reflect Holiday's life, and some believed Ross (a less experienced singer) was inappropriate for depicting Holiday. Among those who opposed the film's casting were Louis McKay (Holiday's former spouse), Leonard Feather (jazz pianist, promoter),[66] and Roger Ebert (white film critic). Ebert's concern was that while Ross could be convincing as Holiday and he knew she could sing, he "couldn't imagine [her] ... reaching the emotional highs and lows of one of the more extreme public lives of our time."[67] Affirming his doubts, Donald Bogle adds:

> Nobody was quite prepared for this screen version of jazz singer Billie Holiday's life. In fact, a number of people were ready to dismiss the film right off the bat as simply a fraud and a travesty. From the moment it had been announced that pop singer . . . Ross would portray Holiday, most thought her all wrong for the role. Where Lady Day had been all stillness and quiet fire . . . Ross was a razzledazzle extrovert, a skinny, high strung live wire who never seemed to stop moving. Then, too, it was feared the movie would whitewash Holiday's drug experiences and her series of love affairs and marriages.[68]

Farah Jasmine Griffin suggests that Ross was unable to recreate a complex personality, effectively reproduce Holiday's music, and convey the Black suffering infused in Holiday's music; most importantly, "Ross had never listened to Holiday's recordings."[69] Despite these concerns, *Ebony* magazine reports, "when Diana Ross curses or sings of heartbreak or fights for a bag of heroin, when Billy Dee Williams scolds and comforts her, and when Richard Pryor has the life savagely beaten from him in a bumbling effort to provide her with the drug that is both life and death, the audience is witness to an epic personality too soon gone, and too soon forgotten."[70] Due to the initial casting concerns, many were surprised that *Lady Sings the Blues* became one of the highest grossing films of 1972. The picture also received five Academy Award nominations; its soundtrack became number one on the *Billboard* music charts and the fastest selling album in Motown's history.[71] Still, many contend that the production, which foregrounds the descent of Holiday's career rather the emergence of a great artist, confirms Holiday's fears that the film industry would be unable to produce an adequate depiction of her life.

CRISIS AND DEVIANT SPACES: AUTOBIOGRAPHY/BIOPIC

Demonstrating how space is utilized to narrativize her ascension and descension as an artist, I argue that *Lady Sings the Blues* (film) employs a reductionist approach in that it confines the protagonist to spaces that minimize her complexity, while the autobiography allows her some degree of agency to challenge and contest the restrictive spaces. More specifically, Holiday/Ross (the character) is more restrained on screen relative to the autobiography, in which Holiday (the person) is allowed more control over her image. Swzed affirms that in the autobiography, Holiday "resists being categorized, typed, and limited by the social constraints placed upon her, and goes to great pains to show how these limitations affected her life and her art."[72] Foucault's views on heterotopias are useful for deconstructing how the film's depiction of certain spaces reveals its inability to appropriately reflect Holiday's complexity, since its restrictive spaces limit a wider exposure to and broader understanding of Holiday's life, while in the autobiography she achieves agency and challenges the restrictions imposed on her and her artistry.

According to Foucault, heterotopias can be placed into two main categories—crisis heterotopias and deviant heterotopias. Crisis heterotopias are "privileged or sacred or forbidden places, reserved for individuals who are, in relation to society and to the human environment in which they live, in a state of crisis: adolescents . . . the elderly, etc."[73] Deviant heterotopias are "those in which individuals whose behavior is deviant in relation to the required mean or norm are placed. Cases of this are rest homes and psychiatric hospitals, and of course prisons."[74] My analysis of *Lady Sings the Blues* considers spaces such as the nightclub, kitchen, bedroom, and bus as crisis heterotopias. It also examines spaces such as the prison and brothel as deviant heterotopias. Unlike Foucault, I do not suggest that one heterotopic space necessarily dissolves into another (even though in some instances this might be the case). Instead, I suggest that spaces depicted in Holiday's autobiography and biopic are sites with multiple modes, so that while there are some parallels in the two representations of Holiday, the autobiography presents the nightclub, kitchen, bedroom, and prison as sites of transformation, whereas the film presents these spaces as more restrictive. Finally, while the bus (a crisis space) and brothel (a deviant space) are two spaces that do not receive comparable attention in the autobiography and the film, they deserve attention because of their significance to the film's overall representation of Holiday.

CRISIS SPACES

Nightclub Space On Screen: A Place of Self-Actualization

In the biopic, the nightclub becomes a place of refuge when, as an adolescent, Holiday/Ross escapes her cleaning duties at a brothel and descends a stairwell that leads to a nightclub below. She observes the entertainment venue from afar and becomes fascinated with the dancers and singers on stage. Since she is underage and rather homely, she is ejected from the establishment, but exposure to the nightclub atmosphere makes her believe she is destined to occupy this entertainment space and reaffirms her desire to become a nightclub singer. Although initially rejected, she returns to the nightclub elegantly dressed in a tight-fitting yellow dress and matching hat to audition as a dancer. When she cannot reproduce the moves required for a line dancer, she is dismissed, but given the chance to audition as a singer, she succeeds due to her talent. The nightclub represents a crisis space in that it signals a turning point in her life, as she transitions from working as a maid in a brothel to seeking safety in a nightclub—a space that marks the beginning of her singing career.

Although the nightclub is initially a place of renewal, it becomes a contradictory space that both enslaves and liberates: on one hand, the small space does not allow for the circulation of her talent; on the other hand, it is within this intimate space that she achieves agency as an artist who exerts control over her art in the manner she desires. This crisis space reflects the contradictory possibilities that stand to be leveraged to subvert the monolithic façade of the dominant culture. Moreover, the nightclub space is contradictory because it encourages the exploitation of her talent, as the dominant patriarchy attempts to control Holiday/Ross's image, career, and art, while also subjecting her to the visceral racial subjugation that existed in the racially segregated United States. In addition, although she achieves some degree of subjectivity in this space, at the same time, the space enslaves her because she is subjected to the gaze of spectators, some of whom disidentify with the singer due to her race. While such disidentification might have occurred in Holiday's own life, the autobiography affirms that Holiday (the person) had more control over how she responded to such hostility.

In comparison to the autobiography, the nightclub space on screen further becomes a contradictory, restrictive crisis heterotopic space in the sequence when Holiday/Ross is informed of her mother's death. After Holiday/Ross performs on stage, she retreats to her dressing room, where she learns of her mother's death, and because her intoxicated state makes her unable to react emotionally, her grief is ventriloquized through the vocal performance of the Piano Man (Richard Pryor). The Piano Man embodies the emotionalism that Holiday/Ross cannot express; he cries, kneels in horror, and becomes the emotional bearer of grief. Despite Holiday/Ross's inability to grieve "appropriately," her mother's death is a turning point because it prompts her to seek treatment for her addiction; she subsequently admits herself to a rehabilitation facility. As Holiday/Ross recuperates in rehab, she is temporarily suspended in happiness when Louis McKay/Billy Dee Williams arrives with gardenias and proposes marriage. This moment of refuge is short-lived; Holiday/Ross descends into tragedy following his departure when white law enforcement authorities arrive to arrest her on drug charges and exhibit a blatant disregard for her ill health. The rehabilitation facility, then, becomes another contradictory crisis space. Moreover, the trauma associated with being returned to jail suggests that even in moments of freedom, Holiday/Ross reverts to a place of pain, suffering, and trauma, demonstrating how the film virtually denies her the legitimate right to enjoy her success.

Nightclub Space in the Autobiography: Artist Achieves Subjectivity

While the film visualizes the nightclub space(s) that Holiday/Ross occupies as both restrictive and liberating, it is in the autobiography that Holiday effectively conveys how she sees herself as an entertainer once she becomes an established star and achieves agency in (both small and large) entertainment spaces. In her autobiography, Holiday clearly negotiates the physical space of performance and utilizes music to achieve agency, whereas the film is less effective in capturing the depth of feeling associated with her musical talent. For example, in the autobiography, Holiday explains that while performing at a small nightclub venue,

> I asked him to play "Trav'lin' All Alone." That came closer than anything to the way I felt. And some part of it must have come across. The whole joint quieted down. If someone had dropped a pin, it would have sounded like a bomb. When I finished, everybody in the joint was crying in their beer, and I picked thirty-eight bucks up off the floor. When I left the joint that night I split [it] with the piano player and still took home fifty-seven dollars.[75]

In this space, Holiday is revered for her talent, her dreams have come true, and the space becomes indicative of her liberation, unlike the confining nightclub spaces depicted on screen that are more often beset with tragedy and trauma. In the autobiography, regardless of the specific venue, the nightclub space becomes a place of liberation for Holiday since it allows her to seek the freedom she desired as an artist.

Vocalizing her own assessment, Holiday affirms how she created such electrifying performances in nightclub spaces when she reflects:

I knew that night I had the future of the whole band riding on me, so I really worked. First, I did "I Cried for You." Then I followed with "Them There Eyes." And then I finished with a thing called "What You Gonna Do When There Ain't No Swing?" . . . When I ended the number, I held on to the word "ain't," then I held "no." Then I held my breath, thinking the jury was out and wondering what the verdict would be, and I sang the word "swing." I hadn't got the word shaped with my mouth when people stood up whistling and hollering and screaming and clapping. There was no arguing. I was the best, so we stayed there for six weeks instead of three.[76]

The autobiography leaves no doubt that Holiday found the nightclub a liberating space and one that provided a mirror image of how she envisioned herself as a celebrated singer. However, the nightclub is not the only space that reveals Holiday's complexities, as the kitchen is another crisis space.

Kitchen Space On Screen: Refusing Subservience

Considering the spaces Holiday/Ross occupies on screen, the kitchen is another crisis space to which she is relegated. When Holiday/Ross as a juvenile leaves Baltimore to travel to New York in search of her absent mother, who is a domestic worker, a white policeman detects that she is without parental guidance, warns her that she should not be walking alone, and then escorts her to the mother's place of employment. But when the mother and daughter are reunited, they retreat to the white employer's kitchen—a space that marks the mother's subservience—where they share a meal and discuss the girl's uncertain future. The kitchen space symbolizes a crisis space and turning point in Holiday/Ross's trajectory because it forces her to acknowledge that if she fails as a singer, she is destined to occupy a space of Black subservience like her mother. However, the kitchen is a contradictory space in that it liberates the adolescent who is reunited with her mother, but also enslaves the adolescent who desires to escape the domesticity and servitude her mother signifies. The film's kitchen space is much more enslaving than the autobiography's, which identifies the kitchen as a more liberating space that contains multiple possibilities; beyond signifying subservience, it can also reflect self-assertiveness and artistic expression.

Kitchen Space in the Autobiography: Liberates and Empowers

Relative to the film, the autobiography's kitchen space is constructed as more liberating, which is made evident when Holiday articulates, "I'd run that kitchen myself. I might not actually cook everything, but I'd oversee it and taste it and see that it's my kind of cooking and that it's straight. I used to laugh when Mom talked about having her own place but look at me now."[77] In this instance, the kitchen space represents a place of retreat and renewal, not one of enslavement or subservience associated with the heteronormative patriarchal white supremacist culture. Affirming how the kitchen space can function for women, scholar Rhiannon Scharnhorst suggests, "Women who choose or prioritize the kitchen . . . as a creative space practice a particular form of resistant cultural work . . . [and for Black women, the kitchen becomes] 'a safe place where [they] could affirm one another and by so doing heal many of the wounds inflicted by racist domination.'"[78] The autobiography depicts the kitchen as self-empowering, whereas the film depicts the space as emblematic of subservience. While the kitchen reflects the exploitation of Black labor (on screen) and liberation (in the autobiography), the bedroom space exemplifies the exploitation of the Black body.

Bedroom Space On Screen: Dreams Tarnished

The bedroom space becomes symbolic of another crisis space, particularly when, as an adolescent, Holiday/Ross is forced to defend herself against the sexual advances of an elderly Black man who follows her home (to her New York City apartment) and traumatizes her. Prior to her exploitation, when Holiday/Ross reaches the safe haven of home, she goes to her bedroom to imitate a singer she hears on a phonograph while looking at herself in the mirror. The young woman gazing into the mirror and engaging in introspection is a significant moment considering Foucault's views. He explains:

> The mirror is, after all, a utopia, since it is a placeless place. In the mirror, I see myself there where I am not, in an unreal, virtual space that opens up behind the surface; I am over there, there where I am not, a sort of shadow that gives my own visibility to myself, that enables me to see myself there where I am absent: such is the utopia of the mirror.[79]

The mirror not only projects the present but also predicts the future; it allows the adolescent to imagine a future in which she is an accomplished singer. Later in the film, other mirror scenes become self-reflexive when Holiday/Ross observes her physiological and psychological demise at various moments in her career. But the adolescent's stare into the mirror reflects her transition from a utopian space (her private bedroom) to a crisis space (where rape is implied) because her gaze is brutally interrupted when the elderly male stalker/pedophile invades her private space. To resist his intrusion, she first gives the impression that she will cooperate, but when he detects her strategy, he chases her around a table, and when she reaches for the door, he manages to grab her at the doorway. Suddenly, the camera cuts away, leading us to believe that he succeeds in his capture and she fails in her escape. Moreover, while the bedroom represents a private space, for Holiday/Ross it is problematic because this is where her dreams are nearly destroyed due to the violence inflicted on her personhood. More than this, the bedroom is a contradictory space, representing crisis and even deviance, given the elderly man's invasion into the adolescent's private space; his violation of her body represents the psychological and physiological trauma the character endures.

Bedroom Space in the Autobiography: Site of Struggle

Both the film and the autobiography acknowledge the sexual abuse the singer endured, but in her autobiography, Holiday describes how she subverted an attempted rape (in a similarly confining space). Further, in direct contrast to the film, she not only retaliates but is rescued. Attesting to how she achieves subjectivity during this episode, Holiday reveals, "My mother and a policeman broke down the door. I'll never forget that night. Even if you're a whore, you don't want to be raped.... It's the worst thing that can happen to a woman."[80] In her autobiography, Holiday's resistance, rescue, and defiance toward sexual abuse demonstrates how she challenged confinement and restriction; she achieves agency and refuses to be victimized. While the biopic constructs Holiday/Ross as a victim, in her autobiography, Holiday challenges such victimization. In the film, the bedroom space of adolescent Holiday/Ross transitions from utopian to traumatic space, whereas the autobiography depicts the bedroom as a transcendent, defiant, self-defining space. Yet both the autobiography and the biopic show that Holiday faced challenges not only in private spaces such as the bedroom but in institutional spaces, such as the prison, as well.

DEVIANT SPACES

Prison Space On Screen: Reduced to Confinement

When *Lady Sings the Blues* (film) opens, Holiday/Ross is fingerprinted, photographed, and escorted to a prison cell (a deviant space) with guards who struggle to hold her upright as her intoxicated body contorts and she attempts to retain some level of consciousness in her delirious state. Holiday/Ross is carried to a cell, where she is locked in solitary confinement and collapses to the floor while her head jerks back and forth; lying on the floor, she screams and cries out while her eyes widen to stare at the ceiling. The overhead camera shot provides spectators with a picture of the disoriented woman that is in stark contrast to the magnanimous, sultry, seductive, and beautiful image Holiday radiated off screen. This introduction to Holiday/Ross is indicative of how the film reduces the artist to her addiction rather than defining her in relation to her art, notoriety, and acclaim. Because the film unfolds through a series of flashbacks, this opening scene, which represents the end of her life rather than its beginning, restricts the talented jazz artist to this deviant space and uses her failings to define her. Since Holiday/Ross is marked in this way, her imprisonment in the film constitutes a deviant space where "those . . . individuals whose behavior is deviant in relation to the required mean or norm are placed."[81] However, the multiple modes of deviant heterotopias are pertinent to the autobiography's depiction of Holiday (the person), who is relegated to this deviant and contradictory space, because here her incarceration both enslaves and, not to glamorize prison life, liberates her from the hostile world outside.

Prison Space in the Autobiography: Asserts Humanity in Confinement

Subverting the prison space in her autobiography, Holiday challenges and contests the space of her incarceration. First, "she describes herself as someone who is not deserving of criminal action but of medical attention"[82] since her addiction is responsible for her imprisonment. Second, unlike the film, she defies this deviant space when she implies that her addiction should not define her. Consistent with these views, biographer O'Meally believes, "Her illness was not just drug addiction but her predicament as a supremely sensitive person who lived in a crassly indifferent world."[83] Admittedly, Holiday was arrested for drug possession, but in the autobiography, she addresses her incarceration. Holiday insists that in response to a prison guard who made it clear she would not receive favors, the singer demonstrated her agency in adamantly declaring that she did not expect favors despite her circumstances. Holiday explains:

> But I was talking about human kindness and she knew it. Sure, I'd been busted again. And I was in jail. But nothing she could say or do could bug me. This went for the whole crew—the fuzz who busted in my hotel room, the magistrate sitting on his bench at dawn waiting for me to [arrive] . . . the police inspector putting out big stories to the papers, the cameramen flashing those bulbs in the face of my little two-pound Chihuahua Pepi as he led me into the clink on his leash.[84]

Holiday clearly asserts her humanity even at this low point in her career, whereas the film defines the artist in relation to the restrictive or deviant spaces that deny her subjectivity. Therefore, while Holiday/Ross (the character) is reduced to such spaces on screen, in the autobiography Holiday (the person) contests these spaces and reframes her own narrative. Holiday's response speaks to what scholar Katherine McKittrick terms "the unresolved geographies of black femininity,"[85] whereby the Black subject engages in resistance and characterizes prison as a place to challenge her dispossession. Moreover, in contrast to the autobiography, the film's emphasis on prison as a restriction also appears in its depiction of the brothel and the bus, spaces that receive far more attention on screen than in the autobiography.

SPACES DEVELOPED ON SCREEN:
BROTHEL (DEVIANT SPACE) AND BUS (CRISIS SPACE)

The virtual erasure of the brothel and bus scenes in the autobiography perhaps suggests Holiday's intent to avoid returning to places of pain and trauma; it might reflect her desire to control her narrative/image or exemplify her resistance to white males disempowering her—an accomplished Black performer. Whatever led her to decenter these spaces in her autobiography, the brothel and the bus are featured in the Hollywood biopic and thus deserve discussion.

Brothel Space On Screen: Propels Escape

The prison marks a deviant space, yet the brothel to which Holiday/Ross is exposed as an adolescent is no less deviant or oppressive. In the film, Holiday/Ross is reduced to working as a maid at a brothel before she begins to actualize her dream of becoming a nightclub performer. The brothel constitutes a deviant space in which women engage in prostitution, and although Holiday/Ross is an adolescent and does not necessarily work as a prostitute, the film suggests that this could or would be her destiny if she fails to become a nightclub singer. In the film, the brothel constitutes a deviant (and contradictory) space that is an integral part of Holiday's life story, but in her autobiography, Holiday empowers herself to tell her story without making the brothel significant. In the biopic, the brothel parallels the bus in that both are traumatic spaces; the brothel signifies body trauma, while the bus represents racial trauma.

Bus Space On Screen: Scene of Racial Hostility

As visualized on screen, Holiday/Ross frequently travels with an all-white band on a bus, a vehicle that becomes indicative of a crisis space. However, when white members of the anti-Black Ku Klux Klan attack the vehicle for transporting this Black female singer alongside white male musicians during an era of racial segregation, the bus becomes politicized, traumatizing, and explosive. At

Billie Holiday (Diana Ross) is protected by band leader Reg Hanley (James Callahan) when the Ku Klux Klan attacks the bus and surrounds it with intimidating signs.

the same time, the bus demonstrates that Holiday/Ross goes from an unknown artist (without a band) to a known artist (with an all-white band), yet this is not to imply that her association with the white band marks her ascension to stardom. The bus symbolizes not only her transition as an artist but also a crisis space since it signals a turning point in her career wherein Holiday/Ross traverses from white acceptance (band members embrace her) to white rejection (Klan members and others reject her).

Holiday/Ross receives white acceptance and protection from the band members, but once the bus stops, she experiences white rejection from a racially hostile world, as when she is not allowed to dine with her fellow musicians, denied access to public facilities, and disavowed occupancy of white spaces. It is not only that Holiday/Ross is denied acceptance among whites outside the bus, but the intimidation tactics of the KKK deter other whites from embracing this Black performing artist since they are determined to enforce the violence of the segregated order and sabotage any possibility for Black acceptance. Thus, the bus becomes a crisis space and a contradictory/contested space that provides the singer with an opportunity to expand her talent but, at the same time, is one in which Holiday/Ross is subjected to racial violence and the singer's talent is exploited to build the white band's reputation.

In one scene, having been denied access to public facilities due to Jim Crow laws, Holiday/Ross exits the bus to relieve herself and witnesses a lynched Black body hanging from a tree. The lynching symbolizes the hatred whites held for Black life, especially Black males. The incident propels her to popularize the lynching song "Strange Fruit," and, more importantly, the scene reflects the trauma she endures and from which she cannot escape. Of course, descending into a world of racial hostility fuels her self-harming behavior, as when she resorts to alcohol and drugs to self-medicate. On screen, the bus space exemplifies the racial trauma Holiday/Ross suffers and explains how she might have internalized this violence, just as the brothel exemplifies the exploitation of women's bodies, another source of trauma. While the biopic graphically visualizes these episodes, Holiday minimizes both types of traumatizing experience in her autobiography. The film's depiction of spaces that are elided in the autobiography complicates representations of Holiday despite her efforts to narrativize her own story and life.

CONCLUSION

This chapter explores how *Lady Sings the Blues* (the film) chronicles Holiday's life relative to her autobiography, making the case that because of her gender, indisputable talent, tragic death, and oppositional behavior, her narrative became appropriate for screen adaptation, even though the reproduction reflected biopic conventions at odds with Holiday's autobiography. Despite the film's limited ability to represent Holiday, the crisis and deviant spaces depicted in both the biopic and autobiography begin to unveil the complexity associated with Holiday's vision of herself. Yet, more often than not, the biopic denies Holiday's complex subjectivity—an outcome that Holiday's fraught relationship with Hollywood had caused her to predict.

When the film was released, many critics recognized that the biopic complicates Holiday's image without offering deeper insight into the artist or surrounding society. For example, *Baltimore Afro-American*'s reviewer enumerates the film's faults, which include the film's "portrayal of complex human conditions without assigning any rank of importance to them and without any meaningful explanation of the causes and effects of the conditions. It emphasizes spectacle rather than thought."[86] This reviewer continues, "Ross is a fine, entertaining singer. But the choice of a fine singer without any acting experience to portray a complex human being who happens to be a singer is itself a typical Nothingness decision."[87] *New Yorker* magazine critic Pauline Kael contends that the film fails "to do justice to the musical life of . . . Holiday" and neglects to exemplify "what made her a star, much less, what made her an artist."[88] Moreover, Kael characterizes the picture as "factually . . . a fraud" even while proclaiming it delivers "emotionally."[89] She insists that the film "avoids the complexity of the race issues in [Holiday's] life, making her strictly a victim."[90] Less critical, *Saturday Review*'s Arthur Knight believes:

> *Lady Sings the Blues* succeeds where so many others have failed because its script by Terence McCloy, Chris Clark, and Suzanne de Passe—never tries to whitewash. It succeeds also because director Sidney Furie and

cinematographer John Alonzo have a remarkable eye for the period and the place and a feeling for the nuances of their story. But most of all the film succeeds because singer Diana Ross . . . has so immersed herself in the Billie Holiday character that her total conviction suffuses the picture.[91]

New York Amsterdam News's James P. Murray opines, "The sprawling document is a landmark film of many firsts, produced with all the trademark spit and polish of a Motown stage act, yet alternately succeeding and failing."[92] Murray adds, "Generally, the casting is a strength that can only be faulted for ignoring at least a score of Black musicians who were so much a part of the songstress' career."[93] *New York Amsterdam News*'s Billie Rowe declares the picture is a "phony story about Billie Holiday . . . that's filled with more fiction than facts. . . . The whole thing really overlooked many people and places [that] added spice to the life and time of Billie Holiday. . . . The biggest wonderment in musical circles is h'cum the music was scored by [French musical composer] Michel Legrand" when so many African American composers could have served in this capacity.[94] Similarly critical, James Baldwin asserts, "The film that has been made is impeccably put together, with an irreproachable professional polish, and has one or two nice moments. It has absolutely nothing to do with Billie, or with jazz, or any other kind of music, or the risks of an artist, or American life, or black life. . . . The script is as empty as a banana peel, and as treacherous."[95] But then Baldwin shifts from criticizing the picture to admonishing the cinema industry; he argues that the actors "might have been treated with more respect by the country to which they gave so much" and sarcastically notes, "but, then, we had to send telegrams to the mayor of New York City, asking him to call off the cops who surrounded Billie's bedside—looking for heroin in her ice cream—and let the lady die in peace."[96] Here, Baldwin exposes the authorities who attempted to arrest Holiday in the hospital where she was being treated prior to her death.[97] However, he further critiques the film and remarks:

> For indeed, the most exasperating aspects of *Lady Sings the Blues*, for me, is that the three principals [Ross, Williams, and Pryor] are, clearly, ready, willing, and able to stretch out and go a distance not permitted by the film. And, even within this straitjacket, they manage marvelous moments, and a truth which is not in the script is sometimes glimpsed through them. Diana Ross, clearly, respected Billie too much to try to imitate her.[98]

Despite the film's mixed reception and its inability to capture Holiday's complexity, the picture reignited appeal for this artist, introduced her to a later generation of viewers, fostered her continuing legacy, and provided an exciting (though somewhat distorted) visualization of the artist. However, it is through her autobiography that Holiday has a voice and empowers herself to exert some control over her image. Furthermore, it is through the autobiography that she resists the restrictions imposed, attempts to achieve agency, and "talks back" to a racially oppressive society. It is her autobiography that suggests why she refused to be "somebody's damn maid" and how she created a destiny that utilized her musical talent and captured the essence of her personhood: a musical genius who exhibited brilliance as a jazz artist and possessed exceptional vocalisms whose execution still haunts, disturbs, intrigues, and fascinates through her image, which continues to circulate in the public imaginary.

Notes

1. Billie Holiday and William Dufty, *Lady Sings the Blues* (Garden City, NY: Doubleday, 1956); I also referenced other editions of Holiday's biography, i.e., Billie Holiday and William Dufty, *Lady Sings the Blues* (London: Barrie & Jenkins, 1973); Donald Clarke, *Billie Holiday: Wishing on the Moon* (Cambridge, MA: Da Capo Press, 2002), 395.

2. George H. Lewis, "Lady in Satin: Billie Holiday and the Invention of Identity," *Popular Music and Society* 18, no. 4 (1994): 97.

3. Lewis, "Lady in Satin," 97.

4. Robert O'Meally, *Lady Day: The Many Faces of Billie Holiday* (New York: Arcade Publishing, 1991), 197; Farah Jasmine Griffin, *If You Can't Be Free, Be a Mystery* (New York: Free Press, 2001), 50. Griffin claims the biography is not a life story of Eleanora Fagan and quite possibly is not the story of Billie Holiday, but Griffin insists "it is a story of Lady Day."

5. Miles M. Jefferson, "The Blues I Got to Sing," *Phylon* (1940–1956) 17, no. 4 (4th quarter, 1956): 398–99.

6. Vera D. Hunton, "Miss Holiday Tries Again," *Journal of Negro Education* 26, no. 2 (Spring 1957): 171.

7. Gilbert Millstein, "Troubled Song," *New York Times*, July 15, 1956, 162.

8. Peter Kramer and Yannis Tzioumakis, eds., *The Hollywood Renaissance: Revisiting American Cinema's Most Celebrated Era* (New York: Bloomsbury Academic Press, 2018), xiii–xviii.

9. Maria DeGuzman, University of North Carolina at Chapel Hill, reviewed parts of the essay and made recommendations (May 2022). Others such as Philip Jeter, Tanya Shields (volume contributor), and Michael Figueroa provided thoughtful suggestions.

10. Michel Foucault and Jay Miskowiec, "Of Other Spaces," *Diacritics* 16, no. 1 (Spring 1986): 26.

11. Dennis Bingham, "I Do Want to Live!" *Cinema Journal* 38, no. 3 (Spring 1999): 3.

12. Bingham, "I Do Want to Live!" 3.

13. Gary Storhoff, "'Strange Fruit': *Lady Sings the Blues* as a Crossover Film," *Journal of Popular Film and Television* 30, no. 2 (2002): 112.

14. O'Meally, *Lady Day*, 168. Historically, Black women were outside the Cult of True Womanhood because enslaved women worked and did not have the privilege of remaining in the domestic sphere.

15. Bingham, "I Do Want to Live!" 22. According to Bingham, "Male filmmakers can tell a female protagonist's story without forcing it into patriarchal structures," but whether or not this film manages to do so is not the essay's primary focus.

16. Griffin, *If You Can't Be Free, Be a Mystery*, 33.

17. Griffin, *If You Can't Be Free, Be a Mystery*, 33.

18. John Szwed, *Billie Holiday: The Musician and The Myth* (New York: Viking, 2015), 53.

19. Bingham, "I Do Want to Live!" 5.

20. Bingham, "I Do Want to Live!" 5.

21. Griffin, *If You Can't Be Free, Be a Mystery*, 46.

22. Clarke, *Billie Holiday*, 396–98.

23. Clarke, *Billie Holiday*, 399.

24. Holiday and Dufty, *Lady Sings the Blues*, 10. Billie Dove was a white actress who appeared in silent and sound pictures. She was cast in *The Black Pirate* (Albert Parker, 1926) and *The Marriage Clause* (Lois Weber, 1926); she became one of the highest-grossing actresses at the box office, exceeding well-known peers such as Mary Pickford, Greta Garbo, and Clara Bow. Denise Lowe, *An Encyclopedic Dictionary of Women in Early American Films, 1895–1930* (New York: Hawthorne Press, 2005), 179–80.

25. Holiday and Dufty, *Lady Sings the Blues*, 52.

26. Clarke, *Billie Holiday*, 83.

27. Larry Richards, *African American Films through 1959: A Comprehensive, Illustrated Filmography* (Jefferson, NC: McFarland, 1998), 169.

28. Holiday and Dufty, *Lady Sings the Blues*, 52.

29. Susan Delson, *Soundies and the Changing Image of Black Americans On Screen: One Dime at a Time* (Bloomington: Indiana University Press, 2021), 55.

30. O'Meally, *Lady Day*, 117.

31. O'Meally, *Lady Day*, 120–21.

32. Arthur Knight, *Disintegrating the Musical: Black Performance and American Musical Film* (Durham, NC: Duke University Press, 2002), 213.

33. Szwed, *Billie Holiday*, 56–58.

34. Bruce Boyd Raeburn, "The Storyville Exodus Revisited, or Why Louis Armstrong Didn't Leave in November 1917, Like the Movie Said He Did," *Southern Quarterly* 52, no. 2 (Winter 2015): 10.

35. See Raeburn's discussion of the myth regarding why jazz musicians departed Storyville in his essay "The Storyville Exodus Revisited," 10–31.

36. Soundtrack credits for *New Orleans* indicate that Holiday sings "Endie" in Paris, but in the film, Louis Armstrong sings the song when his band tours Paris and he is reunited with Miralee. Apparently, Holiday's version of the song was deleted from the film's final version.

37. Holiday and Dufty, *Lady Sings the Blues*, 124–25.

38. Holiday and Dufty, *Lady Sings the Blues*, 125.

39. Holiday and Dufty, *Lady Sings the Blues*, 126.

40. Holiday and Dufty, *Lady Sings the Blues*, 126.

41. Holiday and Dufty, *Lady Sings the Blues*, 127.

42. Stuart Nicholson, *Billie Holiday* (Boston: Northeastern University Press, 1995), 153.

43. Donald Bogle, *Blacks in American Films and Television: An Illustrated Encyclopedia* (New York: Simon & Schuster, 1988), 153.

44. O'Meally, *Lady Day*, 145.

45. Nicholson, *Billie Holiday*, 152–53.

46. O'Meally, *Lady Day*, 145.

47. Szwed, *Billie Holiday*, 60–62. Szwed reports that Herbert Biberman, screenwriter for *New Orleans*, was one of the Hollywood Ten and that when he was called to testify before the House Un-American Activities Committee, this resulted in his imprisonment. Holiday stated in his defense, "He should have shown them *New Orleans*. With all that Uncle Tom stuff in it, and his name on it as one of the authors, he could have beat that mother-huggin' rap." Szwed claims that Black singer Ethel Waters's voice was dubbed for one of Holiday's songs, but the soundtrack credits for the film do not mention Waters, https://www.imdb.com/title/tt0039655/fullcredits/?ref_=tt_ql_cl.

48. Sherrie Tucker, "'White Woman' as Jazz Collector in *New Orleans* (1947)," *Newsletter—Institute for Studies in American Music* 35, no. 1 (Fall 2005): 2.

49. Tucker, "'White Woman' as Jazz Collector in *New Orleans* (1947)," 2.

50. Tucker, "'White Woman' as Jazz Collector in *New Orleans* (1947)," 13.

51. Tucker, "'White Woman' as Jazz Collector in *New Orleans* (1947)," 13.

52. Tucker, "'White Woman' as Jazz Collector in *New Orleans* (1947)," 13.

53. Richards, *African American Films through 1959*, 165–59.

54. Clarke, *Billie Holiday*, 420.

55. Clarke, *Billie Holiday*, 400. Dorothy Dandridge was selected to recreate Holiday on screen, and *Baltimore Afro-American* columnist Dolores Calvin proposed that Dandridge was "a natural for the role, though much thinner, she is a look-alike of Billie, and being a singer herself, she could more easily adapt to the mannerisms than a straight actress." Dolores Calvin, "Dorothy Dandridge Best Bet to Do Lady Day's Life Story," *Baltimore Afro-American*, October 17, 1959, 15. According to the *American Film Institute Catalog*, Lester Cowan along with Anthony Mann had planned to make a version of Holiday's life with Dandridge as the protagonist. "*Lady Sings the Blues*," *American Film Institute Catalog*, https://catalog.afi.com/Catalog/moviedetails/54377.

56. Clarke, *Billie Holiday*, 400.

57. Clarke, *Billie Holiday*, 400. According to Clarke, Ava Gardner may have given Holiday a Chihuahua. Clarke, *Billie Holiday*, 341–42.

58. James Baldwin, *The Price of the Ticket: Collected Nonfiction, 1948–1985* (New York: St. Martin's/Marek Press, 1985), 622.

59. Szwed, *Billie Holiday*, 30, 65.

60. Holiday and Dufty, *Lady Sings the Blues* (London: Barrie & Jenkins, 1973), 103. Note that different printed editions of the autobiography include different page numbers.

61. Louie Robinson, "*Lady Sings the Blues*: Diana Ross Stars in New Movie about Legendary Billie Holiday," *Ebony* 28, no. 1 (November 1972): 40.

62. Robinson, "*Lady Sings the Blues*," 40, 38.

63. Daniel Kremer, *Sidney J. Furie: Life and Films* (Lexington, KY: The University Press of Kentucky, 2015), 156.

64. Kremer, *Sidney J. Furie*, 156–57.

65. Kremer, *Sidney J. Furie*, 156.

66. Kremer, *Sidney J. Furie*, 157.

67. Roger Ebert, "*Lady Sings the Blues* Movie Review," RogerEbert.com, January 1, 1972, http://www.rogerebert.com/reviews/lady-sings-the-blues-1972.

68. Bogle, *Blacks in American Films and Television*, 126–27.

69. Griffin, *If You Can't Be Free, Be a Mystery*, 59.

70. Robinson, "*Lady Sings the Blues*," 43.

71. "To Honor the Star: *Lady Sings the Blues*," *Chicago Defender*, Daily Edition, March 15, 1973, 15; "*Lady Sings the Blues*," *American Film Institute Catalog*; "*Lady Sings the Blues* Is Fastest Selling Album in Motown's History," *Pittsburgh Courier*, December 30, 1972, 19; "*Lady Sings the Blues* Wins NAACP Image Award," *Atlanta Daily World*, November 23, 1972, 3; "Top Black Films of All Times," *Ebony* 54, no. 1 (November 1998): 154; and "*Lady Sings the Blues* Is Biggest Hit," *Chicago Daily Defender*, Daily Edition, December 14, 1972, 17. Ross was nominated for Best Actress; Terrence McCloy, Chris Clark, and Suzanne de Passe for Best Story and Screenplay; Gil Askey for Best Scoring; Bob Mackie, Ray Aghayan, and Norma Koch for Best Costume Design; and Carl Anderson for Best Art Direction. The film lost in the categories of Best Actress, Best Art Direction, and Best Music.

72. Szwed insists Holiday's autobiography "was an act of redemption, an attempt to assert her dignity, as she always did, within a society that had already condemned her to a form of ignominy." Szwed, *Billie Holiday*, 52.

73. Foucault and Miskowiec, "Of Other Spaces," 24.

74. Foucault and Miskowiec, "Of Other Spaces," 25.

75. Holiday and Dufty, *Lady Sings the Blues*, 32.

76. Holiday and Dufty, *Lady Sings the Blues*, 76–77.

77. Holiday and Dufty, *Lady Sings the Blues*, 182.

78. Rhiannon Scharnhorst, "Composing at the Kitchen Table," *GradfoodStudies* 6, no. 1 (June 16, 2019): 2, 4, 7, https://gradfoodstudies.org/2019/06/16/composing-at-the-kitchen-table/. Tanya L. Shields directed my attention to the literature on Black women and the kitchen space.

79. Foucault and Miskowiec, "Of Other Spaces," 24.

80. Holiday and Dufty, *Lady Sings the Blues*, 13.

81. Foucault and Miskowiec, "Of Other Spaces," 25.

82. O'Meally, *Lady Day*, 172.

83. O'Meally, *Lady Day*, 172.

84. Holiday and Dufty, *Lady Sings the Blues*, 200.

85. Katherine McKittrick, *Demonic Grounds: Black Women and the Cartographies of Struggle* (Minneapolis: University of Minnesota Press, 2006), 69.

86. "Movie Review: *Lady Sings the Blues*," *Baltimore Afro-American*, November 18, 1972, 11.

87. "Movie Review," 11.

88. Pauline Kael, "The Current Cinema: Pop Versus Jazz," *New Yorker* 48, no. 37 (November 4, 1972): 152.

89. Kael, "Current Cinema," 152.

90. Kael, "Current Cinema," 154.

91. Arthur Knight, "*SR* Reviews: Films—Two Educations," *Saturday Review* 55, no. 46 (November 11, 1972): 81.

92. James P. Murray, "*Lady Sings the Blues* Is a Hit! Diana Ross Scores in First Movie," *New York Amsterdam News*, October 21, 1972, D1.

93. Murray, "*Lady Sings the Blues* Is a Hit!" D1.

94. Billy Rowe, "Billy Rowe's Notebook," *New York Amsterdam News*, October 28, 1972, C8.

95. Baldwin, *Price of the Ticket*, 620.

96. Baldwin, *Price of the Ticket*, 622.

97. Clarke, *Billie Holiday*, 438. Baldwin, among others, signed a petition directed toward the mayor of New York to prevent law enforcement officials from harassing Holiday during her hospitalization for narcotic violations while she lay on her death bed. They believed hospitals should treat addicts in a humane manner rather than assuming an accusatory position.

98. Baldwin, *Price of the Ticket*, 622–23.

Part IV

Black Literature's Challenge
for Screen Adaptations

Chapter 7

BURBANKING BIGGER AND BETTE THE BITCH

Native Son and *In This Our Life* at Warner Bros.

ELIZABETH BINGGELI

It surprises no one that Richard Wright's novel *Native Son* (1940) was not adapted to film by the Warner Bros. studio. In fact, an analysis of the novel's rejection by Hollywood may seem an exercise in the obvious: Hollywood studios of the classical studio era (1928–1948) were oligopolies invested in producing conservative films thought to be universally consumable. Wright's novel, a fierce critique of the bloody consequences of white racism, seems hardly the kind of presold property for which Hollywood was looking. But rather than accept studio racism as given, I wish here to begin to pry it apart—to interrogate the lesser-known industrial practices that worked to create the well-known industrial product. To begin this interrogation, I will first analyze studio archival records related to the reception of *Native Son* and Ann Petry's *The Street* (1946) to demonstrate the racializing effect of the studio adaptation strategy called "burbanking." Next, I will examine a novel that the studio did see fit to adapt, Ellen Glasgow's Pulitzer Prize–winning *In This Our Life* (1941); like *Native Son*, *In This Our Life* features a Black chauffeur accused of murder and a white woman determined to disregard social restraints on her sexual behavior. Finally, I will argue that the studio culture that rejected plots like *Native Son* and *The Street* and accepted plots like *In This Our Life* gave rise to a specific type of demonized white female star, best exemplified by Warner Bros.'s own Bette Davis.[1]

David Bordwell has shown that the narrative logic of classical Hollywood cinema centers on the psychology and actions of a protagonist who responds to conflict through a chain of cause-and-effect events.[2] The story is generally incited by a temporary threat to social order (an injustice, a crime, a misunderstanding) perpetrated by an inappropriately self-interested antagonist; the story progresses through the actions that the protagonist takes to thwart the antagonist to restore social order. When the studios chose to purchase an existing story, that story would be adapted to this narrative model, to a greater or lesser degree. As Nick Roddick has argued about Warner Bros. film production in the 1930s, "A standard code of practice was adopted in terms of decision-taking, planning, scripting, shooting, editing, publicity, and release. This necessarily involved fitting the variable story material into as regular a narrative pattern and cinematic style as possible, with the crux of the plot . . . illuminated through a central character."[3] If a story presented a corrupt social order as the central character's problem, Hollywood would often resituate the corruption within a single individual, preferring to critique "bad seeds" over bad systems. Because the Warner Bros. West Coast office was in Burbank, California, and this self-styled studio of "social conscience" was particularly fond of this kind of narrative adaptation, the trade newspaper *Variety* dubbed the practice "burbanking." As Roddick and Tino Balio have argued, burbanking had the conservative effect of maintaining current social order because injustice was portrayed as a result of individual villainy that would likely succumb to individual heroism.[4] I would add more specifically that this adaptation practice, which functioned as an ideological narrative technology, rendered Black protagonists unrepresentable in studio-era films.

James Snead argues that in "*all* Hollywood film portrayals of blacks . . . the political is never far from the sexual, for it is both as a political and as a sexual threat that the black skin appears on screen."[5] Of course, the *disappearance* of black skin from the screen had its political and sexual effects as well: conservative studio-era cinema cannot help but be marked by the radical race narratives that it attempts to suppress.

WARNER BROS. READS AND REJECTS *NATIVE SON* AND *THE STREET*

Wright finished a typescript of *Native Son* on June 10, 1939, and less than two weeks later, Paul Reynolds (Wright's literary agent) submitted this version of the novel to Warner Bros.'s New York office; reflecting common practice, the novel was reviewed before it was published.[6] Warner Bros. was not the only studio to consider Wright's work, but its exceptionally complete story department archive provides an illuminating glimpse into industry-wide source acquisition practices.[7] The studio had already reviewed Wright's *Uncle Tom's Children: Four Novellas* (1938), "Bright and Morning Star" (1939), and "Almos' a Man" (1940) and would eventually review "The Man Who Lived Underground" (1944), "Early

Days in Chicago" (1945), *The Outsider* (1953), *Savage Holiday* (1954), and *The Long Dream* (1958).[8] The studio would also consider unpublished Wright works, including a version of *Black Hope*, a story of racial "passing" as well as Wright's only novel with a female protagonist, and *Melody Limited*, an original screenplay about the Fisk University Jubilee Singers.[9] None of Wright's work, however, garnered as much studio attention as *Native Son*.

Warner Bros. story analyst Irving Deakin furnished his superiors with a report on *Native Son* on June 28, 1939. After summarizing the story in some detail, Deakin prepared a memorandum that broadly sketched his impressions of the novel:

> Harper has, as an important novel on their Fall list, a work by Richard Wright entitled NATIVE SON, a report on which I am handing you herewith. It is a fine and powerful novel, telling, in fictional form, the spiritual problem and struggle of the American negro in the face of the restricting white civilization in the United States. Mr. Wright's central character, a negro boy, in revolting against the un-understood restrictions put upon his life in the slums of Chicago, kills a white girl by accident, is caught after a short flight and brought to trial. Only a communist lawyer seems to understand the motives which had prompted him; but a plea for mercy to the judge avails nothing, and the boy awaits death with some satisfaction in the knowledge that for his soul, at least, there would be no further suffering, once he had given his life in the electric chair.[10]

In just this short introduction to Deakin's report, the problems of burbanking Wright's story begin to reveal themselves. At first glance, the protagonist, Bigger Thomas, is depicted as engaged in a psychological "struggle" with forces greater than himself that compel him to action; in this sense, Deakin relates a studio-ready story. On greater inspection, however, we see that the struggle is not Bigger's alone but one common to the "American negro." As such, the story is propelled not by the choices of a purely autonomous individual but by the condition of a social group.

Deakin does not depict this condition in typical burbanking language— as a problematic deviation from an ideal social order perpetrated by an evil individual. Bigger's treatment at the hands of whites is not in fact described as unjust or wrong or immoral; rather, his oppression is a mere "restriction" that is "un-understood." Deakin chooses here to situate the narrative problem not with the oppressors but with the oppressed, whose "spirit" suffers apparently as much from a lack of comprehension of his social situation as from the situation itself.

Despite Wright's own interest in potential theatrical and film adaptations of *Native Son*, he was understandably ambivalent about these venues and predicted how the book might be received. Given "the limitations of the screen and stage in America," he wondered, "can such a book be done in a light that presents Bigger Thomas as a *human being*?"[11] For good reason, Wright's anxiety focused on the depiction of Bigger's "humanity," a common point of contention in the reception of the novel. From Dorothy Canfield Fisher's infamous introduction to the Book-of-the-Month Club edition that likens Bigger to a neurotic lab rat, to James Baldwin's condemnation of Bigger as "Uncle Tom's descendant" embedded in a story haunted by "its rejection of life [and] the human being," critics have been compelled to place the character on a continuum of authentic humanity, where his ability to determine his own fate is measured against his helplessness within social constructs.[12] It can, of course, be argued that with the creation of Bigger, Wright was not capitulating to a racist culture that opposed blackness and individuality; instead, he was graphically illustrating the psychic effects of such an opposition. Among the critics who defended Wright's depiction of the human yet socially constructed Bigger was Alain Locke, who made the point that individualized characters able to transcend social conditions like racism are likely the figures least oppressed by those conditions.[13] A critical or industrial valuation of the "individuality" of a character may be, therefore, merely a code for privileging whiteness. In his monograph, *How Bigger Was Born*, Wright describes his most famous protagonist as a symbol of the bullying, rebellious, defiant, and fascistic tendencies in humankind, Black and white, American and foreign; he creates this symbolic rendering not to strip the character of his humanity but to untether the concept of humanity from the fantasy of unmediated self-determination.[14] It is this fantasy, however, that provides Hollywood with its narrative foundation and creates the need for the burbanking adaptation strategy.

Ross Pudaloff has argued that it is, ironically, the mass media as depicted within the novel that strips Bigger of an "inherent character."[15] Wright is careful, Pudaloff contends, to link Bigger's fate to his obsession with his own representation in media, failing to "distinguish an authentic personal identity from an identity formed by mass culture."[16] Pudaloff makes the case that Bigger's violence, especially against Bessie, is shaped by an emulation of the 1930s hardboiled "tough guy" in film and popular fiction. Because Bigger performs as the mobster-hero, he lives his life "as if it were taking place upon a movie screen, [participating] in the dehumanization of self."[17] Warner Bros. was a primary agent in the popularization of the tough guy in films like *Little Caesar* (Mervyn LeRoy, 1930) and *The Public Enemy* (William A. Wellman, 1931). If Hollywood filmmaking as depicted within the novel is indeed one of the significant forces that robs Bigger of his individuality, how would Hollywood then treat this character, one partially of its own creation, one truly a "native son" of the studios' cultural apparatus?

In his report, Deakin worries that "the technique of [*Native Son*] enables the author to explain much of the inner workings of the boy's mind—a thing which is, of course, difficult to do in pictures."[18] This assessment of the novel's technique is certainly accurate, as is a recognition of the limitations of cinema's visually based narrativity. But studio strategies for transforming a novel's interior monologues were familiar enough, including exteriorization through voiceover, action, or visual symbol. If a novel's reliance on interior monologues in fact presented an insurmountable obstacle to film adaptation, Warner Bros. would have never purchased Glasgow's ponderously psychological *In This Our Life*. Perhaps Deakin's problem with *Native Son*'s interior monologues was not their preponderance but their source: the "inner workings" of a Black man's mind. To adapt a textually represented psychology to a visual medium, the studio would, of course, need first to acknowledge the existence of that psychology and, in so doing, to confront Black male subjectivity.

Deakin asserts that his "instinct and experience [tell him] that this is probably not a subject which would interest us as picture material."[19] But he quickly hedges, declaring that *Native Son* "is, however, a novel with some powerful action, dramatic situations, and a really magnificent characterization in the person of the young negro boy."[20] Deakin might have struggled with an acknowledgment that while *Native Son* would be challenging if not impossible to burbank, the novel does follow a generic structure beloved by his studio at the time: the fugitive drama. The Warner Bros. romance with the fugitive began with the acclaimed film *I Am a Fugitive from a Chain Gang* (Mervyn LeRoy, 1932), an adaptation of Robert E. Burns's experiences as a down-and-out veteran trapped by circumstance into a life in a Georgia prison camp. His story in many ways resembles Bigger's: once escaped, the protagonist laments, "I hide in rooms all day and travel by night. No friends, no rest, no peace." Burns's narrative is also like *Native Son* in that a social system is implicated in the fate of the criminal protagonist. However, while once considered bold in its criticism of a part of the American penal system, the burbanked version of *I Am a Fugitive from a Chain Gang* is not. It suggests, in the words of Balio, "that if the chain gang is removed and the administration of justice in Georgia is reformed, all will be well. Moreover, by focusing on the plight of the protagonist, the film obscures such issues in the story as why the state of Georgia tolerated the chain-gang system, why the federal government turned its back on World War I veterans, and why the economy had turned sour."[21] By 1939, the year Deakin reported on *Native Son*, the studio had burbanked the fugitive genre even further: the 1939 Warner Bros. fugitive dramas *Each Dawn I Die* (William Keighley), *Dust Be My Destiny* (Lewis Seiler), and *They Made Me a Criminal* (Busby Berkeley) each deflected social responsibility for crime by making the white fugitive on the run for murder actually an innocent man wrongly accused. Like Bigger, these fugitives are positioned in conflict with a corrupt social system. But, unlike Bigger, they ultimately find the corruptions to be superficial and surmountable: justice recognizes their innocence in the end. Wright's novel would clearly provide no such miraculous exoneration and no return to a comfortable social order.

Indeed, Deakin contends that it is precisely "because [*Native Son's*] controversial idea presents a splendid social problem, and one worthy of serious treatment, my feeling is that it is the sort of thing which can be done much more dramatically in book form."[22] He continues:

> On the debit side, moreover, racial controversy crops up very strongly towards the end of the book; and for this reason, it is questionable to me whether such a picture would be either in good taste or even good business, for the author, in his brilliant courtroom speech, has implied that unless the white civilization of this country relaxes sufficiently to give underprivileged negroes their chance in the world for life, there lurks a possibility of another Civil War—but this time it would be a war of blacks against whites.[23]

Deakin's earlier vacillations are arrested here, and his warning to the studio is clear.

Deakin's report made its way to Irene Lee, a story editor who would later persuade the studio to purchase the rights to *Everybody Comes to Rick's*, the play that became the film *Casablanca* (Michael Curtiz, 1942). On the basis of Deakin's report, Lee rejected *Native Son* without comment on July 13, 1939. But Lee's history with the novel does not end there. After the rejection of *Native Son*, news soon reached the studio that the Book-of-the-Month Club was interested in the novel and that Harper had pushed the release date from fall 1939 to spring 1940 to allow Wright the time to make the club's required revisions (which, as I explain below, were considerable). When finally published in March 1940, the novel boasted such praise and sales that all of Hollywood was quickly persuaded to reconsider the property.

Amid the buzz generated by the release, Warner Bros. ordered a second review of *Native Son*—this time reading the published Book-of-the-Month Club version. Story analyst Alice Goldberg finished a new report on the novel by March 12, 1940. The synopsis reveals that Goldberg was influenced by the "lab rat" thesis of Fisher's newly added introduction. Goldberg's report functioned for the studio in much the same way that Fisher's introduction functioned for the book club readers: a white mediation for a white audience of a Black author's work. But rather than justifying *Native Son*, Goldberg, like Deakin, constructs in her report an elaborate, escalating case against studio

Native Son and *In This Our Life* at Warner Bros.

consumption of the novel. She begins, however, with praise: "This is a strong, beautifully written book and one of the best on the negro question I have ever read."[24] She then moves quickly to what she sees as the novel's dangers:

My opinion is that it is dynamite for the screen. It is not impossible, but fairly improbable, that this can get across on the screen with the honesty and the impact of the book. The grave danger is that if it misses at all, it is apt to have an exactly opposite effect, and to appear an anti-negro story. This, of course, would be bad policy and bad box office. Once again, I think it will be the most difficult job in the world to explain Bigger to a screen audience and make him sympathetic in terms of psychological and intellectual values, as the book does. For another, this method of presenting the book, could also be interpreted by an audience only as an anti-negro book. To repeat, this is a tremendously dramatic book, but for my money, very, very dangerous dynamite.[25]

A potential adaptation would be "bad policy" for revealing a less-than-ideal model of Black subjectivity and "bad business," perhaps, for revealing Black subjectivity at all. Here Goldberg performs what Thomas Cripps calls "the conscience-liberalism" of studio-era Hollywood, which strummed a "liberal tune while ratifying the status quo."[26] The studios were, for the most part, moving away from the grossest of Black stereotypes of the silent era but were at a loss as to what might stand in their place. Hollywood's "aversion to the racial contradictions in American life," Cripps writes, "reduced African Americans to absent, alibied for, dependent victims of marketing strategies aimed at profitable universality."[27] This "buttering [of] ideological bread on both sides" created a space in which a representation of a "false" Black subjectivity was unacceptably dishonest, and a representation of a "real" Black subjectivity was unacceptably reckless.[28]

Two months after the second Warner Bros. report was written, story editor Irene Lee traveled to Cuernavaca, Mexico, to pay Richard Wright a visit. Although Wright biographer Hazel Rowley identifies Lee as an agent of producer Samuel Goldwyn, she was more likely representing producer Hal Wallis and Warner Bros. at this meeting.[29] Lee visited while Wright was in the process of deciding whom he could trust with the stage rights and theatrical adaptation of the novel. According to Rowley, Lee had some influence on his eventual choice:

[Lee] put the case for [the Mercury Theatre's John] Houseman and [Orson] Welles.... Lee said he would be wiser to put *Native Son* on the stage before they thought about a movie, and there was some latitude in the choice of the person to write the script. Wright mentioned Paul Green, a white dramatist who said he was interested. Lee stressed that

Wright himself should have some input. Wright mentioned Ted Ward as a possible choice for Bigger Thomas. Lee was open to suggestions.[30]

Wright would eventually agree to begin a long and difficult collaboration with Paul Green for the Mercury Theatre stage adaptation. By suggesting that Wright stage the play before selling the film rights, Lee was likely hoping to use the stage as a testing ground before committing studio resources to what was clearly a commercially risky property. Despite Lee's enthusiasm for the play, *Native Son* was again rejected by Warner Bros. on May 24, 1940, shortly after Lee's return from Mexico. Yet the story department continued to watch the evolution of the Mercury Theatre production: it carefully collected news clippings about the play's progress and filed them away with the studio's reports on the novel. While in rehearsals, even the play's director, Orson Welles, considered mounting a film version for RKO. MGM and Fox also indicated an interest in the screen rights.

But after the play opened in March 1941, ticket sales were far less spectacular than had been expected. Rowley describes Hollywood's reaction: "After all the excited talk only one definite bid came in for the picture rights: Metro-Goldwyn-Mayer offered twenty-five thousand dollars to shoot the film with an all-white cast. Wright was horrified."[31] Despite its outrageousness, the possibility that a studio would "whitewash" a prominent Black novel was not unusual. Like MGM, Warner Bros. might have toyed with the idea of using an all-white cast for *Native Son*, as Goldberg's report might suggest: "The book is sufficiently dramatic to make it seem, perhaps, that its main thesis can be discarded, and a picture made based on its plot alone, overlooking the basic racial question, and psychological interpretation of the main character."[32] While Warner Bros. did not ultimately choose to pursue a whitewashed *Native Son*, the studio was not above such a strategy, as its review of Ann Petry's novel *The Street* (1946) suggests.

Warner Bros. story analyst Virginia Volland would, in fact, propose a whitewashing for Petry's novel *The Street* in 1946 and cite *Native Son* in her report. Volland commended Petry's "fast-moving, solidly constructed, and intensely engrossing" novel that "reads with the entertainment value of a whodunit . . . the most satisfactory thing about this author's writing is the feeling of authenticity and life that pervades the pages. This story is real . . . in spite of the fact that it is good entertainment."[33] This "reality" for Volland stems from the author's ability to address issues of race while still presenting the reader with an individuated protagonist; for Volland, it is this particular ability that distinguishes the novel from Wright's work:

One of the most impressive things about [*The Street*] is the treatment of the black/white relationship. Lutie is motivated as an individual, alive, complete, with a racial problem to face, indeed, but she is conceived as a human being, not as a protagonist of racial equality or inequality, as in *Native Son, Black Boy,* etc. It is a story about a woman who happens to be colored . . . and in that is part of its strength.[34]

Lutie is apparently preferred over Bigger because, unlike Wright's character, Petry's protagonist just "happens to be colored" in Volland's estimation; the social conflict of racism is readily excised then, and the character is easy to burbank. Volland continues, "Although one's first reaction is that this is not a book suitable for picture adaptation, because Lutie is a Negress, I believe that it would still hold if the heroine were white. The basic tragedy arises from the lack of money, and if circumstances were evolved that kept a white girl from earning enough to live on decently, the same chain of happenings could apply."[35] The story department at Warner Bros. was clearly operating under two specific assumptions when considering Black characters for studio representation: Black characters needed to be individuated and self-determining to function in burbanked narratives; and if Black characters were individuated and self-determining, they might as well be white.

Not everyone in the story department was as comfortable as Volland with the idea of a white Lutie. Story editor Tom Chapman commented in a memo, "Volland thinks that the girl [Lutie] could be white instead of colored, perhaps a member of a minority group, like the Poles or Shanty Irish. I suppose it is barely conceivable, but the strength of the story lies in its uncompromising presentation of the racial discrimination problem."[36] If Chapman was concerned about what would be left of Petry's novel after such a narrative lobotomy, his concerns did not prevent him from recommending *The Street* to his superiors five days later. His strategy in doing so is particularly revealing: "The author of this is not a Negro. The novel just won the Houghton Mifflin scholarship award. I think you'll find it interesting. Perhaps the woman has possibilities as a writer."[37] We cannot know if Chapman was trying to deceive the recipient of this memo (perhaps to get a less biased reading of the story) or if he truly believed that Petry was "not a Negro"—the later seems more likely, given that when he suggests that Petry would have "possibilities as a writer," he almost certainly means a studio staff writer—and on staff Petry's race would be known. For whatever reason, Chapman's tentative acceptance of a whitewashed *The Street* miraculously extends to the author herself. Apparently, both Lutie and Petry are "incidentally colored." Could this occurrence be attributed to the fact that, within cinematic narrative, race adheres to the Black female body differently than to the Black male body? If Black representation in studio-era cinema was structured around an anxiety about Black male/white female relationships, Black female characters would have no solid representational ground on which to stand, save for being transformed into white women.[38]

Wright understandably rejected the notion of a white Bigger Thomas, and in 1950 he chose to produce and star in the filmed version of *Native Son*.[39] What would—what could—a white Bigger Thomas look like? Such a fantastic transformation seems only laughable until we consider the possibility that the studios produced films like *In This Our Life* in lieu of a white Bigger Thomas. Could Glasgow's predatory villain Stanley Timberlake be the ready-made white Bigger Thomas that Hollywood really wanted?

IN THIS OUR LIFE: A PRE-BURBANKED NOVEL

In March 1943, Warner Bros. story analyst Lucy Land prepared a report on *Chocolate Sailor*, an original story submitted to the studio by Charles Leonard and Langston Hughes.[40] The report tells us that *Chocolate Sailor* charts the rise and fall of a Black chanteuse who leaves the home of her pastor father to pursue a glamorous night club life in the company of gamblers and racketeers; in the end, she realizes her true calling as a US Navy nurse ministering to her fiancé and other patriotic Black wounded soldiers in Guadalcanal. Land writes that "this story is bad, in spite of the honest but limited attempts of the Negro author, Langstan [*sic*] Hughes."[41] Charles Leonard, *Chocolate Sailor*'s white coauthor, apparently does not merit such an elaborate, and backhanded, comment. Land then admonishes *Chocolate Sailor* for exploiting "all the cheap and unattractive aspects of Negro life" and declares that as "our studio has always portrayed the Negro as a human being and not in the traditional subservient manner, we could never be interested in a story of this kind."[42] Land is careful to conclude her report by mentioning an instance when the studio *did* manage to successfully meet its standards of Black representation. Warner Bros., she contends, "stands high in the honor [roll] as an organization to improve racial relations and only recently has been awarded commendation for its outstanding contribution to Democracy by its portrayal of the Negro in 'In This Our Life.'"[43] Thus, Land affirms that the studio *is* interested in depicting Black people, that these depictions are consciously and constructively political (having the effect of improving race relations), and that the studio's shining example of its "contribution to Democracy" is director John Huston's 1942 adaptation of Glasgow's *In This Our Life*.

The fate of *Chocolate Sailor* aside, then, Land's report is useful because it suggests within the studio's discourse of the time a collectively understood figure of what we could call a "Warner Bros. Negro"—a narrative representation of blackness perceived by the studio as profitable. *In This Our Life*'s Parry Clay, as portrayed in the film by Ernest Anderson, is a diligent, polite chauffeur whose dreams are crushed when the scheming daughter of the white family he works for accuses him of killing a child in a hit-and-run accident.[44] He is ultimately exonerated by the patriarch of the white family but is forever psychologically broken.

Despite this ending, the character was welcomed by many Black audience members. One soldier stationed at Fort Bragg sent a postcard to the studio to express his gratitude for the film: "Please give us more pictures like this one, which depict Negroes as flesh and blood human beings, and not as clowns. Thank God you see the light. Thank you."[45] An officer of the Alpha Kappa Sorority wrote, "Our Sorority, composed of four thousand college and university Negro women, offers its heartfelt gratitude and appreciation for the splendid part assigned to Mr. Anderson in 'In This Our Life.'... The type of role portrayed by Mr. Anderson is a step toward the goal of portraying the Negro citizen as a 'normal human being.'"[46] Common in other letters to the studio was the sentiment of one letter writer that with *In This Our Life*, Warner Bros. had "taken a step in democratizing filmland."[47] Another fan promised, "Several million colored movie-goers will be watching future Warner [Bros.] productions with anticipation."[48] The executive editor of the *Pittsburgh Courier* declared:

> A very grievous side of the life of almost every colored American is exposed in the role of Parry Clay. The writer wishes to commend the company for its liberality and courage, recognizing as he does that the people . . . least want to see or hear the truth if it hurts. 'In This Our Life' is a contribution to Americanism; it is a nudge on the way to that better America.[49]

Even Walter White of the NAACP thanked Harry Warner for the "refreshing change" that the depiction of Parry Clay represented.[50] While some writers tempered their praise with criticism of the stereotypes that persisted in the film, the overwhelming response was one of gratitude for what was seen as a progressive step toward positive Black representation.

While acknowledging the barriers broken by Anderson's portrayal of Parry, one must wonder why this supposed representational revolution amounted to so little. The character falls neatly into the conservative role of the Black saint that K. Anthony Appiah describes as "the noble good-hearted black man or woman, friendly to whites, working-class but better educated than most working-class Americans, and oh so decent."[51] A Hollywood relative of the southern "pet negro" that Zora Neale Hurston describes, the Black saint works to satisfy liberal taste while still managing to deny Black subjectivity.[52] Parry's type of Black saint is the tragic mulatto and is described in the novel as a "delicate looking boy, very light in color. . . . Unlike the greater part of Negroes (if, indeed, he could be called a Negro) . . . he was discontented with his lot."[53] The novel suggests that this discontentment stemmed from his racial liminality. The "less colored [that Negroes] are," one of the novel's characters observes,

> the more inscrutable they become, until, when they have so nearly crossed the border line, like this boy Parry, they seem almost to speak another language, and to belong to another species than ours. . . . Even when he smiled, and he had a pleasant smile, there was a shadow of bewilderment—or was it apprehension?—in his expression. Was it . . . the bewilderment of being so nearly white? Or was it the darker apprehension of being so little black?[54]

Glasgow later writes that the "trouble with the boy was that he had no place anywhere."[55] To clarify the novelist's own racial theories, it is worth pointing out that she once praised Carl Van Vechten's *Nigger Heaven* (1926) for being

> the best argument in favor of African slavery that I have ever read. . . . What interested me tremendously [in the book] is the way the Negro reacts to the freedom of Harlem. Only in the father of Mary (a very appealing character) do I find the slightest trace of the Negro that I know. The serene fatalism, the dignity of manner, the spiritual power, all these qualities decayed, it appeared, with the peculiar institution.[56]

Glasgow biographer Susan Goodman describes the author's characters as toilers "within the context of a civilization she believed to be essentially uncivilized, one in which innocent souls suffer undeserved tragedies."[57] The novel's primary tragedies arise because the characters are presented as mere shadows of racist plantation tradition ideals: a poor and impotent white patriarch, a miserable Black servant who does not rejoice in his servility, and a white belle named Stanley who lies, schemes, and runs off with her sister's husband.

But instead of drawing studied conclusions about the decay of southern civility, many readers of Glasgow's novel simply relished the melodramas of husband snatching and racial scapegoating for their own sake and were especially drawn to Stanley, the novel's insatiable id. Glasgow was not pleased with this tendency: "I may confess to annoyance whenever the careless reader appears to regard the soulless little pleasure-seeker, Stanley, as the core of this book."[58] Glasgow's irritation at this "misreading" was extreme enough to lead her to compose *Beyond Defeat* (1966), a sequel to *In This Our Life*, which sought to excise the distracting Stanley from the family so that "careless readers" could no longer be swayed by her influence but would focus instead on the tragedy of the white patriarch.[59]

Where did this "Stanley symptom" come from, one that the author herself was unable to contain? Goodman reveals that the car accident in *In This Our Life* was based on an actual experience involving Glasgow's family: a nephew of hers killed a Black pedestrian in a car accident. If fictionalized more or less as it had occurred in Glasgow's family, the incident would likely be read as Glasgow herself interpreted it: as yet "another assault on a besieged race."[60] Glasgow might have made the white male character such a loathsome individual that his actions would be seen as unrepresentative of whiteness in general, but she allows her male characters in *In This Our Life* significant, if impotent, nobility. Rather than a white man, then, the driver in the novel is recast by Glasgow as a loathsome white woman; the Black male victim of the accident then becomes the Black male victim of the white woman's lies. As revised by Glasgow, the white man becomes not the perpetrator of violence against the Black man but the savior who rescues the Black man from white female predation. Glasgow's reconstruction of the accident provides a miraculous outlet for white liberal guilt about the oppression of Black men without incriminating white men. To return to the earlier question about why the supposedly revolutionary character of Parry amounted to so little, one can answer that the social critique implied by Parry's fate is neatly contained by the character of Stanley. Glasgow burbanks her text from the get-go; she tells a story of racial victimization while deflecting the culpability for that victimization from white hegemony in general and white patriarchy in particular: all blame is placed at the feet of a single white bitch.

Hollywood, of course, couldn't resist. Glasgow decided that $40,000 was the "absolute minimum" she would accept for the film rights, and Warner Bros. gave it to her.[61] Once it was produced, however, Glasgow refused to see the film. She wrote that "the advertisements were enough to make me understand that Hollywood had filmed a very different book, not mine at all, and had entirely missed the point of the novel."[62] Glasgow may have been referring to the poster for *In This Our Life*, which had the teasing tagline: "No One Is Better Than Bette When She's Bad!"[63]

BETTE DAVIS: LETTING THE DEMON GO

In his essay "The Devil Finds Work," James Baldwin explores his complex childhood relationship with Hollywood cinema. At one point, he describes his first reaction to seeing Bette Davis on screen: she "was a *movie star: white* . . . and she was *ugly*."[64] Davis's "ugliness" was not only a creation of Baldwin's identification strategy, as Jane Gaines has argued, but also an ugliness already being performed on film: a strangeness, a symptom of the representational politics of studio-era Hollywood.[65]

A film critic once wrote that Davis "gives that curious feeling of being charged with power which can find no ordinary outlet."[66] Her power was often described as supernatural: a review of the film *Dangerous* (Alfred E. Green, 1935) declares, "Davis would probably have been burned as a witch if she had lived two or three hundred years ago."[67] Of her performance in *Beyond the Forest* (King Vidor, 1949), another critic asserted, "This babe is a witch in spades, diamonds and clubs."[68] Director John Huston called this quality Davis's "demon" and decided that in *In This Our Life*, he would "let the demon go."[69]

Gwendolyn Foster has argued that "the white woman as virginal angel" in film "is an archetype designed to keep hybridity at bay."[70] Perhaps the demon's function becomes a way not to contain hybridity but to express it. Davis, or the cinematic sign audiences have come to know as Davis, certainly expresses gendered hybridity, relying on an ability to play extremes of the attractive and the repulsive, the feminine and the masculine. A critic of one Bette Davis film called her a "tank" in battle with Errol Flynn's "beanshooter"; others praised her "abundance of feminine charm," which somehow manifested itself "manfully."[71] However, Davis is a figure not only of gendered hybridity but of racial hybridity as well.

Several scholars have commented on white female stars' discursive dependence on blackness. Foster suggests that Mae West in *I'm No Angel* (Wesley Ruggles, 1933) performed a kind of "white blackness" in drag, creating a "site of contestation" against racial and heteronormative stereotypes.[72] Writing of the infamous "Hot Voodoo" dance number in Josef von Sternberg's *Blonde Venus* (1932), in which Helen Faraday (Marlene Dietrich) emerges from a gorilla suit, Snead argues that the "very ambiguity of the trope is part of its power: does every beautiful white woman have a primitive, male, black ape-like ardor within her, waiting to be unleashed?"[73] Snead goes on to demonstrate that Davis's performance of the sexy, scheming Julie in *Jezebel* (William Wyler, 1938) is, like Dietrich's Helen, dependent on a backdrop of blackness—only in Julie's case, the gorilla suit is replaced by a household of dutiful slaves. Snead emphasizes that the function of this backdrop "is not mimetic, but rhetorical comparative" and that the Black characters in *Jezebel* "make the narrative point that Miss Julie is in many ways *un*admirable, as if the superfluity of black hands and faces surrounding her, over which she has some control, were meant to symbolize her increasing surplus of vanity over which she has almost no control."[74] Richard Dyer constructs a parallel argument about Davis's performance in *Beyond the Forest*, in which her character's wickedness is linked to her association with a "racial inferior"—her Native American housemaid.[75] bell hooks has made the case that the persona pop star Madonna constructs works to perpetuate white heterosexual patriarchy because her potency as a sign is again and again measured against the purported impotency of nonwhite and

Native Son and *In This Our Life* at Warner Bros.

homosexual people.[76] Ann duCille argues a similar point about Shirley Temple and makes an additional observation: "Temple not only defines her whiteness through a comparison to black characters, she also takes the place of an adult white female when the appearance of an actual mature white woman would be culturally impossible (dancing with a black man, for example)."[77] The nonwhite characters who surround the white female star are reduced to the narrative function of providing "blackdrop." The hyperbolic bitchiness of the Davis star persona is payback for her proximity to these racialized bodies and, in particular, for her "masculine" attempts to dominate those racialized bodies.

The monstrous self-interest that came to be associated with the "bad" Bette Davis is most often defined against and through her characters' dominance of male characters who are racialized, crippled, or both. Her Mildred in *Of Human Bondage* (John Cromwell, 1934) sadistically toys with the clubfooted Philip Carey (Leslie Howard). As the unhinged Marie in *Bordertown* (Archie Mayo, 1935), she ruthlessly attempts to implicate the Mexican American Johnny Ramirez (Paul Muni) in the murder she alone has committed. In *Dangerous*, her drunken Joyce Heath cripples her husband in an intentional car accident. As the calculated killer Leslie Crosbie in *The Letter* (William Wyler, 1940), she guns down her lover, who has become racialized by taking an Asian wife. Her hard-hearted Regina Giddens in *The Little Foxes* (William Wyler, 1941) purposely refuses to fetch heart medication for her wheelchair-bound husband so that he will die and no longer pose a threat to her business schemes. As the flirtatious Fanny Trellis in *Mr. Skeffington* (Vincent Sherman, 1944), she marries the Jewish Job Skeffington for his money alone, truly loving him only when he returns blind from a Nazi concentration camp. Clearly, the racialized or physically enfeebled male presented the demonized Davis with a specific narrative opportunity: patriarchy's anxiety about the castrating female could be expressed in her viciousness but contained by her compromised choice of victim—surely a "whole" white male could not fall prey to her treachery.

Dyer argues that stars as signs always signify in multiple ways: as represented characters and, simultaneously, as "themselves"—as constructed star personas.[78] He explains that stars

> are like characters in stories, representations of people [but] unlike characters in stories, stars are also real people.... Because stars have an existence in the world independent of their screen "fiction" appearances, it is possible to believe that as people they are more real than the characters in stories. This means that they serve to disguise the fact that they are just as much produced images, constructed personalities, as "characters" are. Thus, the value embodied by a star is, as it were, harder to reject as "impossible" or "false," because the star's existence guarantees the existence of the value he or she embodies.[79]

The multiplicity of the star's signification—as both signifier and signified—creates a being that seems to straddle the real and the imaginary and that, therefore, seems to belong nowhere. "The ugly object," in Slavoj Žižek's words, "is an object in the wrong place."[80] Žižek continues, "This does not mean simply that the ugly object is no longer ugly the moment we move it to its proper place. Rather, the ugly object is 'in itself' out of place, on account of the distorted balance between 'representation' and 'existence'. The ugly and out-of-place is *the excess of existence over representation*."[81] If, as Laura Mulvey has argued, Hollywood cinema's scopophilic economy relegates women to object status, female stardom is particularly ugly. As a woman, the white female star has only one place to occupy: the place of the object on the screen. But the stardom of the white female star—her simultaneous existence and signification on and off the screen—disrupts her role as screen object. The ugliness of the white female star, her semiotic instability coupled with her semiotic indispensability, offers a convenient locus for a range of cultural anxieties, including those about race.

In *Native Son*, Wright himself explored the function of the white female star as a vessel for deflected cultural anxiety about race. When he revised the novel to accommodate the taste of the Book-of-the-Month Club, the most considerable alteration was to the early movie theater scene: Wright was asked to eliminate Mary Dalton's appearance in the newsreel and all suggestion of masturbation.[82] Wright did remove the newsreel and references to Bigger "polishing his nightstick," and these changes had the unsurprising effect of occluding the character's sexuality. Significantly, Wright chose to replace the Dalton newsreel with a fictional film of his own creation: *The Gay Woman*, a title that echoes MGM's *The Gay Bride* (Jack Conway, 1934), starring Carole Lombard, and RKO's *The Gay Divorcee* (Mark Sandrich, 1934), starring Ginger Rogers. In the film that Wright creates, Bigger encounters a world in which "amid scenes of cocktail drinking, dancing, golfing, swimming, and spinning roulette wheels, a rich young white woman kept clandestine appointments with her lover while her millionaire husband was busy in the offices of a vast paper mill. Several times Bigger nudged Jack in the ribs with his elbow as the giddy young woman duped her husband and kept from him the knowledge of what she was doing."[83]

Bigger and Jack would have encountered a similar cinematic world had they been watching the early work of MGM star Norma Shearer, whose films *The Divorcee* (Robert Z. Leonard, 1930), *Let Us Be Gay* (Robert Z. Leonard, 1930), and *Strangers May Kiss* (George Fitzmaurice, 1931) highlighted marital infidelity. Also similar was Warner Bros.'s *Three on a Match* (Mervyn LeRoy, 1932), a film that has the married and restless Vivian (Ann Dvorak) leave her wealthy husband to run off with a glamorous underworld gigolo. Wright's imagined film was of a genre and his white female star was of a type that would have been immediately familiar to his readers. Wright apparently recognized that the repulsion the Book-of-the-Month Club readers had for Bigger's desire, which was directed toward the newsreel image of Mary Dalton, did not extend to Bigger's desire directed at the protagonist of *The Gay Woman*. The taste of the club demanded that Mary's celluloid image be protected from Bigger's gaze but allowed his gaze to fall full on the white female star—in particular, the star playing a sexualized, cuckolding pleasure-seeker. Wright emphasizes this contradiction by adorning Bigger's room above the Dalton kitchen with photographs of white stars Ginger Rogers, Jean Harlow, and Janet Gaynor. Wright responds to the censorship of the book club by presenting us with a paradoxical world in which Black male desire for a "real" white woman like Mary is socially unthinkable, but Black male desire for a white female star like Davis is not only tolerated but, arguably, encouraged.

Nowhere is Davis's "ugliness" so explicitly linked to sexuality and race as in *In This Our Life*. In his autobiography, director John Huston's reminiscences of the production flow easily from the character of Parry to the star persona of Bette: "I never cared for *In This Our Life*, although there were some good things about it. It was the first time, I believe, that a black character was presented as anything other than a good and faithful servant or comic relief. Bette fascinated me. There is something elemental about Bette—a demon within her which threatens to break out and eat everybody, beginning with their ears."[84] Surely, there is a link between the two features Huston most remembers about the film: the "positive" representation of the Black male and the "demon" within Davis, which Huston "unleashed." Baldwin's memories of watching *In This Our Life* also link the representation of Parry to Davis's role:

> Davis appeared to have read, and grasped, the script—which must have made her rather lonely—and she certainly understood the role. Her performance had the effect, rather, of exposing and shattering the film, so that she played in a kind of vacuum. . . . Armed with her wealth, her color, and her sex, [Stanley] goes to the prison to persuade [Parry] to corroborate her story: and what she uses, through jailhouse bars, is her sex. She will pay for the chauffeur's silence, any price he demands. Indeed, the price is implicit in the fact that she knows he knows that she is guilty: she can have no secrets from him now.[85]

Both Huston and Baldwin view the film as something of a failure, despite the historic role for Anderson. Both also suggest that this failure is a product of the film's greatest strength: the "demonic" performance of Davis that "shatters" and "exposes." Baldwin situates this shattering at the moment when Stanley visits the jailhouse and coquettishly attempts to persuade Parry to support her lies.

The controversial Warner Bros. adaptation: George Brent as Craig Fleming, Earnest Anderson as Parry Clay, and Bette Davis as Stanley Timberlake.

What is particularly interesting about this scene is that, while easily the most controversial in the film, it did not appear in Glasgow's novel, which has only the men, Craig and Asa, visit Parry at the jailhouse.

CONCLUSION

Why would Warner Bros. engineer a sexually charged face-to-face confrontation between a sympathetic Black male character and the studio's most powerful white female star? The scene that the studio creates is, in a sense, a revision of the scene the studio could never adapt: the death of Mary Dalton in *Native Son*. Terrified that Mary will cry out, Bigger smothers her before she can destroy him. In the parallel scene in Huston's *In This Our Life*, it is rather the white woman who is terrified that the Black man will speak and destroy her. Her weapon against him is her sexuality. Within this scene, many of the studio's narrative goals are accomplished in one stroke. By providing a noble (if emasculated) Black male character unjustly victimized, the studio comfortably portrays itself as politically progressive. In centering a predatory white female star beloved for her badness, the studio burbanks away any potential social critique. And finally, with the tantalizing suggestion that this white female star offers her sexuality as a potential item for barter with the Black man, the studio provides an implicit justification for the doom that awaits such transgressors, both on and off the screen.

Was Bette Davis the white Bigger Thomas that Hollywood really wanted? Her character in *In This Our Life* presents a strategy for deflecting anxieties about race onto anxieties about white femininity. Undoubtedly, Davis's persona of the hyperbolic bitch allowed Warner Bros. a "safe" way to play with the narrative dynamite of miscegenation and racial oppression. But once Bette the bitch was created, studio culture needed to kill her. While Glasgow allowed Stanley a light punishment at the end of *In This Our Life*, Warner Bros. threw the book at her. In the last moments of the film, Stanley dies in a car accident caused by her own recklessness. And Baldwin was correct about Davis's performance having a "shattering" effect on the film: when *In This Our Life* was exhibited, the version shown in Harlem and in southern states had the jailhouse confrontation between Stanley and Parry edited out. Clearly, the figures on either side of the cell bars were unable to contain a repressed narrative of Black male sexuality and rage, and the film, so stressed, literally cracked in two.

Notes

1. A version of this article appeared in *African American Review* 40, no. 3 (Fall, 2006).

2. David Bordwell, "Story Causality," in *The Classical Hollywood Cinema: Film Style and Mode of Production to 1960*, by David Bordwell, Janet Staiger, and Kristen Thompson (New York: Columbia University Press, 1985), 13–23.

3. Nick Roddick, *A New Deal in Entertainment: Warner Brothers in the 1930s* (London: British Film Institute, 1983), 254.

4. Tino Balio, *Grand Design: Hollywood as a Modern Business Enterprise, 1930–1939* (Berkeley: University of California Press, 1993), 281.

5. James Snead, *White Screens/Black Images: Hollywood from the Dark Side* (New York: Routledge, 1994), 8.

6. See Robert Wildof Gustafson, "The Buying of Ideas: Source Acquisition at Warner Bros., 1930–1949" (dissertation, University of Wisconsin, Madison, 1983), 172. While both Warner Bros. offices read submitted stories, the New York office, with its proximity to the publishing and theater worlds, oversaw the acquisition of "pre-sold" properties (such as novels and plays), and the Burbank office oversaw the adaptation of these properties and the generation of original material.

7. During the research for this essay, from 2004 to 2006, Warner Bros. moved the story department files from the University of Southern California's Warner Bros. Collection to the archive of the studio itself in Burbank. Materials were accessed in both locations.

8. See Richard Wright's "Writer's Card," Story Department Files, Warner Bros. Studio Archive, Burbank, CA. Notably absent from this list is *Black Boy: A Record of Childhood and Youth* (1945), which was not read by Warner Bros. until 1978, long after Wright's death (although a studio

164 ELIZABETH BINGGELI

reader did refer to *Black Boy* in her report on Petry's *The Street*, as I discuss in this essay). The fact that *Black Boy* is autobiographical does not explain this omission; Zora Neale Hurston's *Dust Tracks on a Road* (1942) was read and reviewed by the studio the year it was published.

9. See Hazel Rowley, *Richard Wright: The Life and Times* (New York: Holt, 2001), 265; *Black Hope* was scheduled for publication in October 1942 and reviewed by Warner Bros. on October 13, 1942. Rowley reveals that Wright heard the Fisk University Jubilee Singers in 1943 and "visualized a movie portraying the singers' dedication and adventures, the humiliations they endured on tour, and their ultimate triumph." The *Melody Limited* screenplay was written in 1944 and reviewed by Warner Bros. on November 22, 1950. No record remains as to the studio's reaction to either story.

10. Irving Deakin, Memorandum to Irene Lee, June 29, 1939, Story Department Files, Warner Bros. Studio Archive, Burbank, CA.

11. Richard Wright, Letter to John Houseman and Orson Welles, quoted in Rowley, *Richard Wright*, 245.

12. James Baldwin, "Everybody's Protest Novel," *James Baldwin: Collected Essays* (New York: Library of America, 1998), 18. See Richard Wright, *Native Son: Introduction by Dorothy Canfield Fisher* (New York: Harper & Brothers, 1940).

13. Alain Locke, "Of Native Sons, Real and Otherwise," in *Richard Wright: Critical Perspectives Past and Present*, ed. Henry Louis Gates Jr. and Kwame Anthony Appiah (New York: Amistad, 1993), 19.

14. See Richard Wright, *How Bigger Was Born: The Story of Native Son, One of the Most Significant Novels of Our Time, and How It Came to Be Written* (New York: Harper & Brothers, 1940).

15. Ross Pudaloff, "Celebrity as Identity," in *Richard Wright: Critical Perspectives Past and Present*, 156.

16. Pudaloff, "Celebrity as Identity," 164.

17. Pudaloff, "Celebrity as Identity," 160.

18. Deakin, Long Synopsis of *Native Son*, June 28, 1939, Story Department Files, Warner Bros. Studio Archive, Burbank, CA.

19. Deakin, Long Synopsis of *Native Son*, June 28, 1939, Story Department Files.

20. Deakin, Long Synopsis of *Native Son*, June 28, 1939, Story Department Files.

21. Balio, *Grand Design*, 283.

22. Deakin, Long Synopsis of *Native Son*, June 28, 1939, Story Department Files.

23. Deakin, Long Synopsis of *Native Son*, June 28, 1939, Story Department Files.

24. Alice Goldberg, Report on Richard Wright's *Native Son*, March 12, 1940, 1, Story Department Files, Warner Bros. Studio Archive, Burbank, CA.

25. Goldberg, Report on Richard Wright's *Native Son*, March 12, 1940, 1, Story Department Files.

26. Thomas Cripps, *Making Movies Black: The Hollywood Message Movie from World War II to the Civil Rights Era* (New York: Oxford University Press, 1993), 5.

27. Cripps, *Making Movies Black*, 5.

28. Cripps, *Making Movies Black*, 6.

29. Rowley, *Richard Wright*, 203.

30. Rowley, *Richard Wright*, 203–4.

31. Rowley, *Richard Wright*, 247.

32. Goldberg, Report on Richard Wright's *Native Son*, March 12, 1940, Story Department Files.

Native Son and In This Our Life at Warner Bros.   165

33. Virginia Volland, Report on Ann Petry's *The Street*, January 17, 1946, 1. Story Department Files, Warner Bros. Studio Archive, Burbank, California.

34. Volland, Report on Ann Petry's *The Street*, January 17, 1946, 1, Story Department Files.

35. Volland, Report on Ann Petry's *The Street*, January 17, 1946, 1, Story Department Files.

36. Tom Chapman, Memorandum to Ellingwood Kay Regarding Ann Petry's *The Street*, January 23, 1946, 1, Story Department Files. Warner Bros. Studio Archive, Burbank, CA.

37. Tom Chapman, Memorandum to Finlay McDermid Regarding Ann Petry's *The Street*, January 28, 1946, 1, Story Department Files. Warner Bros. Studio Archive, Burbank, CA.

38. See Hazel Arnett Ervin, *Ann Petry: A Bio-bibliography* (New York: G. K. Hall, 1993). Ellingwood Kay rejected *The Street* at Warner Bros. on February 8, 1946. In 1958, Petry would write the screenplay *That Hill Girl* for Columbia as a potential vehicle for Kim Novak.

39. The film *Native Son* (1951) was directed by Pierre Chenal and shot in Argentina.

40. Russian-born Charles Leonard, who worked in Hollywood as a screenwriter and script doctor from the 1920s to the 1940s, collaborated with Hughes on other projects. Leonard was eventually blacklisted for his leftist affiliations.

41. Lucy Land, Report on Charles Leonard's and Langston Hughes's *Chocolate Sailor*, March 6, 1943, 1, Story Department Files. Warner Bros. Studio Archive, Burbank, CA.

42. Lucy Land, Report on Charles Leonard's and Langston Hughes's *Chocolate Sailor*, March 6, 1943, 1, Story Department Files.

43. Lucy Land, Report on Charles Leonard's and Langston Hughes's *Chocolate Sailor*, March 6, 1943, 1, Story Department Files.

44. See Blair Rouse, ed., *Letters of Ellen Glasgow* (New York: Harcourt, Brace, 1958), 302–4; in a letter to Bessie Zaban Jones, June 26, 1942, Glasgow writes that the Clays were modeled on "a family that had belonged to my mother's ancestors for over a hundred and fifty years."

45. James Samuels, Letter to Warner Bros. Studio, June 6, 1942, Production File of *In This Our Life*, Warner Bros. Archive, University of Southern California, School of Cinema-Television Library, Los Angeles.

46. Thomasina Johnson, Letter to Warner Bros. Studio, September 30, 1942, Production File of *In This Our Life*, Warner Bros. Archive, University of Southern California, School of Cinema-Television Library, Los Angeles.

47. Edith P. McDougald, Letter to Warner Bros. Studio, August 10, c. 1942, Production File of *In This Our Life*, Warner Bros. Archive, University of Southern California, School of Cinema-Television Library, Los Angeles.

48. John S. Holley, Letter to Warner Bros. Studio, August 1942, Production File of *In This Our Life*, Warner Bros. Archive, University of Southern California, School of Cinema-Television Library, Los Angeles.

49. P. L. Prattis, Letter to Warner Bros. Studio, June 6, 1942, Production File of *In This Our Life*, Warner Bros. Archive, University of Southern California, School of Cinema-Television Library, Los Angeles.

50. Walter White, quoted in Cripps, *Making Movies Black*, 45.

51. K. Anthony Appiah, "'No Bad Nigger': Blacks as the Ethical Principle in the Movies," in *Media Spectacles*, ed. Marjorie Garber, Jann Matlock, and Rebecca L. Walkowitz (New York: Routledge, 1993), 88.

52. See Cheryl A. Wall, ed., *Hurston: Folklore, Memoirs, and Other Writings* (New York: Library of America, 1995); Zora Neale Hurston's essay "The 'Pet Negro' System" first appeared in *The American Mercury*, May 1943.

53. Ellen Glasgow, *In This Our Life* (New York: Harcourt, Brace, 1941), 26.

54. Glasgow, *In This Our Life*, 27–28.

55. Glasgow, *In This Our Life*, 214.

56. See Rouse, *Letters of Ellen Glasgow*, 80–88; letter to Carl Van Vechten.

57. Susan Goodman, *Ellen Glasgow: A Biography* (Baltimore: Johns Hopkins University Press, 1998), 3.

58. Ellen Glasgow, *A Certain Measure: An Interpretation of Prose Fiction* (New York: Harcourt, Brace, 1943), 259.

59. See Ellen Glasgow, *Beyond Defeat: An Epilogue to an Era* (Charlottesville, NC: University Press of Virginia, 1966). In this posthumously published sequel, Glasgow mentions Stanley only briefly, to indicate that she has chosen exile in California. Stanley's mother "sent her out there, and she was married within a few weeks. Her husband is quite old, but he is very wealthy. He has something to do with the movies." Parry merits even less mention in the sequel.

60. Glasgow, *Certain Measure*, 234.

61. Irving Deakin, Telegram to Hal Wallis, February 21, 1941, Story Department Files, Warner Bros. Studio Archive, Burbank, CA; see Rouse, *Letters of Ellen Glasgow*, 279–80, letter to Stanley Young; previously, Glasgow had sold the film rights of *They Stooped to Folly* (1924) for $25,000 and knew that Hollywood would have little concern for "fidelity" to the source text when adapting it for the screen. However, she still felt compelled to question her editor at Harcourt: "I suppose it is futile to suggest that the movie shall make a kind of 'Mr. Chips' picture, treating Asa Timberlake as the major figure, instead of playing up the subject of callow youth or broken marriages?"

62. See Rouse, *Letters of Ellen Glasgow*, 302–4; letter to Bessie Zaban Jones.

63. Poster advertising *In This Our Life*, Production File of *In This Our Life*, Warner Bros. Archive, University of Southern California, School of Cinema-Television Library, Los Angeles.

64. James Baldwin, "The Devil Finds Work: An Essay," *James Baldwin: Collected Essays* (New York: Library of America, 1998), 482.

65. See Jane Gaines, *Fire and Desire: Mixed-Race Movies in the Silent Era* (Chicago: University of Chicago Press, 2001); Gaines analyzes Baldwin's reaction to Davis as it relates to Black cinema spectatorship.

66. Quoted in Gene Ringgold, *The Films of Bette Davis* (New York: Cadillac, 1966), 65.

67. Quoted in Ringgold, *Films of Bette Davis*, 65.

68. Quoted in Ringgold, *Films of Bette Davis*, 143.

69. John Huston, *Open Book* (New York: Knopf, 1980), 81.

70. Gwendolyn Audrey Foster, *Performing Whiteness: Postmodern Re/Construction in the Cinema* (Albany, NY: State University of New York Press, 2003), 33.

71. Quoted in Ringgold, *Films of Bette Davis*; see the collected reviews of *The Man Who Played God* (John G. Adolfi, 1932), *That Certain Woman* (Edmund Goulding, 1937), *The Private Lives of Elizabeth and Essex* (Michael Curtiz, 1939), and *In This Our Life* (1942).

72. Foster, *Performing Whiteness*, 39.

73. Snead, *White Screens/Black Images*, 72.

74. Snead, *White Screens/Black Images*, 77.

75. Richard Dyer, *White* (New York: Routledge, 1997), 62–63.

76. bell hooks, *Black Looks: Race and Representation* (Boston: South End Press, 1992), 157–64.

77. Ann duCille, "The Shirley Temple of My Familiar," *Transition* 73 (1997): 27.

78. Richard Dyer, *Stars* (London: British Film Institute, 1979), 22.

79. Dyer, *Stars*, 20.

80. Slavoj Žižek, "Love Thy Neighbor? No, Thanks!" in *The Psychoanalysis of Race*, ed. Christopher Lane (New York: Columbia University Press, 1998), 165.

81. Žižek, "Love Thy Neighbor?" 165.

82. Arnold Rampersad, "Introduction," *Native Son* (New York: Perennial Classics, 1998), xviii.

83. Richard Wright, *Native Son* (New York: Library of America, 1993), 491. This edition has Wright's restored text and the citation is from the notes section.

84. Huston, *Open Book*, 81.

85. Baldwin, "Devil Finds Work," 521–22.

Chapter 8

FRANK YERBY AND THE ART AND DISCIPLINE OF RACIAL SUBLIMATION

ELLEN C. SCOTT

Black authors often do not get to write the things they set out to write. Racism prevents it. Black authorship—and indeed, becoming a successful Black figure of one's own making in America more broadly—requires many acts of racial self-censorship. This chapter engages with what happened to a Black author diverted and how he found a way—through repression and indirection—to triangulate his subject. Indeed, this work approaches the very act of Black American writing as a process of adaptation for white eyes, a translational, experimental practice. It argues that American power, especially in the 1940s and 1950s, was garnered through the processes of incredibly intense sublimation and repression. This was both a public and private taming of desire and rage.

Frank Yerby's story, as told by critics, seems simple enough: a Works Progress Administration–trained Black "protest fiction" writer in the mold of Richard Wright failed to get published and therefore abandoned politics to publish cheap, popular historical "costume fiction." But did he? And if the "costume novel" was Yerby's vehicle, what did the costumes disguise? This chapter looks across Yerby's career at his practice of racial sublimation and how it affected the adaptation and legibility of Yerby's works from page to screen. Yerby harnessed the energies of repression to create and articulate otherness through various permissible guises, including history, whiteness, and smallness, but always with the Black situation—and the toxicity of whiteness—deeply in mind. Living out Paul Laurence Dunbar's "We Wear the Mask," Yerby indirectly gave readers some of the deepest themes of Black American life—including enslavement, torture, lynching, interracial sex, and the buoyancy of the runaway and the migrant. What Yerby abandoned was not blackness but direct discussion of contemporary racial issues, and his turn to the popular represents neither a weakening nor a cheapening of his talents. Criticism largely missed Yerby's biggest gift to literature, which was lodged in his facility at politicized indirection.

Yerby employed "infrapolitics"—that practice, dating back to slavery, of tool breaking, running away, and evasion, which remains part and parcel of the daily resistance practices to multifaceted racial oppression.[1]

Yerby was the only Black author of his time to be repeatedly adapted to the Hollywood screen. This chapter examines Yerby's authorial sublimation, how his "costumed" signifiers were cinematized, and then how Yerby's Black audiences interpreted them. It argues that adaptations of Yerby's works were classical Hollywood's most historically accurate representations of Black American enslaved people's experience, though sometimes no Black people appeared in the finished films. But Yerby's disguises were not adequate for Hollywood. In *The Foxes of Harrow* (1946; screen adaptation John M. Stahl, 1947), Yerby wove a narrative of Black life beneath a white dominant narrative, attracting white and Black readers to the text, but Hollywood dared not translate the core of this subnarrative to the screen. With *The Golden Hawk* (1948; screen adaptation Sidney Salkow, 1952) and *The Saracen Blade* (1952; screen adaptation William Castle, 1954), both works provided an increasingly exotic garb and represented a deeper historical dive ensconced in an escaped-slave narrative that the finished films, aided by white leftist screenwriters, heightened rather than abated but that critics, Black and white, largely missed.

Often referred to in the 1940s and 1950s as a contemporary Alexandre Dumas, Yerby was also a bit of a Lin-Manuel Miranda, using history as a mode to reset relations in the present. Described by academic literary critics as a "debunker" of whiteness and a writer of "antiheroic" fiction, Yerby was part of the pulp literary tradition that, like film noir, focused on expelled or marginalized heroes.[2] Unlike many Black authors who trod a path of respectability, Yerby decided to be bad—"bad" sexually, "bad" for white people, and eventually also rebelling against blackness and becoming "bad" for Black people. He was a man whose words bewitched whiteness *and* blackness in his quest for a freedom beyond race. In many ways, then, Yerby predicts the pattern of Blaxploitation. He certainly prefigured its obsessions and the careful deployment of whiteness through the guise of parodic normalcy, even as he performed a blackness that evaded racial rules through disguise, both as author and in his fiction.

BLACK SOLDIERS AND WHITE DUST:
THE SHORT STORIES OF FRANK YERBY

Though Yerby focused on poetry in his early years, by the late 1930s, as he finished his studies at Fisk University, he developed into a short-story writer, winning the O. Henry Award for the best published short story in 1944. Yerby's early stories were razor sharp and prescient in their hardline rage at white injustice, whether that whiteness was figured in human form or inanimately—as white flowers, white monuments, or the white dust that so often covered his Black protagonist. In his earliest story, "Salute to the Flag," a Black veteran of the Great War returns home only to be murdered by a white mob who judges him insufficiently respectful of the American flag, which he had come to regard as a symbol of white supremacy. The narrator's last act before gurgling to death on his own blood is to raise himself up on his ambulance bed to again thumb his nose at a passing American flag.

In "White Magnolia" from 1944, Beth, a white southern debutante, invites Hannah, a Black acquaintance, to lunch at her family's home, only to have her parents openly disparage Hannah, leading Beth to initiate an extended internal critique of whiteness and southern nostalgia that germinates around the magnolia tree in her garden. The duels, hoopskirts, and crinolines she used to imagine at the tree "weren't there any longer. Instead there was only the long line of black men and women in their faded rags moving between stalks of the cotton. And the auctioneer was holding open a Black man's mouth to show his fine teeth. And the slow heartbreaking songs rose from the little cabins and the stench of black flesh drowned out the jasmine."[3] "Health Card," for which Yerby won an O. Henry Award, tells the story of Johnny, a recently married GI preparing for his wife's visit to the town where he's stationed. Johnny is repeatedly challenged about the legitimacy of his marriage and his wife's virtue by innkeepers, his superior officers, and military police, until his rage explodes in a manner that Yerby characterizes in dialect so heavy it might well call into question Yerby's regard for Black people as well as white.

In "Homecoming," World War I veteran Willie returns to his southern hometown and finds himself unable to tolerate the casual racism that he had borne his entire life. His newfound defiance eventually incites a murderous mob that descends on him as he is trying to leave town. His life is saved by an older white man who had been kind to him since his youth, who claims Willie has "combat fatigue" and can't be held responsible for his actions, so instead of being lynched, the story's last image is of Willie being dragged away in a psychiatric ambulance, shouting for his freedom. "My Brother Went to College," similarly a tale of the psychic toll of racism on the dignified Black male hero, focuses on the roaming black sheep of an African American family whose visit to his doctor-brother's idyllic upper-middle-class world is rocked as he discovers that his brother, too, faces racism. Focusing on the embittered Black GI or veteran, in Yerby's works, the white institution—the interracial committee, the asylum, the hospital, or the military—is as much to blame as the white southerner for Black unfreedom. There is an element of unkempt rage in each of these stories—a near-homicidal madness at the powerlessness race makes.

MURIEL FULLER AND THE DEVELOPMENT OF THE SUBLIMATION APPARATUS

These short stories give us a window into what Yerby cared about, who he was, and the deep racial concerns that defined his work. How did Yerby move from enraged, powerful Black soldiers, doctors, and upper-middle-class subjects burned by American inequality to white characters and Black subplots in historical costume dramas? The best evidence of the reasons for this shift come from the historical record. Yerby's correspondence with Muriel Fuller, the "mentor" who ushered him into professional "mainstream" writing, extended from 1943 to the 1970s and consisted of hundreds of pages. With Fuller, Yerby shared many drafts of his never-published *This Is My Own*, a 91,000-word protest novel about a Black boxer and a lynching during World War II, which Yerby eventually discarded after many rejections.

Fuller and Yerby bonded over their mutual critique of Richard Wright—and specifically of Bigger Thomas. "I just hated *Native Son*. I thought as I read it why couldn't he have picked a decent boy," said Fuller of twenty-year-old Bigger. "That lad was rotten in any race. And I felt at the time there was room for a book about a fine colored boy, who had the cards stacked against him, no matter what he did. And now you've written it," Fuller said, referring to Yerby's *This Is My Own*.[4] Yerby replied, "My chief character violates all the taboos: he is intelligent, educated—no 'Bigger Thomas' in any sense of the word. He is myself and a thousand friends and maybe a little bit of all the persecuted minority peoples all over the world."[5] Yerby told Fuller that he considered the "upper-middle-class Negro" the "best source of literary material," one whites would never accept.[6] While Yerby received funds from the AFL-CIO to visit editors in New York, he was simultaneously critiquing Bigger, the heart of Wright's class analysis, dubbing him a "case of a tortured animal" and angling to write literature centered on the middle class.[7]

If Yerby retreated from socially engaged art, his formal shift was not demure but instead punctuated by rage at his white publishing industry critics.[8] His novel was rejected, he asserted, because "one must never present the Negro as a man and a brother. Even when one is entirely sympathetic toward the cause of justice for all men, one must observe this taboo," one even Richard Wright observed, he claimed.[9] Infuriated, he promised Fuller he would write a short story

> about an English flier and an English girl marooned on [a] desert island.
> . . . He's a flying instructor sent over to teach the English lads who are
> training in this country and she's a governess in an English family who
> ran away from the bombings. . . . It will be carefully constructed, and

172   ELLEN C. SCOTT

completely void of anything that might offend anybody, so [some pub-lisher] might take it.[10]

Yerby's promise was more than a bitter joke. It was a plan—an indication of a pattern of deliberate repression and retaliatory retreat from the directness dooming his writing in the white American marketplace that would mark his entire career. When Harper's told Yerby that his book, which included a lynch-ing scene, had "too much stark horror" that "turned the reader's stomach again and again,"[11] he angrily chopped away at his own work:

> I have already begun the revision, which so far has consisted of pure surgery. I am ruthlessly cutting out all . . . sentences beginning with "he thought." . . . How the devil do I know what anybody thought? I only know what they did. . . . I just threw away the last thirty-five pages. I have never been to Africa or England so why should I . . . fake and try to write about them? . . . The lynching scene has been made largely sug-gestive rather than nauseatingly descriptive.[12]

His retreat was an act of refusal as brittle as the reactions of characters in his stories. Fuller's mentorship encouraged this sublimation. His letter, she said, showcased his "poor humor":

> Please don't be bitter. I don't want to lecture you. Anything we [whites] say is simply tripe alongside of what you and others like you who are active in the struggle are doing and saying . . . the one thing you simply <u>must</u> do is get on top of yourself. You have this tremendous driving force that bursts out in words—in writing. Be glad you can express it. You'd probably do something terrible if you couldn't. But . . . the best writing in the world is the restrained writing. Anyone can be swept away with rhetoric—but it doesn't sweep other people away. If you will just harness this gift of yours there isn't anything you can't do. . . . You simply must conquer your gift.[13]

In trying, strategically, to avoid his own "burning opinions," he gave himself—and his reader—a respite from race's modern direction and shape.[14] To be blocked or repressed in his expressions regarding race was just adding another dimension to race's evil snare. So, he avoided it. As he would say later to Fuller of his short stories, "Every time I try to be diplomatic and inoffensive, I get lousy."[15] He adopted the pleasure of evasion. Yerby directly referred to this strategy in a later Black press interview:

Since unfortunately . . . novels of protest reach a small audience with the exception of Dick Wright, it seemed to me that the racial theme would probably get home to a group of the reading public which might never read a novel of protest but might be reached rather deftly by a racial theme as a subplot. . . . I think that I'll reach more people who never read books on racial themes or attend interracial meetings.[16]

It was in this idiom, in 1946, that Yerby penned his first novel, *The Foxes of Harrow*. Fuller had said of Yerby that his planned novel with a closing scene of Marian Anderson singing the national anthem on the steps of the Lincoln Memorial "has both eyes and a foot in Hollywood!"[17] And indeed, within a few years, that is where Yerby's novels—but not the author—would be. But Fuller cautioned again, "Just keep a good tight rein on yourself," arguing that in his best work he "just told the story—you weren't bitter, you didn't lash out—you told it, and it knocked me for a loop."[18]

BLACK AUTHOR, WHITE AUTEUR:
DARRYL F. ZANUCK AND THE STORY OF *FOXES*

Dial Press released *The Foxes of Harrow* with a distinctively color-blind campaign, preselling it without mentioning Yerby's race. At first, Yerby generally avoided white press interviews, carefully chose Black press interviews, and shunned photographs.[19] Southern readers—and booksellers—reportedly did not know Yerby was Black.[20] To Black critics, this trick read more as subversion than "passing," and Yerby himself claimed he was proud of his Black heritage but didn't "flaunt it."[21] Describing the process of creating *Foxes*, which took three years to research and one to write, Yerby rendered himself the protagonist in his own dramatic tale; as he told Black columnist Michael Carter, "By the time I wrote 27 pages, the book was sold. But there followed many short-tempered story conferences and lots of times I wanted to give up. I over-wrote it. . . . It was easier to keep it up than to stop it."[22]

Yerby's novel, which spans 1825–1865, tells the story of Stephen Fox, a white New Orleans gambler and scoundrel who, through his wiles, procures a plantation he names "Harrow," which he builds to decadent heights, using his success to snag an upstanding but "frigid" Creole bride, Odalie, while leaving her cousin Aurore swooning as well.[23] Stephen also has a quadroon mistress, Desiree, a "darker"-skinned, "golden coloured" woman, whose complexion is "gleaming against the ivory white tones of her other [quadroon] companions." He "keeps" Desiree in a house on Rampart Street (a site commonly associated with free women of color in New Orleans and at which, it was said, many white men kept mixed-race mistresses). Stephen, his son Etienne, and the reader all inevitably fall madly in love with Desiree.[24]

As Phyllis Klotman notes, the enslaved people who built the plantation are a major subplot and are "important for what they say about racial arrangements in the antebellum South": Tante Caleen (a brilliant and wise voodoo practitioner feared by white and Black people), her nephew Achille (a brawny, loyal leader of Harrow's fieldworkers), La Belle Sauvage (an enslaved African princess who resists servitude and eventually attempts to kill her son and does kill herself rather than submit to slavery), and "Inch" (Achille and Belle's son, who escapes slavery, becomes an abolitionist, and returns to the South).[25] The Civil War strikes, and, in the wake of it, Inch becomes a policeman in Reconstruction-era New Orleans and marries Desiree, Stephen's former mistress. Though the book focuses on white characters, its clearest moral is spoken by Fox over his ruined plantation: "For a while we lived like gods. Perhaps that was not good for us!"[26]

The book was an unqualified success, selling nearly half a million copies before its release, becoming a Doubleday dollar book club selection, and earning Yerby not only $50,000 in its first year, a blue-chip edition, and a place on the bestsellers list for months to come, but also a six-book deal with Dial Press.[27] By early 1947, Yerby's book sales had exceeded those of any other Black author.[28] The book also had a substantial reception in the Black press. Though Black reviewers either praised or blamed its "lack of racial identification," *all* saw through Yerby's sublimation to the novel's Black liberatory core.[29] The novel sold to Twentieth Century-Fox for six figures, though sources differ on whether it was for $150,000, $250,000, or $500,000.[30]

Foxes's cinematic turn was in keeping with the theatrical vein in Yerby. While at Fisk, he directed plays and wrote his master's thesis on the Black "little theater" movement. He showed an unusual dedication to family pictures and home movies, and, indeed, movies show up in a number of his stories.[31] His early fiction responded not just to southernisms and whiteness but to *Hollywood*'s versions of these constructions. Later, he wrote several unproduced television series, including "County Sheriff" about a deceptively paunchy, aging southern sheriff and "Destination Danger," a spy tale about an "international trouble shooter."[32]

It is little surprise that Yerby, scribe of "costume dramas," found his first novel's cinematic home with Darryl F. Zanuck, the producer who sought to garb social problems in "the glittering robes of entertainment."[33] Indeed, both men plainly told the common, pulpy truth about American history, though, as the course of the filmmaking revealed, they had remarkably different senses of what could be said about American race relations. Yerby's practice of racial sublimation, his crossover into mainstream fiction, and the absence of racial identifiers in promotions or the novel itself gave him access to Hollywood that no earlier Black author had had. Indeed, *The Foxes of Harrow* was one of the first Black-authored titles to make it to the Hollywood screen and the first, certainly, to fetch a six-figure sum.[34] However, production documents reveal that Zanuck, whose "ripped from the headlines" approach to screen stories had minted his reputation at Warner Bros., was still afraid of something in *The Foxes of Harrow*. Yerby told Black reporters that he would not "stand to see any of the colored characters debased. I painted them as they were—human beings with human qualities—and if it's filmed, they must remain that way."[35] But once sold, the book's filming was out of Yerby's hands. Though he wanted to write the *Foxes* screenplay, and Black press sources conjectured he might, Zanuck never hired him to do so.

Perhaps what the studio was afraid of was industry censorship. In conference notes, Zanuck did refer to the Production Code directly. Zanuck pessimistically opined of "the Octoroon (Desiree)," "The Production Code . . . would permit us to use her only if it would be made perfectly clear that nothing happened between her and Stephen, and that neither he nor she ever wanted anything to happen. Under these restrictions, there doesn't seem to be much point of using the girl at all."[36] He did suggest that "Desiree could be just a common girl" rather than an octoroon to avoid Code troubles about her race.[37] Caleen, whom the treatment labels a "spidery, Domingan negress" whose wisdom and magic are the unseen hand behind the success of the Fox family, was originally considered to be a significant film character. It was Caleen whose advice saved the hurricane-threatened crop, who saved Fox and nursed him back to health after his New Orleans arrival, and whose knowing smile was to be the film's close. But Zanuck claimed fear of the "Johnson office" objection to "those scenes in which Caleen plays a dominant part"; these included scenes showing African rituals designed to induce sexual attraction, a scene in which Caleen gives Odalie a "massage" to stimulate her sexually, and a sequence showing an abortion.[38] So, early in the screenwriting, Zanuck pared down both Caleen and Yerby's intricate latticework of Black characters. He eliminated a sequence showing an octoroon ball and all references to "Lagoaster, the great Quadroon tailor" who makes Stephen's clothes.[39] The initial story conference avers Zanuck's intentions to remove the strong Black storyline from the screenplay, and the ensuing drafts of the screenplay submitted in August and September removed Achille, Sauvage, and Inch entirely, including only a muted and servile Caleen. Zanuck himself cut out a scene where a young boy named Josh is sold at auction. He crossed out the scene of La Belle Sauvage being purchased and brought to Harrow. He also seems to have initially cut the entire Margaret Garner–esque scene of La Belle Sauvage attempting to kill her son to avoid his enslavement and killing herself at the scene's conclusion. Nevertheless, nearly all major Black characters, including the controversial Desiree, appear—though diminished—in the finished picture, although Zanuck's memos record reasons for neither cutting (other than the fear of censorship) nor restoring them. Zanuck and his screenwriters mixed and muddled characters. For instance, Zanuck retained light-skinned Zerline, who, unlike Desiree, is played by a Black actor (Helen Crozier, though Dorothy Dandridge and Fredi Washington were reportedly considered). Though safely distanced from Stephen, Zerline still signifies interracial sex because she reveals Stephen and Desiree's affair to her white mistress.

The Production Code Administration certainly affected the adaptation process. However, when Zanuck and director John Stahl publicized the PCA's strictness on *Foxes*, it was likely to justify leaving out content that they were uncomfortable with. A whopping fifty letters passed between the PCA and Twentieth Century-Fox between March and June in 1947, often about the costuming of white and Black characters.[40] The PCA's initial letter informed the studio that the film could not be made as plotted. Its major concerns were "an unpunished murder [when Stephen duels a plantation owner], a suggested rape [Achille of Belle], an objectionable wedding night scene [Stephen breaks the door to Odalie's room, also suggesting rape], an attempted abortion [Odalie attempts to use voodoo to end her pregnancy], and an unmistakable suggestion of adultery treated without the full compensating moral values required by the Code [the relationship between Desiree and Stephen]."[41] Surprisingly, much of the letter pertained to whether Achille was married to Belle and whether or not he raped her. This is of interest in part because earlier, the PCA regarded African Americans' sexual morality differently than white sexual morality, as *Hallelujah* (King Vidor, 1929) exemplified.[42] With *Foxes*, Breen was adamant that for Belle and Achille, two sympathetic characters, to conceive a child, despite their enslaved status and the history of unwedded child conception and outright plantation rape, the scenes in which Achille violently kisses Belle and "the dissolve on Achille carrying the woman into the shadows" that "unmistakably suggests rape" needed to be removed. Likewise, when Stephen says to Achille "She's yours!" if he can get Belle off the wagon that brought her to the plantation, the PCA countered that the union needed more than the master's say-so; it needed the "benefit of clergy."[43] Though the PCA saw Stephen forcing Odalie to have sex on their wedding night as "unacceptable," they did not call it rape. The rest of the letter was mainly dedicated to Desiree, Stephen's kept quadroon. Notably, the PCA did not describe this relationship as "miscegenation" or "rape." However, though the script had already significantly diluted Desiree's race, the letter required further masking: "The lines . . . 'so you know about the <u>house</u> on the Ramparts' and 'that of a poor <u>betrayed</u> wife' definitely indicate that Stephen has committed adultery with Desiree and accordingly they should be changed. The . . . line 'She's twice the woman and thrice the wife that ye ever were, m'dear' is unacceptable."[44] Though these changes were said to be about adultery, the suggested shifts significantly lessened any flavor of interracial love or concubinage from the film, as the location of Rampart Street had a definite connotation with Black concubinage, and Stephen's latter comment suggested that he preferred this Black mistress to his white wife.

Considering that the PCA never mentioned "slavery," its recommended deletions pertained directly to Yerby's condemnation of slavery's system of concubinage and rape—either by or with the sanction of the white plantation owner. The PCA asserted its authority, but Zanuck, aided by Fox public relations chief and former head Hollywood self-censor Jason Joy, pushed back, working hard to maintain indirect suggestion. The Rampart scenes come up at least five times in the finished film, maintaining the suggestion of adultery and interracial sex, though Desiree and Stephen never kiss in the film.

Zanuck fought for deniable references to interracial sex, but he dropped entirely references to Radical Reconstruction that offered a corrective as much to films like *The Birth of a Nation* (D. W. Griffith, 1915) as to Dunning School–era history books, which posited Black Reconstruction as a gross failure.[45] The process of screenplay development seems to have begun with a scene breakdown on July 3, 1946. From the very beginning, however, Yerby's measured inclusion of Black characters was absent: there was little question that this was the story of the life and loves of Stephen Fox. Zanuck's initial observations that the novel was long and that writers should "boil [it] down—take out rambling—draw our story on desire" dovetail with other notes successively reducing Yerby's Black narratives.[46] In later drafts, when screenwriter Wanda Tuchock brought Black characters back, she never attempted to include Yerby's retributive vision of Radical Reconstruction.

Two quite different treatments written by Tuchock on November 4 and November 7 of 1946 showed her facility at mutating the story to fit Zanuck's desire, coring Yerby's original detail to eliminate the insistent specters of Black freedom, critique of white power, and Radical Reconstruction.[47] In both drafts, Stephen marries Odalie, they later fight over the upbringing of their child, and Stephen has a quadroon mistress. In the first draft, however, Odalie, discovering Stephen's infidelity, turns to Tante Caleen to get Stephen back through a "voodoo rite" ceremony "in a cane-brake. . . . It should be a grotesque scene of darkness and fire and snakes and potent libations. It's a scene of sheer horror to Aurore [Odalie's younger cousin], especially when she sees her cousin falling under the spell and swaying and writhing like the Negras [*sic*]."[48] The pyres of these rites catch and, before they know it, Harrow is aflame and Stephen finds his wife with "dress torn" (a signifier of rape), "blackened with smoke."[49] She dies in his arms, and he and Aurore raise their son far from Harrow. In the second treatment written just a few days later, Tuchock removed the voodoo rites and the fire, though not the quadroon ball, and had Odalie regain Stephen's trust, as she would in the finished film, by forcing the enslaved field laborers to work despite an impending storm. Odalie wins back her master, then, through controlling Black labor—by truly becoming the mistress of Harrow.

Tuchock's first continuity draft restored Black characters Zanuck had removed but compounded them with familiar Hollywood southernisms. Achille and Tante Caleen again became prominent figures but, in Tuchock's hands, primarily in relation to Stephen. Tante Caleen is introduced as an "ancient negress" to whose "lean-to" Stephen retires when he is sick and who dresses his wounds and gives him comfort.[50] If Caleen became a kind voodoo-inflected mammy and Achille an enduringly faithful, if atypically strong, field hand, Tuchock, in her way, sought to maintain and build La Belle Sauvage. She gave significant space to Belle's first introduction, including her refusal to be "looked over," a scene that ends in her biting the overseer's hand. Tuchock included sequences to build Belle's character that were not integral to the plot.[51] In one, Belle rankles at the obedient enslaved people who hurriedly prepare for their new mistress's arrival: "Her carriage [is] regal in spite of the Mother Hubbard garment she now wears. . . . She looks around in contempt. 'Slave Nigra!' She spits and walks away swinging her hips like a queen."[52] When Achille tries to dominate her, claiming that she is his woman, she responds, "You no man. . . . My tribe man no make slave. Warrior him, no make slave. Even woman no make slave—die first, killee self first. In my tribe never no slave."[53] When Achille tries to tell her that she is a slave too, she responds, "No slave. . . . No work—no bow down. Still princess, me."[54]

In Yerby's novel, Mike, Stephen's boorish boatman friend, lives on the plantation and rapes enslaved women, including Zerline. This disappeared from the film treatments, but Tuchock crafted a scene where Mike and his gang intrude on Stephen's wedding night, banging gongs until the bride shows herself in her negligee. Stephen refuses to turn him away and instead goes out to meet him. When Fox returns, Odalie is gone, and he and Mike later find her on the levee: "EXT. LEVEE MOONLIGHT: Two figures are outlined in the moonlight. Odalie, lying where she fell on the levee, her lacy negligee in the dirt and standing over her the negro [sic] savage, Belle. At the approach of Mike and Stephen, Belle runs into the shadows."[55] This scene serves not only to tuck the suggestion of rape into the fabric of the narrative but also to align the rebellious running away of the white and Black women.

It also foreshadows the scene on the levee where Belle tries to kill her son, which would become one of the most significant condemnations of slavery in classical Hollywood history. In the cinematic version of this scene, Stephen visits Belle's cabin on the night her son, Inch, is born. When he claims Inch

In the studio adaptation, Black subjectivity becomes visible when Belle (Suzette Harbin) protects her child from the insidious plantation owner (Rex Harrison).

as body servant for his son, Belle angrily pronounces that Inch will never be a slave and desperately runs to the levee to deliver him to death rather than enslavement. Achille wrestles Inch away, and Belle, instead, throws herself into the water to her death. In the original continuity script, Tuchock made several significant changes to this scene; for instance, rather than Belle holding the child throughout the sequence until she plunges into the water, in this version, Stephen takes the child from Belle, and Belle wrests him away.[56] Tuchock also elaborated the character Zerline, developing small moments of subjectivity, as when Zerline surveys the "room which is to shelter her for the rest of her life."[57]

Tuchock developed the Black storyline but was hampered by her own racism. For instance, in the woodland sequence of the voodoo rites, Caleen "makes cabalistic signs over a couple who dance in the clearing before her. The drummers sit in the semi-circle and beyond is a sea of faces whose lips issue the chant: 'Houn! Dance Calinda! Voodoo!'"[58] If this weren't enough, Tuchock instructed: "The whole set-up, including the dance, must be crudely, naively done; but with inspiration. The dancing couple must look and dance like field negroes only a couple of steps removed from animals. If they look like professional dancers in a stage-set, all the mystery and savage sincerity will be lost."[59]

Though Tuchock brought back characters, the novel's hulking second half was removed. And Inch would never grow up—he, who Yerby had made the son of an African princess, who studies law in France, who goes to Boston becoming a figurehead for the abolitionist movement beside Frederick Douglass, who is captured and tried as a runaway slave, who attempts to escape to Canada but is brought back to Harrow, who becomes the police commissioner of New Orleans during Reconstruction, and who, in the novel's final pages, reveals to his former master that he has married Desiree. The book left the white southern protagonists dangling in the midst of a series of reckonings, national and local, personal and political. Though the finished film has Stephen stoically predict slavery's end and encourage his son 'Tienne to study in the North, its finale, quite ironically given Yerby's original conclusion, sees Odalie and Stephen come together through the whip-wrought mastery of the enslaved who've scattered during an economic panic. It is their ability to command Black labor and obedience that promises the couple's survival and provides the film's conclusion. The finished film only vaguely outlines Black rebellion—in Belle, in caricatured forest voodoo rites, and through the violently ended work stoppage.

Similarly, the studio dared to dramatize Belle's suicide and attempted infanticide, but absent good explanation. Still, 'Tienne's death on the decadent, lofty, slave-built staircase shows how the very architecture of planter aggrandizement could also be an instrument of their fatal fall. And when, responding to 'Tienne's illness, the enslaved begrudgingly sing spirituals in the rain, it is an almost parodic deconstruction of Hollywood's image of devotion and fealty. But the film's final lines, which Stephen speaks over 'Tienne's grave, "such a small grave but at least the ground he lies in will always be his," promised that Fox's "Tara" would stay as firmly in "massa's" control as Yerby's words had stayed in Zanuck's. Odalie, who in Tuchock's early drafts was aligned with Black rebellion, gradually became an icon of masterly white supremacist control. Though Yerby's sublimation had worked to produce some of Hollywood's strongest critiques of slavery, it had not managed to produce even a shadow of Radical Reconstruction, choosing instead the plantation's ancient frame.

BLACK SPECULATIVE ENGAGEMENT WITH AND CRITICISM OF FOX'S *HARROW*

Even before *The Foxes of Harrow* was in production, Black journalists engaged in speculative elaboration on what was likely to come of Hollywood's project—a kind of critical projection based on reports from the set, the trades, interviews, and gossip from on-screen extras and bit players. Fredi Washington was perhaps the first commentator to discuss *Harrow*'s screen prospects:

Lively speculation has been going on as to the treatment Hollywood will give this excellent account of the vastly interesting and intriguing era of colorful New Orleans history. . . . The question which is uppermost in our minds is just how does Fox propose to handle the role of "Desiree" the quadroon who becomes the mistress of Stephen Fox, wealthy and fascinating plantation owner? This character is woven into more than half of the story . . . the character . . . went willingly as a virgin to the arms of Stephen Fox with the consent of her mother (the tradition of the era) . . ., was unwillingly seduced by Fox's son, 'Tienne, admired and lusted after by all men who saw her and finally after the Civil War marries "Inch" the former slave manservant of young Fox, who adopts the son she bore for her lover, Stephen Fox.[60]

Perhaps imagining Desiree as the logical, more historically accurate ancestor to the character she played in *Imitation of Life* (John M. Stahl, 1934), Washington saw the film's potential for revealing aspects of Black women's and America's history that the screen had long elided. With prophetic accuracy, a full year before the film would be shot, she predicted:

What will happen with this character in the transferal from book to screen? . . . It boils down to whether or not Fox has the courage to present on the screen the fascinating history which Yerby has rewritten so descriptively. . . . I venture to say that by no [stretch] of the imagination can I conceive of Fox using a Negro girl in the role, though she can be duplicated many times among us. . . . And if a white girl is used it is safe to assume that the role will be so watered [down] that the evil producing conditions which set aside a group of people who are hated and despised by white women, lusted after and opened by white men and held in utter contempt by Negroes of a darker hue will be lessened. The role of Desiree is of course part and parcel, though physically removed, of slavery and its conditions.[61]

Washington saw the importance of Yerby's making visible concubinage and its subjects. Among the least visible of Black women, both because of their status as "kept" and the color of their skin, they were—in their insidiousness to the color line—at the center of Yerby's critique of the South.

Washington also mused about other pathbreaking characters' screen treatment, including Belle Sauvage, "the girl just out of Africa, whose beauty of face and form is a jet black symphony and who has the spirit and litheness of a panther in the jungle," and Inch, who "embodies the super intelligence, freedom-loving Negro who in that age was living proof of the fallacy of the slogan, 'Negroes were like children and needed the care of their slave owners.'"[62] Her questions were beautifully imagined and pointed; sickened by her sense of impending doom, she continued:

> Will, for example, the screen story show those capable Negroes holding positions after the Civil War, or will they show only those field hands who were without the necessary education to prepare them for their new found freedom? In other words, will Twentieth Century Fox make of "The Foxes of Harrow" a significant documentary film which will enlighten the movie going public on the subject of slavery and all its evils, or will they extract its lusty passion and make of it a sensational nonentity which may or may not turn out to be an insult to Negroes?[63]

Built into Washington's rebuke was a critique of Hollywood's ongoing false historiography and its dire effects. Noting that Yerby's book provided a clear window into the fear and stupidity of the ruling class, she opined, "Most of the present-day prejudices and injustices heaped on the Negro in America can be traced directly to ignorance. How much longer are we going to cater to that ignorance?"[64] She ended with a challenge aimed at Zanuck: "In every century there comes a radical who will brave the displeasure of his bigoted brothers by striking out against a vicious, rotten system. The movie industry has become so highly commercialized that it has that kind of system.... Here is the chance for Zanuck to become that radical and make a lasting contribution to the American people and to the industry of which he is a part."[65] Not allowing doubt to choke out hope, Washington powerfully challenged Zanuck in her pointed early column.

Washington's hopes for the film may have been mixed with her desire to play Desiree, an aspiration likely increased by the fact that *Foxes's* director John Stahl had brought Washington—and the Black subplot—to prominence in *Imitation of Life*. The Black press publicized her trip to Hollywood for a screen test. That hope would not come to pass, just as Washington's hope for a clarifying, "documentary" visibility of concubinage was also dashed. When she returned from her Hollywood screen test, it was without a *Foxes* role but not emptyhanded. Washington's critique of the film and Hollywood censorship had matured:

> So far as the race angle of the story is concerned, the censors need not worry. Hollywood has not reached the adult stage of presenting Negroes in any capacity but that which tickles the sadistic egos of the moronic movie-going public . . . my inside information is that the adapters

have pitched out bodily the one or two Negro characters in the story which would give contrast to the usual superstitious slave characters. For instance, the role of the proud and unrelenting African princess, La Belle Sauvage, has been fused with that of the mulatto slave servants. This statement is made purely from my own analysis and it has got to be the right analysis; otherwise Dorothy Dandridge who is to play the role, nor I could never have been considered for La Belle. . . . Hollywood could not bring itself . . . to show a highly intelligent and educated Negro out-thinking and outwitting the white slave owners [as Inch does]. But they could readily transfer the superstitious cunning and unlettered Caleen and her big, good natured son Achille, who can work like hell with his brawn while his brain remains idle, to the screen with no hesitancy.[66]

Early Black press dispatches like Washington's worried about the censorship. Later ones focused on troubles brewing on set. Black actors were "not being treated fairly," and crew members were "making uncomplimentary remarks about Negro participants."[67] A. C. Bilbrew, who played Tante Caleen, rebuked *Foxes*'s detractors, perhaps at the studio's behest. She argued that no one was being mistreated and that the company had hired Black hairdressers, wardrobe attendants, and technicians.[68] Her write-up, however, unwittingly underscored that the problem was significant enough to necessitate public relations: "Some of the local sepia Hollywood writers are showing a little 'beef' in their dispatches over Mrs. A. C. Bilbrew . . . attempting to protect the studio and the production from legitimate press criticism in an article she wrote in a local weekly."[69]

In May of 1947, the studio's racism again emerged as headline news: "After checking the credit sheets that will be transferred to the main title curtain, not one colored actor in 24 major features now shooting has been listed for screen credit."[70] The studio was concerned enough that publicity director Harry Brand invited Black entertainment journalist Harry Levette to the set. During the visit, unit director Sonia Woolson told Levette, "All were touched with the pathos Kenny Washington put into the scene when, with Suzette's limp drenched body in his arms, he says 'You free now.' Director John Stahl [came] over and was introduced to the girls, chatting with them pleasantly."[71] As part of this publicity effort, Levette was given a photo opportunity and a chance to discuss the future of Black actors in Hollywood with actress Vanessa Brown and two of his invitees, actress-pianist Antionette Gibson and soprano Queenie Jackson.[72] These actions indicate the studio's sense of need for public relations to address the Black response to the set controversies.

Nevertheless, by April 1947, the *New Amsterdam News* was reporting as "the hottest" news from Hollywood that "the part of Inch who resisted slavery throughout the book and ended up not only turning the tables on his former master but with Desiree, the gorgeous mulatto gal (who won't be played by a Negro) . . . will be permitted no such exploits on the screen. The characterization of 'Inch' will be stopped at the age of seven!"[73] Black press reviewers were uniformly disappointed in the film and its adaptation. One unnamed reviewer said that *Foxes* was a "plain costume film" whose basis on Yerby's novel "was so slight as to be almost invisible."[74] George E. Brown of the *Courier* said the film "missed its bet as a tolerance document when the anti-slavery sequences were subdued to a whisper."[75] Lois Taylor's full review enumerated and detailed the many missing elements of the film version:

> The film does not show . . . that Stephen Harrow's [*sic*] mistress Desiree, was a daughter of mixed blood parentage, such as those who appeared at the famous quadroon balls. . . . The prospect of a white wife driven to jealous despair by her husband's honey-colored sweetheart was too much for Hollywood to take. . . . Desiree is presented as simply a beauty whom Stephen meets at a public ballroom in a disreputable part of town.[76]

However, her critique went farther than Desiree to the depiction of slavery and resistance:

> Although the movie does show a kind of work-stoppage by the slaves in which Achille . . . proclaims that the white man's day is done and the master-bondsman relationship is over forever, Hollywood could not bear to present on the screen the spectacle of soldiers of color fighting for their freedom during the War Between the States, of the rise of the freedman to positions of authority and influence in the days of Reconstruction . . . [in the book] Etienne is forced to humble himself before his former playmate and servant, Inch. . . . This too is not permitted to happen in the movie.[77]

Beyond what was not shown, Taylor also reviled the film's stereotypes: "Bandannas and religious fervor also are conspicuous . . . in the movie, which generally follows the 'Gone with the Wind' pattern in stressing the romantic beauty of the old South and muting any condemnation of its social system."[78] The only scene Taylor reported enjoying was that of Belle Sauvage, who she said was "faithful to the book, showing spirit and courage on the part of the colored character."[79]

Taylor, who was not a regular film reviewer, demonstrates how *Foxes* provoked a substantial response from Black spectators. Harry Keelan, who had reviewed the novel in the *Afro-American*, called the film a "destruction" of Yerby's novel and found it both "complete and tragic!" Of the novel, he exclaimed,

"Except for Uncle Tom's Cabin, Yerby's novel is the only important one that has condemned the entire social system of the antebellum South, by showing not only how completely unmoral and immoral it was but also how futile!"[80] In the film, by contrast, "Even . . . the colored girl and her environment are so pale that unless one knows New Orleans and understand[s] the reference to Rampart Street, no one in the audience will even suspect that she is colored, but merely any light o'love condemned by these respectable ladies and gentlemen."[81]

While reviewers understood that Yerby's style had been veiled in the novel, they claimed that Hollywood's "camouflage" was "UnYerbyish."[82] Two-thirds of the novel, claimed *Afro-American*'s Bob Queen, was "whacked" out of the film, and the remaining third showed that "powerful book characters, Tante Caleen and Little Inch, the slave who grew into manhood to become an associate of Frederick Douglass, have been relegated to minor roles. The wisdom of Caleen and her witchcraft that was both respected and feared by whites in the novel is projected from the witchcraft angle only," and Desiree's blackness is not only entirely unconfirmed but robbed of its warmth and passion.[83] Queen concluded, "Probably one of the most authentic scenes which didn't require much of 20th Century Fox's nerve to duplicate was the suicide of L[a] Belle Sauvage."[84] *Chicago Defender*'s Lillian Scott likewise found the film a disappointment, noting that Black characters "with minor exceptions" were Hollywood's "same old 'Southern darkie.'"[85] She also imagined Yerby's disdain, noting, "Yerby saw the film at a special screening following the premiere, but would not comment."[86] In her view, the only "saving grace in the film's dialectical handling of Negroes" was Belle, though she also pointed out that "the regal pride which brought her to commit suicide is never cleverly drawn, and the film makes her seem overly hysterical instead of haughty."[87] Scott opined, "The one time a slave rebels . . . she dies for her trouble. And when a group once refused to cut cane, Odalie, Stephen's wife, like a true lady of the old South, whipped them out of hiding. They cut that cane. Yes suh."[88] Ora Lee Brinkley likewise developed an ornate critique of the film's Black characterizations, stating, "There is a large number of Negro actors appearing in the 'Foxes of Harrow' but they seem justifiably uncomfortable in the peculiar roles assigned them. Although Rene Beard, who plays the part of six-year-old 'Little Inch,' displays a lot more self-possession than many of his elders."[89] The Black press was not alone in seeing the film as a failed adaptation. *Time* magazine stated, "All this to-do is as expensively and prettily produced as if anyone could possibly care. Probably because the author of the original best-seller, Frank Yerby, is a Negro, the best thing in the picture is a more than ordinary interest in the slaves and their lives; but even this feature is drowned in ornateness and theatricality."[90]

The film, in its whitewashed state, was not only a financial failure but a cautionary tale to other Black authors seeking the so-called triumph of Hollywood adaptation. Willard Motley, whose film *Knock on Any Door* (Nicholas Ray, 1949) ultimately got a distribution deal with Columbia, considered *The Foxes of Harrow* motivation for securing control over screen adaptation.[91] Zanuck, too, considered the film a failure, even if he hated to fully admit it: "*Captain from Castile* [Henry King, 1947] and *Foxes of Harrow* [1947] . . . were good pictures, but our failure was that we spent more for them than the market could afford. Thus our good judgment in making these pictures was completely nullified by our bad judgment in spending more than we should have. And the result of this is that both pictures stand on the books as failures."[92] This attitude was a foreboding sign for Black Hollywood adaptations, even those wearing racial camouflage. Indeed, despite Yerby's unwavering status as a best-selling author, he would never again have a book purchased by a major studio, let alone for the price *Foxes* fetched.

RKO's and Warner Bros.'s story files give a window into studio decision-making on Yerby's properties. Before rejecting it in December of 1946, Warner Bros.'s story department reviewers recognized the potential of *Foxes*'s "colorful" qualities and financial prospects; one even noted that its "slight undercurrent of racial problems in the South" might "be dropped without wrecking the story."[93] However, writer Robert Buckner, while arguing that the story was the best one they had synopsized in a long while, noted that its expense and "the miscegenation angle" that "is not easily removable without weakening the dramatic structure" made it difficult to film.[94] These story factors—and the bidding war among studios that ensued—were the clearest reasons for Warner Bros.'s decision not to pursue the property.

Given that Yerby was one of America's most popular novelists during this period, many predicted Yerby's Reconstruction era *The Vixens* (1947) would be filmed.[95] One RKO story department reviewer described Yerby's late 1940s novels as "obviously and deliberately picturable."[96] Though Dial art department images appeared on the pages of fan mags exactly a year after *Foxes* premiered, a movie adaptation of *The Vixens* was not to be.[97] Patricia Gordon, story department reader from RKO, said of Yerby's next novel, *The Vixens* (aka *The Core Is Flame*), "it has all the ingredients—handsome hero, suave villain, lush women, gun-play and sword-play; enough grisly details in the torture of Negros to afford the readers chills of horror; enough sex to keep them in a 'gentle dew of anticipation.'"[98] Her appraisal forecast the film's likely box-office success and saw anti-Black brutality as a potentially chilling selling point. However, others from the story department did not agree: a reviewer with the initials W. K. stated, "Big and colorful, expensive to make and touchy as hell for this plays up the post-Civil War situation in the South when intimidation of the Negros by murder 'saved' the South for its old masters. I think this might be excellent reading but . . . [it] probably would be emasculated so severely as to be another story anyway"; another reviewer agreed that the novel was "touchy," and a third mentioned that it was as "controversial as dynamite—by the way, did you know that the author is a Negro?" The company did, however, choose to circulate the materials to the producers.[99]

Challenged by studio decisions about his second Reconstruction-era book, Yerby further developed his practice of racial sublimation. His next novel, *The Golden Hawk* (1948), avoided southern haunts; though other Yerby novels returned to the South, Hollywood avoided these titles. It was only his pre-American novels *The Golden Hawk* (set in the seventeenth-century Caribbean) and *The Saracen Blade* (set in twelfth- and thirteenth-century Italy) that Hollywood adapted. Columbia Pictures Sam Katzman produced both films in cheap Technicolor with white screenwriters. However, in his plots, Yerby never left the Black American experience behind. Rather, he embarked on a reverse colonial journey to find the insidious roots of white supremacy lodged in the histories of Europe. It wasn't a retreat from race, but rather a new hiding place for the story that burned within him.

ADAPTING *THE GOLDEN HAWK*

The Golden Hawk reveals the deadly fraternal wars among England, France, and Spain to control the seventeenth-century Caribbean. Kit, a pirate, is in love with two women: Rouge (herself a pirate) and Bianca (an aristocrat). The colonial novel has virtually no Black subplot, but blackness remains insistently below the surface. First, several white characters are tinged with racial ambiguity: blonde Kit is "bronze" according to the author's description, and Rouge, though white skinned and emerald eyed, has a "Mongolian" look.[100] As with many pirate narratives, *The Golden Hawk* is largely a narrative of successive escapes, with the hero finding his way out of myriad dungeons and tortures. Into this, Yerby works in the stuff of American slave narratives.[101] Black characters are actively ever present in the background, appearing in every ten to twenty pages. Plantations are central, and references to Black women's rape or the sons sired by white men are consistent. The governor of St. Dominique, we learn, was a former slave trader.

Further, the brutality that Black enslaved people suffer often upstages the white drama with an interruptive logic. In one scene, a group of Black enslaved laborers crush sugar cane. Kit watches a young, attractive Englishman cruelly driving them:

> "You black beasts! Get it in there—but in closer or I'll bloody your hides!" . . . Kit saw the young man rise in the saddle and bring the

riding crop down full across the Negro's back. The black man cringed, and gave the stalks a convulsive shove. The next movement Kit heard a scream. It was a terrible sound like a loon nigh-maddened or like a parakeet losing his insane, fiendish laughter. Looking closer, Kit could see that the Negro had caught his hand in the crusher. "Mother of God!" he whispered. "Why doesn't he stop the mules?" But the young Englishman . . . sat there like one stupefied. The great millstones dragged the black's wrists and forearm and upper arm between them so that the slave was pulled round and round the outer rim of the rushers and the cane juice came out red with his blood. "Idiot!" the Englishman shrieked, suddenly completely beside himself with rage. "You've ruined the entire batch! Brutus! Bring the axe!" Kit and Bernardo watched in cold stupefaction while another Negro hurried off to return after a moment with a broad bladed ax. "Set him free!" the young man ordered. Brutus, his black face the color of old ashes, swung the ax skyward. Kit saw it arching against the sky. Then it whistled downward to strike the imprisoned slave's shoulder with a sound like no other sound on earth, except, perhaps, the sound of the poleax in the slaughter pens. The black man lay on the earth, his arm sheared off at the shoulder and the great flood of his life pumped out until all the earth beneath him was muddied. No one made the slightest effort to aid him or to stop the bleeding. Grimly Kit turned to his buccaneers, "All right, men," he said quietly, "burn the field!"[102]

With the grim horror of Yerby's story "Salute to the Flag" combined with the sense of futility in "Homecoming," this brief scene denounces capitalistic slavery's brutal logic—one connecting the plantation to the slaughterhouse. The startling initial whipping with an implement intended for an animal is only worsened as its victim becomes literal grist for the mill and is finally chopped in half to salvage the crop. Slavery's sadistic futility is on full display, as are the deadly consequences of the white colonialist's brutality and stupefaction. Further, Yerby's overseer calls on an ax to "set" the enslaved man "free," equating, as had been done in *Foxes*, freedom with death.[103]

The quickness of the enslaved man's transition from productive to inanimate flesh, as well as the microcosm of wasted human life represented in the spilled blood—the muddying of the earth and the reddening of the cane—is magnified in the next scene as Kit, to thwart the English, burns the very field being cultivated. We later learn that the plantation's destruction, and the accompanying mass Black casualty, is merely a microcosm; legions more enslaved are seized and traded between the warring European powers: "Two hundred and fifty mills and plantations had been destroyed and more than thirteen hundred

Negroes captured."[104] Yerby, historian of scale, moves in these paragraphs from one man's death to the conquering of thousands.

However, these arresting scenes seemingly stolen from American slave narratives were infrequent, with racial narratives and critiques more deeply submerged. And, in contrast to *Foxes*, Black book reviewers seemed bored by *The Golden Hawk*—many even declined to comment. The *Defender's* Gertrude Martin said that it bore "the same formula—a handsome man and two irresistibly beautiful women" but that Yerby's "characters are even less well defined than in his two earlier novels.... In any event, 'The Golden Hawk' will make a wonderful [white] Errol Flynn movie."[105] To maintain Yerby's marketability with white audiences, he seems to have sacrificed—greatly though not completely—his subtle dealing with race history in ways legible to the contemporaneous Black critical community. The script drafts and the PCA file indicate that Columbia never intended to depict slavery or scenes featuring Black people. The PCA was concerned about the fight scenes—kicking and gouging—and the illicit relationships.[106] The PCA noted race only in an Incan dance sequence: "All of the action showing the copper-skinned native girl half clad, doing a 'savage, undisciplined dance,' must be handled carefully."[107]

The finished film, unlike the slavery-laced novel, is a painfully typical swashbuckler, filled to the decks with stock characters and clichés, from pirates with dangling earrings and kerchiefed heads to ladies in busting bustiers—and lots of swordplay above and below deck. Absent from the film is the book's "bronze" skin of the main character, Kit, and it appears Columbia employed not a single Black actor, which rendered the film illegible to most Black press entertainment columnists who tracked and followed Black assignments from Central Casting. The film's only nonwhite characters are the "copper-skinned" Inca and the Chibcha.[108]

In place of the graphic scene of planter violence, the film's scenes of plantation desecration show absolutely no field laborers, a startling omission and a striking contrast with the book where Black death is incredibly visible. In other words, while Yerby consciously visualized slavery's brutality and hulking largeness in European conquest, the film entirely removed any suggestion of slavery whatsoever, sublimating racial specificity to such an extent that it became invisible. However, there is truth in the woodenness of the drama. The conniving and ascendancy of financial and political motives over and above love has its own story to tell about whiteness, colonialism, and the absence of affect in the European "romantic" world of the Caribbean. Perhaps because Yerby's message about Black death had been too thickly camouflaged, his text became a palimpsest for Hollywood screenwriters to inscribe their own trite swashbuckling fantasies of whiteness. The Black press, though it celebrated the film as Yerby's, largely ignored it or cast it as "another case of a good story badly translated from book to film."[109] Delores Calvin opined, "Actor Sterling Hayden and actress Rhonda Fleming could do little to hold up the Columbia production despite the handsome Technicolor."[110]

HIDDEN IN PLAIN SIGHT:
THE BLACK AMERICAN RUNAWAY IN *THE SARACEN BLADE*

With *The Saracen Blade*, Yerby deepened his sublimation of race, going back further historically and shifting his technique. With the accrual of detail that a 328-page book allowed, there was room for signifiers to get lost—and found. In 1951, Yerby, his wife, and their four children moved to France, which perhaps prompted his attention to European history. The novel is the story of Pietro Di Donati, a small, brown Italian boy, son of a rebellious Norman blacksmith and serf, who, aided by bravery and having been born in the same city as Holy Roman Emperor Frederick of Hohenstaufen, rises to become a knight and baron. *The Saracen Blade* represents Yerby's quest for the beginnings of the racist logic that undergirded American slavery and its tortures.

Pietro, the protagonist, is a white man with "brown" skin and blonde hair whose whiteness suggests illegitimacy because it sets him apart from the "black thatched, brown youth, squat, greasy, and smelling forever of sweat and of cattle dung" that surround him in southern Italy where the novel is set.[111] Indeed, his mother, "as dark as a Moor," is accused of being born of a woman "more than a little friendly with a heathen Saracen."[112] The book displays the racially cosmopolitan, literate society of southern Italy, peopled by Jews, Normans, Greeks, Germans, Moors, and "Negroes." One character even exclaims that all Italians are "half-Moors anyhow!"[113] Frederick, soon to become the Holy Roman emperor and the paragon of scientific modernity, is also not purely white: "The sun had burnt him reddish brown, like mahogany, at the same time bleaching his blonde hair to an even lighter shade."[114] Here again, as in earlier novels, whiteness—a concept built upon purity—appears rudderless or, even more disastrously, part Black.

Unmistakably, Yerby traces the horrors of European tortures in ways that Black and white Americans were likely to recognize as American traditions. First, the novel is populated by serfs and slaves, both demeaned in ways similar to American slaves.[115] Serfdom here, like slavery, operates as a caste system, bringing to bear the theme that James Hill has identified as ubiquitous to Yerby's work—that of the outsider.[116] Saidiya Hartman has noted that, at its essence, the word "slave" means stranger, and perhaps the runaway, rolling through an unfriendly world, was the most profound stranger in the taxonomy of the enslaved.[117] This is a connection that Yerby had begun to develop in *The*

Foxes of Harrow but that perhaps matures in *The Saracen Blade*. Yerby deploys a complex politics of the outsider—on the one hand, idealized and desired by the ruling class, but on the other hand, reviled on the principle of his separate status alone.

Early on, Yerby describes the hanging corpses of formerly starving food poachers that have been left out for days on the road as a monument for all to pass and see—all good men who Pietro knows well. Further, Pietro's brown mother almost immediately becomes the target of a white baron's plans for jus primae noctis, a legal rape of peasants by nobles sanctioned by the Church. As Pietro's Norman father flees, he is followed by bloodhounds, yet another tradition legible from the American South. Later, men are boiled in a pot, as was done in Caribbean slavery and as would later be shown occurring in American slavery in *Mandingo* (Richard Fleischer, 1975).[118] When the novel moves to France, we learn that this country, too, is plagued by Crusade-born inhumanity: not only did crusaders bind and burn men, but "they took babes from their mothers and tossed them into the air and caught them upon the points of their swords as they fell. They took toddlers by the feet and swung them against the walls."[119]

When the Crusades bring Pietro to Egypt, the setting allows for even more of the appurtenances of American slavery. On the auction block, as in *Foxes*, women resist enslavement, never demurring.[120] The Egyptian scene also reveals Black people forced to beat fellow slaves against their will.[121] With deep irony, Yerby makes the novel's Black men into eunuchs, avoiding concerns about their proximity to white women.[122] However, he offers a rousing subplot about a Black eunuch who has a wife and child before he is castrated and who Zenobia, a Greek slave, helps to find a place in service for his son after his mother dies. There are further references to the icons of American slavery: people wear bells around their necks "to call down upon them the scorn of the faithful" and must put their faces in the behinds of animals all day as punishment.[123] Zenobia, Pietro, and Pietro's future wife, Io, are all whipped at some point during the novel. Frederick discusses the children who are enslaved and sometimes raped during the Crusades.[124] Throughout the book, the focus on concubinage, the brutal killings of the poor, and the accrual of detail around the slave market in Egypt all pierce the main narrative as signifiers of the debasement that attended American slavery, signifiers that are as discordant to the American consciousness as they are to the white European. The clearest reference to slavery in Yerby's novel, however, comes in an early lynching scene. Pietro's surrogate father, Isaac, is killed:

The good Jew was hanging from one of the parapets. Naked. Upside down. His belly was ripped open, so that the entrails dangled. Other

Sublimating the depiction of American slavery into a narrative about serfdom in medieval European ensured Yerby's "strange fruit" made it to the screen in *The Saracen Blade*.

things had been done to him too. Unspeakable things.... Pietro slumped forward on the neck of his great stallion Amir. He could neither see nor speak but he clung to the destrier's coarse mane. And the wise beast whirled and ran away from there, down a long row of oaks. The wind revived the boy. He straightened. *Then he saw that the trees bore strange fruit.* From each of them, for leagues in the distance, men were hanging. Count Alessandro had had his vengeance.... Pietro mounted. In the saddle, he turned and looked at the thing that had been his father.[125]

Yerby's tale of knighthood and bravery is marked more by torture and brutality than by chivalry. The level of debasement—not just the dirtiness and sordid sexuality but also the murdering of infants—is Yerby's piercing rendering of white colonial history. Though the novel centers on Pietro, his interiority, his love affairs, and his triumphs over his subordinate status, this is the guise—the sophisticated polysemy—through which Yerby continually returns to the mechanisms and machinations of American chattel slavery. Although the book puts the veil of adventure over the mechanisms of torture and human control, the novel's "beats" are the moments of torture that define the protagonists' lives: rape, beating, lynching, maiming—these are the novel's pivotal events. It is, in this way, a kind of horror novel parading as an adventure, and Pietro is a kind of noir empath who is our guide. Though Pietro is an adventurer, there is never the buoyancy of a *Captain Blood* novel here. Yerby's novel is postwar fiction reconciled to the death of dreams.

DeVallon Scott and left-leaning George Worthing Yates adapted *The Saracen Blade* to the screen. In their hands, Yerby's palimpsestic work was stretched in new directions: the script became less the story of class ascent and knighthood and more of class warfare—a serf avenging his father. The film begins with an image of the cross. A narrator's voiceover states that the biggest sin— and the most difficult one to overcome in life—is being born a serf. Though Pietro, played by Ricardo Montalbán, is whitewashed and not visibly brown, his audible accent marks his difference from the rest of the cast of white North American actors. Thus, Hollywood rendered the escaped slave through the othered body of the "Latin lover." If the film removed suggestions of racial mixing, the screenwriters only increased allusions to slavery. The finished film preserved the scene perhaps most highly resonant with the visual and symbolic iconography of Black American slavery: Pietro walks along a road lined with trees, each with a body hanging below. In the film and more so than the novel, this scene becomes *the* moment of Pietro's awakening and the driving force behind his destiny.

The screenwriters describe this scene as a forest filled with

the silence of death . . . CAMERA, CONTINUING TO PAN SLOWLY, that foregrounds the still body of a man standing on air. We cannot see his head and shoulders or the rope by which he hangs from the branching tree. As the PAN CONTINUES we see a strange forest—the perpendicular columns that are rooted in the ground alternating with the perpendicular columns that are rooted in the air.[126]

Pietro looks at the visage of each hanged man:

His face . . . frozen with horror . . . looking up at [one] face [he] gives a violent start—the horror in his eyes intensifies. He stares unbelievingly a moment; then . . . working to keep back the tears, he comes forward, takes one of the limp hands and holds it. . . . Finally there comes into scene the body of Donati, recognizable by his wide, peculiarly-wrought metal belt. Pietro stops, looking up at his father's face. . . . Slowly he sinks to his knees, closes his eyes and bows his head, in a silent, terrible vow.[127]

The screenwriters sharpen attention to this pivotal lynching scene by referring to it several times. For example, Pietro's enemy Enzio is later given the line,

"You will dance your father's dance—on empty air."[128] Pietro, speaking with the emperor, says:

> You had an emperor's might, Sire. I have only these two old friends. (He holds up his hands . . .)
> FREDERICK: But you have a third now, in the person of myself. If you had an emperor's might, against what people would you use it?
> PIETRO: The Siniscolas. (grimly) And when I was done with them, the trees of their forest would once again hang with strange fruit![129]

Like the runaway slave, Pietro has many "lives" and iterations of selves, uncertain and changing parentage, and fictive kinship. Pietro indentures himself to a local lord, only to fall in love; he later escapes with the lord's daughter. He is caught and placed in the dungeon, where we see him disconsolate but still sprightly. He escapes from the dungeon only because his captor has designed his escape for a manhunt, yet another potential reference to slavery. Chased by dogs, Pietro nearly despairs when he is treed by baying hounds, an image that again recalls the iconography of the runaway in the American South. As they sic the dogs on him, Pietro's clothes get dirtier, and the dogs get parts of his clothing; he cleverly escapes by throwing them an article of clothing. The visual of men hunting other men with dogs is even more pronounced in the script and film than in Yerby's book. Pietro passes through swamps and reeds, images common to southern narratives of escape from chain gangs and lynch mobs and prevalent in several slave narratives.

While these depictions are not exact allegories of slavery, the sequences, especially as featured in the film, resonate strongly with this history. Indeed, though all the film's slave references are also present in the book, more emphasis is placed on them in the film. However, the film does not show the book's auction scene, but instead displays a scene strongly infused with the American slave narrative—a scene of a slave being beaten. The *manner* in which the woman is beaten, laid out on the ground with her arms staked to the ground, is a familiar method from scenes of American slavery. Later, another violent motif born of the American slave narrative occurs —the man (in this case, Pietro) is chained to a tree and whipped. Yerby's narrative also bears similarity to the narratives of escaped slaves like William Grimes, for whom escape was not a stable, one-time operation but a way of life. Not only does Pietro's first scene in the desert begin with him watching—and boldly interrupting—the whipping of Zenobia, the slave girl, but Pietro eventually takes her place, suffering a beating at the hands of a Black overseer.

When Pietro becomes the slave of Harum, a wealthy sheik, he participates in the kinds of runaway resistance that John Blassingame and John Hope Franklin ascribe to the runaway.[130] As Pietro is pulled roughly toward Harum's tents, Harum remarks: "Again? Four times in as many months you've tried to get away and as many times you've been brought back flogged. I'll be glad when you're sold at the slave auctions and I'm rid of you!" Pietro replies, "I'll only escape from my new master so why not set me free now!" Harum's reply gels neatly with the history and psychological logic of American plantation slavery: "If I can't get any value from you as a slave, at least I will make an example of you for the others. Twenty lashes don't do any good. Give him thirty!"

The sequence, notably the one farthest from the American and European stage and in a vaguely desert terrain, ends with Zenobia attempting to use the gifts her master has given her to buy Pietro's freedom and her own. The irony of this sale, and the master's reminder that the presumably sexual bond between master and female slave makes her expensive, is highlighted when he states, "How will you buy your own freedom?" With Pietro and Zenobia, Yerby dramatizes the experiences of both the male and female slaves in the American context. Not only is Zenobia Harum's concubine, but the film ends with another revelation of the maiming slavery has wrought, as Zenobia is revealed to have been facially disfigured by Harum. The rarity of these scenes in Hollywood—disfigurement, whipping, and hanging—makes this film, which exploitation filmmaker William Castle directed, even more unique and resonant. The images of dogs treeing a man, Pietro wading through a swamp to evade capture, the "strange fruit" of the Italian poplar trees, and even the secret romances of the lowly slave with the powerful mistress who secretly desires him seem to speak to the secret life of the American slave not pictured on the screen and, furthermore, illustrate the brutality-ridden and elusive life of the runaway slave specifically.

In sum, along with screenwriters Scott and Yates, Yerby captured the life of resistance, revolt, and revolution that had to become the mindset of the escaped slave. Both Pietro and Zenobia embody the pain of loss the runaway must have experienced, the impetus toward perpetual movement away from the hounding of American racial restrictions, and the continued search for freedom. Scott and Yates captured these images, albeit in whiteface, and were bold enough to subversively integrate the popular with social critique. The narrative of the escaped Black American slave in the film is clear, though less apparent in the plot and more apparent in the film's resonant and brutal iconography. Though Pietro is able to overcome the forces that would bind him, it is nevertheless significant that the film represents, in veiled form, the very narrative of the enslaved American runaway that Hollywood found unfilmable.

This time, even fewer reviewers recognized the racial resonances of either the book or the film. *Time Magazine*'s review of *The Saracen Blade* describes the production as a study in triteness—kind of a symptom of the Sirkian moment—overdone and underdone at the same time, a Technicolor film with the "skimpiest crusade in Hollywood history."[131] But against this limpid backdrop, the signifiers of slavery stand out all the more, though it may be that, by this point in Yerby's career and American history, no one was looking for such subtleties.

CONCLUSION

Making history as America's best-selling postwar author and the first African American to become a millionaire from writing, Frank Yerby engineered and created a mode of representing race through history and sublimating its direct representation; he also interjected the internal rage that race had provoked in him. Yerby is often seen as an author who put protest and race behind him— but he never did. Beginning with *The Foxes of Harrow*, Yerby practiced the art of racial sublimation, making Black history into a subplot so as to draw—and even ensnare—readers who would never touch writing on the Black side of the color line. His indirect rendering of race fosters subtle reading of subplots and encourages reading across texts: among the three books and films, there is an undercurrent of images exposing enslavement, torture, and escape that was forbidden in American literature, cinema, and historiography. The blacker Yerby's novels were, the less Hollywood could absorb their images; however, when blackness was guised in bronzed whiteness, Yerby's plots could showcase the storylines of Black history that the screen could not show, though their racial connections often became illegible to Black audiences. In the decades of the 1950s, 1960s, and 1970s, with increasing Black activism, his hidden racial critique gradually seemed to disappear and pass into meaninglessness.

Notes

1. Robin D. G. Kelley, *Race Rebels: Culture, Politics, and the Black Working Class* (New York: Free Press, 1994); James C. Scott, *Domination and the Arts of Resistance: Hidden Transcripts* (New Haven, CT: Yale University Press, 1990).

2. Darwin T. Turner, "Frank Yerby as Debunker," *Massachusetts Review* 9, no. 3 (Summer 1968): 569–77; James Hill, "Anti-Heroic Perspectives: The Life and Works of Frank Yerby" (dissertation, University of Iowa, 1976).

3. Frank G. Yerby, "White Magnolias," *Phylon* 5, no. 4 (1944): 319–26.

4. Muriel Fuller to Frank Yerby, July 23, 1943, Muriel Fuller Papers, Special Collections, Temple University, Philadelphia, PA.

5. Yerby to Fuller, July 22, 1943, Fuller Papers.

6. Yerby to Fuller, November 25, 1943, Fuller Papers.

7. On the CIO, see Yerby to Fuller, October 12, 1943, Fuller Papers.

8. Yerby to Fuller, January 3, 1944, Fuller Papers.

9. Yerby to Fuller, November 25, 1943, Fuller Papers.

10. Yerby to Fuller, November 25, 1943, Fuller Papers.

11. Edward G. Aswell to Frank Yerby, December 28, 1943, Fuller Papers.

12. Yerby to Fuller, January 3, 1944, Fuller Papers.

13. Fuller to Yerby, November 29, 1943, Fuller Papers.

14. Yerby to Fuller, February 23, 1946, Fuller Papers.

15. Yerby to Fuller, March 1, 1944, Fuller Papers.

16. Frank Yerby, Lillian Scott, and Gertrude Martin, "Books and Art," *Headlines and Pictures*, March 1, 1946, 40.

17. Fuller to Yerby, December 29, 1943, Fuller Papers.

18. Fuller to Yerby, December 29, 1943, Fuller Papers.

19. Constance Curtis, "Books Can Make It a Merry Christmas: This Year's Books Mark Banner Year," *New York Amsterdam News*, December 14, 1946, 11; Gertrude Martin, "Bookshelf: Puerto Rican Story," *Chicago Defender*, March 8, 1947, 13; Alfred Smith, "Adventures in Race Relations: Author," *Chicago Defender*, February 15, 1947, 15.

20. Gertrude Martin, "Bookshelf: Puerto Rican Story," *Chicago Defender*, March 8, 1947, 13.

21. Shirley Graham Dubois, "Fotoscope," *People's Voice*, July 27, 1946, 17; "Yerby Calls Writing a Family Enterprise," *Ebony*, February 1, 1955, 32.

22. Michael Carter, "Meet Frank '*Foxes of Harrow*' Yerby: Story about Whites No Social Protest Novel," *Afro-American*, March 2, 1946, 14.

23. Creole, though sometimes used to denote people of mixed African ancestry, in this case refers to a mix of Spanish and French descent.

24. Frank Yerby, *The Foxes of Harrow* (New York: Dial Press, 1946), 167.

25. Phyllis Klotman, "A Harrowing Experience: Frank Yerby's First Novel to Film," *CLA Journal* 31, no. 2 (December 1987): 211.

26. Yerby, *Foxes of Harrow*, 338.

27. On the six-book deal and the number of copies sold before publication, see Ben Burns, "Off the Book Shelf: Frank Yerby Makes His Bow," *Chicago Defender*, February 2, 1946, 15; on the Blue-Chip edition, see "Printer's Ink," *New York Amsterdam News*, February 22, 1947, 26; Van Walters, "Report from New York Staff Correspondence," *Norfolk Journal and Guide*, March 2, 1946, 2.

28. "Georgia Wins High Rank on Race Relations Schomburg Honor Roll: Ellis . . . ," *Atlanta Daily World*, February 11, 1947, 1.

29. S. W. Garlington, "News and Views," *Negro Book Club*, September 1, 1947, 4.

30. "Liberia's First Centennial Will Get U. S. Support Fox Studios Casting *Foxes of Harrow*," *Pittsburgh Courier*, March 22, 1947, 5. This source lists the price as $500,000; "Best Seller Brings $150,000," *Pittsburgh Courier*, May 25, 1946, 1; "Negro Sells His Novel '*Foxes of Harrow*' to Movies, $250,000," *Cleveland Call and Post*, June 22, 1946, 5B; the actual contracts indicate the studio paid Yerby $150,000 for the film; these documents can be found in box 28b, typescript insert 4L, Frank Yerby Papers, Boston University.

31. One letter Flora Yerby (wife) wrote to Muriel Fuller indicates that both Frank and Flora were "confirmed shutterbugs" (Flora Yerby to Muriel Fuller, October 18, 1943, Fuller Papers) and indicates that he was "too interested now in taking pictures of the kids" to finish his short story (Flora Yerby to Muriel Fuller, November 11, 1943, Fuller Papers).

32. On "County Sheriff," see box 22, Frank Yerby Papers, Boston University; on "Destination Danger," see box 18, Frank Yerby Papers, Boston University.

33. Zanuck wrote, "I call upon writers to lead the way—if they have something worthwhile to say, let them dress it in the glittering robes of entertainment and they will find a ready market. . . . No producer who is worthy of the name will reject entertainment and without entertainment no propaganda film is worth a dime." Darryl Zanuck, *Saturday Review of Literature*, October 30, 1943, 12. Yerby wrote, "I write exactly how I feel and think I want to do, but within the framework I try to give pleasure to the reading public . . . the novelist hasn't any right to inflict on the public his private ideas on politics, religion or race. If he wants to preach he should go to the pulpit." "Novelist Frank Yerby Is Just a Name to His Millions of Readers," *Ebony*, February 1, 1955, 31.

34. See Elizabeth Bingelli, "Hollywood Dark Matter: Reading Race and Absence in Studio Era Narrative" (dissertation, University of Southern California, Los Angeles, 2005).

35. Michael Carter, "Meet Frank 'Foxes of Harrow' Yerby," *Afro-American*, March 2, 1946, 14.

36. "Conference with Mr. Zanuck," July 26, 1946, 3, folder 1 of 4, *The Foxes of Harrow*, 20th Century-Fox Collection, USC Cinema-Television Library, Los Angeles.

37. "Conference with Mr. Zanuck," July 26, 1946.

38. "Conference with Mr. Zanuck," July 26, 1946.

39. "Conference with Mr. Zanuck," July 26, 1946.

40. The PCA also met with producer William A. Bacher and director John Stahl in April. The concern that motivated the conference, according to the records, was the "Rampart scenes." Production Code Administration File, Special Collections, Margaret Herrick Library, Beverly Hills, CA.

41. Joseph Breen to Jason Joy, March 25, 1947, Production Code Administration File.

42. Lamar Trotti, the Production Code Administration File's white, southern consultant on Black images said of *Hallelujah*, "If the characters were whites, I would think very definitely that Vidor was treading on very dangerous grounds—that of a renegade parson running off with a strumpet, seeing her die and brutally murdering her lover. But such is the influence of my rearing in the South, I can't get excited about this in the lives of negroes. We think such things happen, everyone seems to accept them as natural and no one bothers about them." Lamar Trotti to Maurice McKenzie, October 19, 1928, *Hallelujah*, Production Code Administration File.

43. Joseph Breen to Joy, March 25, 1947, Production Code Administration File.

44. Joseph Breen to Joy, March 25, 1947.

45. The Dunning School was a historiographic approach modeled at Columbia by William Archibald Dunning and known for its racist distortion of the Reconstruction period as one of failure. For more on the Dunning School, see W. E. B. Du Bois's *Black Reconstruction in America, 1860–1880* (New York: Free Press, 1992). The introduction by David Levering Lewis provides the context for Du Bois's own critique of the Dunning School.

46. Notes written by Zanuck on the front of draft of treatment by Jerome Cady, Revised Synopsis, August 8, Twentieth Century-Fox Collection.

47. Treatment 1, November 4, 1946, *The Foxes of Harrow*, Wanda Tuchock Papers [TP, hereafter], American Heritage Center, University of Wyoming; Treatment 2, November 7, 1946, *The Foxes of Harrow*, Tuchock Papers.

48. Treatment 1, 9, *The Foxes of Harrow*, Tuchock Papers.

49. Treatment 1, 9, *The Foxes of Harrow*, Tuchock Papers.

50. First Draft Continuity, January 10, 1947, 20, *The Foxes of Harrow*, Tuchock Papers.

51. First Draft Continuity, 23, *The Foxes of Harrow*, Tuchock Papers.

52. First Draft Continuity, 27, *The Foxes of Harrow*, Tuchock Papers.

53. First Draft Continuity, 27, *The Foxes of Harrow*, Tuchock Papers.

54. First Draft Continuity, 27, *The Foxes of Harrow*, Tuchock Papers.

55. First Draft Continuity, 30, *The Foxes of Harrow*, Tuchock Papers.

56. First Draft Continuity, 38, *The Foxes of Harrow*, Tuchock Papers.

57. First Draft Continuity, 28, *The Foxes of Harrow*, Tuchock Papers.

58. First Draft Continuity, 33, *The Foxes of Harrow*, Tuchock Papers.

59. First Draft Continuity, 33, *The Foxes of Harrow*, Tuchock Papers.

60. Fredi Washington, "Fredi Says," *People's Voice*, June 15, 1946, 22.

61. Washington, "Fredi Says," 22.

62. Washington, "Fredi Says," 22.

63. Washington, "Fredi Says," 22.

64. Washington, "Fredi Says," 22.

65. Washington, "Fredi Says," 22.

66. Washington, "Fredi Says," *People's Voice*, May 17, 1947, 22.

67. "Rumors of Studio Bias Are Refuted," *New Journal and Guide*, July 5, 1947, 5.

68. "Rumors of Studio Bias Are Refuted," 5.

69. Maria T. Dragna, "This Is Hollywood," *Chicago Defender*, July 12, 1947, 19.

70. Harry Levette, "Screen Credit Denied Top Stars in 24 Major Films," *Afro-American*, May 31, 1947, 8. This story held out hope for *Foxes*, which ultimately denied all Black characters screen credit.

71. Harry Levette, "They Visited in Hollywood," *Chicago Defender*, August 2, 1947, 10.

72. "Photo Standalone 21," *Pittsburgh Courier*, August 30, 1947, 16.

73. "Irving Mills Back to Pick Up More Gold on Cab, Duke," *New York Amsterdam News*, April 26, 1947, 21.

74. "'Foxes' Plain Costume Film," *Los Angeles Sentinel*, October 23, 1947, 20.

75. George F. Brown, "Business Dip, Wax Ban, Bias Fight Mark 1947," *Pittsburgh Courier*, January 3, 1948, 15.

76. Lois Taylor, "Article 1 — No Title," *Afro-American*, November 15, 1947, Ml6.

77. Taylor, "Article 1 — No Title," Ml6.

78. Taylor, "Article 1 — No Title," Ml6.

79. Taylor, "Article 1 — No Title," Ml6.

80. Harry Keelan, "Voice in the Wilderness," *Afro-American*, October 18, 1947, 4.

81. Keelan, "Voice in the Wilderness," 4.

82. Bob Queen, "'Harrow' Film Misses Boat; Sting Absent," *Afro-American*, October 4, 1947, 6.

83. Queen, "'Harrow' Film Misses Boat; Sting Absent," 6.

84. Queen, "'Harrow' Film Misses Boat; Sting Absent," 6.

85. Lillian Scott, "'Foxes of Harrow' Has Little Appeal as a Movie," *Chicago Defender*, October 4, 1947, 17.

86. Scott, "'Foxes of Harrow' Has Little Appeal as a Movie," 17.

87. Scott, "'Foxes of Harrow' Has Little Appeal as a Movie," 17.

88. Scott, "'Foxes of Harrow' Has Little Appeal as a Movie," 17.

89. Ora Lee Brinkley, "On the Brink," *Philadelphia Tribune*, October 11, 1947, 6.

90. "Cinema," *Time Magazine*, October 13, 1947, 105.

91. "*Foxes of Harrow* . . . was faced with the same problems that confront the Motley book. That Yerby agreed to the Hollywood rewrite version is no reason to assume that Motley will do likewise." Hilda See, "Motley Balks Plan to Rewrite His '*Knock on Any Door*' for Films," *Chicago Defender*, March 13, 1948, 8.

92. Darryl F. Zanuck to Henry King, October 20, 1949, in Rudy Behlmer, *Memo from Darryl F. Zanuck: The Golden Years at Twentieth Century Fox* (New York: Grove Press, 1993), 164–65.

93. Ellington Kay to Robert Buckner, October 31, 1945, Warner Bros. Story Files, Accessed courtesy of Elizabeth Bingelli's personal research files.

94. Robert Buckner to Ellington Kay, Memo, October 31, 1945, Warner Bros. Story Files.

95. "Scribes Shy from Pictures: Fall-Off in Hollywood Pitch," *Michigan Chronicle*, August 6, 1947, 1, 18; "Author Yerby's 2nd Novel, 'The Vixens,' May Set Record," *Chicago Defender*, April 19, 1947, 5.

96. Jay Sanford, Reader's Report, April 22, 1948, box SR-140, *The Golden Hawk*, RKO Story Department Files, UCLA Special Collections, Los Angeles.

97. "*The Vixens*," advertisement, *Screenland*, October 1948, 78.

98. Patricia Gordon, Reader's Report, February 3, 1947, box SR-66, Story File, *The Vixens*, RKO Story Department Files.

99. W. K. comments on reader's report, April 21, 1947; W. J. F. comments on reader's report (date illegible); W. N. comments on reader's report, April 22, 1947; Story file for *The Vixens*, February 3, 1947; box SR-66, RKO Story Department Files, UCLA Special Collections, Los Angeles.

100. Frank Yerby, *The Golden Hawk* (New York: Dial Press, 1948), page 12 for description of Kit and page 30 for description of Rouge.

101. "The problem of escape occupied his every waking thought. The tales of the buccaneers ran through his mind, a thousand stories of escape stirred his memory. Kit tried. With a stolen chisel, he and Bernardo worked for four months to loosen the stones through a six-foot section of wall. They were discovered within two feet of freedom, and beaten almost to death. It was three weeks before they could even stand. Upon another occasion they made a break from the quarry but the harquebusier put a ball through Bernardo's thigh. . . . Bearded, filthy and infested with vermin, they resembled nothing human, and the light of Kit's eyes was close to madness." Yerby, *Golden Hawk*, 271.

102. Yerby, *Golden Hawk*, 131–32.

103. Yerby, *Golden Hawk*, 131–32.

104. Yerby, *Golden Hawk*, 138.

105. Gertrude Martin, "Bookshelf: 'The Golden Hawk,'" *Chicago Defender*, April 24, 1948, 14.

106. Joseph Breen to Harry Cohn, August 15, 1951, *The Golden Hawk*, Production Code Administration File. When Kit gives Rouge a gun and says that she can use it in case he does anything she doesn't like, Breen suggested that this increased the film's overall toleration of illicit sexuality.

107. Breen to Cohn, *The Golden Hawk*, Production Code Administration File.

108. Breen to Cohn, *The Golden Hawk*, Production Code Administration File.

109. Dolores Calvin, "Seeing Stars," *Philadelphia Tribune*, October 25, 1952, 16.

110. Calvin, "Seeing Stars," 16.

111. Frank Yerby, *The Saracen Blade* (New York: Dial Press, 1952), 18.

112. Yerby, *Saracen Blade*, 18. "Saracen," a Christian way of referring to Muslims who resided in the south of Italy, has a somewhat epithetical tinge.

113. Yerby, *Saracen Blade*, 56.

114. Yerby, *Saracen Blade*, 84.

115. Yerby, *Saracen Blade*, 19. Further, the protagonist has a Saracen slave named "Abu."

116. Hill, "Anti-Heroic Perspectives," 75.

117. Saidiya Hartman, *Lose Your Mother: A Journey along the Atlantic Slave Route* (New York: MacMillan, 2008), 5.

118. Yerby, *Saracen Blade*, 40.

119. Yerby, *Saracen Blade*, 99.

120. Yerby, *Saracen Blade*, 238.

121. Yerby, *Saracen Blade*, 243.

122. Yerby, *Saracen Blade*, 236.

123. Yerby, *Saracen Blade*, 132.

124. Yerby, *Saracen Blade*, 132.

125. Yerby, *Saracen Blade*, 43–45; emphasis added.

126. DeVallon Scott and George Worthing Yates, *The Saracen Blade: Final Draft*, September 25, 1953, 27.

127. Scott and Yates, *Saracen Blade: Final Draft*, 27.

128. Scott and Yates, *Saracen Blade: Final Draft*, 50.

129. Scott and Yates, *Saracen Blade: Final Draft*, 68.

130. John Blassingame, *The Slave Community* (New York: Oxford, 1972); John Hope Franklin, *Runaway Slave: Rebels on the Plantation* (New York: Oxford, 2000).

131. "New Pictures," *Time Magazine*, June 14, 1954, 112.

Part V

Black Auteurs Defying Dominant Norms

Chapter 9

ADAPTING BLACK MASCULINITY IN MELVIN VAN PEEBLES'S *THE STORY OF A THREE DAY PASS*

PRISCILLA LAYNE

Since the birth of film in the late nineteenth century, only a handful of African American directors have made a mark on the industry. This is largely because of racial and structural inequalities within the film industry. During its nascence, film was, like other areas of entertainment, a space in which white Americans wanted to control the narrative, portraying African Americans according to their prejudices. It was even common to cast white actors in blackface, rather than actually casting African American actors in Black roles. Nevertheless, even at this time, a few Black directors responded with their own narratives. As Jacqueline Stewart writes in *Migrating to the Movies*, "Early Black film images should be read as being polyphonic, 'speaking of' and 'speaking to' constructions of blackness produced by both whites and African Americans at the turn of the twentieth century. As whites produced and consumed images of Black subservience, ignorance, and inferiority, Black people responded by refuting limiting stereotypes and by constructing new images for themselves and their white observers."[1] But for an African American director to make a film, they would have needed both the know-how and the finances to make this possible. Oscar Micheaux was one of the first to break through this barrier. He serves as a pioneer on whose shoulders subsequent African American directors stand. But the focus of this chapter is on a different pioneer, one who would help usher in a new kind of film in the post–civil rights era: Melvin Van Peebles.

Van Peebles (1932–2021), whose directing career spanned from the 1950s until his last film in 2012, was known for films that address race in a controversial manner, such as one of his more well-known films *Watermelon Man* (1970), a comedy about a bigoted white man who wakes up one day to discover he has become Black. Racquel Gates writes that although *Watermelon Man* was Van Peebles's only Hollywood film and he was subject to the pressure of white studio executives during filming, he "used the very tools of Hollywood representation, such as conventions around whiteness and American identity, to reveal deeper truths about racism, white privilege, and Hollywood."[2] Though Van Peebles directed seventeen films, he is perhaps best known for *Sweet Sweetback's Baadasssss Song* (1971), as it marked a turning point in American cinema, introducing a militant, resistant Black protagonist who was ready to use violence to take on racism. The film's protagonist, a sex worker turned cop-killing vigilante, offered a direct contrast to what had become the dominant image of African American men—namely, the subservient, harmless type Sidney Poitier often depicted. *Sweetback* sent such shockwaves through the American film industry that in critics' enthusiastic reception, it was incorrectly seen as the first film shot by an African American director. However, it was not the first film that an African American directed and was not even Van Peebles's first film. His first feature-length film was actually *The Story of a Three Day Pass*, which was shot in France in 1967 and based on a short story Van Peebles wrote in French the same year called *La Permission* (The Permission). Van Peebles had been residing in France for seven years before the film's release. He had been living in Europe, Holland specifically, because after having made a few short films while in San Francisco, he did not feel Hollywood was supportive of his work. In this chapter, I will explore how the formal aesthetics of the film—which include antirealist aesthetics and jump cuts—compare to Van Peebles's original short story *La Permission*, which is written in the first person and includes devices like stream of consciousness. *The Story of a Three Day Pass*, which premiered in the United States in 1968, can be considered a close adaptation that remains fairly faithful to the text, which is no doubt aided by the fact that Van Peebles is the author of both.

As Elizabeth Reich notes in her monograph *Militant Visions*, Hollywood in the early 1960s was *not* interested in risking "its reputation on edgy politics and 'flights of radical daring.'"[3] Film historian Thomas Cripps describes this era as the "age of Sidney Poitier," which was, "if not a political ice age, at least a politics of cool, buttoned-down style."[4] As Reich remarks, politically daring images of African Americans would not reach the screen until the early 1970s. This is the sociohistorical background for why Van Peebles left the United States. By the time he settled in France, for decades the country had been considered a kind of utopian space for African American artists and expatriates like Josephine Baker, James Baldwin, and Richard Wright, who all felt they had more intellectual and physical freedoms there than in the United States.[5] Van Peebles was also aware that in France a law existed that allowed a published author to receive support to direct a film.[6] Thus, after spending about a year in Holland, where he studied astronomy and acting, his marriage problems with his wife, Maria Marx, motivated him to move to France.[7] It was there that he penned *La Permission* and laid the groundwork for his first feature-length film. He would eventually return to the United States, specifically to the San Francisco Film Festival as a French delegate with his film in tow, where he won the festival's Critics' Choice Award.[8] And based on the film's success, he "secured a three-picture deal with Columbia."[9] Since his passing, a Melvin Van Peebles Trailblazer Award has been established by the Critics Choice Association.

VAN PEEBLES'S ASTUTE POLITICAL COMMENTARY AND DARING AESTHETIC CHOICES

The Story of a Three Day Pass centers on an African American soldier named Turner, played by Guyanese actor Harry Baird, who is stationed in France following World War II. During the American occupation of France following World War II, African American soldiers were overly represented in the Communications Zone (ComZ) because of their assignment to service units. Marie Louise Roberts notes that, for example, "the Oise base section (part of ComZ in north-central France including Reims) had a total white strength of 29,154 and a total Black strength of 14,060 or about thirty-three percent."[10] After being promoted in the military, Turner's captain grants him a three-day pass for some time off prior to taking on his new responsibilities. During a night on the town in Paris, Turner happens to meet Miriam (Nicole Berger), a young white woman, in a jazz club, and the two begin an affair. But this endangers his career in the US military, which though desegregated, still maintained a very racist culture. For his remaining time off, Miriam calls into work sick so that she and Turner can take a trip to the coast of France, where they stay in a deserted hotel and spend time together on the beach. However, during one of these trips to the beach, Turner encounters several white officers he knows, and these officers inform his captain that he is involved with a white woman. Upon Turner's return to base, his promotion has been revoked and he is tasked with showing a tour group of African American women who are visiting the base to see how Black soldiers are being treated. During the tour, Turner steps away to call Miriam's work to inform her he will be accompanying the women to Paris. However, when her employer tells him she has called in sick, he immediately knows she has moved on to another suitor.

By entangling the politics of race, gender, sex, and military culture, *The Story of a Three Day Pass* examines the existential crisis of Black men in the period following World War II but before the onset of the civil rights movement. For many African Americans, serving in the military offered one of the few opportunities for social mobility; it offered stable employment, responsibility, and respect. However, in *What Soldiers Do: Sex and the American GI in World*

War II France, Roberts describes all the hardships Black GIs faced in the service during this time, including in the European Theater of Operations (ETO) following World War II. As she explains, "While the War Department famously claimed that no distinctions were made between white and black troops other than segregation, in practice blacks in the army suffered discrimination in every aspect of their military lives. . . . Rather than receive full basic training, black soldiers were often sent out to do menial labor."[11] Thus, despite his success in the service, Turner remains at the mercy of white men, whatever their rank. By having an affair with Miriam, he breaks a sacred rule against miscegenation that had long been ingrained in American society and was exported to France with the military. Roberts writes:

> Black GIs with passes into town would often get stuck on base because their white peers, allowed to get on buses first, would either leave them no room at the back or refuse to let them ride at all. Even getting into town would not guarantee a relaxing evening, as black soldiers looked in vain for a "colored" restaurant, bar, or theater. The results were deeply demoralizing. . . . While questions of access to resources fueled racial tensions in all theaters, the most dangerous color line to cross was, without a doubt, sexual relations with white women.[12]

By offering us a first-person narration of Turner's experience, Van Peebles's film gives a voice to the many Black men in the United States in the 1960s whose desire for respect and self-determination continued to be sabotaged by white supremacy and structural racism.

In addition to its political content, one of the most notable aspects of the film is its avant-garde aesthetics. As Reich points out, one can clearly see the influence of French New Wave and Brechtian techniques of framing reflected in the film, making it a kind of bridge between European new wave cinema and Black independent filmmaking. Subsequently, *The Story of a Three Day Pass* also stands out for its challenges to realism. Not only does the film contain several fantasy sequences to convey Turner's and Miriam's thoughts, but Turner's "double consciousness" appears as a talking mirror image that sometimes mocks him about being an "Uncle Tom" or warns him that though he may be abroad, American racism will still punish him if he steps out of line.

While the formal aesthetics of the film compare to Van Peebles's short story *La Permission*, *The Story of a Three Day Pass* represents an adaptation that provides a slightly different perspective of the central character. Of course, I am aware that, as John M. Desmond and Peter Hawkes state, "Even when the adapter attempts to transfer the original story to film as closely as possible, film is another medium with its own conventions, artistic values, and techniques, and so the original story is transformed into a different work of art."[13] Desmond and Hawkes also point out that while textual language is abstract and variable, the language of film is concrete and specific. As they explain, "The unfixed language of the literary text will become fixed in exact screen images chosen by the filmmaker."[14] Thus, when one reads a text like a short story, the words on the page can invoke all types of images in a person's mind, depending on the reader.

Translation theory is useful to consider here because it poses a similar interpretive problem. For example, in Walter Benjamin's seminal essay "The Task of the Translator," he notes, "In the words *Brot* ["bread" in German] and *pain* ["bread" in French], what is meant is the same but the way of meaning it is not. The difference in the way of meaning permits the word *Brot* to mean something other to a German than what the word *pain* means to a Frenchman, so that these words are not interchangeable for them."[15] Thus, when a German and a Frenchman read the word "bread" in a text, they imagine different things. The German might imagine a loaf of rye bread, while the Frenchman might imagine a baguette. And they are free to imagine what they please when encountering a word on paper. But as soon as someone attempts to film a text, they must choose an image to represent the "bread," and whatever image they choose therefore eliminates all other possibilities one might have imagined. Nevertheless, adapting a text to a film does not *just* mean fixed photographic images but rather, in Robert Stam's understanding, it is a movement from one track—a text—to five tracks, and those five tracks consist of "moving photographic image, phonetic sound, music, noises, and written materials."[16] Another important distinction between a text and a film adaptation is story versus discourse. According to Seymour Chatman, "The story is the *what* in a narrative that is depicted, discourse the *how*."[17]

I am most interested in how discrepancies in discourse between the text and the film emerge in Van Peebles's choices of perspective, editing, and sound. There are two particular distinctions between *La Permission* and *The Story of a Three Day Pass* that interest me. First, in the short story, which is written in the third person with a narrator, Van Peebles has distinct literary elements at his disposal in order to explore Turner's psychological state in ways that encourage readers to understand his predicament as being subject to American-specific structural racism. In the short story, Van Peebles uses straightforward interior monologue so that we hear a lot of transparent emotion from Turner about his state of mind in tense, racially charged situations. The narrator himself also occasionally comments on the action of the story and how it relates to race relations. In the film, however, we hear less from Turner. Rather than simply conveying the character's experience of racist reactions to the interracial affair through prose transplanted to the film via voiceover, Van Peebles shifts the point of view, from a third-person perspective in the story to a camera that frequently adopts Turner's perspective in the film, collapsing the Black soldier's and the viewers' perspectives into one.[18] Second, as I mentioned above, in the film Van Peebles frequently relies on antirealist visual aesthetics and discordant music. The visual abstraction also aligns the viewers' perspective with Turner's, so they can feel his sense of powerlessness in the face of white supremacy.

It was quite daring for Van Peebles to make these aesthetic choices for *The Story of a Three Day Pass*, particularly because it has never been easy for Black directors to stray from realism. In his book *Welcome to the Jungle*, Kobena Mercer writes that Black independent film is frequently expected to emphasize the "real" in order to provide "a counter-discourse against those versions of reality produced by dominant voices."[19] Mercer worries that this emphasis on the "real" often inhibits Black independent filmmakers from antirealist depictions. What further influences the drive toward realism is that, in the past, Black independent filmmakers had to function outside of Hollywood and had to make do with low-budget productions. *The Story of a Three Day Pass* is an interesting exception to this tendency toward a realism overdetermined by discrimination-based economic constraints, considering that it was shot for only $200,000 in 1967. And yet, despite its attention to important sociohistorical issues and its aesthetic experimentation, Reich contends that "almost no critical attention has been paid" to the film.[20]

I argue that the formal differences between Van Peebles's text and film are not just a result of adapting between media; rather, they indicate a change in the way we are meant to view Turner. It strikes me that Turner in the film is at times portrayed as much more confident and self-assured than in the story because we can no longer hear his interior dialogue and we do not have a narrator to fill in what we don't know about his feelings. By conveying his emotions through perspective, sound, and editing, Van Peebles arguably relies on formalist techniques from traditions of leftist cinema that intend to get the audience to act rather than passively empathize with Turner.

DIFFERENT AUDIENCES, SOMEWHAT DIFFERENT DEPICTIONS OF BLACK MASCULINITY

The first remarkable difference between the story and the film is the audiences targeted. In the case of the film, it is clear that Van Peebles is targeting an African American audience. The film's themes of structural racism, forbidden interracial love, and naïve white allies would all have been familiar to an African American audience. And there is a certain kind of humor Van Peebles includes in the film that is very culturally specific. An example thereof is the

Black church ladies from the First African Methodist Episcopal (AME) Church of Harlem, who at the film's end come to the base for a tour and are quite taken with Turner and hope to help him get back in his captain's good graces. The ironic, exaggerated manner in which the women speak locates them in the archetype of the Black Christian proponent of respectability politics—the kind of character we would later see parodied in Blaxploitation flicks.[21] In several short scenes with the group's leader, Mrs. Abernathy (Tria French), the irony is that if these respectable Black women knew Turner was being punished for having an affair with a white woman, they might be less likely to help him. Thus, in these brief moments, Van Peebles is able to showcase some of the conflicts within the African American community, which I believe only an African American audience would be attuned to.

I would argue that, in contrast to the film, the short story is targeted at a white French audience. This is evident first and foremost in the ways the two narratives begin. The short story starts with a description of the French town where the American base is located, and it offers some context regarding the American occupation. The sociohistorical context of the American occupation after World War II and the local color conveyed in how the town is described would be most interesting to a French audience. In contrast, the film begins with a close-up of the month of November on a calendar, with two circles that fade in and show us the three days Turner will have off, the tenth through twelfth. Thus, most important to the African American film audience is not the sociohistorical context of the American occupation of France but rather this particular moment in the life of the Black protagonist. The Black audience will know what is at stake for Turner regarding both his promotion in the military and how he spends his three days of freedom away from the scrutiny of white Americans.

Another important difference is the interiority and depth of Turner's character. As I mentioned above, in the short story, we gain insight into how Turner is feeling at any given moment and that he is often rather insecure about the situation. For example, prior to first going out on the town during his three-day vacation, Turner puts on a pair of shades. In the short story, we are told he wears the shades to look cool *and* to hide his racial insecurity. In the film, however, there is no voiceover to tell us about his mental state in this moment, nor does he appear to be insecure. He is playful, forward, and on the prowl for women. His shades and fedora also conform to a style we see worn by other young men who are out on the town.

A part of the more confident Turner apparent in the film compared to the short story is a scene that takes place at a public restroom in the park. In the short story, this scene addresses the permeable border between gay and straight men in a manner that invokes questions about Turner's insecure masculinity and anxious heterosexuality. Prior to first meeting Miriam in a jazz club, Turner takes a stroll in a park, where he stops at a public restroom to urinate. Here the narrator gives us a detailed description of how an American man holds his penis to urinate and why this might be misconstrued by gay men as an invitation to sex. The narrator states, "An American holds his cock from below or from the side with two or three fingers, allowing the best part of it to be visible. The guy next to Turner in the urinal is in the process of determining if the way Turner is holding his penis is an invitation or not."[22]

The way the narrator describes the scene, there is a moment of ambiguity and possibility. We do not know for sure if Turner might also be interested in men. We have no idea how he would react to a possible advance from a gay man. But then the tension is resolved when a third man enters the restroom and is said to be offering much clearer cues. As the short story narrator explains, "Before he can get up the courage to take the chance and ask Turner, another man enters the restroom and stands on the other side of Turner and presents his assets in a manner that is more clear than ambiguous."[23] The narrator even proceeds to explain that the reason gay men in France must be so covert when soliciting sex is because of a law introduced by Napoleon prohibiting pederasty. In the film, this plays out much differently. The camera perspective adopts that of the external narrator, focused first on one French man, then another. The attention to detail about the French culture of cruising in the story is conveyed simply in close-ups of the two French men standing on either side of Turner. Their gaze at each other is a small indication that they might be looking for something beyond a place of relief. When the camera cuts to Turner, who is revealed to be standing in the middle, he simply backs up and walks away. Compared to the story, we do not hear the perspective of either gay man, and for that reason the possibility of Turner being an object of desire in this instance is not even introduced.

It is possible that Van Peebles intentionally left out this possibility because of the film's American audience in contrast to the short story's French audience. While contemporary France clearly had homophobic biases, for potentially Black American audiences, these biases would have additionally intersected with race. Although, as Roderick Ferguson has pointed out, there have always been queer folx in the African American community, the extent to which queer folx, and gay Black *men* especially, have been accepted depends on the social context. During the 1960s, some very homophobic views were normalized among Black men fighting for civil rights. Eldridge Cleaver, for example, stated in *Soul on Ice* that homosexuality was not "natural" for Black men and that gay Black men were suffering from a kind of self-hatred that made them want to be objectified by white men.[24] Since these homophobic views circulating in the Black community associated gayness with emasculation, it is possible that Van Peebles avoided any ambiguity about Turner in the film, because he meant for Turner to be presented as a strong, masculine figure in contrast to the emasculated roles in which Black men typically had been cast.

In Reich's analysis of *The Story of a Three Day Pass*, she reads "Turner's performances of black masculinity and Van Peebles's *avant-garde* aesthetics [as offering] something new by demonstrating instability in categories of race and masculinity."[25] However, when one compares the film to the short story, I would argue that, in the film, there seems to be less room for ambiguity about Turner's sexuality. In the film, as Reich describes, we experience Turner as "the picture of cool and composed masculinity—a new kind of man" or arguably a new kind of Black man.[26] But the short story is less invested in making Turner appear to be cool and confident, perhaps precisely because of its different audience.

While in the short story it is Turner's insecurity that sometimes delays his actions, in the film it is his overconfidence that foils his plans. In the story, when Turner first sees Miriam at the bar and decides to approach her, he imagines a very romantic scenario of the two spotting each other from across the room, their gazes cutting through the crowd: "The dancers, those listening to the orchestra, the waiters, everyone realizes that this is a historic moment and that when he goes toward HER everyone will respectfully step aside as they advance, like Moses parting the waves of the Red Sea, to allow the passage of the Hebrews."[27] In the film, this romantic element is no longer present. In fact, Turner first eyes a blonde friend of Miriam's. At this moment, he is not nervous at all, he is super cool, and his doppelganger breaks off from his body and approaches her. The room of people still split down the middle to allow him to walk through—but in this case they appear impressed by his coolness, rather than understanding that fate has brought Turner and Miriam together. In the short story, he envisions Miriam welcoming him with open arms and the two of them running toward each other. But it turns out that was merely a fantasy. In the story, Turner also appears more aware of his precarious situation as a Black man in Paris. Although the hat and shades make him feel good, he ultimately sets them aside for fear he might be profiled as a suspected rapist recently reported wearing the same accessories and possessing a dark "Mediterranean" complexion. The narrator informs us that this suspected rapist turned out to be a fictional story made up by the woman to make her boyfriend jealous.[28] This indicates to us the kinds of stereotypes that have existed in France about racialized, dark-skinned men.

While both the short story and the film employ fantasy to show the conflict between Turner's imagination and the reality, in each case Turner emerges differently as a character. In the short story, Turner is much more of a romantic. Even before he meets Miriam, the narrator refers to her in capital letters as ELLE, which could be translated as SHE or HER depending on the grammatical context. Thus, although the readers have no specific woman in mind, we know that Turner is searching for his great love—a woman who stands out from all the rest—and he believes he will find her in Paris. At one point, the narrator reports that while Turner is in a bar, "Suddenly he believes he hears THAT voice. The girl is so beautiful that he is convinced that it can only be her."[29] Even though Turner has no idea *what* he's looking for, he believes fate will bring him together with the right girl. The story also makes it clear that Turner views being with a white woman as giving him a certain kind of recognition he wouldn't otherwise have access to.

The narrator states that when he is with Miriam at the bar, "he closes his eyes with joy. . . . He is transformed he becomes another."[30] Turner's reaction recalls Frantz Fanon's views about recognition and interracial relationships in *Black Skin, White Masks*. Fanon chastises the Black man who seeks to be recognized by white society and becomes a quasiwhite man through a romantic relationship with a white woman.[31] The fact that this is acknowledged in the story reveals a little more insecurity and vulnerability on Turner's part. In the film, Turner's fantasy about meeting "the one" has nothing to do with love. It is more of a tongue-in-cheek critique of Turner's coolness. He thinks the crowd will part, not in awe of their romantic chemistry but in awe of his coolness. And this cool persona will soon fall flat as he proceeds to hit on Miriam's friend, who flat out ignores him, which is the only reason he ends up talking to Miriam. In the short story, Turner does not have the courage to invite Miriam directly to take a trip with him. He merely blurts out while they are dancing, "Tomorrow, I think I might go to the sea. . . . Maybe I'll go to the sea."[32] The way Turner phrases this desire, making it conditional rather than a declaration, and the fact that Turner repeats himself show some insecurity on his part. It is Miriam who seizes this opportunity to indirectly invite herself: "You're lucky! I also like the sea. . . . But it's so far."[33]

Another discrepancy between the story and the film is that, in the film, there are a lot of quick cuts, interrupting Turner and Miriam's conversation at the club. The film does not provide an in-depth conversation like that offered in the story, and therefore we get less of Turner's interiority and his nervousness.

Even though Miriam eventually accepts his invitation to come with him to the sea, Turner's insecurity resurfaces that night, in both the story and the film, after they have parted ways and agreed to meet in the morning. In his room, Turner imagines seeing his "cool" alter ego in the mirror. His mirror image tries to raise doubts about if Miriam will come tomorrow, saying, "Don't sell the bearskin before killing it," which can be interpreted as meaning "Don't count your chickens before they've hatched."[34] Turner is pleasantly surprised the next day when Miriam does, in fact, show up at the meeting point they agreed upon. But in the story, Turner's insecurity leads him to make a potentially damaging move when he asks Miriam, "How much do I have to pay you for these two

After meeting Miriam at the beach, Turner's alter ego raises doubt as to whether she will come with him in Melvin Van Peebles's *The Story of a Three Day Pass* (1967).

days," insinuating that she is a prostitute.[35] Interestingly, in the film, his question is provoked when Miriam makes the comment that it can be expensive to have a (girl)friend. Luckily for Turner, Miriam laughs off this accusation.

During the car ride to the sea, Miriam confides in him about her life, explaining that she works in a store but is an aspiring teacher. Miriam confesses that working in the store is difficult, and she tries to take time off as often as possible. Turner is really touched by her troubles. In the story, the scene is described as very romantic with "soft and tender" music playing on the radio and Turner thinking "for him she was the purest girl."[36] When they stop to eat at a restaurant, the way the sun shines behind her makes her glow. In contrast, the film downplays romance and instead stresses the sexual tension between the two. In the film, the entire car scene only shows Turner's perspective, with close-ups of Miriam's face from different angles. There are a few brief shots of Turner's eyes in the rearview mirror, indicating that he steals a glance at Miriam while he is driving.

Toward the end of the car ride, though, his mind does seem to get distracted. There are many shots of her bare legs beneath her skirt; the film freezes and jumps to another shot. The shots of her legs are always accompanied by a distorted guitar sound. These are the techniques Van Peebles uses since he does not have a narrator. The point Van Peebles is making both to his French audience (via the text) and to his African American audience (via the film) is that it is both dangerous and exhilarating for an African American man to view a white woman in this sexual manner. But for a French audience, Van Peebles would have to be much more explicit with his words. Meanwhile, an African American audience would already be familiar with the larger context of the history of race in the United States and would not need such an explicit statement to accompany the images and sound.

The way the film presents their ride to the beach, Turner is clearly fixated on Miriam's body, but at the same time he seems afraid to look. But rather than reflecting an inner insecurity, his fragmented gaze appears the result of his conflicted self. He desires to look at Miriam but has been conditioned by the rules regulating race that prohibit him to look. In the short story, however, the narrator clearly indicates both how turned on Turner is by Miriam in the car and how shy he is about actually initiating sex when they reach the hotel room. On the car ride, we are told, "Miriam changes her position again, Turner's pants become very tight," and "She changes her position again, she can't sit still . . . it stretches, her breasts struggle with her blouse."[37] Turner is so distracted by Miriam's body that he even has a hard time listening to what she's saying: "He knew she had spoken to him because her lips had moved but his ears were buzzing so much that he missed her words."[38]

Another moment when weak or anxious masculinity seems a focal point in the short story is when Turner and Miriam first check into the hotel in Normandy. The hotel employee asks the couple how many beds they would like. The narrator informs us that Turner "didn't want to say what he wanted. He made vague gestures with his hands."[39] But then Miriam just bursts out and asks for a single bed. In the film, she also answers the hotel employee, but this is attributed to Turner misunderstanding something in the translation, trying to express his desire for a room with a view of the water.

In the short story, the narrator depicts Miriam and Turner's first time alone in the hotel room as both exciting and uncomfortable. They are both clearly interested in each other romantically, but the situation is awkward. There is a lot of uncertainty—laughing, kidding, drooling. The entire experience feels like "the longest moment in life."[40] In the film, their feelings are conveyed through an aerial view perspective that shows the awkwardness of their encounter.

Part of this experience of their first time being intimate is that both Miriam and Turner have distinct fantasies of what it will be like sleeping with someone from a different race and culture. In the short story, we are told, "For him, she is a countess and he by analogy a count with a large castle, [yet] she sees herself surrounded by forty big-cocked [N]egroes with bowler hats raping her."[41] These strikingly different fantasies clearly convey that while Turner sees his relationship with Miriam as elevating his social status, Miriam fantasizes that being with a Black man entails a certain sexual aggression that she only associates with Black men. In the film, Van Peebles uses silent film techniques—background piano, trick photography, freeze-frame—to convey Turner's excitement about sleeping with Miriam. While in the story, he only imagined himself as a duke in a manor, in the film, trick photography is used to show him becoming different personae, until he finds the one he feels most confident and comfortable with. In this way, the film uses humor to convey his insecure masculinity rather than using interior dialogue.

BLACK MASCULINITY:
HELD IN SUSPENSION AS RACISM REASSERTS ITSELF

There are two final moments of significance toward the film's end that are important for how perspective is treated differently in the film compared to the short story and how the two narratives present Turner as a protagonist. Miriam and Turner's love story takes a fateful turn when they decide to go to the beach one day and white soldiers from his barracks happen to arrive. At first, the beach appears to be deserted. In the short story, Turner indicates he is well aware of the risk he is taking by being with Miriam. As he lies on the beach and Miriam asks why he is grinning, he replies, "I was just thinking of my captain, if he could see me now."[42] In retrospective, this becomes a serendipitous or nearly prophetic moment. During their car ride to the beach, he has revealed that though his captain was generous enough to give him a pass, he did so because he thinks Turner is a "good Black." As Turner explains, "For my Captain, that means a Negro . . . a Black man who . . . eh . . . eh . . . is happy . . . docile . . . fearful . . . and who never, never speaks with a white woman, who will never have a white female friend."[43] In the film, the impending threat of the white soldiers' presence is heightened, because the shot of Turner grinning on the beach is immediately followed by an iris shot of the three white soldiers heading to the beach. Using an iris shot to introduce these characters obscures some of the detail and context. We do not immediately know who these men are, but the darkness surrounding them suggests they will mean something bad for Turner—they are ominous. His teasing remark, "If the captain could see me now," is foreshadowing, because the white soldiers function as the captain's eyes.

In the short story, the narrator tells us Turner has fallen asleep, which is why he does not see the men approach; he is only awakened when they start jokingly dropping pebbles on him. In the film, however, we do not know that Turner is asleep. And because of where the camera is placed, offering a low angle of the white soldiers, when we see the white soldiers approaching, we assume the perspective is Turner's. It is only when we get a reverse shot of them looking down at Turner that we realize he is asleep and unaware of this impending intrusion. The film uses photography and camera angles to establish both a power imbalance between Turner and the white soldiers and animosity between them.

In the short story, we are told that the soldiers are initially happy to see Turner, though their interaction does leave some ambiguity:

- You're a little far from home said the second soldier.
No further than you, said Turner.
(Everyone laughs.)
- Do you want us to take you back to base?
. . .
Thanks, but I'm free until tomorrow and I have my car here anyway.
- You're on duty Monday, said the third soldier.
Yes, every Monday, Turner replies.
- The Captain has appointed Turner to a new post, said the aide-de-camp.
(The second and third soldiers are very enthusiastic, they congratulate
Turner and say well done, all three smile at him.
On the beach, Miriam runs up to them.)
I'm taking advantage of this rest . . . that is, until you arrived. . . . Ha ha. . . .
(Turner laughs nervously and leans back hoping that they will go away.)
- Let's go guys, my father always said, we must not disturb a man who is
resting, said the first soldier.
(They are about to get up, when the third soldier adds,)
- There is nothing to do in this village except to rest.[44]

This exchange reveals that Turner is worried the white soldiers might see him with Miriam. In the short story, their passive-aggressive comments about Turner being far from home indicate that they may have already witnessed the romantic pair together. The white soldiers' celebration of Turner's promotion could just be a sadistic way of mocking him, knowing that once they report back to the captain he will lose his promotion. They know that Turner's "resting" involves spending time with Miriam, who unfortunately jumps on top of Turner just before the white soldiers leave. The soldiers react negatively: "The first looks shocked, the second both angry and amused and the aide-de-camp disgusted."[45] Unfortunately, Miriam cannot read the tension of the situation, nor would she understand why the soldiers are reacting this way. So, she continues to act intimately with Turner, putting her arm around him and scratching his back. When she invites the soldiers to stay, their response reveals their jealousy: "The captain didn't give us three days off, said the second soldier. . . . No, we don't have permission . . . said the aide-de-camp."[46]

The aide-de-camp's mention of "permission" without any direct object implies that he might be referring to the social acceptance of having a relationship with a white woman, which *Turner* does not have. In the film, one of the white soldiers departs with the comment, "We'll let you get back to your thing. But we'll tell everybody we saw you"—which could definitely be read as a threat. Turner tells Miriam after they leave, "I just lost my promotion."[47] But

Miriam approaches in the background, while Turner (Harry Baird) talks to the white soldiers in Van Peebles's cinematic adaptation of his short story *La Permission* (1967).

Miriam is convinced nothing bad will come of it—they will not tell—and she encourages Turner to enjoy the rest of the day at the beach with her.

An important difference between the short story and the film is that in *La Permission* the scene is told from Turner's perspective, but in the film, we have an anonymous perspective of a voyeur. So, when Turner awakens after the two soldiers throw pebbles, we have no idea if he is scared or happy to see the soldiers. Another major difference that adds to the suspense in the film is how Miriam is revealed to the white soldiers. In the short story, while Turner and the soldiers talk, we know Miriam is somewhere on the beach, but we are not sure where she is until she suddenly, playfully jumps on him. In the film, the camera angle allows us to see Miriam slowly approaching as the men talk. This delay builds suspense as we wait for their relationship to be revealed and for the white men to react.

Both the story and the film spend a significant amount of time detailing what a romantic time Miriam and Turner have after frolicking on the beach, hitching a ride with a farmer, exploring nature, grabbing something small to eat, and eventually watching the rain from within their hotel room. This leaves Turner feeling more positive: "I'm not going to worry anymore.... I'm sure they won't do anything."[48] In both the story and the film, he even tells her he loves her, and she suggests that she will never take sick leave from work again with anyone but him. In both texts, the next morning, his mirror image expresses skepticism about their relationship. And this skepticism about her true feelings toward him is confirmed when he tries to call her.

Turner's future plans with Miriam are disrupted because of the punishment he receives from his captain for his transgressions. In both the film and the story, we get a detailed account of how his captain reacts to what he has been told. In the short story, the Captain tells Turner, "I was sure I could trust you, the captain said to Turner—and you cheated on me. . . . This is not the first time that my trust in a man has been betrayed. . . . I do not hesitate to admit my mistake. . . . My support for your advancement has been withdrawn! A three-day leave is not a permission for everything!"[49] In the film, his words are intensified by the framing: we get a close-up of the captain screaming at Turner. We do not get a reverse shot to show us Turner's reaction, because Turner's response doesn't matter. Turner has no opportunity to defend himself or offer his version of the story. The only account that matters is that of his white fellow soldiers; the only authority that matters is the white captain's.

Part of Turner's punishment is he is unable to leave the base. Additionally, his captain orders him to act as a tour guide for a group of Black women from the First AME Church of Harlem. According to their tour bus, they are the "Royal Crusading Angels" on a "European Tour."[50] Reich remarks that their presence in the film signifies "a stereotypical element of black American culture that has, thus far in the film, been absent."[51] In the short story, the exchange is very matter of fact. The leader of the group introduces herself: "'My name is Madame Abernathy. So, you're the young man who is going to walk us? That's nice, very nice.' She takes Turner's arm with a pretty gesture."[52]

In the film, the way that Madame Abernathy/Tria French faces the camera and repeats her words, one gets the sense that Turner sees her in a rather patronizing manner. Like his captain, she is there to monitor his behavior and would likely frown on his interracial relationship with Miriam, as he is representing "the race" abroad. In the film, the exaggerated speech and affect of the Black church ladies, which is absent in the short story, indicates that the film is directed toward an African American audience, who will recognize such tropes. Madame Abernathy feels bad when she hears about Turner's punishment, which now has lasted for two weeks, and she goes to the captain to appeal that he permit Turner to accompany the women to Paris.

In Turner's final interactions with the women, after Madame Abernathy gets his punishment reversed, Turner does not remain to hear their pleas to have him accompany them in town. In this scene, it is clear that these women cannot fathom what Turner's actual transgression was and that they also falsely believe going into town with them will cheer him up. For them, Turner is

A moment that anticipates the film's allegorical ending in which Turner (Harry Baird) remains frozen in midair, suspended supernaturally.

probably lonely as the sole African American stuck on a European base, and he should be thrilled to have some familiar Black faces from home. But Turner has one goal in mind: to call Miriam and make plans to see her. In the film, as the church ladies continue to speak, Turner simply turns and runs to the nearest phone both. The camera's perspective is a moving shot facing Turner as he runs toward the camera and away from the women, possibly symbolizing Turner's intention of leaving American race relations behind and returning to the utopian space of interracial love that he found with Miriam. However, Turner is soon disappointed when he calls Miriam's job and discovers that she has taken another sick day, likely with her new suitor. Disappointed, Turner decides not to go to Paris with the Black women. He simply returns to his barracks to lie down on his bed.

Though the film ends with an unusual shot of Turner frozen in midair while collapsing onto his bed, the story actually ends the exact same way, with the narrator stating, "But in the dark, the shadow played a trick and it seemed like Turner was not lying down but was stopping at an impossible angle neither here nor there, in an untenable position, not that he lacked the habit of doing this kind of thing since he was black and everything."[53] In both cases, Van Peebles may be trying to convey how Turner is caught in between—in between American and French cultures, in between civilian life and military life, in between pleasing his white superiors and being true to himself. While this freeze-frame shot does not seem like an odd way to end a film, for the short story, this description of him frozen in space leaves more questions open, insinuating that there is something supernatural about African Americans because of how they are required to navigate different spaces. This supernatural element at the short story's end offers additional insight into why Van Peebles uses so many nonrealistic techniques in the film.

CONCLUSION

In this chapter, I hope to have demonstrated how the differing perspectives offered by the story and the film result in a slightly different protagonist. The manner in which Van Peebles toys with perspective in the film heightens the antagonism between Turner and his surroundings. Turner is also presented as more confident and self-assured in the film than in the short story. I would argue that because the short story is directed at a French audience intending to *inform* them of the experience of Black men in France, as a character, Turner must contend less with hegemonic African American ideals of masculinity and can be a less rigidly defined character. In contrast, I believe the film is directed at an African American audience whom Van Peebles wishes to impel to action, often using affect and sensation to have them experience what Turner is going through.

If the stakes for an African American audience are to present a Black male protagonist who is desirable and can confidently act on his desires for white women, perhaps Van Peebles minimized the doubt and ambiguity associated with an unconventional masculinity present in the story. Interestingly, this is precisely the kind of Black masculinity that will resurface in *Sweet Sweetback's Baadasssss Song*. Thus, perhaps *The Story of a Three Day Pass* was the film for Van Peebles to get his foot in the door, providing a way for him to test a radical vision of Black masculinity that broke with white conventions, which made it possible for him to push even more boundaries with the character Sweetback.

Notes

1. Jacqueline Stewart, *Migrating to the Movies: Cinema and Black Urban Modernity* (Berkeley: University of California Press, 2005), 31.

2. Racquel Gates, "Subverting Hollywood from the Inside Out: Melvin Van Peebles's Watermelon Man," *Film Quarterly* 68, no. 1 (2014): 12.

3. Elizabeth Reich, *Militant Visions: Black Soldiers, Internationalism, and the Transformation of American Cinema* (New Brunswick, NJ: Rutgers University Press, 2016), 158.

4. Thomas Cripps, *Making Movies Black: The Hollywood Message Movie from World War II to the Civil Rights Era* (New York: Oxford University Press, 1993), 282–3.

5. See Tyler Stovall, *Paris Noir: African Americans and the City of Light* (Boston: Houghton Mifflin, 1996).

6. Reich, *Militant Visions*, 165.

7. Melvin Donalson, "Melvin Van Peebles," in *Encyclopedia of African-American Literature*, second edition, ed. Wilfred D. Samuels (New York: Facts on File, 2013), 19.

8. Reich, *Militant Visions*, 160. For a list of Van Peebles's awards, see "Melvin Van Peebles," *Who's Who among African Americans* (Farmington Hills, MI: Gale, 2021) or "Melvin Van Peebles," Internet Movie Database, https://www.imdb.com/name/nm0887708/awards?ref_=nm_awd.

9. Reich, *Militant Visions*, 165.

10. Mary Louise Roberts, *What Soldiers Do: Sex and the American GI in World War II France* (Chicago: University of Chicago Press, 2013), 203.

11. Roberts, *What Soldiers Do*, 199–200.

12. Roberts, *What Soldiers Do*, 201.

13. John M. Desmond and Peter Hanke, *Adaptation: Studying Film and Literature* (New York: Mc Graw Hill, 2006), 1–2.

14. Desmond and Hanke, *Adaptation*, 35.

15. Walter Benjamin, "The Task of the Translator," in *Walter Benjamin: Selected Writings, vol. 1*, ed. Marcus Bullock and Michael W. Jennings (Cambridge, MA: Belknap Press, 2002), 257.

16. Robert Stam, "Beyond Fidelity: The Dialogics of Adaptation," in *Film Adaptation*, ed. James Naremore (New Brunswick, NJ: Rutgers University Press, 2000), 59.

17. Seymour Chatman, *Story and Discourse: Narrative Structure in Fiction and Film* (Ithaca, NY: Cornell University Press, 1978), 19.

18. Reich, *Militant Visions*, 170.

19. Kobena Mercer, *Welcome to the Jungle: New Positions in Black Cultural Studies* (New York: Routledge, 1994), 57.

20. Reich, *Militant Visions*, 160.

21. For respectability politics, see Evelyn Brooks Higginbotham, *Righteous Discontent: The Women's Movement in the Black Baptist Church, 1880–1920* (Cambridge, MA: Harvard University Press, 1993).

22. Melvin Van Peebles, "La Permission" (Paris: Le Gadenet, 1967), 24–25. All translations from French to English are by the author.

23. Van Peebles, "La Permission," 25.

24. Eldridge Cleaver, *Soul on Ice* (New York: Delta Book, 1991), 128–29.

25. Reich, *Militant Visions*, 180.

26. Reich, *Militant Visions*, 172.

27. Van Peebles, "La Permission," 31–32.

28. Van Peebles, "La Permission," 33.

29. Van Peebles, "La Permission," 31.

30. Van Peebles, "La Permission," 40.

31. Frantz Fanon, *Black Skin, White Masks* (New York: Grove Press, 1967), 45.

32. Van Peebles, "La Permission," 37.

33. Van Peebles, "La Permission," 40.

34. Van Peebles, "La Permission," 41.

35. Van Peebles, "La Permission," 42.

36. Van Peebles, "La Permission," 44.

37. Van Peebles, "La Permission," 46–47.

38. Van Peebles, "La Permission," 47.

39. Van Peebles, "La Permission," 48.

40. Van Peebles, "La Permission," 50.

41. Van Peebles, "La Permission," 51.

42. Van Peebles, "La Permission," 58.

43. Van Peebles, "La Permission," 46.

44. Van Peebles, "La Permission," 59–60.

45. Van Peebles, "La Permission," 60.

46. Van Peebles, "La Permission," 60.

47. Van Peebles, "La Permission," 61.

48. Van Peebles, "La Permission," 65.

49. Van Peebles, "La Permission," 67.

50. Reich, *Militant Visions*, 178.

51. Reich, *Militant Visions*, 178.

52. Van Peebles, "La Permission," 69.

53. Van Peebles, "La Permission," 74.

Chapter 10

BLACK AUTONOMY ON SCREEN AND OFF

Gordon Parks's *The Learning Tree* (1969) and *Shaft* (1971)

CYNTHIA BARON AND ERIC PIERSON

Gordon Parks arrived in post-studio-era Hollywood with substantial clout and a thirty-year background in creating candid, empathetic visual narratives about African American lives.[1] He had been a professional photographer since the late 1930s, known for his photojournalism, celebrity photos, and fashion photography. In the early 1940s, he had participated in "one of the era's most important creative communities—Chicago's legendary Black Renaissance of painters, sculptors, writers, poets, and dancers working around the South Side Community Art Center."[2] In 1942, as a member of the US Farm Security Administration (FSA) staff, Parks photographed Ella Watson to create *American Gothic, Washington, D.C.*, which reimagines the 1930 Grant Wood painting that depicts a pair of white farmers.[3] In Parks's photograph, the thin African American woman, whose cleaning jobs included the building housing the FSA office, stands behind a tall upturned broom on one side and an inverted mop on the other while a huge American flag in the background looms above, dwarfing her slight frame. The image, which remains one of the twentieth century's most salient and troubling photographs, exemplifies the compassion and astute social commentary in Parks's work as a photographer and filmmaker.

In subsequent 1940s freelance work, Parks's celebrity photos and ground-breaking photo-essays on racial inequality were published in *Ebony* and *Life* magazines; his appealing fashion photography appeared in *Glamour* and *Vogue*. In 1949, Parks's multidimensional abilities in portraiture led him to become the first Black staff photographer at *Life*, which was mid-twentieth-century America's leading news, entertainment, and lifestyle magazine. In the 1960s, Parks directed three television documentaries on race and poverty in the United States and Latin America: *Flavio* (1964), *Diary of a Harlem Family* (1968), and *The World of Piri Thomas* (1968).[4] His literary work added to the collection of

Black autobiographies expressly or implicitly associated with the American civil rights movement. His 1963 autobiographical novel, *The Learning Tree*, was a best seller, and his 1965 memoir, *A Choice of Weapons*, was well received.[5]

Parks's opening pair of Hollywood films, *The Learning Tree* (1969) and *Shaft* (1971), exemplify a moment in Hollywood cinema when social and financial factors combined to create a window of opportunity for Black creative talent. *The Learning Tree* represented the first time an African American directed a Hollywood production, and *Shaft* was the most commercially successful Black-directed studio film of the early 1970s until *Super Fly*, the directorial debut of his son Gordon Parks Jr., surpassed it in 1972.[6]

In 1989, *The Learning Tree* was among the twenty-five productions selected for the National Film Registry its inaugural year. In 2000, Parks's production of *Shaft*, starring Richard Roundtree, was added to the registry.[7] Yet *The Learning Tree* and *Shaft* received varied reviews when they were released, and the films continue to elicit differing responses. Initial reviews of *The Learning Tree* praised the film for "creating a black character who was not scarred and embittered by racism," but they also criticized it for "propagating 'Uncle Tomism' during a period of heightened racial consciousness among African Americans."[8] In subsequent scholarship, Thomas Cripps compares *The Learning Tree* to *Nothing But a Man* (Michael Roemer, 1964) and *Sounder* (Martin Ritt, 1972), finding that these films "personalize and humanize [the] black plight and rage" but in doing so pander to dominant society to make the films "palatable for [white] audiences."[9] Expressing an opposing view, Ed Guerrero argues, "In an eleven-year period between *Nothing But a Man* in 1964 and [Michael Schultz's] *Cooley High* in 1975, the only commercial films that showed the complex humanity of black people versus formulas and stereotypes were *The Learning Tree*, [Ossie Davis's 1972 film] *Black Girl*, and *Sounder*."[10]

When *Shaft* was released, many reviewers saw the film as a "breakthrough production in terms of expanding black representation in commercial cinema."[11] Yet others believed the film implicitly fostered a "containment of black social or political aspirations."[12] Some viewers found "an entertaining black hero in the James Bond tradition [while others] saw an exploitative black male stereotype thrown on-screen to increase Hollywood's profits."[13] Ensuing scholarly assessments of *Shaft* also featured an array of viewpoints. Describing the film as a black "cover" of a white genre film, Cripps finds that it inserts Richard Roundtree into a "Dick Powell role [like] those in *Murder My Sweet* or other 1940s *films noir* [and retailors] the lingo, dress, and body English to fit the new black circumstances."[14]

Mark Reid also sees Shaft as based on a white model, contrasting him with the hero in *Sweet Sweetback's Baadasssss Song* (Melvin Van Peebles, 1971) and emphasizing that while Sweetback "rebelled against authority figures, Shaft

[will] fight only against those outside the law."[15] Other scholars identify different relationships between Shaft and Sweetback. James Naremore argues that Parks and Van Peebles give "new life to old forms by turning the black male into a sexually potent hero."[16] In his view, both directors "created black supermen [who represented a response] to decades of emasculated or nearly invisible black people on the screen."[17] Echoing Naremore's point, Eithne Quinn sees a "superstud coding of black masculinity . . . powerfully consecrated in *Sweetback* and *Shaft*" and, further, finds that "the misogyny onscreen runs deep" in these two films.[18] Yet questioning the notion that Shaft is solely aligned with dominant white society, Quinn finds that both *Sweetback* and *Shaft* explore "some degree of collaboration between individualist heroes and activists."[19]

To explore these issues from a new angle, this chapter considers *The Learning Tree* and *Shaft* in relation to one other and in light of Parks's professional background as an accomplished visual storyteller. The chapter's delimited auteur study proposes that the two films are grounded in Black literary traditions and Parks's ability to depict African Americans as individuals continuously engaged in both reflection and action. To describe Parks's contributions to cinematic representations of blackness, the discussion analyzes the contrasting adaptation processes that led to the two films, showing that the cinematic version of *The Learning Tree* represents a distillation of Parks's novel, whereas the filmic iteration of *Shaft* constitutes a transformation of Ernest Tidyman's pulp fiction. To clarify how Parks acquired the agency necessary to infuse both films with his vision, the chapter sets aside discussions of Black family dramas and Blaxploitation to examine the role of Black activism and Black creative talent in the productively turbulent context of the Hollywood Renaissance in late 1960s and early 1970s.[20] Together, these considerations illuminate the autobiographical dimension of both adaptations and their shared vision of Black caring, integrity, and self-mastery as essential to survival, agency, and autonomy in white-dominated America.

DISTILLATION: PARKS'S PROCESS ADAPTING *THE LEARNING TREE*

There is no question that Parks is *the* creative force behind the literary and filmic versions of *The Learning Tree*. Both emerge from his life as a Black youth in early twentieth-century Fort Scott, Kansas, which the novel and film call Cherokee Flats to acknowledge Indigenous land rights.[21] The unshakable dignity of the story's central character, fifteen-year-old Newton "Newt" Winger, captures the resolve and self-reliance that distinguished the Parks family and other pioneering Exodusters, who migrated from southern states to Kansas, Oklahoma, and Colorado after Reconstruction collapsed in 1877.[22] In both novel and film, the representations of young love, unfailing family support, racialized social and economic disparity, and a white police officer's unchecked prerogative to kill Black citizens are grounded in Parks's personal history.

The literary and filmic versions of *The Learning Tree* reveal the influence of Black autographical narrative traditions, which include "autobiographies constructed to read as novels."[23] Like such work, Parks's novel and film emphasize connections between blackness, resistance, and intellectual sophistication to generate a counterdiscourse to the narratives that dominant white society has generated about African Americans.[24] Parks's autobiographical novel and film have points of contact with a range of publications, including Richard Wright's *Black Boy* (1945), James Baldwin's *Go Tell It on the Mountain* (1953), Martin Luther King Jr.'s *Stride Toward Freedom* (1958), *Nigger: An Autobiography by Dick Gregory* (1964) coauthored with white journalist Robert Lipsyte, *The Autobiography of Malcolm X* (1965) coauthored with Black journalist Alex Haley, Margaret Walker's *Jubilee* (1966), and Anne Moody's *Coming of Age in Mississippi* (1968).

The literary and filmic versions of *The Learning Tree* echo W. E. B. Du Bois's 1903 autobiographical narrative in *The Souls of Black Folk* because, in all cases, the landscape is "a figurative space" and an "arena" in which the authors fashion their lives.[25] The narratives of Du Bois and Parks also seem to share the hope that whites will work with African Americans to "forge a new community."[26] Yet in contrast to *The Souls of Black Folk*, the central character in Parks's story does not travel to or from a land of freedom but instead learns that Cherokee Flats is a place of freedom *and* oppression for Black Americans. Newt's family home and the surrounding prairie offer nurturance and the means for self-sufficiency, whereas the school, courthouse, white homes, and white businesses in town are sites of racial inequality. Even the river, a place of freedom for Black youths to skinny-dip on hot Sunday afternoons, is subject to white supremacist violence, which Parks underscores by bookending his novel and film with scenes of death at the river. In an early scene, the town sheriff shoots an unarmed Black man in the back; red blood colors the water as the man's body sinks and disappears. At the close of the story, the bigoted sheriff guns down a Black youth in the same spot, and red blood on the surface of the water is the last evidence of his tortured life.[27]

Parks's longtime interest in creatively revisiting the place where he had been raised is evident in the series of Fort Scott photographs he took in 1950, which *Life* magazine commissioned for a photo-essay that was eventually shelved.[28] Assigned to document segregation in other southern locales, Parks created another body of photographs taken in and around Mobile, Alabama, for a September 1956 *Life* magazine photo-essay titled "Restraints: Open and Hidden." The images feature members of an extended African American family in everyday settings that illustrate how segregation shapes their daily lives, and his novel and film would include scenes that recall this series of photographs.[29] Prior to the publication of *The Learning Tree*, Parks traveled again to Fort Scott, this time staging and photographing specific scenes in the novel. In August 1963, *Life* magazine published these photographs alongside passages from Parks's novel in a two-part feature titled "How It Feels to be Black." The photo-essays gave witness to African American lives in rural America and essentially served as storyboards for Parks's film, which recreates scenes found in the photo-essays.[30]

Despite Parks's comprehensive involvement in the literary and filmic iterations of *The Learning Tree*, it is possible to qualify his attribution as sole author. Genevieve Young, the Harper & Row editor assigned to Parks when he was writing *The Learning Tree*, was known for her ability to restructure stories to generate the greatest emotional impact, and interview material suggests that Young worked with Parks on each chapter of his novel.[31] Similarly, the film's opening credits list Young as the story consultant, suggesting that she helped distill the novel's multifaceted story to create the film's dramatic structure, which presents Newt Winger (Kyle Johnson), who enjoys the support of a loving family, and Marcus Savage (Alex Clarke), who is Newt's abused and poverty-stricken peer, as two opposing roles for young Black men. Young, who became romantically involved with Parks when he was writing *The Learning Tree* and married him in 1973, perhaps edited other Parks projects, including the various audio versions of Parks reading his novel.[32] Young and Parks remained friends and intellectual colleagues despite their divorce in 1979, and she established the Gordon Parks Foundation in 2006 to preserve and foster his artistic legacy.

Even with Young's editorial contributions, *The Learning Tree* is imbued with Parks's personal history and the themes to which he would return throughout his multifaceted career. Echoing his powerful photo-essays and documentaries on racial inequality, Parks presents the story's "tragic figures, Marcus and Arcella, [as] victims of a horrific system of racism [and] with such dignity and love that their fates hurt even more."[33] He also shows how African Americans in the early twentieth century lived with the specter of white rampages like the 1921 Tulsa Massacre, as the fear of widespread white reprisal against Black people in Cherokee Flats leads Newt to delay telling anyone he witnessed Marcus's father kill white farmer Jack Kiner. At the same time, Parks provides an alternative to narratives that frame African Americans as little more than victims. As a novel and film, *The Learning Tree* illuminates the loving and self-reliant life of a Black family on the American plains, offering striking scenes of Black pioneers who ride horses and herd cattle on the open prairie.

Instilled with his family's integrity and self-reliance, Newt Winger (Kyle Johnson) has the strength of character to confront the town's racist sheriff (Dana Elcar) in *The Learning Tree*.

The literary and cinematic iterations of Parks's coming-of-age narrative create a "complex, knowing, and compassionate portrayal of African American characters," which includes the depiction of Newt's girlfriend, Arcella (Mira Waters).[34] Distilling a collection of scenes in the novel, on screen "Arcella and Newt's love story gets a romantic, lyrical montage heretofore unseen for Black characters."[35] Parks's poetic vision of Black romantic love would carry into another series of images not seen before in mainstream American cinema—namely, the discreet montage of Shaft and his girlfriend, Ellie (Gwenn Mitchell), making love. The scene begins with Shaft reading an issue of *Essence* magazine as he is tucked into the fur-lined couch in her apartment.[36] Its brief dialogue conveys her concern for him and his need for comfort, and it ends with a tactful image of her face that conveys her physical and emotional pleasure.[37]

In their depiction of complex Black characters, Parks's novel and film present Newt's mother, Sarah (Estelle Evans), as the family member who "really kept things together."[38] It is her vision that Newt has been "born into the start of a new world" and that education is "more powerful than guns or money" that shapes Newt's upbringing.[39] In the novel and the film, it is Sarah's wisdom that keeps the threat of the lynching tree at bay so that Newt will focus on the metaphor of the learning tree, which she sees as a reminder that "we gotta do things for ourself."[40] Together with Newt's father, Sarah instills a sense of dignity in her children, with the result that in the novel and the film, the family members all "have self-respect and pride, and [they] are unafraid to talk back to their oppressors."[41] Starting on the opening page, the novel repeatedly highlights the dignity of self-reliance and the characters' pride in being Black; the film condenses these moments to include Newt's last quiet but defiant statement to the bigoted sheriff: "I can make it by myself."[42]

TRANSFORMATION: PARKS'S APPROACH TO ADAPTING *SHAFT*

Any assistance Parks received in creating the literary and cinematic versions of *The Learning Tree* led to the novel and film having a shared vision of the characters and themes. In comparison, the radical differences between Tidyman's novel and the film version of *Shaft* signal Parks's profound authorial intervention. It is true that white author Ernest Tidyman created a basis for the plot in his 1970 novel and contractually received credit as screenplay coauthor along with white journeyman TV writer John D. F. Black. However, comparative analysis of Tidyman's novel and the 1971 film shows that Parks completely reimagined the angry, isolated, misogynistic hard-boiled detective in Tidyman's novel to create a personable, intelligent character who is adept at his profession, kind to vulnerable people, comfortable in bustling New York City, emotionally connected to his bright, caring Black girlfriend, in touch with the survival skills he developed as a youth growing up in a rough neighborhood, and psychologically equipped to smoothly navigate a range of social environments.

These worlds include the disparate domains of Harlem kingpin Bumpy Jonas (Moses Gun), the Black activists who support Shaft's boyhood friend Ben Buford (Christopher St. John), and the Black middle-class family that briefly provides a safe haven for Buford after the Italian mobsters murder his comrades.[43] The varied locales that Shaft easily occupies include the busy Midtown Manhattan district that offers an efficient location for his one-man business office; the bohemian neighborhood of Manhattan's Greenwich Village, which is well suited to Shaft's bachelor pad/auxiliary office; and the run-down precinct quarters of white detective Vic Androzzi (Charles Cioffi), who respects Shaft's abilities and seems to be the only decent cop in the notoriously corrupt mid-twentieth-century New York Police Department.[44]

In Tidyman's pulp fiction, Shaft is ruthless and prone to violent outbursts. A Vietnam vet suffering from post-traumatic stress disorder, Tidyman's central character sometimes feels "almost without control . . . as if he were being asked to walk across an empty stage, under the blinding beam of an arc light, while an auditorium of hostile strangers" judge his performance.[45] He acts on instinct; as he explains, "That's the way he was. Circumstance and response. Cause and effect. . . . There was no room for thought, reflection or perspective."[46] Fueled by anxiety and rage, the events that allow him to rescue the Harlem gangster's daughter from the white mobsters leave him "fucking tired and lonely, puzzled by the sweeping assault of doubt."[47]

His appearance reflects his surly, hard-boiled nature. He has a "saddle-stitch scar [running] down his forehead toward his eyes," lives in a filthy apartment, and wears a rumpled gray suit throughout most of the story.[48] In addition, Tidyman keeps Shaft and Black activist Ben Buford continually at odds, but

Parks creates an evolution in their relationship, which leads to Shaft entrusting the kidnapped girl to Buford after she has been rescued.[49] In Tidyman's pulp fiction, Ellie is a sexually adventurous white woman with a maid. The woman provides recreational sex but no emotional support. In the novel, the Harlem kingpin takes care of Shaft after he is beaten by the white mobsters, but Parks has Buford take Shaft to Ellie's apartment for care. In the novel, Shaft finds some solace spending time with the family of his middle-class accountant, whereas early on, Parks has Shaft seek emotional refuge at Ellie's place, which has framed pictures of the couple on a living room end table.[50] Further, in place of the homophobia that permeates the novel, Parks presents Shaft as friends with Billy (Ron Tannas), a gay bartender at the pub across the street from his apartment.

Other, seemingly minor, changes in Parks's film create significant differences in Shaft's characterization. For example, when Shaft first meets the white mobster who will take him to confirm that the kidnapped girl is still alive, the novel conveys Shaft's hostile way of moving through the world as Shaft starts the conversation, calling the man "a wop punk," to which the man replies in kind, "I'd know you anywhere, n----r."[51] In contrast, the filmic version depicts the white mobster as the inherently hostile character, first referring to Shaft as a "n----r," which then prompts Shaft to call him a "wop."

The film version of *The Learning Tree* retains the novel's themes, key dramatic developments, and vision of the central characters, even though it reduces the times Newt contends with the presence of death, and it eliminates subplots such as the one in which Newt's parents participate in the Black townspeople's protests of the inequality in their children's education. In sharp contrast, the literary and filmic versions of *Shaft* reveal entirely different influences. Tidyman's model for Shaft is white hard-boiled detective Mike Hammer, the racist, homophobic, and misogynistic hero of Mickey Spillane's best-selling mid-twentieth-century novels.[52] Modeled on Spillane's pulp fiction, Tidyman's novel retains the conventional perspective in which the private detective enters a world of crime and darkness that constitutes a deviation from the white norm. Tidyman's superficial change of Shaft's racial identity makes his detective an alien, without any connection to white society or communities of color.[53] Unveiling his character's uncomfortable blackface existence, Tidyman ends his novel with Shaft in a cab headed for the airport to anywhere that will allow him to "get out of his own skin."[54]

As in his autobiographical novel, Parks reverses the standard white gaze, so that "rather than looking at a dark, mysterious world . . . audiences see the machinations of a white world through the eyes of a black individual."[55] In the novel and film of *The Learning Tree*, Parks captures the flagrant historical violations against African Americans in his characterizations of both the town sheriff who kills Marcus and the judge's profligate son who rapes and impregnates Newt's beloved girlfriend, Arcella. Parks crystallizes the bigotry shaping his own public education in Fort Scott, Kansas, in the character of Newt's guidance teacher Miss McClintock, who instructs Newt to take easy classes since she assumed "colored kids [would always] wind up porters and maids."[56] In *Shaft*, Parks conveys the callous cruelty of mid-twentieth-century white society in his depictions of the well-armed white mobsters and the smug white cops surrounding Vic. He also illustrates white women's objectification of handsome Black men in the era of the swinging sixties through his character-ization of the Greenwich Village woman who throws herself at Shaft the night he finds the mobsters at his local bar staking out his apartment.[57]

Parks's film uses Black detective fiction and his personal experiences as a photographer as his guides for envisioning John Shaft and the story's thematic exploration of Black self-reliance. His film implicitly builds on work such as John Edward Bruce's *The Black Sleuth* (1907–1909), one of the first instances of a Black detective in literature, and Oscar Micheaux's *Murder in Harlem* (also known as *Brand of Cain* and *Lem Hawkin's Confession*, 1935), an early example of a Black detective in cinema. More specifically, Parks's intermixing of levity and grittiness shows the influence of African American novelist Chester Himes, whose Harlem Detective series features Black detectives Grave Digger Jones and Coffin Ed Johnson, who have a "sense of community and family that doesn't exist in the mainstream detective tradition."[58] Individually and together, Himes's detective stories reveal racial inequality's toxic effects on African Americans.[59] Himes's work was an integral part of mid-twentieth-century Black literature, and the Harlem Detective series included *For Love of Imabelle* (also known as *A Rage in Harlem*, 1957), *The Real Cool Killers* (1959), *The Crazy Kill* (1959), *The Big Gold Dream* (1959), *All Shot Up* (1960), *The Heat's On* (1961), *Cotton Comes to Harlem* (1965), and *Blind Man with a Pistol* (1969).[60] Himes's importance as a contemporary Black author led his work to be the basis for the second Black-directed Hollywood film, Ossie Davis's *Cotton Comes to Harlem* (1970), starring Godfrey Cambridge and Raymond St. Jacques.

Parks's reconceptualization of John Shaft and other aspects of Tidyman's novel also depended on his familiarity with the imagery and dynamics of criminal life in the New York neighborhood of Harlem. In the 1940s, he spent three years doing research with "his friend [literary figure] Ralph Ellison, who had been working on an article titled 'Harlem Is Nowhere,' about the intricate connections among poverty, race, and mental health in the area."[61] While "Harlem Is Nowhere" was never published, *Life* magazine featured a November 1948 photo-essay titled "Harlem Gang Leader," which included a selection of the photographs Parks was able to produce because of the many hours he and Ellison "walked the streets and together . . . documented the hostile environment."[62] Later, *Life* magazine commissioned Parks to create the photographs for a September 1957 photo-essay titled "The Atmosphere of Crime," which included a sampling from the hundreds of color photographs Parks took in New York, Chicago, San Francisco, and Los Angeles. Notably, his images "rejected clichés of delinquency, drug use and corruption, opting for a more nuanced view that reflected the social and economic factors tied to criminal behavior and a rare window into the working lives of those charged with preventing and prosecuting it."[63]

As in his direction of *The Learning Tree*, Parks's photographs, this time of distressed urban settings and individuals whose lives intersect in some way with criminal life, provided a basis for images and scenes in his production of *Shaft*. In addition, Parks used his experiences traveling the globe and professional background as a fashion and celebrity photographer to develop and visualize Shaft's cosmopolitan outlook. As observers have noted, Shaft "bears more than a passing resemblance to the director himself, from his clothing to his ease moving between Harlem and Greenwich Village."[64] Parks's autobiographical conception of the Black detective complicates interpretations that see Shaft as aligned with dominant white culture simply because he works as a private eye who has dealings with law enforcement. The Parks-Shaft connection also destabilizes the notion that the character is modeled on the Black buck stereotype and is like other "aggressive, pistol-packing, sexually-charged urban cowboys" of the early 1970s.[65] Insofar as Shaft is modeled on Parks's life as a twentieth-century Renaissance man, the character's multicultural perspective is best understood as anticipating what Trey Ellis has described as "an openended New Black Aesthetic" that shapes the social and aesthetic choices of contemporary "cultural mulattoes [who] no longer need to deny or suppress any part of [their] complicated and sometimes contradictory cultural baggage to please either white people or black."[66]

The opening moments of the film illustrate how completely Parks reimagined the unkempt, anxiety-ridden character in the novel. In the scenes of Shaft/Roundtree traversing busy New York streets, "Parks reveals John Shaft's attitude, suaveness, and sexuality through camera shots that constantly frame Richard Roundtree's features and athletic frame."[67] The images integrate "Shaft into the environment, making him inseparable from the allure and edginess of the urban community."[68] Instead of seeing a scowling, scar-faced Black man in a lifeless gray suit, audiences are presented with a handsome African American male who walks with energy and purpose. His fitted cashmere turtleneck, bronze-brown tweed slacks, and tailored, three-quarter-length brown leather topcoat convey his professionalism, mental balance, and smart sense of sartorial style.

The music and lyrics of Isaac Hayes's Oscar-winning "Theme from Shaft" amplify the impressions that the images create. The funky and hard-driving but melodic and elegantly orchestrated score suggests John Shaft's deft blending of

Richard Roundtree in *Shaft* (1971): an embodiment of the integrity and intelligence Gordon Parks saw as essential to African American self-sufficiency and influence in America.

toughness and humanity. The lyric segment's call-and-response format presents the character as a member of the African American community and an iconic figure in African Diasporic storytelling traditions. The lyrics themselves capture Shaft's salient qualities: sexually attractive to women, brave enough to risk his life to protect another, ethical and principled to the core, and a complex man in a meaningful relationship with a woman who truly loves and understands him.

In the opening sequence, Shaft's brief encounter with a man selling a stolen watch reveals that he's a detective who does not terrorize petty criminals or enforce (white property) laws. Roundtree's amused smile as he passes through the small group of protesters on a sidewalk conveys that Shaft has a healthy sense of humor. His first verbal exchange in the film, with Marty, the blind newsstand vendor (Lee Steele), shows that Shaft is on good terms with people around him. His simple gesture of casually lifting a heavy stack of newspapers and placing it next to the papers Marty is selling to the stream of morning pedestrians communicates his innate goodwill and underscores the profound contrast with the novel's anger-filled character. Subsequent scenes confirm that Shaft is "mellow but assertive and unintimidated by whites" or people of color.[69]

Parks's film adaptations of *The Learning Tree* and *Shaft* feature the specific iconography of their respective settings, yet both are firmly grounded in his photography and personal experiences. For *The Learning Tree*, the adaptation process required little more than selecting the characters and scenes essential to retaining the novel's meaning. However, to create the film version of *Shaft*, Parks replaced the white template in Tidyman's novel with perspectives and thematic elements drawn from Black detective fiction, knowledge he had acquired as a crime photographer, and life experiences that had taken him from the slums of

Rio de Janeiro to the fashion salons of Paris. As a result, Parks was able to create a character whose makeover as a Black private eye was more than cosmetic. Especially if one decouples his adaptation from subsequent Black action films with urban settings, instead considering it in relation to Parks's body of work, it is possible to see his depiction of Shaft as another autobiographical project.

AGENCY AND AUTONOMY: BLACK CREATIVE LABOR DURING THE HOLLYWOOD RENAISSANCE

A constellation of factors contributed to Parks's authorial agency as a Hollywood director. The 1960s and early 1970s represented a time of change in the mainstream film industry as studios competed with and then co-opted television production, filmmakers incorporated the aesthetics of foreign art films, and studios turned to independent creative talent as they moved more exclusively into distribution.[70] Film content and audience expectations shifted as the Production Code was decommissioned in 1966 and the rating system was established in 1968. The 1971 Revenue Act, which allowed "income tax credits on film losses and reintroduced tax credits for domestic film production," facilitated experimentation, including the increased production of Black-themed and Black-directed films.[71] In addition, Parks's adaptations of *The Learning Tree* and *Shaft* belong to a time when mainstream films reflected the polarized social climate. Films such as *Bonnie and Clyde* (Arthur Penn, 1967), *The Graduate* (Mike Nichols, 1967), and *Easy Rider* (Dennis Hopper, 1969) were popular with counterculture audiences, whereas vigilante films like *Joe* (John G. Avildsen, 1970), *Dirty Harry* (Don Siegel, 1971), and *Walking Tall* (Phil Karlson, 1973) resonated with conservatives.[72]

Further, even audiences that supported efforts to increase racial justice had conflicting responses to the work of star actor Sidney Poitier, who had made movie history as the first African American to win a Best Actor Academy Award for his performance in *Lilies of the Field* (Ralph Nelson, 1963). Reflecting the approval of many ostensibly liberal viewers, *To Sir, with Love* (James Clavell, 1967), *In the Heat of the Night* (Norman Jewison, 1967), and *Guess Who's Coming to Dinner* (Stanley Kramer, 1967) made Poitier "the biggest box-office star of the year."[73] The films also garnered mainstream critical acclaim: *In the Heat of the Night* won five Oscars, including Best Picture; *Guess Who's Coming to Dinner* received two Oscars. Yet at the height of Poitier's career, scores of Black-authored articles criticized his sanitized star image and the simplistic narratives in which he embodied "sterile paragons of virtue."[74] These critiques of Hollywood representations signaled new audience expectations. To create products that would sell in the changing marketplace, the studios employed Parks and other Black artists. Further, while executives continued to focus on minimizing costs to enhance profits, the agency Parks secured for his productions of *The Learning Tree* and *Shaft* is indicative of the Hollywood Renaissance period when new creative laborers enjoyed a degree of autonomy far beyond the opportunities in the earlier "producer-unit" system of classical Hollywood cinema.[75]

Summarizing how the 1960s' focus on race relations affected the entertainment industry, Quinn observes that the "assassination of Martin Luther King Jr., the social unrest and urban rebellions, the rise of black nationalism, the attempts to implement civil rights laws, and the stirring white backlash gave race politics enormous salience in America."[76] Thus, along with Hollywood's decision to greenlight and promote films starring Poitier, television shows featuring Black actors became part of the commercial landscape. Raymond St. Jacques was cast in the 1965–1966 season of *Rawhide* (CBS 1959–1966), and Bill Cosby costarred with white actor Robert Culp in *I Spy* (NBC 1965–1968). The news program *Black Journal* (NET 1968–1970, PBS 1970–1977); *The Outcasts* (ABC 1968–1969), a Western costarring Otis Young; *Julia* (NBC 1968–1971) starring Diahann Carroll; and *Mod Squad* (ABC 1968–1973) with Clarence Williams III were additional TV shows with African American content or leading actors.

The cultural interest in race relations led to various independent and studio-produced Black-themed films with white directors. *Shadows* (John Cassavetes, 1959), *A Raisin in the Sun* (Daniel Petrie, 1961), *Nothing But a Man* (1964), *Sweet Love, Bitter* (Herbert Danska, 1967), and *Uptight* (Jules Dassin, 1968) are some of the earlier films in this group. *Slaves* (Herbert Biberman, 1969), *The Lost Man* (Robert Alan Aurthur, 1969), *Putney Swope* (Robert Downey Sr., 1969), *The Liberation of L.B. Jones* (William Wyler, 1970), and *The Great White Hope* (Martin Ritt, 1970) illustrate the era's disparate race-related films with white directors.[77] Productions featuring Black actors such as Harry Belafonte, Ruby Dee, Brock Peters, Woody Strode, Cicely Tyson, Bernie Casey, Jim Brown, and Fred Williamson confirm the studios' interest in what white executives saw as marketable material in the Hollywood Renaissance period.

However, during the 1960s, Black artists and critics had become increasingly concerned about white-directed, Black-themed films. In 1968, the proposed studio adaptation of William Styron's bigoted novel *The Confessions of Nat Turner* prompted the formation of the activist group that became known as the Black Anti-Defamation Association (BADA), which included Black novelist Louise Meriwether and Black actor-director Ossie Davis as its leaders. As Quinn shows, protests of the Styron adaptation project "helped 'pave the way' for the late entry of a few black filmmakers into Hollywood"[78] because the activism put pressure on the studios to include "meaningful black creative input" on Black-themed films.[79] Quinn explains that the "salience of black culture around the end of the 1960s and the belated realization of white filmmakers and executives of the need for black talent as a source of marketing legitimacy, thematic value, and formal innovation generated some new leverage for African Americans."[80]

Black writers found work in Hollywood. Bill Gunn was hired to write and direct *Stop!* (1970), which Warner Bros. shelved after the film received an X rating, and he wrote the screenplays for the white-directed films *The Landlord* (Hal Ashby, 1970) and *Angel Levine* (Ján Kadár, 1970), a HarBel production starring Harry Belafonte.[81] Lonne Elder III wrote the screenplays for African American editor-director Hugh A. Robertson's *Melinda* (1972) and white director Martin Ritt's film *Sounder* (1972), for which he received the first Oscar nomination awarded to a Black screenwriter.

Black-directed, studio-distributed films released due to the sound box-office performance of films such as *The Learning Tree* and *Shaft* include *Super Fly*, *Buck and the Preacher* (Sidney Poitier, 1972), *Come Back, Charleston Blue* (Mark Warren, 1972), *Shaft's Big Score!* (Gordon Parks, 1972), *Trouble Man* (Ivan Dixon, 1972), *Gordon's War* (Ossie Davis, 1973), and *The Spook Who Sat by the Door* (Ivan Dixon, 1973). African American directors also contributed to the era's independently distributed film productions, as shown in work such as *Sweet Sweetback's Baadasssss Song* (1971), *Black Girl* (1972), *Together for Days* (Michael Schultz, 1972), *Blacula* (William Crane, 1972), *The Limit* (Yaphet Kotto, 1972), *Top of the Heap* (Christopher St. John, 1972), and *The Final Comedown* (Oscar Williams, 1972).

The comparative autonomy that Parks attained to make *The Learning Tree* and *Shaft* parallels the agency Ossie Davis and Melvin Van Peebles fought for and won as pioneer African American directors in Hollywood. Davis, who cowrote and directed the United Artists production of *Cotton Comes to Harlem* (1970), used his leverage to hire Black crew members[82] and embellish the adaptation's ending to include a warmly comedic scene, which reveals that beloved minor character Uncle Budd (Redd Foxx) quietly left Harlem with the missing trove of ill-gotten cash that had set the plot in motion.

Similarly, as director of the Columbia Pictures production *Watermelon Man* (1970), Van Peebles obtained "a significant degree of control . . . taking on the role of score composer and negotiating important changes to the film's narrative."[83] For the film's story of a racist insurance salesman who wakes up one morning and sees that he has suddenly become a Black man, the studio had planned to use a white actor in blackface, even though the character is white in only the first few scenes. Van Peebles "insisted that the lead be African American, and actor-comedian Godfrey Cambridge was soon signed on, and he performs these early scenes whited up."[84] Like Davis, Van Peebles reworked the story's conclusion, with the formerly white character "fully affirming his new identity, becoming a black nationalist, and opening a successful community business."[85] As Quinn explains, "Van Peebles's insistence on changing [white screenwriter Herbert] Raucher's original screenplay to introduce an ending featuring independent black wealth echoes Ossie Davis's script intervention on *Cotton* with Uncle Budd. In both, there is a utopian dream of abundant black wealth generation replacing exploited black labor."[86]

The influence that Davis and Van Peebles exerted in their Hollywood directorial debuts suggests the comparatively more artist-centered approach that studio executives took in the late 1960s and early 1970s. Corporate restructuring had "installed younger studio leaders, who shifted away from traditional product lines . . . to attract the increasingly youthful [and diverse] cinema-going market."[87] Warner Bros.-Seven Arts (1967–1969), the studio that produced and distributed *The Learning Tree*, exemplifies the era's interest in attracting counterculture audiences, releasing films such as *Bonnie and Clyde* (1967), *Cool Hand Luke* (Stuart Rosenberg, 1967), *Petulia* (Richard Lester,1968), and *I Love You, Alice B. Toklas* (Hy Averback, 1968) prior to Parks's first feature film. The films of Warner Bros.-Seven Arts reflected the independent background of Seven Arts Productions, which had created offbeat films like *Lolita* (Stanley Kubrick, 1962) and *What Ever Happened to Baby Jane?* (Robert Aldrich, 1962). When Seven Arts cofounder Eliot Hyman became the chairman of Warner Bros.-Seven Arts, he named his son Kenneth Hyman the head of production. Prior to leading the Warner Bros.-Seven Arts film production unit, Kenneth Hyman had produced *The Hill* (Sidney Lumet, 1965) with Ossie Davis and *The Dirty Dozen* (Robert Aldrich, 1967), featuring Jim Brown, both Metro-Goldwyn-Mayer releases that suggest his interest and experience in making films involving Black creative talent.

The hard-earned authorial agency that Davis secured at United Artists and Van Peebles attained at Columbia echoed Parks's arrangement at Warner Bros.-Seven Arts when he became the first African American to direct a studio picture. White actor-director John Cassavetes, who had been in *The Dirty Dozen*, directed the Black-themed independent film *Shadows* (1959), and was familiar with Parks's work as a writer and photographer, arranged a meeting between Gordon Parks and Kenneth Hyman.[88] In their first meeting, Hyman commissioned Parks to direct *The Learning Tree*, adapt the novel, compose the film score, and serve as one of the film's producers.[89] Parks secured positions for African American crew members and selected the department heads, including white cinematographer Burnett Guffy, the Oscar-winning director of photography for *Bonnie and Clyde*, which was shot in rural northeast Texas six hours south of Fort Scott. That experience, along with Parks's photographs, served as references for Guffy, who had recently been the cinematographer for *The Split* (Gordon Flemyng, 1968), starring Jim Brown and Diahann Carroll.

Parks chose the cast for *The Learning Tree* and grounded his low-key directing approach in his long experience photographing subjects ranging from impoverished children to actors such as Ingrid Bergman, Laurence Olivier, Joan Crawford, James Cagney, and Bette Davis.[90] He also made his quietly maverick stance visible from the film's opening moments forward. The bright-blue credits over warm pastoral images feature Newt/Kyle Johnson walking through patches of Kansas wild sunflowers, along a quiet riverbank, and through a field of tall sorghum. These images, of a thoughtful Black youth in pleasant rural settings, signal the film's break with Hollywood conventions. The content of the credits is also revolutionary. Along with Parks's credits as writer, producer, director, and composer, two unknown Black actors, Kyle Johnson and Alex Clarke, receive top billing; the cast consists primarily of African American actors; and Black vocal artist O. C. Smith, who had achieved commercial and critical success with his 1968 recording of "Little Green Apples," is listed as singing the theme song that Parks composed.

In his memoir *A Hungry Heart* (2005), Parks recounts the often race-based obstacles he faced during the production of *The Learning Tree.* Yet he found ways to handle the racist white townspeople in Fort Scott where the film was shot and bigoted film producer William Conrad, who eventually withdrew from the project. The release was modestly successful, with the $3.15 million in theatrical rentals covering the $1.9 million spent on production and marketing costs.[91]

Parks's professionalism in his feature directorial debut led to his work on *Shaft* for Metro-Goldwyn-Mayer (MGM), yet another studio interested in Black-themed films and Black creative labor. Prior to *Shaft*, MGM had released *The Hill* (1965), with Ossie Davis, and a series of films starring Jim Brown: *The Dirty Dozen* (1967), *The Split* (1968), *Dark of the Sun* (Jack Cardiff, 1968), *Ice Station Zebra* (John Sturges, 1968), *Kenner* (Steve Sekey, 1969), and *Tick, Tick, Tick* (Ralph Nelson, 1970). However, in contrast to the artist-friendly environment of Warner Bros.-Seven Arts during its two-year existence (1967–1969), MGM became known for firing employees and canceling productions after business-man Kirk Kerkorian took control of MGM in 1969 with the goal of liquidating the studio's film and real estate resources. James T. Aubrey Jr., who served as MGM president under Kerkorian from 1969 to 1973, gained notoriety for cutting budgets and overriding creative artists, especially during postproduction. Tasked with liquidating the studio to fund Kerkorian's hotel and cruise ship ventures, Aubrey saw value only in productions with budgets under $2 million. Thus, Parks's time at MGM reflected the tension between the studio's interest in attracting younger, more diverse audiences and its draconian cost-control methods. Eric Pierson's chapter in *Beyond Blaxploitation* (2016) details the ongoing challenges Parks faced during the production and marketing of *Shaft*.[92] Yet Parks prevailed, and the film produced for under $2 million garnered a reported $12 million in box-office receipts and received the NAACP Image Award for Film of the Year.

Notably, Parks's transformational adaptation process depended on African American creative talent, including Richard Roundtree, who received an NAACP Image Award nomination for Best Actor, and editor Hugh A. Robertson, who had recently completed the New York City film *Midnight Cowboy* (John Schlesinger, 1970) and become the first African American to receive an Oscar nomination for Best Film Editing. Most famously, Parks collaborated with Isaac Hayes, who became the first African American to win an Academy Award for Best Original Song. Hayes also won a Golden Globe for Best Score Motion Picture and two Grammy Awards, Best Instrumental Arrangement and Best Original Score Written for a Motion Picture or a Television Special.[93] To create his authorial vision of John Shaft during production and without reference to the racist book and screenplay iterations, Parks also worked with collaborative white filmmakers, including producer Joel Freeman, who received the NAACP Image Award for Producer of the Year, and cinematographer Urs Furrer, who had shot the New York–based counterculture films *The Fat Black Pussycat* (Harold Lee, 1963) and *The Sidelong Glances of a Pigeon Kicker* (John Dexter, 1970).

CONCLUSION

The Learning Tree and *Shaft* extend the rich and varied tradition of African American cinema. In addition, like the pioneering films of Black directors such as Ossie Davis and Melvin Van Peebles, they contribute to the Hollywood Renaissance, challenging aesthetic and cultural norms in ways that parallel the work of directors like Arthur Penn, Dennis Hopper, and Martin Scorsese.[94] Importantly, both of Parks's films reflect his personal experience. As he explains, the characters' interactions in *The Learning Tree* illustrate his formative years in rural Kansas, while the New York City characters that detective John Shaft encounters resemble individuals Parks had studied as a *Life* magazine photographer taking pictures "with homicide squads, vice squads, and dope squads in the night."[95] Just as Parks chose a camera as his weapon to fight systemic racism, the fictional character John Shaft makes private detective work his choice of weapon in a world that requires someone to keep a cool head when other people display the cruelty and callousness that privilege fosters or the anger and inertia that hopelessness creates.

Although *The Learning Tree* is a coming-of-age story whereas *Shaft* belongs to the tradition of Black detective fiction, they share thematic common ground. Both films begin with Black male characters easily traversing their environments and then present events that endanger the characters and test their integrity. Throughout the films, Parks illuminates "the grit it takes for a black man [or youth] to maintain his cool in a racially embattled America."[96] Echoing Parks's photographic portraits of African American men as "objects of derision, sexual fascination, or artistic greatness," Parks's motion pictures convey the elegance and underlying tension of Black male figures who strive to define themselves in a white-dominated society.[97] As both stories close, the central characters have not rooted out the racism that mars their worlds, but their encounters in their respective locales have given them new confidence to navigate the inevitable challenges they will face as Black men in America. In addition, *The Learning Tree* and *Shaft* communicate a message that Parks conveys throughout the varied forms of his artistic practice—namely, that African Americans are an integral part of America, despite the efforts of dominant white culture to confine them to a separate society.

Notes

1. Some publications refer to Gordon Parks (1912–2006) as Gordon Parks Sr. to distinguish him from his son Gordon Parks Jr. (1934–1979), who was killed in a plane crash. Parks Sr. was accomplished in many artistic fields, including music, his primary focus before his photography career began in 1937.

2. Earl A. Powell III and Peter W. Kunhardt Jr., "Director's Foreword," in *Gordon Parks: The New Tide: Early Work 1940–1950*, ed. Philip Brookman (Washington, DC: National Gallery of Art, 2018), 13.

3. In October 1942, the renowned Historical Section of the FSA was moved from the US Department of Agriculture to the US Office of War Information. Parks resigned in December 1943 after the US military blocked his assignment to photograph and travel with the 332nd Fighter Group, the group of African American pilots who fought in World War II and became known as the Tuskegee Airmen.

4. For *Flavio*, Parks received directing and writing credit. *Diary of a Harlem Family* consists of images Parks had shot for a photo-essay titled "A Harlem Family," published in *Life* magazine in March 1968. Project supervisor Josef Filipowic is sometimes listed as the film's director. Yet Parks is the creative force behind the project. He found and established a rapport with the family and spent weeks with them as he shot the images for the photo-essay and the film; he also composed the narration and provided an evocative reading of it that runs throughout the film, https://www.austinfilm.org/2020/11/watch-this-gordon-parks-diary-of-a-harlem-family/. For *The World of Piri Thomas*, Parks is generally given regular directing credit; he is listed in the film's credits as directing its special sequences (visualizations that accompany Piri Thomas's reading of his poetry), https://archive.org/details/theworldofpirithomas and https://archive.org/details/theworldofpirithomas/theworldofpirithomasreel2.mov.

5. See James Baldwin, *Go Tell It on the Mountain* (1953), in *James Baldwin: Early Novels and Stories*, ed. Toni Morrison (Washington, DC: The Library of Congress, 1998). The title of Parks's 1965 memoir recalls James Baldwin's *Go Tell It on the Mountain*, in which the central character acquires "if not a weapon at least a shield" (18) when a school principal recognizes his intelligence. Parks's memoir provides the title for *A Choice of Weapons: Inspired by Gordon Parks* (John Maggio, 2021), an HBO documentary on his career. Parks's other memoirs are *To Smile in Autumn* (1979), *Voices in the Mirror* (1990), and *A Hungry Heart* (2005).

Parks's *The Learning Tree* (1969) and *Shaft* (1971)   243

6. Information about the budget and box office receipts for *Shaft* varies. The budget figures range from $500,000 to $1.8 million, and the box office numbers range from $4 million to $12 million. Prior to the release of *Shaft*, studio-produced films *Cotton Comes to Harlem* (Ossie Davis, 1970) and *Watermelon Man* (Melvin Van Peebles, 1970) had box office receipts of $5.2 and $1.1 million dollars, respectively. The box office gross of *Super Fly* is reported as ranging from $24.8 to $30 million. Melvin Van Peebles's independent feature *Sweet Sweetback's Baadasssss Song* (1971), released in April, a few months before *Shaft*, secured a box office gross of $15.2 million.

7. In 1989, *The Learning Tree* was the only film with a Black writer, director, cast, and story among the first group of films identified as a culturally, historically, and aesthetically significant American production.

8. Charlene Regester, "*The Learning Tree*," in *The Encyclopedia of Novels into Film*, ed. John C. Tibbets and James M. Welsh (New York: Facts on File, 1998), 231.

9. Thomas Cripps, "Film," in *Split Image: African Americans in the Mass Media*, ed. Jannette L. Dates and William Barlow (Washington, DC: Howard University Press, 1993), 167.

10. Ed Guerrero, *Framing Blackness: The African American Image in Film* (Philadelphia: Temple University Press, 1993), 104.

11. Guerrero, *Framing Blackness*, 93.

12. Guerrero, *Framing Blackness*, 93.

13. Melvin Donalson, *Black Directors in Hollywood* (Austin: University of Texas Press, 2003), 11.

14. Cripps, "Film," 169.

15. Mark A. Reid, *Redefining Black Film* (Berkeley: University of California Press, 1993), 85.

16. James Naremore, *More Than Night: Film Noir in its Contexts*, updated and expanded ed. (Berkeley: University of California Press, 2008), 243.

17. Naremore, *More Than Night*, 244.

18. Eithne Quinn, *A Piece of the Action: Race and Labor in Post-Civil Rights Hollywood* (New York: Columbia University Press, 2020), 158, 178–79.

19. Quinn, *Piece of the Action*, 161.

20. See Quinn, *Piece of the Action*, 80. See also Walter Metz, "From Harlem to Hollywood: The 1970s Renaissance and Blaxploitation," in *Beyond Blaxploitation*, ed. Novotny Lawrence and Gerald R. Butters Jr. (Detroit: Wayne State University Press, 2016), 225–45. See Cynthia Baron and Yannis Tzioumakis, *Acting Indie: Industry, Aesthetics, and Performance* (New York: Palgrave Macmillan, 2020) for additional research that frames the work of Black filmmakers as integral to American cinema movements typically identified with white male directors.

21. Parks saw his formative years on the Kansas prairie as so crucial to his identity that he chose to be buried in Fort Scott.

22. See Nell Irvin Painter, *Exodusters: Black Migration to Kansas after Reconstruction* (New York: W. W. Norton, 1986). Parks's film shows the same key events as his novel, but in the book, Newt goes from age twelve to fifteen.

23. Jennifer Jensen Wallach, *"Closer to the Truth Than Any Fact": Memoir, Memory, and Jim Crow* (Athens: University of Georgia Press, 2008), 8.

24. Adetayo Alabi, *Telling Our Stories: Continuities and Divergences in Black Autobiographies* (New York: Palgrave Macmillan, 2005), 142.

25. Robert B. Stepto, *From Behind the Veil: A Study of Afro-American Narrative*, 2nd ed. (Chicago: University of Illinois Press, 1991), 77.

26. Stepto, *From Behind the Veil*, 91.

27. Parks refers to the river as Gunn's River in his memoir *A Hungry Heart*; contemporary maps show the Marmaton River circling the perimeter of Gunn's Park in Fort Scott.

28. See Karen Haas, *Back to Fort Scott: Gordon Parks* (Boston: Museum of Fine Arts, Boston, 2015).

29. See Michael E. Shapiro and Peter W. Kundardt Jr., eds., *Gordon Parks: Segregation Story* (Atlanta: High Museum of Art, 2014).

30. The Criterion Collection release of *The Learning Tree* includes a booklet with the first installment of Gordon Parks's August 1963 *Life* magazine photo-essay titled "How It Feels to Be Black."

31. "Genevieve Young Interview—*A Choice of Weapons: Inspired by Gordon Parks*," Kunhardt Film Foundation, February 18, 2022, video, https://www.youtube.com/watch?v=yVmzZagmMEM.

32. See *Gordon Parks Reads The Learning Tree* (1970), https://www.youtube.com/watch?v=fYttW9hvgEw.

33. Odie Henderson, "*The Learning Tree*: Personal History," *Current*, February 9, 2022, https://www.criterion.com/current/posts/7685-the-learning-tree-personal-history.

34. Henderson, "*The Learning Tree*."

35. Henderson, "*The Learning Tree*."

36. *Essence* was established in 1970 as a magazine for African American women. Parks was on the magazine's editorial board for its first three years.

37. Viewers in the 1970s and subsequent eras tend to see this intimate moment as recreational sex, even though parallel scenes in other films with white actors are recognized as moments of emotional bonding. Parks's interest in depicting Black women as dignified individuals carries over into the changes he made to the representation of the kidnapped girl. In the novel, she is a drug addict who has had a child out of wedlock, whereas in the film, she is young woman on her way to college who is interested in the Black nationalist movement.

38. Gordon Parks, *The Learning Tree* (New York: Ballantine Books, 1963), 218.

39. Parks, *The Learning Tree*, 62, 65.

40. Parks, *The Learning Tree*, 29.

41. Henderson, "*The Learning Tree*."

42. Parks, *The Learning Tree*, 229. See also 1, 29, 43, 68, 104, 111, 195.

43. In the novel, the Harlem gangster is named Knocks Persons, whereas in the film, his name, Bumpy Jonas, creates an association with actual Harlem kingpin Bumpy Johnson.

44. The Knapp Commission Report on Police Corruption published in 1972 detailed the massive corruption that whistleblower NYDP patrolman Frank Serpico identified. The whistle-blower's story is the basis for the 1973 film *Serpico* (Sidney Lumet) starring Al Pacino.

45. Ernest Tidyman, *Shaft* (Mt. Laurel, NJ: Dynamite Entertainment, 2016), 17; first published in 1970. See also 35, 36.

46. Tidyman, *Shaft*, 126.

47. Tidyman, *Shaft*, 191; see also 204.

48. Tidyman, *Shaft*, 9. For a description of the apartment, see 140–41; for clothing descriptions, see 2, 8, 10, 73, 101, 132.

49. Tidyman, *Shaft*, 97, 104, 185.

50. See Tidyman, *Shaft*, 171, 202. In Parks's film, Shaft has a framed photo of Ellie in his office.

51. Tidyman, *Shaft*, 155.

52. See Naremore, *More Than Night*, 45, 151.

53. See Tidyman, *Shaft*, 81 and 173; Tidyman describes Shaft as having a "Polynesian" face and green eyes, perhaps emphasizing that he embodies the racist tropes of a tragic mulatto.

54. Tidyman, *Shaft*, 206.

55. Cynthia Baron, *Denzel Washington* (London: British Film Institute, 2015), 115.

56. Parks, *The Learning Tree*, 134.

57. Most scholars take the Greenwich Village liaison as illustrating a pattern in Shaft's behavior and as arising from his initiation. However, in contrast to the novel, in which Shaft talks about having sex with various sexually adventurous white women, the Greenwich Village episode is the only instance of emotionally disengaged sex with a woman shown or suggested in the film. Moreover, while misogyny pervades the novel, Parks's film frames Shaft's Greenwich Village sex partner and an inept white waitress (at the café where Shaft meets the mobster) in a negative light but shows the Black female characters, Jonas's daughter and Ellie, in a positive one.

58. Stephen Soitos, *The Blues Detective: A Study of African American Detective Fiction* (Amherst: University of Massachusetts Press, 1996), 31.

59. See Manthia Diawara, "Noirs by Noirs: Toward a New Black Realism," in *Shades of Noir: A Reader*, ed. Joan Copec (New York: Verso, 1993), 263.

60. Himes's series also includes the unfinished novel *Plan B*, which was published posthumously in 1993.

61. Philip Brookman, "Gordon Parks: The Sphere of Conscious History," in *Gordon Parks: The New Tide: Early Work 1940–1950*, ed. Philip Brookman (Washington, DC: National Gallery of Art, 2018), 252.

62. Brookman, "Gordon Parks," 252.

63. Nicole Fleetwood and Bryan Stevenson, overview of *Gordon Parks: The Atmosphere of Crime, 1957*, ed. Sarah Hermanson Meister (New York: The Museum of Modern Art, 2020), https://steidl.de/Books/The-Atmosphere-of-Crime-1957-0017233350.html.

64. Henderson, "*The Learning Tree*." Parks's refined clothing style and relaxed demeanor are visible in his cameo appearance as a Harlem landlord who tells Shaft that he is also looking for Ben Buford because the political activist owes him rent.

65. Donald Bogle, *Toms, Coons, Mulattoes, Mammies, and Bucks: An Interpretive History of Blacks in American Films*, 4th ed. (New York: Continuum, 2004), 232.

66. Trey Ellis, "The New Black Aesthetic," in *Platitudes & "The New Black Aesthetic"* (Northeastern University Press, 2003), 187, 189.

67. Donalson, *Black Directors in Hollywood*, 12.

68. Donalson, *Black Directors in Hollywood*, 12.

69. Bogle, *Toms, Coons, Mulattoes, Mammies, and Bucks*, 239.

70. See Christopher Anderson, *Hollywood TV: The Studio System in the Fifties* (Austin: University of Texas Press, 1994); Denise Mann, *Hollywood Independents: The Postwar Talent Takeover* (Minneapolis: University of Minnesota Press, 2008); Tino Balio, *The Foreign Film Renaissance on American Screens, 1946–1973* (Madison: University of Wisconsin Press, 2010).

71. Quinn, *Piece of the Action*, 170. See Quinn 194; the Tax Reform Act of 1976, which ended tax-shelter financing, contributed to the declining opportunities for Black filmmakers.

72. See Guerrero, *Framing Blackness*, 82, 104.

73. Guerrero, *Framing Blackness*, 72.

74. Guerrero, *Framing Blackness*, 72.

75. Mann, *Hollywood Independents*, 216.

76. Quinn, *Piece of the Action*, 59.

77. *Lady Sings the Blues* (Sidney J. Furie, 1972) and *The Mack* (Michael Campus, 1973) are examples of white-directed, Black-themed films released after *The Learning Tree* and *Shaft*. Bogle categorizes *The Learning Tree* with white-directed films *Uptight, Slaves, The Lost Man, Putney Swope*, and *The Reivers* (Mark Rydell, 1969) due to the films' similar release dates.

78. Quinn, *Piece of the Action*, 67.

79. Quinn, *Piece of the Action*, 68.

80. Quinn, *Piece of the Action*, 61.

81. Harry Belafonte established HarBel Productions in 1957. It was the first mainstream production company with an African American founder.

82. Quinn, *Piece of the Action*, 75.

83. Quinn, *Piece of the Action*, 76.

84. Quinn, *Piece of the Action*, 83.

85. Quinn, *Piece of the Action*, 83.

86. Quinn, *Piece of the Action*, 89–90.

87. Quinn, *Piece of the Action*, 60.

88. George Alexander, *Why We Make Movies: Black Filmmakers Talk about the Magic of Cinema* (New York: Harlem Moon, 2003), 6.

89. See Alexander, *Why We Make Movies*, 6.

90. Gordon Parks, *A Hungry Heart: A Memoir* (New York: Atria Books, 2005), 280. *My Father: Gordon Parks* (Meyer Odze, 1968), which features behind-the-scenes footage of Parks directing *The Learning Tree*, includes scenes that illustrate Parks's prepared but easygoing directing style. The Odze film is included in the Criterion Collection DVD package.

91. Quinn, *Piece of the Action*, 71.

92. Eric Pierson, "In the Beginning There Was *Shaft*," in *Beyond Blaxploitation*, ed. Novotny Lawrence and Gerald R. Butters Jr. (Detroit: Wayne State University Press), 77–101.

93. In addition, Henry Bush, Ron Capone, and Dave Purple won the Best Engineered Recording (Non-classical) Grammy for the "Theme From *Shaft*."

94. See Quinn, *A Piece of the Action*, 60, 242. See Quinn, xix; Quinn notes that in *The Hollywood Renaissance: Revisiting American Cinema's Most Celebrated Era* (London: Bloomsbury, 2018), Peter Krämer and Yannis Tzioumakis "draw self-reflective attention to the white (male) identities of both Hollywood Renaissance filmmakers and most scholars who examine such films, identifying an 'extreme white male bias' in Hollywood Renaissance canon formation."

95. MGM, "Multi-Talented Parks," *Shaft* Pressbook 1971, *Shaft* Production File, Margaret Herrick Library, Beverly Hills, CA. See Eric Lichtenfeld, *Action Speaks Louder: Violence, Spectacle, and the American Action Movie* (Westport, CT: Praeger, 2004), 11, 284.

96. Hilton Als, "Through a Lens," *The New Yorker*, March 27, 2006, https://www.newyorker.com/magazine/2006/03/27/through-a-lens.

97. Als, "Through a Lens."

Chapter 11

DEVIL IN A BLUE DRESS

Aesthetic Strategies That Illuminate "Invisibility" and Continue Black Literary Traditions

CYNTHIA BARON

Devil in a Blue Dress is the first book in Walter Mosley's fourteen-volume detective series featuring Ezekiel "Easy" Rawlins, who represents one of the many African Americans who migrated to Los Angeles during or just after World War II. Mosley's 1990 novel belongs to literary traditions featuring Black writers such as Ralph Ellison, Chester Himes, Iceberg Slim (Robert Beck), and Donald Goines. Like the work of Barbara Neely, Gar Anthony Haywood, and other Black detective writers who gained recognition in the 1990s, the Easy Rawlins novels contrast with classical and hard-boiled detective fiction by depicting ways that African Americans negotiate a society built on white supremacy.[1]

Taking a parallel path, Carl Franklin's 1995 adaptation starring Denzel Washington uses noir conventions, specifically those featured in black noir films such as *Eve's Bayou* (Kasi Lemmons, 1997). In contrast to traditional noir productions with white protagonists, black noir films examine society through the eyes of their central Black characters and cogently reveal Black Americans' historically "invisible" experiences and perspectives. Black noir films also effectively illustrate the matrix of laws and social conventions that reflect the systemic racism "invisible" to white Americans.[2] With Easy Rawlins's race-inflected experiences and wise ruminations on society and human behavior integral to both novel and film, his character is arguably an "avatar of earlier slave narratives that [explore] the mystery or conundrum of who stole the African American's soul."[3] In addition, the novel and film continue the cultural-aesthetic project initiated by the *Narrative of the Life of Frederick Douglass* (1845), because they, too, trace "an individual's moral, spiritual, and intellectual progress" while also illustrating "both the horror and the great quest of the African American experience."[4]

Analyzing the parallel aesthetic strategies in the literary and filmic versions of *Devil in a Blue Dress*, this chapter shows how Mosley and Franklin illuminate Rawlins's subjectivity and the social realities "invisible" to white Americans due to socioeconomic segregation, unequal treatment in society, and racial indifference.[5] To illustrate the ethical questions that fill Easy's thoughts in the novel and film, the discussion explores various aspects of Rawlins's defining relationship with his friend Raymond "Mouse" Alexander; Mosley had created these two intertwined characters in his (belatedly published) novel *Gone Fishin'*, which features Easy's compelling account of some unsettling experiences with Mouse when the two are young men in Texas.[6] Considering ways that *Devil in a Blue Dress*, as a novel and film adaptation, deftly plumbs white supremacy in America, the chapter analyzes the first-person narration in Mosley's novel, which carries into Franklin's film, and considers the novel (and film) in relationship to Black literary traditions. The chapter also shows how Franklin's aesthetic choices create meanings and perspectives that parallel those generated by Mosley's prose; analyzing the film's music and performance details, it explains how these elements communicate the thoughts, feelings, and aspirations of Easy Rawlins, a Black citizen-sleuth who finds ways to negotiate racist mid-twentieth-century America.

FIRST-PERSON NARRATION AND BLACK LITERARY TRADITIONS

In the novel and film, Rawlins's first-person narration features the "lucidity, modesty, honesty, and economy" valued in personal accounts from Douglass's time forward.[7] These qualities reflect the narrator's mature outlook; as *A Red Death* (1991), the second book in the Easy Rawlins series, reveals, Rawlins's narration in *Devil in a Blue Dress* is from the temporal distance of the 1980s and the perspective of a man in his sixties.[8] Notably, the narrator's wiser, distanced viewpoint creates a mystery story that is not "a simple matter of locating a murderer or saving a potential victim, but rather an intricate problem in moral perception."[9]

Rawlins is the young fellow in the story *and* the older man recounting the events. As a result, not only is the narration autodiegetic (the narrator is the protagonist of the story), but it also has homodiegetic dimensions (the narrator is a character who bears witness to the experiences or actions of the protagonist). The narration is also complex because Rawlins's longtime friend, Mouse, is not the protagonist, but his major presence in Easy's memories and ruminations make Mouse the figure whose actions raise the moral dilemmas with which Easy contends. Mouse personifies the aspects of Easy that trouble his conscience, in part because Mouse's "formidable efficacy . . . imperils the synthesis that Easy doggedly attempts to forge" from his aspirational, middle-class values that make property owning important and his survival strategies that had saved him as a child and during the war.[10]

In one sense, Easy and Mouse are "character types who represent alternative and often conflicting strategies to combat racialist authoritarian discourses."[11] Yet due to his actions in war, Easy knows he can be as ruthless as Mouse. In addition, Easy's ruminations on differences between Mouse and himself highlight the shared obstacles they face as Black men in white-dominated America. Moreover, the seasoned narrator rejects the ostensive opposition between reason and instinct, finding instead that both approaches are valid. As in Mosley's earlier novel *Gone Fishin'*, the complex narration illuminates Easy's active conscience, revealing his soft, introspective nature and his resolve that Mouse's survival-focused approach is right when the "invisible" systemic forces of racism become overwhelming.

The sociological analysis and the ethical quandaries that *Devil in a Blue Dress* examine align the novel and film with a tradition in which *Narrative of the Life of Frederick Douglass* is a touchstone. The novel's social and moral considerations also reflect Mosley's longstanding interest in Albert Camus's *The Stranger*, "a 'crime' story that condemns its hero to an existential sense of responsibility and suffering that Easy would understand."[12] Mosley's novel illustrates his view that crime stories are "the ones that really ask the existentialist questions such as 'How do I act in an imperfect world when I really want to be perfect?'"[13] Likewise, the film reveals Franklin's sustained interest in using mystery narratives to explore universal and culturally specific existential questions; along with *Devil in a Blue Dress*, his work includes the crime thrillers *One False Move* (1992), *High Crimes* (2002), and *Out of Time* (2003).

Mosley's novel and Franklin's film align with a popular narrative tradition that reaches back to Pauline Hopkins's serial novel *Hagar's Daughter: A Story of Southern Caste Prejudice* (1901–1902) and John Edward Bruce's mystery *The Black Sleuth* (1907–1909), which employs "a Black Atlantic perspective to evaluate white prejudice and racial injustice in the United States and elsewhere."[14] In both early works, the central characters' innate abilities and awareness of social masks combine with the "low opinion most whites have of blacks" to help them solve the immediate mysteries but not "the greatest conspiracy of all—that of prejudice against people of color."[15] *Devil in a Blue Dress* echoes these stories because it also suggests that the defeat of prejudice depends on "black solidarity."[16] In both novel and film, Mouse reminds Easy, "You gotta have somebody at yo' back, man," and they conclude with Rawlins's longtime friend Odell Jones confirming, "All you got is your friends, Easy."[17]

DAPHNE'S IDENTITY, EASY'S DOUBLE, AND
BLACK NOIR COMPLICATIONS

In *Devil in a Blue Dress*, Rawlins is a twenty-eight-year-old World War II veteran, recently laid off from his good-paying job as a defense industry worker. His education in human nature and ethical development are the heart of this postwar Los Angeles story. At the urging of his friend, African American bar proprietor Joppy Shag, Easy agrees to locate white-passing Daphne Monet for DeWitt Albright, a white man whose initial handshake Easy describes as "strong but slithery, like a snake coiling around my hand."[18] In the story, nothing is as it seems. Easy eventually learns that Joppy involved him in the search for Daphne simply to complicate Albright's search for the elusive character. In obstructing Albright's mission, Joppy sought to garner favor with Daphne and protect his illegal business dealings with her half-brother, African American bootlegger Frank Green. Similarly, in both the novel and the film, Albright tells everyone he is helping a friend find Daphne. Yet in the novel, he is truly intent on taking the large sum of money she possesses; in the film, he turns out to be an agent in a blackmail scheme. In addition, as the novel and film eventually reveal, Daphne is not a society woman from the white enclaves of West Los Angeles but Ruby Hanks from Lake Charles, Louisiana, a biracial woman in love with Todd Carter, a wealthy white man running for mayor of Los Angeles against a pedophile named Matthew Teran in the novel and Matthew Terrell in the film.[19]

In the novel, Teran drops out of the mayoral race due to pressure from Carter. In retaliation, Teran tells Carter that Daphne is biracial and threatens to make the information public. This causes Daphne to flee with $30,000 of Carter's money, a development that leads Albright to track her down. The film changes these plot points so that Carter drops out of the race after learning the truth about Daphne. Genuinely in love with Carter, Daphne fights back, getting photographs that prove Terrell is a pedophile, hoping that the evidence will help Carter prevail over Terrell *and* secure her place with him and his wealthy white family. Her effort to assist Carter is successful, but her hope to cross the color line is not; eliding the novel's look at the incest shaping Ruby's young life, the film explores the tragedy arising from the "social transgression" associated with her desire to marry a prominent white man in 1948 America.[20]

In Mosley's fiction, Mouse reveals Daphne's identity to Easy, whereas the film gives Daphne more agency so that she is the one who tells Easy that Frank Green is her half-brother. Franklin's adaptation also eliminates the scenes of sexual intimacy between Easy and Daphne. This change reflects the race-based censorship that has long characterized Hollywood cinema, but it also supports Franklin's sense that Daphne has sincere feelings for Carter and is desperate and determined to act when her biracial identity is revealed. Explaining why the film deletes the Easy-Daphne liaison, Franklin points out that the narration in the novel frames all of Daphne's actions in a sympathetic light, whereas depictions of Daphne sleeping with Easy would have made her seem licentious and thus unsympathetic to film audiences.[21]

The novel and film both emphasize that African Americans are vulnerable in public and even private spaces, since whites can intrude whenever they please. Albright's entrance into Joppy's bar is the first of many invasions of Black space. Albright's subsequent insistence that Easy meet him at the whites-only Santa Monica Pier puts Easy in a threatening situation, which Albright escalates with his impulsive, gun-wielding behavior. Following this incident, two white cops accost Easy at his home and take him to the local police station for questioning and a beating. Later, walking home along a city street, Easy is forced into a menacing meeting with mayoral candidate Teran/Terrell. Soon after, Daphne's request that Easy take her to a house in whites-only Hollywood puts him at risk again; the danger escalates when he becomes stranded at the house, which is the scene of a white man's murder. Later, Albright and his thugs take over Rawlins's home, terrorizing him to get information about Daphne. This harrowing series of events leads Easy to call his beloved friend EttaMae in Houston to get help from Mouse, her estranged husband, because as Rawlins-the-narrator explains, "The only time in my life that I had ever been completely without fear was when I ran with Mouse."[22] Described in a subsequent Rawlins mystery *Bad Boy Brawly Brown* as "a guardian angel from hell,"[23] Mouse arrives just in time to save Easy from Daphne's half-brother Frank, who is about to slit Easy's throat during yet another invasion of Rawlins's cherished home.

Far from being a sidekick or secondary character, Mouse functions in the novel and film as Easy's double, his "brother" from Houston who embodies the pragmatic agency that troubles Rawlins's ethical conscience and aspirational desires.[24] Easy and Mouse resemble the twin brothers, Jackson and Goldy, in Chester Himes's *A Rage in Harlem* (*For Love of Imabelle*, 1957), in which devout, college-educated Jackson turns to street-smart, cross-dressing Goldy to survive. The contrast between introspective Easy and charismatic Mouse is reflected in film critics' comments about Don Cheadle's scene-stealing portrayal of Mouse.[25] Yet the close, existential connection between Easy and Mouse is not only "the most important and complex friendship" in the novel and film but also "one of the most innovative features of Mosley's mystery series."[26] The two distinct but entangled characters in some fashion reflect Du Bois's evolving vision of double consciousness; Mouse serves as a conscience, role model, and cautionary tale for Easy as he attempts to survive in a white-dominated society and prosper in a country in which African Americans are surrounded by a white world.[27]

Despite the differences between the novel and film, both reflect Mosley's aim to model Rawlins after Ralph Ellison's "infamous unnamed narrator in

Devil in a Blue Dress reveals that Easy Rawlins's friend Mouse (Don Cheadle) is his guardian angel, who embodies the ruthlessness sometimes required to survive in a white world.

1952's *Invisible Man*."[28] Like Ellison's central character, Easy is largely invisible: "Other black characters identify Easy as one of them, and see nothing particularly special, or threatening, about him"; the "white characters see him as simply one of a horde of nameless, faceless, brainless blacks over whom they maintain control."[29] Yet with Mouse's help, Easy uses invisibility as a cloak while gathering evidence to solve the mystery and save himself from wrongful imprisonment. As in Ellison's novel, the first-person narration in Mosley's fiction and the voiceover in Franklin's film make Rawlins's beliefs, doubts, aspirations, and memories visible and thus counter the idea that he is brainless or nothing special.

Rawlins's experiences in the novel and film shed light on "the everyday oppression and harm done to African Americans trying to live unexceptional lives in the years after World War II."[30] His encounters and his reflections on them show that being a Black man in America makes him "an immediate suspect, subjected to sudden arrests, imprisonment, 'legal' violence, and police harassment."[31] Writing about the film and making a point that applies to Mosley's novel as well, Philippa Gates observes that *Devil in a Blue Dress* "updates the history of *noir* by bringing to the genre the black subjectivity its label implies but ignores."[32] Dan Flory extends this observation, finding that a number of films reimagine noir conventions to "expose the injustices and inequities that typically frame black experience in the United States."[33] Black detective fiction and Black noir films such as *Devil in a Blue Dress* illustrate "the inadequacies of racialized understandings of humanity, justice, and morality."[34] In doing so, they contribute to a cultural-aesthetic tradition grounded in work such as the *Narrative of the Life of Frederick Douglass*.

BLACK LITERARY TRADITIONS AND MOSLEY'S NOVEL

Rudolph Fisher's detective novel *The Conjure Man* (1932), featuring John Archer in Harlem, restarted the work begun by novelists Pauline Hopkins and John Edward Bruce in the early twentieth century. In the 1940s, Black writers involved in the "literary resistance to racism" began to employ noir tropes to dismantle "white supremacy and racial hierarchy."[35] This work includes Chester Himes's Los Angeles novels *If He Hollers Let Him Go* (1945) and *Lonely Crusade* (1947) and his series of detective novels initiated by *A Rage in Harlem* (1957). Broadly speaking, it includes works as different as Ann Petry's *The Street* (1946) and Richard Wright's *The Outsider* (1953). The literary tradition includes the bleak Iceberg Slim novels *Pimp: The Story of My Life* (1969) and *Trick Baby* (1970) and the gritty Donald Goines novels *Dopefiend* (1971) and *Black Girl Lost* (1974).

Himes's work in particular provides a foundation for Mosley's *Devil in a Blue Dress*. The depiction of "black male teamwork and rage" in Himes's first detective story, "He Knew" (1933), anticipates the rage that eventually prompts Easy to see a partnership with Mouse as the only way to escape the trap in which he finds himself.[36] Himes's novels *If He Hollers Let Him Go* and *Lonely Crusade* are especially pertinent to *Devil in a Blue Dress*, because they, too, bear "painful witness to the migration of blacks into wartime Los Angeles to work in the defense industry."[37] For these Black Americans, the West Coast's promise of freedom never materialized, since its racism turned out to be "as brutal as anything [they had] experienced in the South or the Midwest."[38] Virulent racism actually expanded in the postwar period because the "Japanese attack on Pearl Harbor [in 1941 had] intensified West Coast nativism and xenophobia."[39] During the war and the postwar period, Mexican Americans endured "brutal beatings in downtown Los Angeles and discrimination against blacks—in housing and jobs—reached a sickening level."[40]

If He Hollers Let Him Go sets several precedents for *Devil in a Blue Dress*. As in Mosley's novel, the narrator and central character, defense industry worker Robert "Bob" Jones, has migrated to Los Angeles. Anticipating Rawlins's emotional investment in his house, Bob takes great pride in his car; Bob explains, "My car was proof of something to me, a symbol."[41] As in Mosley's novel, the vivid first-person narration not only gives readers a clear sense of how Bob sees other people and the world around him but also takes readers into his vivid nightmares. Both novels feature an intense pace and fateful events occurring in a compressed period. They also center on a young Black man who finds himself drinking excessively to cope with the overwhelming experiences and whose aspirations for upward mobility involve a light-skinned Black woman who can pass for white. Bob's upper-class fiancée from the Jefferson Park neighborhood of Los Angeles is a model for Daphne's refined, sensitive persona; Franklin's film sustains this narrative thread with T-Bone Walker's "West Side Baby" as the song in the opening credit sequence. The events in both novels, combined with their Black character's candid first-person narration, illuminate the peril of living in a white supremacist society and the injustice of American judicial and socioeconomic systems. As Bob explains in the closing pages of Himes's novel, he could see that the "whole structure of American thought was against" him.[42]

Himes's writing anticipates themes in all of Mosley's books about Easy Rawlins. The feverishly paced coming-of-age novel *Gone Fishin'* concludes with Easy's reflections as a Black solider preparing to leave Paris at World War II's end.[43] Despite being a war hero, the whole structure of American thought is against him. As Easy explains, there "were gangs of white American soldiers roaming the streets, killing solitary [Black] enlisted men," and every step of the way home "could mean death to a black man" like him.[44] *Devil in a Blue Dress* is filled with equally somber observations. For example, Easy explains, "A job in a factory is an awful lot like working on a plantation in the South. The bosses see all the workers like they're children [and] Benny thought he'd teach me a little something about responsibility because he was the boss and I was the child."[45]

Like *Gone Fishin'*, *Devil in a Blue Dress* traces Rawlins's evolution as a young Black man in white America, in this case from factory plant(ation) laborer to self-employed detective. Notably, *Gone Fishin'* provided the template for Mosley's subsequent characterizations of Easy and Mouse. It reveals that they were both orphaned as children and that as teenagers they saved each other's lives. Yet Mouse terrifies and disturbs Easy, since Mouse is ruthless while Easy is not; as Momma Jo, the powerful and mysterious character in *Gone Fishin'*, explains, "They is somethin' diff'rent in you, Easy, somethin' soft."[46] Yet Easy and Mouse are hardly opposites because Easy can become like Mouse. In *Devil in a Blue Dress*, Easy gets some answers once he finally decides to be assertive like Mouse, a move signaled by his call to EttaMae in Houston.

Stephen Soitos highlights Black detective fiction's "curious amalgam" of classical (amateur, rational) detective and hard-boiled (private eye, instinctive) detective novels.[47] Incorporating classical and hard-boiled traditions, *Devil in a Blue Dress* features Easy, who is more closely associated with rational modes of detection, and Mouse, who effectively uses instinct to reach objectives. Easy's place as the central character and narrator leads readers to identify with his coolheaded approach, yet Mosley complicates this alignment by making Mouse a persuasive, engaging figure. The novel shows that Easy understands and even respects Mouse's "repudiation of middle class respectability."[48] It also offers Mouse's pointed criticism of Easy and Daphne, as he finds them mistaken in their belief that accommodating behavior will help them succeed in white society. As Mouse explains, "You learn stuff and you be thinkin' like white men be thinkin.' You thinkin' that what's right fo' them is right fo' you [but] brother you don't know that you both poor n----rs."[49] The myriad challenges that white society poses in *Devil in a Blue Dress* (novel and film) give credence to Mouse's cynical but candid assessment.

BLACK NOIR AND MUSIC IN FRANKLIN'S FILM

The ethical and existential complexities Mosley explores in his Black detective fiction structure Franklin's Black noir adaptation. Contextualizing Black noir films, Manthia Diawara notes that classic (white) noir films feature "tropes of blackness as metaphors for the white characters' moral transgressions and falls from grace."[50] Yet Black detective fiction established an alternative for filmmakers; as Diawara explains, Chester Himes's novel *A Rage in Harlem* vividly illustrates "a way of life that has been imposed on black people through social injustice."[51] Moreover, Himes's novel subverts the main tenet of classic (white) noir—namely, "that blackness is a fall from whiteness."[52] Himes shows that racist values and institutions create a world in which "black people are living in hell and white people are in heaven not because the one colour is morally inferior to the other, but because black people are held captive."[53]

Franklin's film builds on the Black noir tradition that Himes and other authors established, using music and performance to illustrate social realities from a Black perspective. "West Side Baby," the blues song featured in the film's opening, brings audiences into the world of the Texas and Louisiana migrants who made a home in south Los Angeles in the postwar years. The song's prominent placement in the initial credit sequence sets the film's "moods and tonalities,"[54] as the cool blues sound foretells both passion and pain for the Black characters. Signaling the transplanted community's vibrancy, the film also immerses audiences in the story world with up-tempo jump blues songs like Wynonie Harris's "Good Rockin' Tonight," Amos Milburn's "Chicken Shack Boogie," and Lloyd Glenn's "Chica Boo." The film fleshes out the characters' world with blues songs like Jimmy Witherspoon's "Ain't Nobody's Business" and Memphis Slim's "Messin' Around," as well as big-band swing numbers featuring Bull Moose Jackson and Duke Ellington. Together, these musical selections help to recreate the postwar setting for a chapter in Easy's moral, spiritual, and intellectual progress as a Black man in white America and his deepening understanding of Mouse's reminder, "You gotta have somebody at yo' back, man."

Franklin's film also features an Elmer Bernstein score that is not from the period or milieu. As with "all background music in Hollywood films, [this score] provides continuity, unity, and narrative cuing."[55] Importantly, Bernstein's score includes a theme that becomes associated with Rawlins, his situations, and his emotions, as it evolves and contributes "to the dynamic flow of the narrative."[56] This multidimensional musical theme includes "American elements [that] come from folk song, from jazz and popular music, and from the Americana phase of Aaron Copland's work."[57] At certain times in the film, as when Rawlins makes the pivotal decision to meet Todd Carter to get information about his job to locate Daphne, the theme plays under Washington's voiceover; the combination creates a strong connection between Rawlins's reflections and the emotions that the music conveys, with the plaintive melody suggesting both the pain of knowing that powerful forces have placed him in jeopardy *and* his firm desire to succeed despite the odds.

Some moments in the multipart musical theme are fully orchestrated Copland-like passages featuring strings that communicate Rawlins's aspiration for respect and his desire for peace. Others are simple, cool jazz-inflected passages with piano and flute that lead into a solemn trumpet melody (with supporting strings) that conveys Rawlins's aching sense of loss. Another part of Bernstein's musical theme features a Copland-like string orchestration that takes up the trumpet melody and later a solo trumpet that carries the suggestion of hope. Bernstein's trumpet melody bears some resemblance to the melancholy trumpet solo that distinguishes the theme Jerry Goldsmith wrote for *Chinatown* (1974). Yet, overall, the theme for *Devil in a Blue Dress* is much more like Copland's "Lincoln Portrait" (1942), employed in *He Got Game* (Spike Lee, 1998), and in both instances, the music underscores the fact that African American stories are *American* stories. In *Devil in a Blue Dress*, Bernstein's theme not only complements the blues and swing music that immerses audiences in the story's 1948 world but also functions much like the narration in Mosley's novel, which reflects the perspective of the older and wiser Easy Rawlins. The music selections thus allow Franklin to capture a crucial aspect of Mosley's complex narration, in which the narrator is the story's central character and a character, Easy's older self, who bears witness to the events.

BLACK NOIR AND PERFORMANCES IN FRANKLIN'S FILM

The film's casting and performance choices also parallel key aesthetic strategies in the novel. Washington's embodiment of Rawlins establishes a contrast with (white) noir and neo-noir, for the central character in the narrative and "the voice that tells the story, literally, in a voice-over narration" is African American.[58] Due to Washington's embodiment of the character, Mosley's source material, and Franklin's faithful adaptation, the film literally and figuratively replaces noir's conventional exploration of exotic, shadowy domains with a candid look at sordid realities visible to anyone who has been the target of white-dominated institutions. Moreover, with Mosley and Franklin providing the content and as voiced by Washington, the emotions that color the film's narration convey each step in Easy's deepening understanding of not just the case but also human behavior in a racialized world.

Like the film's voiceover, performances in *Devil in a Blue Dress* illuminate Black perspectives because key portrayals feature observable contrasts between the physical and vocal expressions meant for other characters and those designed for audiences alone. For instance, when Easy first looks for information about Daphne (Jennifer Beals) in the speakeasy that is a community gathering space, the bemused smirk that Lisa Nicole Carson (as Coretta) offers in response to his questioning lets only the audience know that she has information about Daphne and that Easy is doing a terrible job concealing his attempt to locate her friend. Such moments function as "Shakespearean asides" that connect characters and audiences.[59]

Similarly, in portraying Rawlins, Washington's physical and vocal expressions frequently send out "dual signals," some for the audience, others for the characters.[60] Reflecting the demands of the noir narrative, his performance involves the observable depiction of disguise and concealment.[61] His portrayal makes Easy's inner life visible because it conveys (to the audience) times when the character works to conceal or disguise his thoughts and feelings from other characters. Washington's performance also communicates the inner pressure created by restraining anger; capturing the film's connection with Chester Himes's writings from "He Knew" (1933) forward, Ed Guerrero explains that Washington imbues Rawlins with "social vulnerability and caution mixed with a persistent toughness that gradually builds into a cunning, assertive rage against injustice as the narrative evolves."[62]

Just as the voiceovers reveal Easy's "subjectivity and 'interiority,'" the distinction between Washington's "ostensive" emotions shown to other characters and "suppressed" emotions revealed to the audience illuminate Easy's complexity.[63] Washington's ways of moving, gesturing, and speaking in unguarded moments serve as a point of reference. When the film introduces Rawlins, he is calmly enjoying a cigarette and a whiskey while reading a newspaper. There is a smooth, even, direct quality to Washington's inflections in the voiceover that works in tandem both with the quick, light, and relaxed way he takes a drag off his cigarette and his effortless pose that balances the focused way he scans the newspaper. Notably, he masks his relaxed, natural disposition the moment he meets Albright (Tom Sizemore). Later, audiences are privy to a play-within-a-play sequence that shows soft-spoken, clean-cut Easy Rawlins pretend to be a loud-mouthed lowlife in a club, pool hall, and liquor store, all performances meant to get bootlegger Frank Green's attention. Whereas

Rawlins naturally moves and speaks in a measured way, his performance as a lazy drunk in these scenes features rapid, irregular vocal expressions that make him seem testy, hot-tempered, and not very bright.

Washington's light, relaxed manner when embodying Easy in unguarded moments also contrasts with the qualities in his physical and vocal expression when Rawlins finally gets the answers he needs—namely, who killed his erstwhile lover Coretta and what Terrell (Maury Chaykin) has on Daphne. When Daphne reveals that Joppy (Mel Winkler) killed Coretta and that Terrell knows she is a mixed-raced woman, the strong, direct qualities in Washington's body and voice become heavy, weighted energy that shows the information is more troubling than Easy had expected. The contrast, between performance details here and the opening scene when he reads his newspaper, allows audiences to trace the character's existential journey, especially as seen by his mature self.

Between Easy's first scene and Daphne's revelation, Washington's performance gives depth to his character by revealing his private responses to tight situations, as when Rawlins finds himself most threatened by Albright and his thugs. The scene begins with Rawlins returning home in the early morning and seeing Albright's car parked outside his house. Washington's quick, light movements as he puts his car in park, rolls up the window, and closes the car door convey Rawlins's initial confidence that he can handle Albright. Shifting to slower, more weighted movements, he shows Rawlins's growing concern at the sound of several voices in his house. Showing Easy's resolve as he enters the house, Washington goes on the offensive, essentially flicking away Albright's men as he objects to them being in his house. Yet Albright throws Easy off-balance, calling him "n----r" and threatening him with a knife.

With Easy forced to back down, Albright instructs him to write down Daphne's address, "if [he] can write." Washington's tightly bound movements convey the rage Easy feels at being insulted in his own home. Moments later, in response to Albright/Sizemore instructing Easy to get him some whiskey, Washington shows Rawlins refusing to be submissive; his line delivery is quiet but very direct when he states, "Get it your own damn self." Holding himself tall, Washington trembles with anger and his eyes glisten with emotion, but he "conceals" that feeling from the other characters by averting his eyes and lowering his voice to a whisper. After the thugs leave, Washington relaxes his body in a moment of relief. Then, collecting his energy to convey Rawlins's newfound resolve, he slams his fist on the table and strides forward, his head up, shoulders open. It is time to contact Mouse and deal with threats to his survival the way Mouse (and his instinctual self) would.

Capturing the complexity of Mosley's prose, Washington's scenes with Cheadle reveal the ambivalence Easy feels about Mouse's methods *and* his own survival instincts. Paralleling the nuanced narration in Mosley's novel, the actors' portrayals show that Easy could never be Mouse, because his softness and internal conflicts preclude the possibility of being cool and efficient. Embodying Mouse, Cheadle's physical and vocal expressions are distinguished by their force and economy. Everything is precise, focused, and without wasted effort. In contrast, despite the calm coherence that pervades Washington's depiction in the opening moments of the film, as the story develops, his portrayal involves moments in which Easy is not only off-balance but flailing about.

For example, when Mouse arrives at Rawlins's house and discovers that Frank Green (Joseph Latimore) has Easy pinned to the floor, Cheadle's face is focused but calm, and he speaks quietly but with quick efficiency as he asks, "You want me to shoot this son-of-a-bitch, Easy?" Once Frank lets Easy get up, Cheadle/Mouse becomes more assertive but remains measured and self-contained as he tells Frank, "Goddamn, I'm goin' blow your head off." In counterpoint, Washington/Easy stammers loudly, "No wait, no, no, don't shoot him." The actors continue to depict the differences between their characters as they negotiate with Frank: Washington pleads loudly, while Cheadle uses a lower volume and pitch, striking a firm but congenial tone until the moment he suddenly shoots Frank in the shoulder. Seeking to disrupt this violent course of action, Washington/Easy bumps into Cheadle/Mouse. His clumsy move allows Frank to escape. In the next moments, Washington uses large, ineffectual gestures (he takes a handkerchief from his pocket and slaps it against his leg) to convey Rawlins's frustration, whereas Cheadle's precise, self-contained movements to prepare for the next fight suggest how Mouse will work toward solving his friend's problems.

A subsequent scene, in which Easy and Mouse question Black speakeasy bouncer Junior Fornay (David Fonteno) about the murder of the white man in the Hollywood hills, features the same rhythmic contrast and harmonic interdependence in the Washington and Cheadle performances. Washington gestures broadly and speaks in a rushed, higher pitched voice, while Cheadle's gestures are distinguished by precision and economy, his vocal expressions succinct and at a lower pitch. The actors also employ counterpointed portrayals in the shootout at Albright's cabin late in the film. Forming a complementary team, Washington/Easy enters the fray in tentative fashion, whereas Cheadle/Mouse enters decisively on cue to make the crucial shots. In the shootout's aftermath, the performances again convey the characters' distinct but intertwined temperaments and philosophies; Cheadle embodies pragmatic agency, calmly reiterating the characters' need to leave the scene as quickly as possible, whereas Washington shows there is "somethin' soft" about Easy as he drops to the ground to mourn Joppy's death at the hands of Mouse.

MOSLEY AND FRANKLIN: BLACK ARTISTS ILLUMINATING BLACK REALITIES AND SUBJECTIVITIES

In a concluding scene in Franklin's film, Mouse exits Rawlins's house and cheerfully hops into a cab, ready for his next challenge. Yet soon after, Easy quietly ruminates on the recent events as he watches neighborhood kids jump rope, sell ice tea, and have their pictures taken on a pony. In this moment of calm, Easy's neighborhood offers "camaraderie and contentment."[64] Yet multiple threats remain. The headline on the newspaper that Odell (Albert Hall) reads as he sits on Rawlins's porch announces, "Negroes Angered by New Property Restrictions." The cops who had beaten Rawlins earlier in the story cruise menacingly down his street. Like the scene's visual mixture of respite and threat, Washington's voiceover has a relaxed, confident tone, whereas Bernstein's theme "suffuses the sequence with a certain sadness."[65] Thus, through music and performance details, the film once again captures the novel's remarkable accomplishment of immersing readers in the world of Rawlins-the-character while also conveying the sage perspective of Rawlins-the-narrator. In accord with Mosley's novel, the emotion in Washington's body and voice show that Easy's salient feeling is warm appreciation for his home and the moment of peace with his friend Odell. Yet also echoing Mosley's novel, the emotion in the musical theme shows that for the narrator, the moment is bittersweet, for he sees the toll that life takes on a Black man in America and, looking back, feels compassion for his younger self and all the "invisible" Black people trying to do the right thing in an imperfect world.

Mosley's novel and Franklin's film reveal ways that Black artists use the aesthetic tools of their respective art forms to shed light on the realities that have allowed white Americans to willfully ignore the humanity of African Americans and be indifferent to the nexus of laws and socioeconomic practices that maintain white supremacy.[66] Deftly illuminating the experiences of Black amateur sleuth Easy Rawlins, the literary and filmic iterations of *Devil in a Blue Dress* give lie to the threadbare "invisibility" of the racial prejudices shaping customs and institutions in American society. Using art rather than argumentation, Mosley and Franklin vividly illustrate their central character's observations, ethical quandaries, abiding aspirations, and astute analysis of the surrounding white world. Considered within larger cultural-aesthetic contexts, the novel and its adaptation nourish the rich tradition of Black detective fiction that features the central characters' keen intellect and shrewd understanding of human behavior. In addition, Mosley's and Franklin's exploration of the character dynamics that fuel Rawlins's insights and retrospective reflections sustain traditions of candid African American accounts that trace back to the work of Frederick Douglass.

Devil in a Blue Dress concludes with Easy Rawlins (Denzel Washington) enjoying a moment of bittersweet camaraderie with friends in his amiable but vulnerable neighborhood.

Notes

1. Writers gaining notice in the 1990s include Eleanor Taylor Bland, Grace F. Edwards, Robert Greer, Gary Hardwick, Hugh Holton, Glenville Lovell, Penny Mickelbury, Gary Phillips, Valerie Wilson Wesley, and Paula L. Woods.

2. See Michelle Alexander, *The New Jim Crow: Mass Incarceration in the Age of Colorblindness* (New York: The New Press, 2012), 241. See Dan Flory, *Philosophy, Black Film, Film Noir* (University Park: The Pennsylvania State University Press, 2008). There are noir elements in films by Oscar Micheaux, Spencer Williams, Ralph Cooper, Blaxploitation films, and a host of contemporary productions.

3. Gilbert H. Muller, "Double Agent: The Los Angeles Crime Cycle of Walter Mosley," in *Los Angeles in Fiction*, rev ed., ed. David Fine (Albuquerque: University of New Mexico Press, 1995), 294.

4. John W. Blassingame, "Introduction," in *Narrative of the Life of Frederick Douglass, an American Slave, Written by Himself*, ed. John R. McKivigan, Peter P. Hinks, and Heather L. Kaufman (New Haven, CT: Yale University Press, 2016), xiii, xl.

5. Alexander, *New Jim Crow*, 203.

6. Mosley wrote *Gone Fishin'* before *Devil in a Blue Dress*, but the novel was not published until 1997.

7. Blassingame, "Introduction," xvi.

8. Walter Mosley, *A Red Death* (New York: W. W. Norton, 1991), 275.

9. Muller, "Double Agent," 294.

10. Laura Quinn, "The Mouse Will Play: The Parodic in Walter Mosley's Fiction," in *Finding a Way Home: A Critical Assessment of Walter Mosley's Fiction*, ed. Owen E. Brady and Derek C. Maus (Jackson: University Press of Mississippi, 2008), 127.

11. Albert U. Turner Jr., "Collaboration and Community in Easy Rawlins Series," in *Finding a Way Home: A Critical Assessment of Walter Mosley's Fiction*, ed. Owen E. Brady and Derek C. Maus (Jackson: University Press of Mississippi, 2008), 113.

12. Muller, "Double Agent," 294. Mosley acknowledges the influence of Dashiell Hammett, Raymond Chandler, and Ross MacDonald but compares Easy Rawlins to the authors of hard-boiled stories rather than their fictional creations. See Walter Mosley, interview by Christin Ayers, *Black Renaissance*, KPIX TV, https://www.youtube.com/watch?v=nZ9PVfNdNTE. In this 2016 television interview, Mosley identifies Chester Himes, Donald Goines, Iceberg Slim, and Ishmael Reed as key influences.

13. D. J. R. Bruckner, "Mystery Stories are Novelist's Route to Moral Questions," *New York Times*, September 4, 1990, C13.

14. John Cullen Gruesser, "Introduction," in *The Black Sleuth*, ed. John Cullen Gruesser (Boston: Northeastern University Press, 2002), ix.

15. Gruesser, "Introduction," xxi, xxii.

16. Gruesser, "Introduction," xxii.

17. Walter Mosley, *Devil in a Blue Dress* (New York: Washington Square Press, 1990), 156, 219.

18. Mosley, *Devil in a Blue Dress*, 2.

19. Carl Franklin, "Director's Commentary," *Devil in a Blue Dress* (Culver City: Tri-Star Pictures, 2006). Franklin changed Teran's name because it seemed implausible that a character with a name sounding Middle Eastern could run for Los Angeles mayor in 1948.

20. Mark L. Berrettini, "Private Knowledge, Public Space: Investigation and Navigation in *Devil in a Blue Dress*," *Cinema Journal* 39, no. 1 (Fall 1999): 79.

21. Franklin, "Director's Commentary."

22. Mosley, *Devil in a Blue Dress*, 50.

23. Walter Mosley, *Bad Boy Brawly Brown* (New York: Little, Brown, 2002), 237.

24. Quinn, "Mouse Will Play," 125.

25. Desson Howe, "*Devil in a Blue Dress*," *Washington Post*, September 29, 1995; Kristine McKenna, "The 'Mouse' in 'Devil' is Roaring: Movies: A Scene-Stealing Performance as a Dangerous but Lovable Sociopath Could Be a Breakthrough Role for Don Cheadle," *Los Angeles Times*, September 30, 1995.

26. John Cullen Gruesser, "An Un-Easy Relationship: Walter Mosley's Signifyin(g) Detective and the Black Community," in *Multicultural Detective Fiction: Murder from the "Other" Side*, ed. Adrienne Johnson Gosselin (New York: Garland, 1999), 249.

27. John Pittman explains, "Any account of double consciousness rooted in the sweep of Du Bois's writings must acknowledge his taking it as both a state of consciousness of individual African-Americans as members of an oppressed group and also as a form of social recognition of an entire social situation in which that group finds itself [since Du Bois does not use the term 'double consciousness' after 1903] because he wants to resist the impression that this is simply and only a problem *of* consciousness, unconnected with any palpable social facts." John P. Pittman, "Double Consciousness," in *The Stanford Encyclopedia of Philosophy*, Summer 2016 edition, ed. Edward N. Zalta (Stanford, CA: Center for the Study of Language and Information, 2016), https://plato.stanford.edu/entries/double-consciousness/. See Roger A. Berger, "'The Black Dick': Race, Sexuality, and Discourse in the L.A. Novels of Walter Mosley," *African American Review* 31, no. 2 (1997): 291; Robert Crooks, "From the Far Side of the Urban Frontier: The Detective Fiction of Chester Himes and Walter Mosley," in *Crisscrossing Borders in Literature of the American West*, ed. Reginald Dyck and Cheli Reutter (New York: Palgrave Macmillan, 2009), 53.

28. Charles E. Wilson Jr., *Walter Mosley: A Critical Companion* (Westport, CT: Greenwood Press, 2003), 20. See Kelly C. Connelly, "The Visible Man: Moving Beyond False Visibility in

Ralph Ellison's *Invisible Man* and Walter Mosley's Easy Rawlins Novels," in *Finding a Way Home: A Critical Assessment of Walter Mosley's Fiction*, ed. Owen E. Brady and Derek C. Maus (Jackson: University Press of Mississippi, 2008), 71.

29. Wilson, *Walter Mosley*, 20.

30. Flory, *Philosophy, Black Film, Film Noir*, 215.

31. Samuel Coale, *The Mystery of Mysteries: Cultural Differences and Designs* (Bowling Green, OH: Bowling Green State University Popular Press, 2000), 176.

32. Philippa Gates, *Detecting Men: Masculinity and the Hollywood Detective Film* (Albany: State University of New York Press, 2006), 212.

33. Flory, *Philosophy, Black Film, Film Noir*, 1. These include other films with Washington. In *Ricochet* (Russell Mulchay, 1991), his character's middle-class life is almost destroyed by a white man determined to exact revenge for his perceived victimization. In *Virtuosity* (Brent Leonard, 1995), *Fallen* (Gregory Hoblit, 1998), and *The Bone Collector* (Phillip Noyce, 1999), Washington's characters also become the singular targets of malevolent white men.

34. Flory, *Philosophy, Black Film, Film Noir*, 4.

35. Flory, *Philosophy, Black Film, Film Noir*, 27.

36. John Cullen Gruesser, *Race, Gender and Empire in American Detective Fiction* (Jefferson, NC: McFarland, 2013), 4.

37. David Fine, *Imagining Los Angeles: A City in Fiction* (Albuquerque: University of New Mexico Press, 2000), 196.

38. Fine, *Imagining Los Angeles*, 197.

39. Fine, *Imagining Los Angeles*, 196.

40. Fine, *Imagining Los Angeles*, 197.

41. Chester B. Himes, *If He Hollers Let Him Go* (Chatham, NJ: Chatham, 1973; originally published 1945), 31.

42. Himes, *If He Hollers Let Him Go*, 187.

43. As Priscilla Lane's essay in the volume illustrates, writer-director Melvin Van Peebles explores the complicated experiences of an African American veteran in postwar Europe.

44. Walter Mosley, *Gone Fishin'* (New York: Washington Square Press, 1997), 198.

45. Mosley, *Devil in a Blue Dress*, 64.

46. Mosley, *Gone Fishin'*, 163.

47. Stephen F. Soitos, *The Blues Detective: A Study of African American Detective Fiction* (Amherst: The University of Massachusetts Press, 1996), 24.

48. Quinn, "Mouse Will Play," 131.

49. Mosley, *Devil in a Blue Dress*, 209.

50. Manthia Diawara, "Noir by Noirs: Toward a New Black Realism," in *Shades of Noir: A Reader*, ed. Joan Copec (New York: Verso, 1993), 262.

51. Diawara, "Noir by Noirs," 263.

52. Diawara, "Noir by Noirs," 263.

53. Diawara, "Noir by Noirs, 263.

54. Claudia Gorbman, *Unheard Melodies: Narrative Film Music* (Bloomington: Indiana University Press, 1987), 11.

55. Krin Gabbard, *Jammin' at the Margins: Jazz and the American Cinema* (Chicago: University of Chicago Press, 1996), 291.

56. Gorbman, *Unheard Melodies*, 4.

57. William Darby and Jack Du Bois, *American Film Music: Major Composers, Techniques, Trends, 1915–1990* (Jefferson, NC: McFarland, 1990), 461.

58. Gates, *Detecting Men*, 210.

59. James Naremore, *Acting in the Cinema* (Berkeley: University of California Press, 1988), 75.

60. Naremore, *Acting in the Cinema*, 76.

61. Richard deCordova, "Genre and Performance: An Overview," in *Film Genre Reader*, ed. Barry Keith Grant (Austin: University of Texas Press, 1986), 135.

62. Ed Guerrero, "*Devil in a Blue Dress*," *Cineaste* 22, no. 1 (1996): 40.

63. Steve Neale, *Genre and Hollywood* (New York: Routledge, 2000), 168; Naremore, *Acting in the Cinema*, 80.

64. Flory, *Philosophy, Black Film, Film Noir*, 218.

65. Flory, *Philosophy, Black Film, Film Noir*, 219.

66. Alexander, *New Jim Crow*, 203, 241.

ABOUT THE CONTRIBUTORS

Cynthia Baron is a professor in the Department of Theatre and Film at Bowling Green State University. She is the author of *Modern Acting: The Lost Chapter of American Film and Theatre* (2016) and *Denzel Washington* (2015). She is the coauthor of *Acting Indie: Industry, Aesthetics, and Performance* (2020), *Appetites and Anxieties: Food, Film, and the Politics of Representation* (2014), and *Reframing Screen Performance* (2008). She is coeditor of *More Than a Method: Trends and Traditions in Film Performance* (2004), editor of the *Journal of Film and Video*, and the BGSU Research Scholar of Excellence 2017–2020.

Elizabeth Binggeli teaches at Immaculate Heart High School in Los Angeles. She received her PhD from the University of Southern California; her dissertation was titled "Hollywood Dark Matter: Reading Race and Absence in Studio Era Narratives." Her articles appear in *Cinema Journal* and *Arizona Quarterly: A Journal of American Literature, Culture, and Theory*. Her anthology contributions include chapters in *Mary Pickford: Queen of the Movies* (2012) and *"The Inside Light": New Critical Essays on Zora Neale Hurston* (2010). She is the coproducer of the documentary *Palace of Silents* (2010), a history of silent movie theaters in Los Angeles.

Kimberly Nichele Brown is an associate professor of gender, sexuality, and women's studies at Virginia Commonwealth University. She is the author of *Writing the Black Revolutionary Diva: Women's Subjectivity and the Decolonizing Text* (2010). She is working on two books, *IncogNegro Stances: Cross-racial Espionage in Contemporary Literature and Film* (University Press of Mississippi) and *Through Ebony Eyes: A Black Feminist and Ethical Praxis of Viewing Contemporary Film*. Her essays appear in anthologies such as *Slavery in the Post-Black Imagination* (2020), *African American Cinema through Black Lives Consciousness* (2019), and *Hollywood's Africa after 1994* (2012).

Terri Simone Francis is an associate professor of cinematic arts at the University of Miami. She is the author of *Josephine Baker's Cinematic Prism* (2021), which illustrates Baker's conscious shaping of her celebrity and African Americans' interest in cinema and efforts to gain equality. Her research appears in *Feminist Media Histories, Film History, Film Quarterly, Black Camera*, and other journals. In her former role as director of the Black Film Center/Archive at Indiana University, she curated series on Classic Black Films of the 1970s, Black Cinematic Imaginations of Outer Space, and other topics.

Priscilla Layne is an associate professor in the Department of Romance Languages at the University of North Carolina at Chapel Hill and an adjunct associate professor of African and Afro-American studies. She is the author of *White Rebels in Black: German Appropriation of Black Popular Culture* (2018) and the coeditor of *Rebellion and Revolution Defiance in German Language History and Art* (2010). Her forthcoming book, *Out of this World: Afro-German Afrofuturism*, analyzes Afrofuturist concepts in the work of Afro-German writers and playwrights. Her essays appear in *Camera Obscura, Popular Music and Society, Seminar: A Journal of Germanic Studies*, and *Television & New Media.*

Eric Pierson is a professor in the Department of Communication Studies at the University of California, San Diego. His publications appear in anthologies such as *From Madea to Media Mogul: Theorizing Tyler Perry* (2016) and *Watching While Black: Centering the Television of Black Audiences* (2013). He is the author of "A National Concern: Remembering and Teaching the Death of Emmett Till" in Novotny Lawrence's *Documenting the Black Experience: Essays on African American History, Culture, and Identity in Nonfiction Films* (2015). His articles appear in *Journal of Mass Media Ethics, Screening Noir: A Journal of Black Film, Television, & New Media Culture*, and other journals.

Charlene Regester is an associate professor in the Department of African, African American, and Diaspora Studies and affiliate faculty with the Global Cinema Minor at the University of North Carolina at Chapel Hill. She is the author of *African American Actresses: The Struggle for Visibility, 1900–1960* (2010) and coeditor with Mae Henderson of *The Josephine Baker Critical Reader* (2017). Her essays have appeared in *In the Shadow of "The Birth of a Nation": Racism, Reception and Resistance* (2023), *Resetting the Scene: Classical Hollywood Revisited* (2021), and *Hollywood at the Intersection of Race and Identity* (2020).

Ellen C. Scott is an associate professor and head of the Cinema and Media Studies Program in the School of Theater, Film, and Television at the University of California, Los Angeles. In 2016, she was awarded the Academy of Motion Picture Arts and Sciences Film Scholars Grant for her project "Cinema's Peculiar Institution," which investigated the representation of slavery on screen. She is the author of *Cinema Civil Rights: Race, Repression, and Regulation in Classical Hollywood Cinema* (2015). Her publications appear in *Film History, African American Review, American History, Black Camera,* and other journals.

Tanya L. Shields is an associate professor in the Department of Women's and Gender Studies at the University of North Carolina at Chapel Hill. She is the author of *Bodies and Bones: Feminist Rehearsal and Imagining Caribbean Belonging* (2014) and the editor of *The Legacy of Eric Williams: Into the Postcolonial Moment* (2015). Her forthcoming book, *Gendering the Manager: Sex, Race, and Power on Plantations Owned by Women,* is a study of the women who owned plantations in the Caribbean and the US South. She is the editor of a special issue in *Cultural Dynamics* and has published in journals such as *Souls* and anthologies, including *Caribbean Literature in Transition, 1970–2020.*

Judith E. Smith is a professor emerita of American studies at the University of Massachusetts, Boston. Her books include *Becoming Belafonte: Black Artist, Public Radical* (2014), *Visions of Belonging: Family Stories, Popular Culture, and Postwar Democracy, 1940–1960* (2004), and *Family Connections: A History of Italian and Jewish Immigrant Lives in Providence, Rhode Island, 1900–1940* (1985). Her publications include essays on Ruby Dee, *A Raisin in the Sun, Nothing But a Man,* live television drama, and radio in the 1930s and 1940s. She is the historical consultant on many documentaries, including *Sighted Eyes/Feeling Heart* (2018) on Lorraine Hansberry.

Robin G. Vander is an associate professor in the Department of English at Xavier University of Louisiana. She is the coeditor of *Percival Everett: Writing Other/Wise* (2014) and *Perspectives on Percival Everett* (2013). She is the coeditor of two issues of the *Xavier Review:* "Celebrating Jesmyn Ward: Critical Readings and Scholarly Responses" (2018) and "Reading the Intersections of Sex and Spirit in the Creative Arts" (2007). Her article "The African American Population in New Orleans after Hurricane Katrina" appears in *The Review of Black Political Economy* (2011).

INDEX

adaptation, 4, 14, 14n1; adaptation scholarship, 5–9; Black literary/film adaptations, 9–14, 17, 18, 47, 69, 95, 118, 145, 168, 208, 227, 248; translation theory, 209

Aldrich, Robert, 239

American Gothic, Washington, D.C., 225

American Writers Congress (AWC), 102

Anderson, Ernest, 154, 155, 161, 162

Angel Levine, 238

anticommunism, 11, 99, 108, 112n46. *See also* blacklist

antifascism, 11, 98, 110

Antwone Fisher, 15n9

Argentine Sono Films, 36

Armstrong, Louis "Satchmo," 121, 122, 123, 124

Aubrey, James T., Jr., 240

Aurthur, Robert Alan, 237

Autobiography of Malcolm X, The, 8, 228

Baartman, Sarah, 68

Bad Boy Brawly Brown, 251

Baird, Harry, 207, 219, 221

Baker, Josephine, 206

Baldwin, James, 7, 89n46, 91n71, 125, 138, 142n97, 148, 157, 161–63, 166n65, 206, 228, 242n5

Beals, Jennifer, 257

Beard, John Relly, 96

Belafonte, Harry, 69, 74, 77, 91n71, 108, 237, 238, 246n81

Beloved (film), 7

Beloved (novel), 7

Berger, Nicole, 207

Bernstein, Elmer, 255, 256, 260

Betrayal, The, 21

Beyond Defeat, 156, 166n59

Beyond the Forest, 158

Biberman, Herbert, 123, 141n47, 237

Bilbrew, A. C., 183

Billie Holiday, 125

Bingham, Dennis, 8, 118, 140n15

biopic, 8, 11, 115–19, 123, 125, 126, 128, 129, 133, 135, 137

Bizet, Georges, 67, 68, 72, 77, 80, 83, 87n7

Black agency, 97; authorial/directorial, vii, 238, 239; characters, 12, 104, 105, 250, 251, 259; female sexuality, 10, 46, 69, 71, 74–82, 88n22; Holiday, 128, 129, 130, 133, 134, 139; Parks, 227, 236, 237

Black Anti-Defamation Association (BADA), 237

Black Boy, 153, 163n8, 228

Blacker the Berry, The, 22

Black Girl, 226, 238

Black Girl Lost, 253

Black Hope, 147, 164n9

Black Jacobins, The, 97, 109n10

Black Journal, 237

blacklist, 99, 100, 108, 110n26, 111n41, 123, 165n40. *See also* anticommunism

black magic, 47, 64n2, 64n9. *See also* vodou; voodoo

Black nationalism, 71, 73, 75, 76, 77, 88, 237, 238, 244n37

Black Orpheus, 7
Black republic, 48, 95–97, 100, 105, 107. *See also* Haiti
Black Sleuth, The, 233, 249
Blacula, 238
Blankfort, Michael, 100–103, 111n41, 112n46, 112n55, 112n57
Blassingame, John, 194
Blaxploitation, 8, 169, 211, 227, 240, 161n2. *See also* Hollywood Renaissance
Blonde Venus, 158
Blood of Jesus, The, 46
Bogle, Donald, 17, 36, 60, 82, 90n65, 123, 127, 246n77
Bonnie and Clyde, 236, 239
Bontemps, Arna, 25, 28, 96
Bordertown, 159
Brand of Cain, 233
Breen, Joseph, 33, 176, 200n106
Broken Arrow, 101, 111n41
Brown, Jim, 237, 239, 240
Bruce, John Edward, 13, 233, 249, 253
Buck and the Preacher, 238
Buckner, Robert, 186
burbanking, 11, 145–49, 153, 154, 157, 163
Burns, Robert E., 149

Cambridge, Godfrey, 233, 238
Caribbean, 10, 27, 45–57, 63, 64, 99, 105, 109, 187, 189, 191; Afro-Caribbean, 52, 60; Haitian-Caribbean, 57
Carmen, 10, 67–85, 87n3, 87n7, 88n19, 88n22, 90n64, 91n65, 91n71
Carmen (novella), 10, 67, 71, 85. See also *Karmen Geï*; *UCarmen eKhayelitsha*
Carmen (opera), 67, 68, 71, 72, 77, 87n7
Carmen: A Hip Hopera, 69, 90n61, 90n64, 91n71
Carmen Jones, 68, 69, 74, 77–80, 89n29, 89n46, 91n71, 125
Carroll, Diahann, 126, 237, 239
Carson, Lisa Nicole, 257
Casablanca, 150
Casey, Bernie, 237
Cassavetes, John, 237, 239
Castle, William, 5, 32, 169, 195

censorship, 4, 12, 18, 20, 21, 27, 31, 99, 115, 161, 175, 176, 182, 183, 250; self-censorship, 3, 33, 168, 177. *See also* Production Code Administration
Chapman, Tom, 29, 153
Chaykin, Maury, 258
Cheadle, Don, 251, 252, 258, 259
Chenal, Pierre, 15n9, 36, 165n39
Chesnutt, Charles Waddell, 9, 16, 18, 19–20, 22
Chocolate Sailor, 154
Choice of Weapons, A (film), 242n5
Choice of Weapons, A (memoir), 226
Christophe, Henri, 108
Cioffi, Charles, 231
civil rights, 10, 98, 205, 207, 212, 226, 237
Civil War, 174, 181, 182, 186
Clarke, Alex, 229, 240
Cold War, 11, 102. *See also* anticommunism
Colmeiro, José F., 68, 87n3
colonialism/colonial, vii, ix, 3, 6, 9, 10, 11, 48, 51, 52–54, 58, 60, 64, 73–75, 84, 96, 104, 187, 188, 189, 192. *See also* decolonization; imperialism
color line, 47, 54, 181, 196, 208, 250. *See also* segregation
Color Purple, The (film), 7
Color Purple, The (novel), 7
Columbia Pictures, 33, 34, 165n38, 186, 187, 189, 190, 207, 238, 239
Come Back, Charleston Blue, 238
Coming of Age in Mississippi, 228
coming of age narrative, 230, 241, 254
communism, 99, 123, 147; Communist Party, 102, 108. *See also* anticommunism
Conjure Man, The, 253
Conjure Woman, The, 19
Conquest, The, 21
Conrad, William, 240
Cook, Fielder, 15n9
Cooley High, 226
Copland, Aaron, 256
costume drama/fiction, 4, 12, 30, 168, 171, 174, 184
Cotton Comes to Harlem (film), 8, 233, 238, 239, 243n6
Cotton Comes to Harlem (novel), 8, 233

Count Basie and His Sextet, 125

Crane, William, 238

Creole, 48, 54, 173, 197n23

Crime Partners, 15n9

Cripps, Thomas, 151, 206, 226

Crozier, Helen, 176

Cry, the Beloved Country (1951 film), 8

Cry, the Beloved Country (1995 film), 8

Cry, the Beloved Country (novel), 8

Dandridge, Dorothy, 68, 69, 74, 77, 79, 82, 90n65, 91n71, 125, 141n55, 176, 183

Dangerous, 158, 159

Daniels, Lee, 8

Danska, Herbert, 237

Dark of the Sun, 240

Dassin, Jules, 237

Davies, Carole Boyce, 71

Davis, Bette, 145, 157–59, 161–63, 166n65, 240

Davis, Ossie, 8, 126, 226, 233, 237–41, 243n6

Deakin, Irving, 147, 149, 150

decolonization, 10, 11, 67, 69, 70, 71, 80, 82, 85, 95. *See also* colonialism/colonial

Dee, Ruby, 237

de Lisser, Herbert G., 5, 10, 48, 49, 52, 54, 62

de Passe, Suzanne, 137, 142n7

Dessalines, Jean-Jacques, 47, 100

detective fiction, 13, 231–35, 241, 247, 252–55, 260

Devil in a Blue Dress (film), 5, 7, 8, 13, 249, 252, 255–57, 260, 261

Devil in a Blue Dress (novel), 7, 8, 13, 247–50, 252–55, 260, 261n6

Devil's Daughter, The, 5, 10, 45–50, 52, 53, 55–64

Diary of a Harlem Family, 225, 242n4

Diatta, Aline Sitoe, 76

Diawara, Manthia, 255

Dickerson, Ernest R., 15n9

Dirty Dozen, The, 239, 240

Divorcee, The, 160

Dixon, Ivan, 9, 238

Dopefiend, 253

Dornford-May, Mark, 76, 89n29

Douglass, Frederick, 13, 180, 185, 260

Dove, Billie, 120, 140n24

Dovey, Lindiwe, 7, 8, 78

Downey, Robert, Sr., 237

drumming, 10, 45, 49–53, 55, 58, 65n14, 105

Du Bois, W. E. B., 198n45, 228, 251, 262n27

Dufty, William, 11, 115, 120, 139n1

Duke, Bill, 15n9

Dunbar, Paul Laurence, 9, 16, 18–19, 20, 22, 168

Dunham, Katherine, 96

Dunne, Philip, 100, 103, 111nn31–32, 111n35, 112n55, 112n57

Dunning School, 177, 198n45

Dust Be My Destiny, 149

Dyer, Richard, 158, 159

Each Dawn I Die, 149

Eisenstein, Sergei, 24

Elder, Lonne, III, 238

Ellington, Duke, 120, 255

Ellison, Ralph, 13, 233, 247, 251, 252

Emperor Jones, The, 46, 120

erotics/eroticism, 10, 45–48, 53–56, 59, 62, 63, 64n1, 72, 73, 79, 84, 85

Eurocentricism, 71, 85

Evans, Estelle, 230

Everybody Comes to Rick's, 150

Eve's Bayou, 247

Exile, The, 21

exoticism, 46, 56, 57, 59, 63, 71, 87n7, 95, 96, 100, 105, 107, 108, 169, 256

Fanon, Frantz, 214

Farm Security Administration (FSA), 225

fascism, 98

Faulkner, William, 7, 16

Fauset, Jessie, 28

Feather, Leonard, 127

Fences, 15n9

Final Comedown, The, 238

Fisher, Dorothy Canfield, 148, 150

Fisher, Rudolph, 253

Flavio, 225, 242n4

Fonteno, David, 259

Fools (film), 7

Fools (novella), 7

For Colored Girls, 15n9

INDEX

For Love of Imabelle, 233, 251. See also *Rage in Harlem, A*

Foucault, Michel, 117, 128, 132

Foxes of Harrow, The (film), 5, 12, 31, 32, 169, 173, 174, 176, 180, 182, 184–86, 189, 199n70

Foxes of Harrow, The (novel), 30, 169, 173, 175, 186, 188, 190, 191, 196

Fox studio. *See* Twentieth Century-Fox

Foxx, Redd, 238

Foy, Bryan, 22, 24

Frankie "Sugar Chile" Robinson, 125

Franklin, Aretha, 68, 87n6

Franklin, Carl, 5, 7, 13, 14, 247–52, 254–57, 260, 262n19

Franklin, John Hope, 29, 40n66, 194

Freedman, Jerrold, 15n9

Freeman, Joel, 241

French, Tria, 211, 220

Fuller, Muriel, 171–73

Furie, Sidney J., 5, 11, 115, 126, 127, 137, 246n77

Furman, Abraham L., 22

Furrer, Urs, 241

Gardner, Ava, 125, 126, 141n57

Gay Bride, The, 160

Gay Divorcee, The, 160

Gentleman's Agreement, 99

Glaser, Joe, 122

Glasgow, Ellen, 12, 145, 149, 154, 156, 157, 162, 163, 165n44, 166n59, 166n61

Glover, Danny, 108

Goines, Donald, 247, 253, 262n12

Goldberg, Alice, 150, 151, 152

Golden Hawk, The (film), 5, 12, 32, 169

Golden Hawk, The (novel), 32, 169, 187, 189

Goldwyn, Samuel, 151

Gone Fishin', 248, 249, 254, 261n6

Gone with the Wind (film), 6, 184

Gone with the Wind (novel), 6, 31

Gordon's War, 238

Gordy, Berry, Jr., 126, 127

Go Tell It on the Mountain, 228, 242n5

Grapes of Wrath, The, 98

Great White Hope, The, 237

Green, Paul, 35, 151, 152

Greenlee, Sam, 9

Griffin, Farah Jasmine, 119, 127, 139n50

Grimes, William, 194

Guess Who's Coming to Dinner, 236

Guèye, Ndèye, 76

Guffy, Burnett, 239

Gun, Moses, 231

Gunn, Bill, 238

Hagar's Daughter: A Story of Southern Caste Prejudice, 249

Haitian Revolution, 95–101, 103–5, 108, 109

Haiti/Haitians, 10, 11, 47–50, 52, 53, 55, 57, 64, 95–101, 103–8

Haley, Alex, 228

Hall, Albert, 260

Hall, Rebecca, 15n9

Hallelujah, 46, 176, 198n42

Handy, W. C., 7

Hansberry, Lorraine, 8, 26

Harbin, Suzette, 179

Harlem Detective series, 233

Harlem Renaissance, 16, 17, 22, 28

Harrison, Rex, 179

Hate U Give, The, 15

Hayes, Isaac, 234, 241

Hays Code. *See* Production Code Administration

Haywood, Gar Anthony, 247

He Got Game, 8, 256

heterotopia/heterotopic space, 117, 128, 129, 134

Hidden Figures, 15n9

High Crimes, 249

High School Girl, 24

Hill, The, 239, 240

Himes, Chester, 8, 13, 28, 233, 245n60, 247, 251, 253–55, 257, 262n12

Hoffberger Company, J. H., 46

Holiday, Billie, 11, 115–39, 139n4, 140n36, 141n47, 141n55, 141n57, 142n72, 142n97

Hollywood Renaissance, 13, 116, 227, 236, 237, 241, 246n94

Hollywood Writers Mobilization, 98

Homesteader, The (film), 21

Homesteader, The (novel), 21

Hopkins, Pauline, 13, 249, 253

Horne, Lena, 125
House Behind the Cedars, The (film), 19, 20
House Behind the Cedars, The (novel), 19, 20
House Committee on Un-American
  Activities (HUAC), 99, 111n44, 112n46
How Bigger Was Born, 148
How Green Was My Valley, 98
How Stella Got Her Groove Back (film), 8
How Stella Got Her Groove Back (novel), 8
How Tasty Was My Little Frenchman, 6
Hudson-Weems, Clenora, 75, 88n25
Hughes, Langston, 8, 9, 16, 22, 24–26, 28, 30,
  96, 154, 165n40
Hungry Heart, A, 240, 242n5, 244n27
Hurst, Fannie, 8, 16, 27
Hurston, Zora Neale, 7, 9, 16, 22, 26–28, 30,
  39n53, 40n59, 155, 163n8, 165n52
Huston, John, 5, 154, 158, 161, 162
Hyman, Eliot, 239
Hyman, Kenneth, 239

I Am a Fugitive from a Chain Gang, 149
Iceberg Slim (Robert Beck), 247, 253, 262n12
Ice Station Zebra, 240
If Beale Street Could Talk (film), 7
If Beale Street Could Talk (novel), 7
If He Hollers Let Him Go, 253
I Know Why the Caged Bird Sings, 15n9
Imitation of Life (1934 film), 8, 27, 46, 59, 181,
  182
Imitation of Life (1959 film), 8, 27, 126
Imitation of Life (novel), 8, 27
Immigration Act of 1924, 96
I'm No Angel, 158
imperialism, 10, 24, 53, 54, 60, 62–64, 75, 101.
  See also colonialism/colonial
Interne, The, 22–24
In the Heat of the Night, 236
In this Our Life (film), 5, 11, 154, 155, 157, 158,
  161–63
In this Our Life (novel), 12, 145, 149, 154, 156,
  157, 163
Intruder in the Dust (film), 7
Intruder in the Dust (novel), 7
Invisible Man, 252
I Spy, 237

Jamaica/Jamaicans, 10, 47, 48, 50, 52, 62
James, C. L. R., 97
James, Ida, 45, 47, 50, 56–58
James, Olga, 77
Jenkins, Barry, 7, 15n9
Jewison, Norman, 236
Jezebel, 158
Jim Crow, 98, 100, 102, 121, 136, 261n2. *See
  also* segregation
Johnson, Kyle, 229, 230, 240
Johnson, Rashid, 15n9
Johnston, Eric, 34, 42n107
Jonah's Gourd Vine, 27, 28, 40n59
Joy, Jason, 177
Jubilee, 228
Julia, 237

Karmen Geï, 5, 8, 10, 67, 69, 70–72, 74, 77, 80,
  82–84, 86. See also *Carmen* (novella)
Kastel, Kumba, 76, 81
Katzman, Sam, 187
Kenner, 240
Killens, John Oliver, 108
King, Woodie, Jr., 15n9
Klotman, Phyllis, 22, 25, 32, 174
Knight, Arthur, 120, 137
Knock on Any Door (film), 32, 34, 35
Knock on Any Door (novel), 32, 35, 186
Kotto, Yaphet, 238
Krims, Milton, 99
Kumina/Pukkumina, 48

Lady Sings the Blues (autobiography), 11,
  115–18, 120, 125, 128–39
Lady Sings the Blues (film), 5, 11, 115–19,
  127–39
Lafayette Players, 18, 25
La Genèse, 8
Land, Lucy, 154
La Permission, 13, 206–9, 219. See also *Story
  of a Three Day Pass, The*
Latimore, Joseph, 259
Lawrence, Jacob, 96
League of American Writers, 102, 112n46
Learning Tree, The (film), 5, 13, 225–32,
  234–42, 243n7, 244n30, 246n77, 246n90

INDEX

Learning Tree, The (novel), 13, 226–29, 231, 232, 241, 242
Lee, Canada, 35
Lee, Irene, 150–52
Lee, Spike, 7, 8, 256
Lem Hawkin's Confession, 233
Lemmons, Kasi, 247
Leon, Kenny, 15n9
Leonard, Arthur H., 5, 45
Leonard, Charles, 154, 165n40
Leonard, Sheldon, 50
LeRoy, Mervyn, 148, 149, 160
Letter, The, 159
Let Us Be Gay, 160
Levy, Robert, 18, 19
Lewis, George, 115
Liberation of L.B. Jones, The, 237
Life in a Haitian Valley, 97
Lilies of the Field, 236
Limit, The, 238
Lipsyte, Robert, 228
Little Caesar, 148
Little Foxes, The, 159
Lively Lady, 97
Locke, Alain, 148
Lonely Crusade, 253
Long Dream, The, 147
Long Night, The, 15n9
Lord, Robert, 33
Lorde, Audre, 79
Lost Man, The, 237, 246n77
Louverture, Francois-Dominique Toussaint, 96, 98, 100, 102–7, 114n86
Love Wanga, The, 5, 10, 45–56, 58–64, 66n39
Lubin, Arthur, 11, 121
Lumet, Sidney, 239, 244n44
Lydia Bailey (film), 5, 11, 95, 98–109, 109n1, 111nn31–32, 113nn81–82
Lydia Bailey (novel), 95–98
Lying Lips, 46
lynching, 54, 55, 136, 168, 170–72, 191–94, 230

Macunaíma (film), 7
Macunaíma (novel), 7
Magic Island, The, 48, 49, 65n18
Malcolm X, 8, 228

Mandingo, 191
Mandler, Anthony, 15n9
Ma Rainey's Black Bottom, 15n9
Marrow of Tradition, The, 19
Marshall, William, 103, 104, 107, 108, 114n83
Marson, Una, 47, 48, 52, 58
Martens, Emiel, 60, 64n1
Martin, Darnell, 15n9, 28
masculinity, 10, 12, 85, 158, 159, 210, 211, 213, 216, 217, 222, 227
Matheus, John Frederick, 47, 48, 52
Mayfield, Curtis, 87n6
Mayfield, Julian, 108
McClary, Susan, 68, 71, 72, 80, 85, 87n7, 88n19
McCloy, Terence, 137, 142n71
McCuller, Carson, 7
McKay, Claude, 28
McKay, Louis, 127, 130
McKinney, Nina Mae, 10, 45–50, 56–58, 64
McMillan, Terry, 8
McQueen, Steve, 15n9
McRae, Carmen, 123
Melfi, Theodore, 15n9
Melinda, 238
Melody Limited, 147, 164n9
Member of the Wedding, The (film), 7
Member of the Wedding, The (novel), 7
Mentasti, Artillo, 36
Mérimée, Prosper, 10, 67, 68, 71, 72, 83, 86, 88n19
Meriwether, Louise, 237
Metro-Goldwyn-Mayer (MGM), 22, 34, 96, 152, 160, 239, 240
Micheaux, Oscar, 8, 9, 18–22, 27, 46, 205, 233, 261n2
miscegenation, 12, 55, 56, 63, 87n3, 163, 176, 186, 208. *See also* segregation
misogyny/misogynoir, 13, 68, 73, 77, 81, 227, 231, 232, 245n57
Mitchell, Gwenn, 230
Mitchell, Margaret, 6, 16
Mod Squad, 237
Monster, 15n9
Montalbán, Ricardo, 193
Moody, Anne, 228
Moonlight, 15n9

Moses, Man of the Mountain, 27, 28

Mosley, Walter, 5, 7, 13, 14, 247–58, 260, 261n6, 262n12

Motion Picture Association of America (MPAA), 34, 42n107, 99

Motley, Willard, 9, 30, 32–35, 37, 41n96, 41n113, 186, 199n91

Motown Records, 126, 127, 138

Mr. Skeffington, 159

Muccino, Gabriele, 15n9

Mules and Men, 27

Murder in Harlem, 233

Murphy, Dudley, 46, 120

Muse, Clarence, 18, 25

Napoleon I, 96, 101, 103, 105, 107, 212

narration, 208, 242n4, 248, 249, 251–58; narrator, 50, 68, 71, 72, 88n19, 209, 210, 212–17, 221, 248, 249, 251, 253, 254, 256, 260; stream of consciousness, 206; voiceover, 149, 193, 209, 211, 252, 256, 257, 260

Narrative of the Life of Frederick Douglass, 247, 249, 252

National Association for the Advancement of Colored People (NAACP), 40n76, 98, 155, 240, 241

Native Son (1951 film), 15n9, 36, 37, 153, 165n39

Native Son (1986 film), 15n9

Native Son (2019 film), 15n9

Native Son (novel), 7, 11, 29, 35, 36, 42n113, 145, 147, 149–53, 160, 162, 171

Native Son (play), 152

Ndebele, Njabulo S., 7

Neely, Barbara, 247

Negulesco, Jean, 5, 95, 101–3, 111n41, 112n55

Nelson, Ralph, 236, 240

Never Die Alone, 15n9

New Orleans, 11, 121–23, 125, 140n36, 141n47

Nicholson, Stuart, 123

Nigger: An Autobiography by Dick Gregory, 228

Nigger Heaven, 156

noir, 7, 8, 12, 13, 29, 169, 193, 226, 247, 250, 252, 253, 255–57, 261n2, 263n33

Northwest Passage (film), 109n3

Northwest Passage (novel), 96

Nothing But a Man, 226, 237

O, 7

Obeah, 48–49, 52, 58, 61, 62, 64n9

Of Human Bondage, 159

Ogunyemi, Chikwenye, 75, 76, 88n25, 89n36

O'Meally, Robert, 115, 119, 120, 124, 134

One False Move, 249

opera, 47, 48, 49, 52, 67, 68, 71–74, 77, 87n7, 89n29, 121, 124

Othello, 6

ouanga, 47, 54, 61

Ouanga (film), 45. See also *Love Wanga*, *The Ouanga!* (opera), 47, 48

Outcasts, The, 237

Out of Time, 249

Outsider, The, 147, 253

Palcy, Euzhan, 15n9, 109

Pan-Africanism, 75, 76

Paramount Pictures, 25, 26, 111n41, 126, 127

Parks, Gordon, 5, 13, 225–42, 242n1, 242nn3–5, 243nn21–22, 244n27, 244n30, 244nn36–37, 244n50, 245n57, 245n67, 246n90

Parks, Gordon, Jr., 226, 242n1

Passing, 15n9

Peregini, Frank, 46

performance/acting, 14, 29, 36, 72, 73, 81, 91n71, 124, 129, 130, 137, 158, 161–63, 206, 231, 236, 248, 255–58, 260

Perry, Tyler, 15n9

Peters, Brock, 91n71, 237

Petrie, Daniel, 15n9, 26, 237

Petry, Ann, 5, 9, 12, 22, 28–30, 145, 152, 153, 163n8, 165n38, 253

pigmentocracy, 52, 53, 55, 56, 62

Pimp: The Story of My Life, 253

Pinky, 99, 111n31

plantation, 12, 26, 45, 46, 51, 57, 61–63, 65n14, 156, 174, 180, 187–89, 195, 254; Black female ownership, 45–47, 49–51, 53–55, 57–64; plantocracy, 50, 62

Pocomania, 47, 48, 58

Poitier, Sidney, 26, 206, 236, 237, 238

postcolonialism/postcolonial, 68, 70, 73, 84. *See also* colonialism/colonial

Powrie, Phil, 68, 74, 83, 84, 87n7

Prabhu, Anjali, 70, 75, 76, 78, 80, 83, 84, 86, 87

Precious, 8, 15n8

Preminger, Otto, 68, 69, 74, 77, 78, 81, 82, 89n29, 89n46, 90n65, 125

primitivism, 46, 47, 49, 50, 55, 63

Prince-Bythewood, Gina, 7, 8

Production Code Administration (PCA), 12, 24, 33, 112n57, 175–77, 189, 198n40, 198n42, 236. *See also* censorship

protest fiction, 12, 168, 171, 173

Pryor, Richard, 127, 129, 138

Public Enemy, 148

Pudaloff, Ross, 148

pulp fiction, 12, 13, 169, 227, 231, 232

Pursuit of Happyness, The, 15n9

Push: A Novel, 8. See also *Precious*

Putney Swope, 237, 246n77

Quinn, Eithne, 227, 237, 238, 245n71, 246n94

racism, 9, 12, 13, 75, 123, 145, 148, 153, 168, 170, 179, 183, 206, 208–10, 217, 226, 229, 241, 242, 247, 249, 253

Raengo, Alessandra, 6–8

Rage in Harlem, A, 233, 251, 253, 255

Raisin in the Sun, A (1961 film), 8, 15n9, 26, 237

Raisin in the Sun, A (1989 film), 15n9

Raisin in the Sun, A (2008 film), 15n9

Raisin in the Sun, A (play), 8, 26

Ramaka, Joseph Gaï, 5, 8, 10, 69–85, 87, 88n9, 89n45, 91n79

Rampersad, Arnold, 25, 26

Rangle River, 46

rape, 32, 132, 133, 176, 177, 178, 187, 191, 192, 232

Raucher, Herbert, 239

Rawhide, 237

Ray, Nicholas, 34, 186

Reconstruction, 174, 177, 180, 184, 186, 187, 198n45, 227

Red Death, A, 248

Reol Productions, 18

Reynolds, Paul, 146

Ritt, Martin, 226, 237, 238

RKO Pictures, 28, 152, 160, 186

Roberts, Kenneth, 11, 95–98, 109n4, 109n10

Roberts, Marie Louise, 207, 208

Robertson, Hugh A., 238, 241

Robeson, Paul, 46, 108, 114n83, 120

Roemer, Michael, 226

Roots: The Saga of an American Family, 15n9

Ross, Diana, 11, 126–38, 142n71

Roundtree, Richard, 226, 234, 235, 241

Rowley, Hazel, 151, 152, 164n9

Sack Amusement Enterprises, 46

Salkow, Sidney, 5, 32, 169

Sanders of the River, 46

Sands, Diana, 126

Sapphire, 8

Saracen Blade, The (film), 5, 12, 32, 169, 192, 193, 195

Saracen Blade, The (novel), 32, 187, 190, 191, 200n112, 200n115

Savage Holiday, 147

Scar of Shame, 46

Schermer, Jules, 101–3

Schultz, Michael, 226, 238

Scott, DeVallon, 193

Screen Writers Guild, 100, 101, 111n30

Seabrook, William Buehler, 48, 49, 52, 54–56, 65n18

Secret Life of Bees, The, 7, 8

segregation, 20, 95, 102, 107, 135, 208, 228, 229, 248

Sembene, Ousmane, 71

Seven Arts, 239

sexuality, 60, 103, 145, 160–63, 175, 192, 195, 200n106, 208, 213, 215, 216, 234, 250; bisexuality, 82, 83, 90n62; Black female, 10, 45, 51, 56, 58, 59, 67–73, 75–82, 85, 86, 87n3, 88n22, 90n64; and blackness, 48, 51, 74, 89n46, 105, 124, 146, 176; heterosexuality, 32, 59, 71, 77–79, 81, 83, 85, 158, 211; Holiday, 118, 132, 133; homophobia, 212, 232; homosexuality, 73, 83, 159, 90n62, 212; lesbianism, 83–86; queerness, 46, 50, 70, 78, 83, 87, 212

Shadow of Chinatown, 46

276 INDEX

Shadows, 237, 239

Shaft (film), 5, 13, 225–27, 231–38, 240–42, 243n6, 244n50, 246n77, 246n93

Shaft (novel), 13, 227, 231–33, 245n53

Shaft's Big Score!, 238

short stories, 39n50; Hughes, 24, 25; Van Peebles, 206–22; Wright, 146, 147; Yerby, 12, 169, 171, 172, 197n31

Show Boat, 125

Siegel, Sol, 99

Sirk, Douglas, 8, 27, 126, 195

Sissoko, Cheick Oumar, 8

Sizemore, Tom, 257, 258

slavery, 12, 17, 45, 62, 103, 156, 169, 177, 178, 180–82, 184, 189–96

Slaves, 237, 246n77

Slim, Iceberg (Robert Beck), 247, 253, 262n12

Smith, Bessie, 120

Smith, J. Jesses, 15n9

Smith, O. C., 240

Snead, James, 146, 158

Souls of Black Folk, The, 228

Sounder, 226, 238

Sound of Jazz, The, 125

spirituality, 48, 64, 86, 126, 147, 247, 255; spiritual power, 10, 45, 50, 52, 54, 76; spiritual practice, 48, 49, 51, 60

Split, The, 239, 240

Spook Who Sat by the Door, The (film), 9, 238

Spook Who Sat by the Door, The (novel), 9

Sport of the Gods, The (film), 18, 19

Sport of the Gods, The (novel), 18

Stahl, John M., 5, 8, 27, 30, 46, 169, 176, 181–83, 198n40

Stam, Robert, 6, 7, 209

Stevedore, 102

St. Jacques, Raymond, 233, 237

St. John, Christopher, 231, 238

St. Louis Blues, 46

Stobie, Cheryl, 76, 78, 83, 85

Stop!, 238

Story, Tim, 15n9

Story of a Three Day Pass, The, 5, 12, 13, 205–10, 213, 215, 222. See also *La Permission*

Stowe, Harriet Beecher, 16, 17

Strangers May Kiss, 160

Street, The, 12, 28, 29, 145, 146, 152, 153, 163n8, 165n38, 253

Stride Toward Freedom, 228

Strode, Woody, 237

studio era, 5, 145, 146, 151, 153, 157, 225

Sugar Cane Alley, 15n9

Suleman, Ramadan, 7

Sullivan, Kevin Rodney, 8

Super Fly, 226, 238, 243n6

Sweet Love, Bitter, 237

Sweet Sweetback's Baadasssss Song, 13, 206, 222, 226–38, 243n6

Symphony in Black: A Rhapsody of Negro Life, 120

Szwed, John, 119, 124, 141n47, 142n72

television, 30, 111n30, 114n83, 174, 225, 236, 237, 241

Tell My Horse, 27

Terwilliger, George, 5, 45, 47

Their Eyes Were Watching God (film), 15n9

Their Eyes Were Watching God (novel), 27, 28

They Made Me a Criminal, 149

Think Like a Man, 15n9

This Is My Own, 171

Three on a Match, 160

Thurman, Wallace, 9, 16, 22–24, 26, 30, 39n32

Tick, Tick, Tick, 240

Tidyman, Ernest, 227, 231–33, 235, 244n48, 245n53

Tillman, George, Jr., 15

Together for Days, 238

Tomorrow's Children, 22, 23

Toomer, Jean, 28

Top of the Heap, 238

To Sir, with Love, 236

Townsend, Robert, 69, 90n61

Trick Baby, 253

Trouble Man, 238

Tuchock, Wanda, 177–80

Turner, Lana, 126

12 Years a Slave, 15n9

Twentieth Century-Fox, 22, 30, 31, 96, 98–100, 102, 103, 105, 106, 111n41, 112n57, 152, 174, 176, 177, 180–82, 185

Tyson, Cicely, 237

UCarmen eKhayelitsha, 69, 89n29. See also
  Carmen (novella)
Uncle Tom's Cabin (film), 16
Uncle Tom's Cabin (novel), 7, 16, 17, 185
Uncle Tom's Children: Four Novellas, 146
Underground Railroad, The, 15n9
United Artists, 30, 238, 239
Universal Studios, 33, 111n41
Uptight, 237, 246n77

Van Peebles, Melvin, 5, 12, 13, 205–13, 215, 216,
  219, 221, 222, 223n8, 226–39, 241, 243n6,
  263n43
Veiled Aristocrats, 19, 20
Vernot, Henry J., 18
Vidor, King, 46, 109n3, 158, 176, 198n42
Vixens, The, 186
vodou, 47, 64n2, 97, 100, 104. *See also* voodoo
Volland, Virginia, 29, 152, 153
voodoo, 10, 49, 50, 52–55, 58, 60–63, 63n2,
  64n9, 100, 104, 105, 107, 158, 174, 176–80.
  See also vodou

Waiting to Exhale (film), 8
Waiting to Exhale (novel), 8
Walker, Alice, 7, 75
Walker, Margaret, 36, 228
Walker, T-Bone, 254
Wallis, Hal, 151
Ward, Ted, 152
Warner Bros., 7, 11, 12, 28, 29, 111n41, 145–55,
  157, 160, 162, 163, 163n6, 163n8, 164n9, 175,
  186, 238
Warner Bros.-Seven Arts, 239, 240
Warren, Mark, 238
Washington, Denzel, 15n9, 247, 257–59, 261,
  263n33
Washington, Fredi, 10, 45–48, 50, 56, 59, 64,
  176, 180–82
Washington, Kenny, 183
Watermelon Man, 205, 238, 243n6
Waters, Ethel, 124, 141n47
Waters, Mira, 230
Watson, Ella, 225
Way Down South, 25, 26
Weber, Lois, 46, 140n24

Welles, Orson, 35, 121, 151, 152
Weston, Jay, 126
Whitaker, Forest, 8
White, Clarence Cameron, 47
White, Walter, 98, 155
White Heat, 46
whiteness, 9, 14, 56, 59, 62, 148, 157, 159,
  168–70, 174, 189, 190, 196, 206, 255
White Witch of Rose Hall, The, 10, 48, 54,
  58, 61
White Zombie, 49
Wilbur, Crane, 22, 23
Williams, Billy Dee, 127, 130, 138
Williams, Clarence, III, 237
Williams, Oscar, 238
Williams, Spencer, 46, 261n2
Williamson, Fred, 237
Willkie, Wendell, 98, 101, 110nn18–19
Wilson, 99
Wilson, Eileen, 125
Wind from Nowhere, The, 21
Winkler, Mel, 258
Wolfe, George C., 15n9
womanism, 75, 88n25, 89n36
Woolfalk, Saya, 75, 79, 85, 86
World of Piri Thomas, The, 225, 242n4
World War I, 149, 170
World War II, 10, 11, 13, 30, 69, 95, 98, 171, 207,
  208, 211, 242n3, 247, 250, 252, 254
Wright, Richard, 5, 7, 9, 11, 12, 28–30, 32, 35–37,
  42n113, 145–48, 150–53, 160, 161, 163n8,
  164n9, 168, 171, 173, 206, 228, 253
Writers' Congress of 1943, 98, 108
Wyler, William, 158, 159, 237

Yates, George Worthing, 193, 195
Yerby, Frank, 5, 9, 12, 30–32, 35, 37, 168–75,
  177–82, 184–96, 197nn30–31, 198n33,
  199n91
Young, Genevieve, 229
Young, Otis, 237

Zanuck, Darryl F., 30, 98, 100, 101, 103, 104,
  108, 111n39, 114n83, 173–78, 182, 186,
  198n33
zombie, 49, 50, 60, 61

Printed in the USA
CPSIA information can be obtained
at www.ICGtesting.com
LVHW041558160324
774517LV00002B/209